T0309432

℣ Lord, open our lips.
℟ And we shall praise your name.

Invitatory Psalm

A CALL TO PRAISE GOD   PSALM 94(95)

Come, ríng out our jóy to the Lórd;
háil the Gód who sáves us.†
Let us cóme before him gíving thánks,
with sóngs let us háil the Lórd.

A míghty Gód is the Lórd,
a gréat king abóve all góds.
In his hánd are the dépths of the éarth;
the héights of the móuntains are hís.
To hím belongs the séa, for he máde it,
and the drý land sháped by his hánds.

Come ín; let us bów and bend lów;
let us knéel before the Gód who máde us
for he is our Gód and wé
the péople who belóng to his pásture,
the flóck that is léd by his hánd.

O that todáy you would lísten to his vóice!
'Hárden not your héarts as at Meríbah,
as on that dáy at Mássah in the désert
when your fáthers pút me to the tést;
when they tríed me, thóugh they saw my wórk.

For forty yéars I was wéaried of these péople
and I said: "Their héarts are astráy,
these péople do not knów my wáys."
Thén I took an óath in my ánger:
"Néver shall they énter my rést." '

Alternative Invitatory Psalm

THE JOY OF THOSE WHO ENTER
   THE TEMPLE OF THE LORD   PSALM 99(100)

Cry out with jóy to the Lórd, all the éarth†
Sérve the Lórd with gládness.*
Come befóre him, sínging for jóy.

Know that hé, the Lórd, is Gód.†
He máde us, we belóng to hím,*
we are his péople, the shéep of his flóck.

Gó within his gátes, giving thánks.†
Enter his cóurts with sóngs of práise.*
Give thánks to him and bléss his náme.

Indéed, how góod is the Lórd,†
etérnal his mérciful lóve.*
He is fáithful from áge to áge.

Alternative Invitatory Psalm

THE LORD COMES TO HIS TEMPLE   PSALM 23 (24)

The Lórd's is the éarth and its fúlness,*
the wórld and áll its péoples.
It is hé who sét it on the séas;*
on the wáters he máde it fírm.

Who shall clímb the móuntain of the Lórd?*
Who shall stánd in his hóly pláce?
The mán with clean hánds and pure héart,†
who desíres not wórthless thíngs,*
who has not swórn so as to decéive his néighbour.

He shall recéive bléssings from the Lórd*
and rewárd from the Gód who sáves him.
Súch are the mén who séek him,*
seek the fáce of the Gód of Jácob.

O gátes, lift hígh your héads;†
grow hígher, áncient dóors.*
Let him énter, the kíng of glóry!

Whó is the kíng of glóry?†
The Lórd, the míghty, the váliant,*
the Lórd, the váliant in wár.

O gátes, lift hígh your héads;†
grow hígher, áncient dóors.*
Let him énter, the kíng of glóry!

Who is hé, the kíng of glóry?†
Hé, the Lórd of ármies,*
hé is the kíng of glóry.

Alternative Invitatory Psalm

O Gód, be grácious and bléss us*
and let your fáce shed its líght upón us.
So will your wáys be knówn upon éarth*
and all nátions learn your sáving hélp.

Let the péoples práise you, O Gód;*
let áll the péoples práise you.

Let the nátions be glád and exúlt*
for you rúle the wórld with jústice.
With fáirness you rúle the péoples,*
you guíde the nátions on éarth.

Let the péoples práise you, O Gód;*
let áll the péoples práise you.

The éarth has yíelded its frúit*
for Gód, our Gód, has bléssed us.

May Gód still gíve us his bléssing*
till the énds of the éarth revére him.

Let the péoples práise you, O Gód;*
let áll the péoples práise you.

A SHORTER
MORNING AND
EVENING PRAYER

Other editions of *The Divine Office* available:

The Divine Office, complete in 3 volumes
Daily Prayer
Morning and Evening Prayer

Also available from Collins:
The Sunday Missal
The Weekday Missal
Study Lectionary vols 1-3

A SHORTER
MORNING AND
EVENING PRAYER

The Psalter of
The Divine Office

with selected texts for the Seasons,
Feasts of the Lord and Solemnities

Collins
SINCE 1819

Collins, a division of HarperCollins*Publishers*
1 London Bridge Street, London SE1 9GF

www.williamcollinsbooks.co.uk

HarperCollins*Publishers*
Macken House, 39/40 Mayor Street Upper, Dublin 1, D01 C9W8, Ireland

First printed 1983
This edition printed in 2022

ISBN 978-0-00-721987-2

Taken from *The Divine Office,* a translation of *Liturgia Horarum,* approved by the Episcopal Conferences of Australia, England and Wales, Ireland, Scotland.

Also approved for use in Gambia, Ghana, India, Kenya, Liberia, Malaysia and Singapore, New Zealand, Nigeria, Zimbabwe, Sierra Leone, Tanzania, Uganda.

Concordat cum originali: John P Dewis
                   Denis J Hart

Imprimatur: Mgr Ralph Brown VG
                Westminster, 6 January 1983

                +James Cardinal Freeman
                Archbishop of Sydney
                25 January 1983

Printed in India

CONTENTS

ACKNOWLEDGEMENTS

The Publishers are grateful to the following for permission to reproduce copyright material:

SCRIPTURE TEXTS
The following versions have been used:
Knox Bible, © 1945, 1949, the Hierarchy of England and Wales.
New English Bible, 2nd edition copyright 1970, Oxford and Cambridge University Presses.
Revised Standard Version, Common Bible, copyrighted © 1973, by the Division of Christian Education, National Council of the Churches of Christ in the USA. Special permission has been obtained to use in this publication the 'you-your-yours' forms of the personal pronoun in the address to God.
Today's English Version (*Good News for Modern Man*), United Bible Societies of America and Collins Publishers, London.
Psalm texts are translated from the Hebrew by The Grail, © The Grail (England) 1963, and published by Collins. They are reprinted from the Singing Version first published in Fontana Books in 1966.
The practical needs of choral recitation prompted a number of revisions in the psalms and canticles of this Breviary. These revisions are made with the agreement of The Grail.

HYMNS
Geoffrey Chapman, a division of Cassell Publishers, for James Quinn SJ, 'Blessed be the Lord our God', 'Day is done but love unfailing', 'I am the holy vine', 'Sing all creation'.
Chatto & Windus and the literary estate of Eleanor Henrietta Hull, for 'It were my soul's desire'.
Oxford University Press, for 'Father, we praise thee, now the night is over', © translation Percy Dearmer 1867-1936, from *The English Hymnal*.
Benedictine Nuns of Stanbrook Abbey, from *Stanbrook Abbey Hymnal*, 'In the beginning God created heaven', 'Lord God, your light which dims the stars', 'O Christ the light of heaven', 'The day is filled with splendour', 'The Father's glory, Christ our light', 'Transcendent God in whom we live', 'We bless you, Father, Lord of life', 'When God had filled the earth with life', 'When God made man, he gave him all the earth'.

SCRIPTURE VERSIONS USED
FOR CANTICLES

Grail Version

Exodus 15:1-4a,8-13,17-18	Daniel 3:52-57
Deuteronomy 32:1-12	3:57-88 56
1 Samuel 2:1-10	Hab 3:2-4,13a,15-19
Sirach 36:1-7,13-16	Luke 1:46-55
Isaiah 12:1-6	1:68-79
45:15-26	2:29-32
Jeremiah 31:10-14	

Revised Standard Version

1 Chron 29:10-13	Isaiah 66:10-14a
Tobit 13:1-5b,7-8	Jeremiah 14:17-21
13:8-11,13-15	Ezekiel 36:24-28
Judith 16:2-3a,15-19	Daniel 3:3,4,6,11-18
Wisdom 9:1-6,9-11	Ephesians 1:3-10
Isaiah 2:2-5	Philippians 2:6-11
26:1-4,7-9,12	Colossians 1:12-20
33:13-16	1 Timothy 3:16
38:10-14,17-20	1 Peter 2:21-24
40:10-17	Revelation 4:11; 5:9,10,12
42:10-16	11:17-18; 12:10b-12a
61:10-62:5	15:3-4
	19:1-2.5-7

PREFACE

This Book contains a selection of material from Morning and Evening Prayer from The Divine Office. It may serve as an introduction to the Prayer of the Church, (the Liturgy of the Hours) for lay people, who may find the entire Office somewhat daunting; and as a convenient pocket companion for travellers who would normally use either *Daily Prayer* or *The Divine Office* in its complete form.

It contains:

* the complete four week Psalter

* sufficient material from the Proper of Seasons to allow for seasonal variation: a week of proper material for each of the Seasons; complete Morning and Evening Prayer for Christmas Day (which may be used during the Octave); Palm Sunday (which may be used during Holy Week); Holy Thursday Evening Prayer and Good Friday Morning Prayer; Easter Sunday Morning and Evening Prayer (which may be used during the Octave)

* for the Feasts of the Lord and Solemnities during the Seasonal Cycle or in Ordinary Time, for Sundays in Ordinary Time and for Solemnities from the General Calendar of Saints, the antiphons for the Gospel Canticles and Concluding Prayers are given: in this way the 'flavour' of the day may be captured in a simple form.

* the Office for the Dead and the Saturday Memorial of the Blessed Virgin Mary are given to meet particular devotional needs.

For further information about Morning and Evening Prayer, with helps for the reader and a complete Commentary on the Psalms and Canticles, please refer to *The School of Prayer: An Introduction to the Divine Office for All Christians*, by John Brook (HarperCollins, 1992).

STRUCTURE OF
MORNING AND EVENING PRAYER

MORNING PRAYER	EVENING PRAYER
INTRODUCTION	
℣ Lord, open our lips.	℣ O God, come to our aid.
℟ And we shall praise your name.	℟ O Lord, make haste to
[Invitatory Psalm (Pss 94, 99, 66	help us
or 23) with its antiphon]	
HYMN	
PSALMODY	
Antiphon 1	Antiphon 1
A 'morning' psalm	A psalm
Antiphon repeated	Antiphon repeated
(*Silent Prayer*)	(*Silent Prayer*)
Antiphon 2	Antiphon 2
Old Testament canticle	A psalm
Antiphon repeated	Antiphon repeated
(*Silent Prayer*)	(*Silent Prayer*)
Antiphon 3	Antiphon 3
A psalm of praise	New Testament canticle
Antiphon repeated	Antiphon repeated
(*Silent Prayer*)	(*Silent prayer*)
SCRIPTURE READING	
(*Silent Prayer*)	
SHORT RESPONSORY	
GOSPEL CANTICLE	
Benedictus antiphon	Magnificat antiphon
Canticle of Zachariah	Canticle of Mary
Antiphon repeated	Antiphon repeated
INTERCESSIONS	
Invocations of praise	Prayers of intercession
	(*final prayer always for*
	the faithful departed)
(*Silent Prayer*)	
The Lord's Prayer	
CONCLUDING PRAYER	
BLESSING	

STRUCTURE OF NIGHT PRAYER

INTRODUCTION
℣ O God, come to our aid
℟ O Lord, make haste to help us.
(*Examination of conscience   Act of Repentance*)

HYMN

PSALMODY
Antiphon
Psalm
Antiphon

SCRIPTURE READING
(*Silent Prayer*)

SHORT RESPONSORY

GOSPEL CANTICLE
Antiphon
Canticle of Simeon
Antiphon repeated

CONCLUDING PRAYER

BLESSING

ANTHEM TO THE BLESSED VIRGIN

THE CYCLE OF THE FOUR WEEK PSALTER

Each year, begin using Psalter Week 1 on:

First Sunday of Advent
Monday after the Baptism of the Lord
First Sunday of Lent
Easter Sunday

Each year on Monday after Pentecost, examine this TABLE and begin using Psalter of the appropriate week as follows:

YEAR	PSALTER WEEK	YEAR	PSALTER WEEK
2020	1	2029	3
2021	4	2030	2
2022	2	2031	1
2023	4	2032	3
2024	3	2033	2
2025	2	2034	4
2026	4	2035	2
2027	3	2036	1
2028	1	2037	4

INTRODUCTION

*Why we pray Morning and Evening Prayer in the
Liturgy of the Hours*

The Apostolic Constitution promulgating the revision of the Divine
Office after the Second Vatican Council states that the revised Office
has been composed so that it becomes the prayer not only of the
clergy but of the whole People of God. Its revised form can be fitted
into the actual hours of people's daily lives. The Constitution says:

The most important "Hours" are Morning Prayer and Evening
Prayer. These become the two hinges, as it were, of the daily office.

At Morning Prayer intercessions are given to consecrate the day in
order to prepare for the work of the day; while at Evening Prayer
supplications have been added following the pattern of the Prayer of
the Faithful.

The revision of the official prayer of the Church, taking into
account both the oldest traditions and the needs of modern life will,
it is hoped, renew and vivify all Christian prayer and serve to
nourish the spiritual life of the People of God. We hope, therefore,
that the command of our Lord Jesus Christ to his Church to pray
without ceasing will be fulfilled. The Liturgy of the Hours will be of
great assistance in this, especially when a group assembles together
for this purpose and thus presents an unmistakable sign of the
Praying Church.

Christian prayer is primarily the prayer of the entire community
of mankind joined to Christ himself. Each individual has his part in
this prayer which is common to the one Body, and it thus becomes
the voice of the beloved Spouse of Christ, putting into words the
wishes and desires of the whole Christian people and making
intercession for the necessities common to all mankind. It obtains its
unity from the heart of Christ himself. Our Redeemer, as he himself
entered into life through his prayer and sacrifice, wishes that this
should not cease throughout the ages in his Mystical Body, the
Church, and so the official prayer of the Church is at the same time
the *very prayer which Christ himself, together with his Body,
addresses to the Father*. Thus when the Divine Office is said, our
voices re-echo in Christ and his in us.

In order that this shall come about it is necessary that *that warm and living love for Scripture* which emanates from the Liturgy of the Hours shall be renewed among all, so that in truth Sacred Scripture becomes the principal source of all Christian prayer. The psalms especially, showing as they do the action of God in the history of salvation, must be better understood by the People of God, and this will come about more easily if among the clergy there is promoted a deeper study of the psalms as they are used in the liturgy, and if this is then handed on to the faithful by efficient catechesis. Then this more fruitful use of the Scriptures in the Mass and in the Liturgy of the Hours will bring about a continuous meditation on the history of salvation and its continuation in the life of men.

Since the life of Christ in his Mystical Body perfects and elevates the personal life of each of the faithful, there can be no opposition between the prayer of Christ and the personal prayer of the individual, but instead the relationship between them is strengthened by the Divine Office. Mental prayer is nourished by the readings and psalms and other parts of the Liturgy of the Hours; and if the method and form of the celebration is chosen which most helps the persons taking part, one's personal, living prayer must of necessity be helped. Then the prayer of the Office as it becomes truly personal prayer forms a clear link between the liturgy and the whole life of the Christian, since every hour of the day and night is itself a kind of *leitourgia* wherein they give themselves to the ministry of the love of God and their fellow-men, and are joined to the actions of Christ who by his life among men and by his sacrifice sanctified the life of men. This deepest truth of the Christian life is shown forth and at the same time brought about by the Liturgy of the Hours, and so it is offered to all the faithful.

from *Apostolic Constitution*, nn 2,8
POPE PAUL VI

FREQUENTLY RECURRING TEXTS

INTRODUCTION TO THE DAILY OFFICE

This is used at the beginning of the day, but may be omitted, together with the invitatory psalm.

℣ Lord, open our lips.
℞ And we shall praise your name.

The invitatory psalm is then said, ps 94, p 3, with its antiphon. It is preferable to repeat the antiphon at the beginning of the psalm and after each strophe, GI no. 34 (Introduction no. 3). In recitation on one's own it suffices to say the antiphon once at the beginning of the psalm.

¶ *Pss 99, 66 or 23 may be said in place of ps 94. When one of them occurs in the Office which follows it should be replaced there by ps 94. For the ordinary Sundays and Weekdays of the Year the invitatory antiphon is given in the psalter at the beginning of each day.*

For convenience, the antiphons for the seasons, which are used on more than one occasion, are printed below.

Invitatory Antiphon

The Proper of Seasons

ADVENT
I (*to 16 Dec.*): Let us adore the Lord, the king who is to come.
II (*17-23 Dec.*): The Lord is at hand: come, let us adore him.

CHRISTMASTIDE
I (*before Epiphany*): Christ has been born for us: come, let us adore him.
II (*after Epiphany*): Christ has appeared to us; come, let us adore him.

LENT
I (*including Holy Week*): Christ the Lord was tempted and suffered for us: come, let us adore him.
II (*alternative, except in Holy Week*): O that today you would listen to his voice: harden not your hearts.†

EASTERTIDE
I (*to the Ascension*): The Lord has truly risen, alleluia.
II (*Ascension to Pentecost*): Christ the Lord has promised us the Holy Spirit: come, let us adore him, alleluia.

Invitatory Psalm

A CALL TO PRAISE GOD   PSALM 94(95)
Every day, as long as this 'today' lasts, keep encouraging one another
(Heb 3:13)

Come, ríng out our jóy to the Lórd;
háil the Gód who sáves us.
†Let us cóme before him, gíving thánks,
with sóngs let us háil the Lórd. (*Antiphon*)

A míghty Gód is the Lórd,
a gréat king abóve all góds.
In his hánd are the dépths of the éarth;
the héights of the móuntains are hís.
To hím belongs the séa, for he máde it,
and the drý land sháped by his hánds. (*Antiphon*)

Come ín; let us bów and bend lów;
let us knéel before the Gód who máde us
for hé is our Gód and wé
the péople who belóng to his pásture,
the flóck that is léd by his hánd. (*Antiphon*)

O that todáy you would lísten to his vóice!
'Hárden not your héarts† as at Meríbah,
as on that dáy at Mássah in the désert
when your fáthers pút me to the tést;
when they tríed me, thóugh they saw my wórk. (*Antiphon*)

For forty yéars I was wéaried of these péople
and I said: "Their héarts are astráy,
these péople do not knów my wáys."
Thén I took an óath in my ánger:
"Néver shall they énter my rést." ' (*Antiphon*)

Glory be to the Father and to the Son and to the
 Holy Spirit.
As it was in the beginning, is now, and ever shall be,
 world without end. Amen. (*Antiphon*)

3

Alternative Invitatory Psalms

THE JOY OF THOSE WHO ENTER   PSALM 99(100)
THE TEMPLE OF THE LORD

The Lord calls all those he has redeemed to sing a hymn of victory (St Athanasius)

> Cry out with jóy to the Lórd, all the éarth.†
> Sérve the Lórd with gládness.*
> Come befóre him, sínging for jóy.
>
> Know that hé, the Lórd, is Gód.†
> He máde us, we belóng to hím,*
> we are his péople, the shéep of his flóck.
>
> Gó within his gátes, giving thánks.†
> Enter his cóurts with sóngs of práise.*
> Give thánks to him and bléss his náme.
>
> Indéed, how góod is the Lórd,†
> etérnal his mérciful lóve.*
> He is fáithful from áge to áge.

ALL THE PEOPLES WILL GIVE PRAISE TO THE LORD   PSALM 66(67)
Let it be known to you that this salvation from God has been sent to all peoples (Acts 28:28)

> O Gód, be grácious and bléss us*
> and let your fáce shed its líght upón us.
> So will your wáys be knówn upon éarth*
> and all nátions learn your sáving hélp.
>
> Let the péoples práise you, O Gód;*
> let áll the péoples práise you.
>
> Let the nátions be glád and exúlt*
> for you rúle the wórld with jústice.
> With fáirness you rúle the péoples,*
> you guíde the nátions on éarth.
>
> Let the péoples práise you, O Gód;*
> let áll the péoples práise you.
>
> The éarth has yíelded its frúit*
> for Gód, our Gód, has bléssed us.

4

May Gód still gíve us his bléssing*
till the énds of the éarth revére him.

Let the péoples práise you, O Gód;*
let áll the péoples práise you.

THE LORD COMES TO HIS TEMPLE PSALM 23(24)
*The gates of heaven were opened to Christ because he was lifted up in
the flesh* (St Irenaeus)

The Lórd's is the éarth and its fúlness,*
the wórld and áll its péoples.
It is hé who sét it on the séas;*
on the wáters he máde it fírm.

Who shall clímb the móuntain of the Lórd?*
Who shall stánd in his hóly pláce?
The mán with clean hánds and pure héart,†
who desíres not wórthless thíngs,*
who has not swórn so as to decéive his néighbour.

He shall recéive bléssings from the Lórd*
and rewárd from the Gód who sáves him.
Súch are the mén who séek him,*
seek the fáce of the Gód of Jácob.

O gátes, lift hígh your héads;†
grow hígher, áncient dóors.*
Let him énter, the kíng of glóry!

Whó is the kíng of glóry?†
The Lórd, the míghty, the váliant,*
the Lórd, the váliant in wár.

O gátes, lift hígh your héads;†
grow hígher, áncient dóors.*
Let him énter, the kíng of glóry!

Who is hé, the kíng of glóry?†
Hé, the Lórd of ármies,*
hé is the kíng of glóry.

INTRODUCTION TO EACH HOUR

℣ O God, come to our aid.
℟ O Lord, make haste to help us.
Glory be to the Father and to the Son and to the Holy Spirit, as it was in the beginning, is now, and ever shall be, world without end. Amen. Alleluia.

This introduction is omitted a) when the Invitatory is used, and b) when the Hour follows immediately on another Hour. Alleluia is omitted during Lent.

THE GOSPEL CANTICLES

The following canticles are used daily in the Divine Office

THE BENEDICTUS
The Canticle of Zechariah

LK 1:68-79

The Messiah and the one who was sent before him

Blessed be the Lord, the God of Israel!*
He has visited his people and redeemed them.

He has raised up for us a mighty saviour*
in the house of David his servant,
as he promised by the lips of holy men,*
those who were his prophets from of old.

A saviour who would free us from our foes,*
from the hands of all who hate us.
So his love for our fathers is fulfilled*
and his holy covenant remembered.

He swore to Abraham our father to grant us,*
that free from fear, and saved from the hands of our foes,
we might serve him in holiness and justice*
all the days of our life in his presence.

As for you, little child,*
you shall be called a prophet of God, the Most High.
You shall go ahead of the Lord*
to prepare his ways before him,

To make known to his people their salvation*
through forgiveness of all their sins,
the loving-kindness of the heart of our God*
who visits us like the dawn from on high.

He will give light to those in darkness,†
those who dwell in the shadow of death,*
and guide us into the way of peace.

Glory be to the Father and to the Son and to the Holy Spirit.*
As it was in the beginning, is now, and ever shall be,
    world without end. Amen.

This is said at Morning Prayer with its antiphon.

*On Sundays and during Advent, Christmastide, Lent and Eastertide
the antiphon each day is proper.*
*On ordinary Weekdays of the Year the antiphon is taken from the
psalter.*

The Glory be to the Father *is said after every canticle unless ex-
pressly noted to the contrary.*

THE MAGNIFICAT
The Canticle of Mary
LK 1:46-55

My soul rejoices in the Lord

My soul glorifies the Lord,*
my spirit rejoices in God, my Saviour.
He looks on his servant in her lowliness;*
henceforth all ages will call me blessed.

The Almighty works marvels for me.*
Holy his name!
His mercy is from age to age,*
on those who fear him.

He puts forth his arm in strength*
and scatters the proud-hearted.
He casts the mighty from their thrones*
and raises the lowly.

He fills the starving with good things,*
sends the rich away empty.

He protects Israel, his servant,*
remembering his mercy,
the mercy promised to our fathers,*
to Abraham and his sons for ever.

This is said at Evening Prayer with its antiphon. The choice of antiphon is determined in the same way as is that of the Benedictus antiphon.

THE NUNC DIMITTIS
The Canticle of Simeon
LK 2:29-32

Christ is the light of the nations and the glory of Israel

At last, all-powerful Master,†
you give leave to your servant*
to go in peace, according to your promise.

For my eyes have seen your salvation*
which you have prepared for all nations,
the light to enlighten the Gentiles*
and give glory to Israel, your people.

This canticle is said at Night Prayer with its antiphon.

THE LORD'S PRAYER

The Lord's Prayer is said by all at Morning and Evening Prayer after the intercessions and before the concluding prayer. It may be introduced in this manner:

Let us now pray in the words our Saviour gave us: *Our Father ...*

or by some similar formula, e.g.

I

Let us now pray to the Father, in the words our Saviour gave us: *Our Father ...*

2

As we look to the coming of God's kingdom, let us say: *Our Father ...*

3

Let us sum up our praise and petitions in the words of Christ, saying: *Our Father ...*

4

Let us give a sure foundation to our praise and petitions by the Lord's Prayer: *Our Father ...*

5

Let us, once more, praise the Father and pray to him in the words of Christ himself, saying: *Our Father ...*

6

(*Addressed to Christ*) Lord, remember us in your kingdom, as following your teaching we say: *Our Father ...*

7

Following our Lord's teaching, let us say with faith and trust: *Our Father ...*

8

Let us fulfil our Lord's instruction, and say: *Our Father ...*

9

Let us now together say those words which the Lord gave us as the pattern of all prayer: *Our Father ...*

Our Father, who art in heaven,
hallowed be thy name.
Thy kingdom come.
Thy will be done on earth, as it is in heaven.
Give us this day our daily bread,
and forgive us our trespasses,
as we forgive those who trespass against us
and lead us not into temptation,
but deliver us from evil.

THE CONCLUDING PRAYER

The concluding prayer is prefixed with Let us pray *when said at Night Prayer. At Morning and Evening Prayer it is said after the Lord's Prayer, without this introduction.*

Conclusion of this prayer at Morning and Evening Prayer:

(We make our prayer) through our Lord Jesus Christ, your Son,
who lives and reigns with you and the Holy Spirit,
God, for ever and ever.
R̸ Amen.

The lead words only are usually given in the text.
If a different conclusion is to be used it is set out in full in the text.

At Night Prayer the following short conclusions are said:

1 When the prayer is addressed to the Father:
   Through Christ our Lord.

2 When the prayer is addressed to the Father, but ends with a mention of the Son:
   Who lives and reigns for ever and ever.

3 When the prayer is addressed to the Son:
   Who live and reign for ever and ever.

During Advent, Christmastide, Lent and Eastertide the prayer proper to each day concludes all the Hours of the Divine Office except Night Prayer.

On ordinary Sundays of the Year the same rule holds; but on week-days, prayers are given in the psalter for all the Hours.

On the Solemnities and Feasts of Saints the prayer of the celebration is used at all the Hours of the Divine Office except Night Prayer.

CONCLUSION OF THE HOURS

Morning and Evening Prayer

¶ *When a priest or deacon presides over the Office and no other Hour follows:*

The Lord be with you.

R̷ And also with you.

May almighty God bless you, the Father, and the Son, and the Holy Spirit.   R̷ Amen.

Another form of blessing may be used as in the Missal.

The people are then invited to leave:

Go in the peace of Christ.

R̷ Thanks be to God.

¶ *When no priest or deacon is present, or in recitation on one's own, the conclusion is as follows:*

The Lord bless us, and keep us from all evil, and bring us to ever-lasting life.   R̷ Amen.

Night Prayer

Night Prayer concludes with a blessing:

The Lord grant us a quiet night and a perfect end.   R̷ Amen.

Then, at Night Prayer, one of the final anthems to the Blessed Virgin is said or sung.

THE FOUR WEEK PSALTER

WEEK 1: SUNDAY

EVENING PRAYER I

℣ O God, come to our aid.
℞ O Lord, make haste to help us.
Glory be to the Father and to the Son and to the Holy Spirit, as it was in the beginning, is now, and ever shall be, world without end. Amen. Alleluia.

HYMN

O Light serene of God the Father's glory,
To you, O Christ, we sing,
And with the evening star, at hour of sunset,
Our worship bring.

To Father, Son and God's most Holy Spirit,
Eternal praise is due.
O Christ, who gave your life, the world gives glory
And thanks to you.

PSALMODY

ANTIPHON I
Advent: Proclaim it, say to the peoples: Behold, God will come and save us.
Lent, Sunday 1: Accept us, Lord, since we come with contrite heart and humbled spirit. Let our sacrifice be pleasing to you today, Lord God.
Lent, Sunday 5: I will put my law into their hearts; I will be their God and they shall be my people.
Eastertide: Let the raising of my hands in prayer please you like the evening oblation, alleluia.

Through the Year: Lord, let my prayer rise before you like incense.

12

PRAYER IN TIME OF DANGER   PSALM 140(141):1-9
*The smoke of incense rose before God with the prayers of the saints
from the hand of the angel (Rev 8:4)*

I have cálled to you, Lórd; hásten to hélp me!*
Héar my vóice when I crý to yóu.
Let my práyer aríse befóre you like íncense,*
the ráising of my hánds like an évening oblátion.

Sét, O Lórd, a guard óver my móuth;*
keep wátch, O Lórd, at the dóor of my líps!
Do not túrn my héart to thíngs that are wróng,†
to évil déeds with mén who are sínners.*

Néver allów me to sháre in their féasting.
If a góod man stríkes or repróves me it is kíndness;†
but let the óil of the wícked not anóint my héad.*
Let my práyer be éver agáinst their málice.

Their prínces were thrown dówn by the síde of the róck:*
thén they understóod that my wórds were kínd.
As a míllstone is sháttered to píeces on the gróund,*
so their bónes were stréwn at the móuth of the gráve.

To yóu, Lord Gód, my éyes are túrned:*
in yóu I take réfuge; spáre my sóul!
From the tráp they have láid for me kéep me sáfe:*
kéep me from the snáres of thóse who do évil.

Glory be to the Father and to the Son and to the Holy Spirit,*
As it was in the beginning, is now, and ever shall be, world without
    end. Amen.

*This doxology is said after each psalm and canticle unless otherwise
noted.*

Ant. Through the Year: Lord, let my prayer rise before you like
incense.

Ant. Advent: Proclaim it, say to the peoples: Behold, God will
come and save us.

Advent, Ant. 2: Behold the Lord will come, and all his holy ones with him. On that day a great light will appear, alleluia.

Ant. Lent, Sunday 1: Accept us, Lord, since we come with contrite heart and humbled spirit. Let our sacrifice be pleasing to you today, Lord God.
Ant. 2: If you call, the Lord will hear you; if you cry to him, he will say, 'Here I am.'

Ant. Lent, Sunday 5: I will put my law into their hearts: I will be their God and they shall be my people.
Ant. 2: I count everything as loss because of the surpassing worth of knowing my Lord Jesus Christ.

Ant. Eastertide: Let the raising of my hands in prayer please you like the evening oblation, alleluia.
Ant. 2: You have brought me out from prison to give praise to your name, alleluia.

Ant. 2: Through the Year: You are my refuge, Lord; my heritage in the land of the living.

YOU ARE MY REFUGE   PSALM 141(142)
All these things were fulfilled by the Lord at the time of his passion
(St Hilary)

> With all my vóice I crý to the Lórd,†
> with all my vóice I entréat the Lórd.*
> I póur out my tróuble befóre him;
> I téll him áll my distréss†
> while my spírit fáints withín me.*
> But yóu, O Lórd, know my páth.
>
> On the wáy where Í shall wálk*
> they have hídden a snáre to entráp me.
> Lóok on my ríght and sée:*
> there is nó one who tákes my párt.
> I have nó méans of escápe,*
> not óne who cáres for my sóul.

14

I crý to yóu, O Lórd.†
I have sáid: 'Yóu are my réfuge,*
all I háve in the lánd of the líving.'
Lísten, thén, to my crý*
for Í am in the dépths of distréss.

Réscue me from thóse who pursúe me*
for théy are strónger than Í.
Bríng my sóul out of this príson*
and thén I shall práise your náme.
Aróund me the júst will assémble*
becáuse of your góodness to mé.

Ant. *Through the Year:* You are my refuge, Lord; my heritage in the land of the living.

Ant. *Advent:* Behold the Lord will come, and all his holy ones with him. On that day a great light will appear, alleluia.
Ant 3: The Lord will come with great might and all flesh will see him.

Ant. *Lent, Sunday 1:* If you call, the Lord will hear you; if you cry to him, he will say, 'Here I am.'
Ant. 3: Christ suffered for our sins. Innocent though he was, he suffered for the guilty, to lead us to God. In the body he was put to death; in the spirit he was raised to life.

Ant. *Lent, Sunday 5:* I count everything as loss because of the surpassing worth of knowing my Lord Jesus Christ.
Ant. 3: Although he was the Son of God, he learned to obey through suffering.

Ant. *Eastertide:* You have brought me out from prison to give praise to your name, alleluia.
Ant. 3: The Son of God learned to obey through suffering, and he became the source of eternal salvation for all those who obey him, alleluia.

15

Ant. 3, Through the Year: The Lord Jesus humbled himself; therefore God has highly exalted him for ever.

CHRIST, THE SERVANT OF GOD   CANTICLE: PHIL 2:6-11

Though he was in the form of God,*
Jesus did not count equality with God a thing to be grasped.

He emptied himself,†
taking the form of a servant,*
being born in the likeness of men.

And being found in human form,†
he humbled himself and became obedient unto death,*
even death on a cross.

Therefore God has highly exalted him*
and bestowed on him the name which is above every name.

That at the name of Jesus every knee should bow,*
in heaven and on earth and under the earth,

And every tongue confess that Jesus Christ is Lord,*
to the glory of God the Father.

Ant. Through the Year: The Lord Jesus humbled himself; therefore God has highly exalted him for ever.

Ant. Advent: The Lord will come with great might and all flesh will see him.

Lent, Sunday 1: Christ suffered for our sins. Innocent though he was, he suffered for the guilty, to lead us to God. In the body he was put to death; in the spirit he was raised to life.

Lent, Sunday 5: Although he was the Son of God, he learned to obey through suffering.

Eastertide: The Son of God learned to obey through suffering, and he became the source of eternal salvation for all those who obey him, alleluia.

¶ *In Advent, Christmastide, Lent and Eastertide all from the Scripture Reading, inclusive, is from the Proper of Seasons.*

THROUGH THE YEAR

Scripture Reading *Rom 11:33-36*

How great are God's riches! How deep are his wisdom and know-ledge! Who can explain his decisions? Who can understand his ways? As the scripture says, 'Who knows the mind of the Lord? Who is able to give him advice? Who has ever given him anything, so that he had to pay it back?' For all things were created by him, and all things exist through him and for him. To God be glory forever! Amen.

Short Responsory

Cantor: How great are your works, O Lord.
All: How great are your works, O Lord.
Cantor: In wisdom you have made them all.
All: How great are our works, O Lord.
Cantor: Glory be to the Father and to the Son and to the Holy Spirit.
All: How great are your works, O Lord.

Magnificat antiphon from the Proper of Seasons.

Intercessions

Glory be to the one God, Father, Son, and Holy Spirit as we humbly pray: R⁷ Lord, be with your people.
Almighty Father, bring justice to our world,—that your people may live in the joy of your peace. R⁷
Bring all peoples into your kingdom,—that all mankind may be saved. R⁷
Give to married people the strength of your peace, the guidance of your will,—and the grace to live together in constant love. R⁷
Be the reward of all who have given us their help,—and grant them eternal life. R⁷
Have mercy on those who have lost their lives through warfare or violence,—and receive them into your rest. R⁷
Our Father

The concluding prayer from the Proper of Seasons.
Conclusion of the Hour as above, pp 11.

¶ *In the Offices which follow, all texts not otherwise designated are those of the time: Through the Year.*

Invitatory

℣ Lord, open our lips.

℟ And we shall praise your name.

Ant. Through the Year: Come, ring out our joy to the Lord; hail the God who saves us, alleluia.†

Invitatory Psalm, p 3.

MORNING PRAYER

℣ O God, come to our aid.

℟ O Lord, make haste to help us.

Glory be to the Father and to the Son and to the Holy Spirit, as it was in the beginning, is now, and ever shall be, world without end. Amen. Alleluia.

This versicle is omitted when the Invitatory immediately precedes this Hour.

HYMN

Transcendent God in whom we live,
The Resurrection and the Light,
We sing for you a morning hymn
To end the silence of the night.

When early cock begins to crow
And everything from sleep awakes,
New life and hope spring up again
While out of darkness colour breaks.

Creator of all things that are,
The measure and the end of all,

Forgiving God, forget our sins,
And hear our prayer before we call.

Praise Father, Son and Holy Ghost,
Blest Trinity and source of grace,
Who call us out of nothingness
To find in you our resting-place.

Alternative hymn
  Christ is the world's redeemer,
  The lover of the pure,
  The font of heavenly wisdom,
  Our trust and hope secure,
  The armour of his soldiers,
  The Lord of earth and sky,
  Our health while we are living,
  Our life when we shall die.

  Down in the realm of darkness,
  He lay a captive bound,
  But at the hour appointed
  He rose a victor crowned.
  And now, to heaven ascended,
  He sits upon a throne,
  Whence he had ne'er departed,
  His Father's and his own.

  All glory to the Father,
  The unbegotten One,
  All honour be to Jesus,
  His sole-begotten Son;
  And to the Holy Spirit,
  The perfect Trinity,
  Let all the worlds give answer,
  Amen—so let it be.

PSALMODY

ANTIPHON I

Advent: On that day the mountains will run with sweet wine. The hills will flow with milk and honey.

Lent, Sunday 1: I will bless you all my life, Lord; in your name I will lift up my hands.

Lent, Sunday 5: You, my God, have become my help.

Eastertide: Let anyone who is thirsty come and drink the water of life, a free gift for those who desire it, alleluia.

Through the Year: To you, O God, I keep vigil at dawn, to look upon your power, alleluia.

A SOUL THIRSTING FOR GOD   PSALM 62(63):2-9
Let the man who has put away the deeds of the night watch for God

O Gód, you are my Gód, for you I lóng;*
for yóu my sóul is thírsting,
My bódy pínes for yóu*
like a drý, weary lánd without wáter.
So I gáze on yóu in the sánctuary*
to sée your stréngth and your glóry.

For your lóve is bétter than lífe,*
my líps will spéak your práise.
So I will bléss you áll my lífe,*
in your náme I will líft up my hánds.
My sóul shall be fílled as with a bánquet,*
my móuth shall práise you with jóy.

On my béd I remémber yóu.*
On yóu I múse through the níght
for yóu have béen my hélp;*
in the shádow of your wíngs I rejóice.
My sóul clíngs to yóu;*
your ríght hand hólds me fást.

Ant. To you, O God, I keep vigil at dawn, to look upon your power, alleluia.

Ant. Advent: On that day the mountains will run with sweet wine. The hills will flow with milk and honey.
Ant. 2: The mountains and hills will sing praise to God, and all the trees of the countryside will clap their hands, for the Lord will come and he will reign for ever, alleluia.

Ant. Lent, Sunday 1: I will bless you all my life, Lord; in your name I will lift up my hands.
Ant. 2: Sing and praise God for ever.

Ant. Lent, Sunday 5: You, my God, have become my help.
Ant. 2: Deliver us by your wonderful works; save us from the power of death.

Ant. Eastertide: Let anyone who is thirsty come and drink the water of life, a free gift for those who desire it, alleluia.
Ant. 2: Worship the maker of heaven and earth and the sea and every spring of water, alleluia.

Ant. 2: The three sang with one voice in the heart of the fire: Blessed be God, alleluia.

LET EVERY CREATURE PRAISE THE LORD
CANTICLE
DAN 3:57-88, 56

Praise our God, all you his servants (Rev 19:5)

O all you works of the Lord, O bless the Lord.*
To him be highest glory and praise for ever.
And you, angels of the Lord, O bless the Lord.*
To him be highest glory and praise for ever.

And you, the heavens of the Lord, O bless the Lord.*
And you, clouds of the sky, O bless the Lord.
And you, all armies of the Lord, O bless the Lord.*
To him be highest glory and praise for ever.

And you, sun and moon, O bless the Lord.*
And you, the stars of the heav'ns, O bless the Lord.
And you, showers and rain, O bless the Lord.*
To him be highest glory and praise for ever.

21

And you, all you breezes and winds, O bless the Lord.*
And you, fire and heat, O bless the Lord.
And you, cold and heat, O bless the Lord.*
To him be highest glory and praise for ever.

And you, showers and dew, O bless the Lord.*
And you, frosts and cold, O bless the Lord.
And you, frost and snow, O bless the Lord.*
To him be highest glory and praise for ever.

And you, night-time and day, O bless the Lord.*
And you, darkness and light, O bless the Lord.
And you, lightning and clouds, O bless the Lord.*
To him be highest glory and praise for ever.

O let the earth bless the Lord.*
To him be highest glory and praise for ever.

And you, mountains and hills, O bless the Lord.*
And you, all plants of the earth, O bless the Lord.
And you, fountains and springs, O bless the Lord.*
To him be highest glory and praise for ever.

And you, rivers and seas, O bless the Lord.*
And you, creatures of the sea, O bless the Lord.
And you, every bird in the sky, O bless the Lord.†
And you, wild beasts and tame, O bless the Lord.*
To him be highest glory and praise for ever.

And you, children of men, O bless the Lord.*
To him be highest glory and praise for ever.

O Israel, bless the Lord. O bless the Lord.*
And you, priests of the Lord, O bless the Lord.
And you, servants of the Lord, O bless the Lord.*
To him be highest glory and praise for ever.

And you, spirits and souls of the just, O bless the Lord.*
And you, holy and humble of heart, O bless the Lord.
Ananias, Azarias, Mizael, O bless the Lord.*
To him be highest glory and praise for ever.

Let us praise the Father, the Son, and Holy Spirit:*
To you be highest glory and praise for ever.
May you be blessed, O Lord, in the heavens.*
To you be highest glory and praise for ever.

The Glory be *is not said after this Canticle, as it contains a doxology.*

Ant. The three sang with one voice in the heart of the fire: Blessed be God, alleluia.

Ant. Advent: The mountains and hills will sing praise to God, and all the trees of the countryside will clap their hands, for the Lord will come and he will reign for ever, alleluia.
Ant. 3: Behold, a great Prophet will come and he will renew Jerusalem, alleluia.

Ant. Lent, Sunday 1: Sing and praise God for ever.
Ant. 3: The Lord takes delight in his people. He crowns the poor with salvation.

Ant. Lent, Sunday 5: Deliver us by your wonderful works; save us from the power of death.
Ant. 3: Now the hour has come for the Son of Man to be glorified.

Ant. Eastertide: Worship the maker of heaven and earth and the sea and every spring of water, alleluia.
Ant. 3: Let the saints rejoice in glory, alleluia.

Ant. 3: Let Sion's sons exult in their king, alleluia.

THE SONG OF JOY OF THE SAINTS   PSALM 149
The members of the Church, God's new people, will rejoice in their king, who is Christ (Hesychius)

Síng a new sóng to the Lórd,*
his práise in the assémbly of the fáithful.
Let Ísrael rejóice in its Máker,*
let Síon's sons exúlt in their kíng.
Let them práise his náme with dáncing*
and make músic with tímbrel and hárp.

For the Lórd takes delíght in his péople.*
He crówns the póor with salvátion.

23

Let the fáithful rejóice in their glóry,*
shout for jóy and táke their rést.
Let the práise of Gód be on their líps*
and a twó-edged swórd in their hánd,

to déal out véngeance to the nátions*
and púnishment on áll the péoples;
to bínd their kíngs in cháins*
and their nóbles in fétters of íron;
to cárry out the séntence pre-ordáined:*
this hónour is for áll his fáithful.

Ant. Let Sion's sons exult in their king, alleluia.

Ant. Advent: Behold, a great Prophet will come and he will renew Jerusalem, alleluia.

Lent, Sunday 1: The Lord takes delight in his people. He crowns the poor with salvation.

Lent, Sunday 5: Now the hour has come for the Son of Man to be glorified.

Eastertide: Let the saints rejoice in glory, alleluia.

THROUGH THE YEAR

Scripture Reading   *Rev 7:10,12*

Victory to our God, who sits on the throne, and to the Lamb! Praise and glory and wisdom and thanksgiving and honour and power and strength to our God for ever and ever. Amen.

Short Responsory

Cantor: You are the Christ, the Son of the living God. Have mercy on us.

All: You are the Christ, the Son of the living God. Have mercy on us.

Cantor: You are seated at the right hand of the Father.

All: You are the Christ, the Son of the living God. Have mercy on us.

Cantor: Glory be to the Father and to the Son and to the Holy Spirit.

All: You are the Christ, the Son of the living God. Have mercy on us.

Benedictus antiphon from the Proper of Seasons.

Intercessions

Let us pray to Christ the Lord, the sun who enlightens all men, whose light will never fail us: ℟ Lord our Saviour, give us life!

Lord of the sun and the stars, we thank you for the gift of a new day;—and we celebrate the day of resurrection. ℟

Lead us by your Spirit to do your will;—guide and protect us by your wisdom. ℟

Bring us to share with joy this Sunday's eucharist;—nourish us by your word, and by your body. ℟

Lord, grant us your gifts, though we are unworthy;—with all our hearts we thank you. ℟

Our Father

The concluding prayer from the Proper of Seasons.
Conclusion of the Hour as on p 11.

EVENING PRAYER II

℣ O God, come to our aid.

℟ O Lord, make haste to help us.

Glory be to the Father and to the Son and to the Holy Spirit, as it was in the beginning, is now, and ever shall be, world without end. Amen. Alleluia.

HYMN

Praise to the holiest in the height,
And in the depth be praise,
In all his words most wonderful,
Most sure in all his ways.

O loving wisdom of our God!
When all was sin and shame,
A second Adam to the fight
And to the rescue came.

25

O wisest love! that flesh and blood
Which did in Adam fail,
Should strive afresh against their foe,
Should strive and should prevail.

And that a higher gift than grace
Should flesh and blood refine,
God's presence and his very self,
And essence all divine.

O generous love! that he who smote
In man for man the foe,
The double agony in man
For man should undergo.

And in the garden secretly,
And on the cross on high,
Should teach his brethren, and inspire
To suffer and to die.

Praise to the holiest in the height,
And in the depth be praise,
In all his words most wonderful,
Most sure in all his ways.

Alternative hymn
In the beginning God created heaven,
The dark and empty earth;
His Spirit moved across the sombre waters
And stirred them with his breath.

Then God created light, and with its coming
The dark was swept away;
The morning came, and then the quiet evening:
The end of God's first day.

To God the Father of the world give glory,
With Christ his only Son,
Who with the Spirit govern all creation:
Blest Trinity in One.

PSALMODY

ANTIPHON I

Advent: Rejoice greatly, daughter of Sion, shout with gladness, daughter of Jerusalem, alleluia.

Lent, Sunday 1: You must worship the Lord, your God, and serve him alone.

Lent, Sunday 5: As Moses lifted up the serpent in the desert, so the Son of Man must be lifted up.

Eastertide: The Lord has risen and sits at the right hand of God, alleluia.

Through the Year: The Lord will send his mighty sceptre from Sion, and he will rule for ever, alleluia.

THE MESSIAH IS KING AND PRIEST PSALM 109(110):1-5,7
He must be king so that he may put all his enemies under his feet
(1 Cor 15:25)

The Lórd's reveláton to my Máster:†
'Sít on my ríght:*
your fóes I will pút beneath your féet.'

The Lórd will wíeld from Síon†
your scéptre of pówer:*
rúle in the mídst of all your fóes.

A prínce from the dáy of your bírth†
on the hóly móuntains;*
from the wómb before the dáwn I begót you.

The Lórd has sworn an óath he will not chánge.†
'You are a príest for éver,*
a príest like Melchízedek of óld.'

The Máster stánding at your ríght hand*
will shatter kíngs in the dáy of his wráth.

He shall drínk from the stréam by the wáyside*
and thérefore he shall líft up his héad.

27

Ant. The Lord will send his mighty sceptre from Sion, and he will rule for ever, alleluia.

Ant. Advent: Rejoice greatly, daughter of Sion, shout with gladness, daughter of Jerusalem, alleluia.

Ant. 2: Christ our King will come. He is the Lamb that John announced.

Ant. Lent, Sunday 1: You must worship the Lord, your God, and serve him alone.

Ant. 2: Now is the favourable time; this is the day of salvation.

Ant. Lent, Sunday 5: As Moses lifted up the serpent in the desert, so the Son of Man must be lifted up.

Ant. 2: The Lord of hosts protects and rescues; he spares and he saves.

Ant. Eastertide: The Lord has risen and sits at the right hand of God, alleluia.

Ant. 2: He has freed us from the power of darkness and has given us a place in the kingdom of his Son, alleluia.

Ant. 2: The earth trembled before the Lord, alleluia.

ISRAEL IS FREED FROM EGYPT   PSALM 113A(114):1-8
You, who have renounced this world, have also been led forth from Egypt (St Augustine)

When Ísrael came fórth from Égypt,*
Jacob's sóns from an álien péople,
Júdah becáme the Lord's témple,*
Ísrael becáme his kíngdom.

The séa fléd at the síght:*
the Jórdan turned báck on its cóurse,
the móuntains léapt like ráms*
and the hílls like yéarling shéep.

Whý was it, séa, that you fléd,*
that you túrned back, Jórdan, on your cóurse?

Móuntains, that you léapt like ráms,*
hílls, like yéarling shéep?

Trémble, O éarth, before the Lórd,*
in the présence of the Gód of Jácob,
who túrns the róck into a póol*
and flínt into a spríng of wáter.

Ant. The earth trembled before the Lord, alleluia.

OUTSIDE LENT

Ant. Advent: Christ our King will come. He is the Lamb that John announced.
Ant. 3: Behold I am coming soon to reward every man according to his deeds, says the Lord.

Ant. Eastertide: He has freed us from the power of darkness and has given us a place in the kingdom of his Son, alleluia.
Ant. 3: Alleluia, the Lord, our God, is King; let us rejoice and give glory to him, alleluia.

Ant. 3: The Lord is King, our God, the Almighty! alleluia.

When chanted, this canticle is sung with Alleluia *as set out below. When recited, it suffices to say* Alleluia *at the beginning and end of each strophe.*

THE MARRIAGE FEAST OF THE LAMB   CANTICLE: REV 19:1,2,5-7
    Alleluia.
    Salvation and glory and power belong to our God,*
    (R̦ Alleluia.)
    His judgments are true and just.
    R̦ Alleluia (alleluia).

    Alleluia.
    Praise our God, all you his servants,
    (R̦ Alleluia.)
    You who fear him, small and great.
    R̦ Alleluia (alleluia).

29

Alleluia.
The Lord our God, the Almighty, reigns,*
(R̷ Alleluia.)
Let us rejoice and exult and give him the glory.
R̷ Alleluia (alleluia).

Alleluia.
The marriage of the Lamb has come,*
(R̷ Alleluia.)
And his bride has made herself ready.
R̷ Alleluia (alleluia).

Ant. The Lord is King, our God, the Almighty! alleluia.

Ant. Advent: Behold I am coming soon to reward every man according to his deeds, says the Lord.
Eastertide: Alleluia, the Lord, our God, is King; let us rejoice and give glory to him, alleluia.

LENT

Ant. Lent, Sunday 1: Now is the favourable time; this is the day of salvation.
Ant. 3: Now we are going up to Jerusalem, and everything that is written about the Son of Man will come true.

Ant. Lent, Sunday 5: The Lord of hosts protects and rescues; he spares and he saves.
Ant. 3: He was wounded for our faults, he was bruised for our sins. Through his wounds we are healed.

CHRIST, THE SERVANT OF GOD,	CANTICLE
FREELY ACCEPTS HIS PASSION	I PET 2:21-24

Christ suffered for you,†
leaving you an example*
that you should follow in his steps.

He committed no sin;*
no guile was found on his lips.

30

When he was reviled,*
he did not revile in return.

When he suffered,*
he did not threaten;
but he trusted to him*
who judges justly.

He himself bore our sins*
in his body on the tree,
that we might die to sin*
and live to righteousness.

By his wounds you have been healed.

Ant. Sunday 1: Now we are going up to Jerusalem, and everything that is written about the Son of Man will come true.
Sunday 5: He was wounded for our faults, he was bruised for our sins. Through his wounds we are healed.

THROUGH THE YEAR

Scripture Reading   *2 Cor 1:3-4*
Let us give thanks to the God and Father of our Lord Jesus Christ, the merciful Father, the God from whom all help comes! He helps us in all our troubles, so that we are able to help those who have all kinds of troubles, using the same help that we ourselves have received from God.

Short Responsory
Cantor: Blessed are you in the vault of heaven.
All: Blessed are you in the vault of heaven.
Cantor: You are exalted and glorified above all else for ever.
All: Blessed are you in the vault of heaven.
Cantor: Glory be to the Father and to the Son and to the Holy Spirit.
All: Blessed are you in the vault of heaven.

Magnificat antiphon from the Proper of Seasons.

31

Intercessions

Christ is the Head of his body, the Church, and we are the members of that body; gathered this evening to pray in his name, we say:
℟ Your kingdom come!

May your Church be a light to the nations, the sign and source of your power to unite all men:—may she lead mankind to the mystery of your love. ℟

Guide the Pope and all the bishops of your Church:—grant them the gifts of unity, of love, and of peace. ℟

Lord, give peace to our troubled world—and give to your children security of mind and freedom from anxiety. ℟

Help us to bring your compassion to the poor, the sick, the lonely, the unloved;—lead us to find you in the coming week. ℟

Awaken the dead to a glorious resurrection:—may we be united with them at the end of time. ℟

Our Father

The concluding prayer from the Proper of Seasons.
Conclusion of the Hour as on p 11.

WEEK 1: MONDAY

Invitatory ant. Let us come before the Lord, giving thanks.
Psalm, p 3.

MORNING PRAYER

HYMN

The day is filled with splendour
When God brings light from light,
And all renewed creation
Rejoices in his sight.

The Father gives his children
The wonder of the world

In which his power and glory
Like banners are unfurled.

With every living creature,
Awaking with the day,
We turn to God our Father,
Lift up our hearts and pray:

O Father, Son and Spirit,
Your grace and mercy send,
That we may live to praise you
Today and to the end.

PSALMODY

The first antiphon given with each psalm is used Through the Year and, except for Eastertide, during the other seasons unless otherwise noted.

Ant. 1: It is you whom I invoke, O Lord. In the morning you hear me.
Eastertide: In you they rejoice, those who love your name, alleluia.

MORNING PRAYER FOR HELP　　　　　　　　　　PSALM 5:2-10,12-13
Those who have received the Word of God which dwells within will rejoice for ever.

To my wórds give éar, O Lórd,*
give héed to my gróaning.
Atténd to the sóund of my críes,*
my Kíng and my Gód.

It is yóu whom I invóke, O Lórd.*
In the mórning you héar me;
in the mórning I óffer you my práyer,*
wátching and wáiting.

Yóu are no Gód who loves évil;*
no sínner is your guést.
The bóastful shall not stánd their gróund*
befóre your fáce.

33

You háte áll who do évil:*
you destróy all who líe.
The decéitful and blóodthirsty mán*
the Lórd detésts.

But Í through the gréatness of your lóve*
have áccess to your hóuse.
I brów down befóre your holy témple,*
fílled with áwe.

Léad me, Lórd, in your jústice,†
because of thóse who lie in wáit;*
make cléar your way befóre me.

No trúth can be fóund in their móuths,*
their héart is all míschief,
their thróat a wíde-open gráve,*
all hóney their spéech.

All thóse you protéct shall be gládd*
and ríng out their jóy.
You shélter them; in yóu they rejóice,*
those who lóve your náme.

It is yóu who bless the júst man, Lórd:*
you surróund him with fávour as with a shíeld.

Ant. It is you whom I invoke, O Lord. In the morning you hear me.
Eastertide: In you they rejoice, those who love your name, alleluia.

Ant. 2: Lord our God, we praise the splendour of your name.
Eastertide: Yours is the kingdom, O Lord, and you are exalted as
head above all, alleluia.

TO GOD ALONE BE HONOUR AND GLORY   CANTICLE
I CHRON 29:10-13
Blessed be the God and Father of our Lord Jesus Christ (Eph 1:3)

Blessed are you, O Lord,†
the God of Israel our father,*
for ever and ever.

Yours, O Lord, is the greatness, and the power,†
and the glory, and the victory, and the majesty;*
for all that is in the heavens and in the earth is yours;

Yours is the kingdom, O Lord,*
and you are exalted as head above all.

Both riches and honour come from you,*
and you rule over all.
In your hand are power and might;*
and in your hand it is to make great and to give strength to all.

And now we thank you, our God,*
and praise your glorious name.

Ant. Lord our God, we praise the splendour of your name.
Eastertide: Yours is the kingdom, O Lord, and you are exalted as head above all, alleluia.

Ant. 3: Adore the Lord in his holy court.
Eastertide: The Lord is enthroned as king for ever, alleluia.

PUBLIC PRAISE OF THE WORD OF GOD   PSALM 28(29)
A voice was heard from heaven, saying, 'This is my beloved Son'
(Mt 3:17)

O give the Lórd you sóns of Gód,*
give the Lórd glóry and pówer;
give the Lórd the glóry of his náme.*
Adore the Lórd in his hóly court.

The Lord's vóice resóunding on the wáters,*
the Lórd on the imménsity of wáters;
the vóice of the Lórd, full of pówer,*
the vóice of the Lórd, full of spléndour.

The Lord's vóice sháttering the cédars,*
the Lord shátters the cédars of Lébanon;
he makes Lébanon léap like a cálf*
and Sírion like a yóung wild-óx.

35

The Lord's vóice fláshes flames of fíre.†

The Lord's vóice sháking the wílderness,*
the Lord shákes the wílderness of Kádesh;
the Lord's vóice rénding the óak tree*
and strípping the fórest báre.

The Gód of glóry thúnders.*
In his témple they áll cry: 'Glóry!'
The Lórd sat enthróned over the flóod;*
the Lórd sits as kíng for éver.

The Lórd will give stréngth to his péople,*
the Lórd will bless his péople with péace.

Ant. Adore the Lord in his holy court.
Eastertide: The Lord is enthroned as king for ever, alleluia.

THROUGH THE YEAR

Scripture Reading   *2 Thess 3:10b-13*
We gave you a rule when we were with you: not to let anyone have
any food if he refused to do any work. Now we hear that there are
some of you who are living in idleness, doing no work themselves
but interfering with everyone else's. In the Lord Jesus Christ, we
order and call on people of this kind to go on quietly working and
earning the food that they eat. My brothers, never grow tired of
doing what is right.

Short Responsory
R̸ Blessed be the Lord from age to age. *Repeat* R̸
V̸ He alone has wrought marvellous works. R̸ Glory be. R̸

Benedictus ant. Blessed be the Lord, our God.

Intercessions
As the new day begins let us praise Christ, in whom is the fulness of
grace and the Spirit of God. R̸ Lord, give us your Spirit.
We praise you, Lord,—and we thank you for all your blessings. R̸
Give us peace of mind and generosity of heart;—grant us health
and strength to do your will. R̸

May your love be with us during the day;—guide us in our work. ℟
Be with all those who have asked our prayers,—and grant them all
their needs. ℟
Our Father

Concluding Prayer
Lord, be the beginning and end
of all that we do and say.
Prompt our actions with your grace,
and complete them with your all-powerful help.
(We make our prayer) through our Lord.

Conclusion of the Hour as on p 11.

EVENING PRAYER

HYMN

Come, praise the Lord, the Almighty, the King of all nations!
Tell forth his fame, O ye peoples, with loud acclamations!
His love is sure;
Faithful his word shall endure,
Steadfast through all generations!

Praise to the Father most gracious, the Lord of creation!
Praise to his Son, the Redeemer who wrought our salvation!
O heav'nly Dove,
Praise to thee, fruit of their love,
Giver of all consolation.

PSALMODY

Ant. 1: The Lord cares for the weak and oppressed.
Eastertide: Courage! The victory is mine; I have conquered the
world, alleluia.

37

THE LORD HAS GIVEN SECURITY　　　　　　　　　PSALM 10(11)
TO THE UPRIGHT MAN
*Blessed are those who hunger and thirst for what is right: they shall
be satisfied* (Mt 5:6)

In the Lórd I have táken my réfuge.†
Hów can you sáy to my sóul:*
'Flý like a bírd to its móuntain.

See the wícked brácing their bów;†
they are fíxing their árrows on the stríng*
to shóot upright mén in the dárk.
Foundátions once destróyed,* what can the júst do?'

The Lórd is in his hóly témple,*
the Lórd, whose thróne is in héaven.
His éyes look dówn on the wórld;*
his gáze tests mórtal mén.

The Lórd tests the júst and the wícked:*
the lóver of víolence he hátes.
He sends fíre and brímstone on the wícked;*
he sends a scórching wínd as their lót.

The Lórd is júst and loves jústice:*
the úpright shall sée his fáce.

Ant. The Lord cares for the weak and oppressed.
Eastertide: Courage! The victory is mine; I have conquered the
world, alleluia.

Ant. 2: Blessed are the pure in heart: they shall see God.
Eastertide: He shall live in your tabernacle; he shall dwell on your
holy mountain, alleluia.

WHO SHALL BE WORTHY TO STAND　　　　　　　PSALM 14(15)
BEFORE THE LORD?
You have come to Mount Sion to the city of the living God (Heb 12:22)

Lord, whó shall be admítted to your tént*
and dwéll on your hóly móuntain?

Hé who wálks without fáult;*
hé who ácts with jústice
and spéaks the trúth from his héart;*
hé who does not slánder with his tóngue;

hé who does no wróng to his bróther,*
who cásts no slúr on his néighbour,
who hólds the gódless in disdáin,*
but hónours those who féar the Lórd;

hé who keeps his plédge, come what máy;†
who tákes no ínterest on a lóan*
and accépts no bríbes against the ínnocent.
Such a mán will stand fírm for éver.

Ant. Blessed are the pure in heart: they shall see God.
Eastertide: He shall live in your tabernacle; he shall dwell on your holy mountain, alleluia.

Ant. 3: God chose us in his Son and made us his adopted sons.
Eastertide: When I am lifted up from the earth, I shall draw all men to myself, alleluia.

GOD, THE SAVIOUR   CANTICLE: EPH 1:3-10
Blessed be the God and Father*
of our Lord Jesus Christ,
who has blessed us in Christ*
with every spiritual blessing in the heavenly places.

He chose us in him*
before the foundation of the world,
that we should be holy*
and blameless before him.

He destined us in love*
to be his sons through Jesus Christ,
according to the purpose of his will,†
to the praise of his glorious grace*
which he freely bestowed on us in the Beloved.

In him we have redemption through his blood,*
the forgiveness of our trespasses,
according to the riches of his grace*
which he lavished upon us.

He has made known to us†
in all wisdom and insight*
the mystery of his will,
according to his purpose*
which he set forth in Christ.

His purpose he set forth in Christ,*
as a plan for the fulness of time,
to unite all things in him,*
things in heaven and things on earth.

Ant. God chose us in his Son and made us his adopted sons.
Eastertide: When I am lifted up from the earth, I shall draw all men
to myself, alleluia.

THROUGH THE YEAR

Scripture Reading   *Col 1:9b-11*
We ask God to fill you with the knowledge of his will, with all the
wisdom and understanding that his Spirit gives. Then you will be
able to live as the Lord wants, and always do what pleases him.
Your lives will be fruitful in all kinds of good works, and you will
grow in your knowledge of God. May you be made strong with all
the strength which comes from his glorious might, so that you may
be able to endure everything with patience.

Short Responsory
R̸ Heal my soul for I have sinned against you. *Repeat* R̸
V̸ I said: 'Lord, have mercy on me.' R̸ Glory be. R̸

Magnificat ant. My soul magnifies the Lord, since God has had
regard for my humble state.

Intercessions
God our Father has bound himself to us in an everlasting covenant.

In thankfulness and faith, we pray to him: R̷ Lord, bless your people!

In Christ you have given a new covenant to men:—may they know the greatness which they have inherited. R̷

Gather into one all who bear the name of Christian,—that the world may believe in the Christ you have sent. R̷

Pour out your love on our friends, and on all whom we know;—may they carry with them the gentleness of Christ. R̷

Comfort the dying;—may they know your saving love. R̷

Show your mercy to the dead;—may they find their rest in Christ. R̷

Our Father

Concluding Prayer

Let our worship give you glory, Lord,
who for our salvation looked upon
the lowliness of Mary your handmaid:
raise us up to share with her
the fulness of redemption.
(We make our prayer) through our Lord.

Conclusion of the Hour on p 11.

WEEK 1: TUESDAY

Invitatory ant. The Lord is a great king: come, let us adore him.
Psalm, p 3.

MORNING PRAYER

HYMN

O Christ, the Light of heaven
And of the world true Light,
You come in all your radiance
To cleave the web of night.

41

May what is false within us
Before your truth give way,
That we may live untroubled,
With quiet hearts this day.

May steadfast faith sustain us,
And hope made firm in you;
The love that we have wasted,
O God of love, renew.

Blest Trinity we praise you
In whom our quest will cease;
Keep us with you for ever
In happiness and peace.

PSALMODY

Ant. 1: The man with clean hands and pure heart will climb the mountain of the Lord.
Eastertide: He who came down is he who has now risen higher than all the heavens, alleluia.

When the following psalm has been used at the Invitatory, ps 94, p 3, is said here in place of it.

THE LORD COMES TO HIS TEMPLE   PSALM 23(24)
The gates of heaven were opened to Christ because he was lifted up in the flesh (St Irenaeus)

The Lórd's is the éarth and its fúlness,*
the wórld and áll its péoples.
It is hé who sét it on the séas;*
on the wáters he máde it fírm.

Who shall clímb the móuntain of the Lórd?*
Who shall stánd in his hóly pláce?
The mán with clean hánds and pure héart,†
who desíres not wórthless thíngs,*
who has not swórn so as to decéive his néighbour.

42

He shall recéive bléssings from the Lórd*
and rewárd from the Gód who sáves him.
Súch are the mén who séek him,*
seek the fáce of the Gód of Jácob.

O gátes, lift hígh your héads;†
grow hígher, áncient dóors.*
Let him énter, the kíng of glóry!

Whó is the kíng of glóry?†
The Lórd, the míghty, the váliant,*
the Lórd, the váliant in wár.

O gátes, lift hígh your héads;†
grow hígher, áncient dóors.*
Let him énter, the kíng of glóry!

Who is hé, the kíng of glóry?†
Hé, the Lórd of ármies,*
hé is the kíng of glóry.

Ant. The man with clean hands and pure heart will climb the mountain of the Lord.
Eastertide: He who came down is he who has now risen higher than all the heavens, alleluia.

Ant. 2: Praise the king of the ages in all your deeds.
Eastertide: Keep these days with joy and give glory to the Lord, alleluia.

GOD PUNISHES AND ALSO SAVES   CANTICLE: TOB 13:1-5B,7-8
Blessed be the God and Father of our Lord Jesus Christ! Because of his great love we have been born anew (1 Pet 1:3)

Blessed is God who lives for ever,*
and blessed is his kingdom.
For he afflicts, and he shows mercy;†
he leads down to Hades, and brings up again,*
and there is no one who can escape his hand.

Acknowledge him before the nations, O sons of Israel;*
for he has scattered us among them.
Make his greatness known there,*
and exalt him in the presence of all the living;
because he is our Lord and God,*
he is our Father for ever.

He will afflict us for our iniquities;*
and again he will show mercy,
but see what he will do with you;*
give thanks to him with your full voice.
Praise the Lord of righteousness,*
and exalt the King of the ages.

I give him thanks in the land of my captivity,*
and I show his power and majesty to a nation of sinners.
Turn back, you sinners, and do right before him;*
who knows if he will accept you and have mercy on you?

I exalt my God;†
my soul exalts the King of heaven,*
and will rejoice in his majesty.
Let all men speak,*
and give him thanks in Jerusalem.

Ant. Praise the king of the ages in all your deeds.
Eastertide: Keep these days with joy, and give glory to the Lord, alleluia.

Ant. 3: Praise is fitting for loyal hearts.
Eastertide: The Lord fills the earth with his love, alleluia.

PRAISE OF THE PROVIDENCE OF THE LORD   PSALM 32(33)
All things were made through him (Jn 1:3)

Ring out your jóy to the Lórd, O you júst;*
for praise is fítting for lóyal héarts.

Give thánks to the Lórd upon the lýre*
with a tén-stringed hárp sing him sóngs.

O síng him a sóng that is néw,*
play lóudly, with áll your skíll.

For the wórd of the Lórd is fáithful*
and áll his wórks to be trústed.
The Lórd loves jústice and ríght*
and fílls the éarth with his lóve.

By his wórd the héavens were máde,*
by the bréath of his móuth all the stárs.
He colléts the wáves of the ócean;*
he stóres up the dépths of the séa.

Let all the éarth féar the Lórd,*
all who líve in the wórld revére him.
He spóke; and it cáme to bé.*
He commánded; it spráng into béing.

He frustrátes the desígns of the nátions,*
he deféats the pláns of the péoples.
His ówn designs shall stánd for éver,*
the pláns of his héart from age to áge.

They are háppy, whose Gód is the Lórd,*
the péople he has chósen as his ówn.
From the héavens the Lórd looks fórth,*
he sées all the chíldren of mén.

From the pláce where he dwélls he gázes*
on áll the dwéllers on the éarth,
he who shápes the héarts of them áll*
and consíders áll their déeds.

A kíng is not sáved by his ármy,*
nor a wárrior presérved by his stréngth.
A váin hope for sáfety is the hórse;*
despíte its pówer it cannot sáve.

The Lórd looks on thóse who revére him,*
on thóse who hópe in his lóve,
to réscue their sóuls from déath,*
to kéep them alíve in fámine.

Our sóul is wáiting for the Lórd.*
The Lórd is our hélp and our shíeld.
In hím do our héarts find jóy.*
We trúst in his hóly náme.

May your lóve be upón us, O Lórd,*
as we pláce all our hópe in yóu.

Ant. Praise is fitting for loyal hearts.
Eastertide: The Lord fills the earth with his love, alleluia.

THROUGH THE YEAR

Scripture Reading   *Rom 13:11b,12-13a*
You know what hour it is, how it is full time now for you to wake
from sleep. The night is far gone, the day is at hand. Let us then
cast off the works of darkness and put on the armour of light; let us
conduct ourselves becomingly as in the day.

Short Responsory
R̷ My helper is my God; I will place my trust in him. *Repeat* R̷
V̷ He is my refuge; he sets me free. R̷ Glory be. R̷

Benedictus ant. The Lord has raised up a mighty saviour for us, as
he promised through the lips of his prophets.

Intercessions
As Christians called to share the life of God, let us praise the Lord
Jesus, the high priest of our faith. R̷ You are our Saviour and our
God.
Almighty King, you have baptized us, and made us a royal priest-
hood:—may we offer you a constant sacrifice of praise. R̷
Help us to keep your commandments;—so that through your Holy
Spirit we may dwell in you, and you in us. R̷
Everlasting Wisdom, come to us:—dwell with us and work in us
today. R̷
Help us to be considerate and kind;—grant that we may bring joy,
not pain, to those we meet. R̷
Our Father

Concluding Prayer
Look with favour on our morning prayer, Lord,
and in your saving love
let your light penetrate the hidden places of our hearts.
May no sordid desires darken our minds,
renewed and enlightened as we are by your heavenly grace.
(We make our prayer) through our Lord.

EVENING PRAYER

HYMN

O Strength and Stay upholding all creation,
Who ever dost thyself unmoved abide,
Yet day by day the light in due gradation
From hour to hour in all its changes guide,

Grant to life's day a calm unclouded ending,
An eve untouched by shadows of decay,
The brightness of a holy death-bed blending
With dawning glories of the eternal day.

Hear us, O Father, gracious and forgiving,
Through Jesus Christ thy co-eternal Word,
Who, with the Holy Ghost, by all things living
Now and to endless ages art adored.

PSALMODY

Ant. 1: The Lord will give victory to his anointed one.
Eastertide: Now our God reigns, and power belongs to Christ, his
anointed, alleluia.

PRAYER FOR A KING BEFORE BATTLE   PSALM 19(20)
Whoever calls upon the name of the Lord will be saved (Acts 2:21)

May the Lord ánswer in tíme of tríal;*
may the náme of Jacob's Gód protéct you.

May he sénd you hélp from his shríne*
and gíve you suppórt from Síon.
May he remémber áll your ófferings*
and receive your sacrifice with favour.

May he gíve you your héart's desíre*
and fulfíl every óne of your pláns.
May we ríng out our jóy at your victory†
and rejóice in the náme of our Gód.*
May the Lórd gránt all your práyers.

I am súre nów that the Lórd*
will give victory tó his anóinted,
will replý, from his hóly héaven*
with the mighty victory of his hánd.

Sóme trust in cháriots or hórses,*
but wé in the náme of the Lórd.
Théy will collápse and fáll,*
but wé shall hóld and stand fírm.

Give victory to the king, O Lórd.*
give ánswer on the dáy we cáll.

Ant. The Lord will give victory to his anointed one.
Eastertide: Now our God reigns, and power belongs to Christ, his anointed, alleluia.

Ant. 2: We shall sing and praise your power.
Eastertide: You have assumed your great power, you have begun your reign, alleluia.

THANKSGIVING FOR A KING'S VICTORY   PSALM 20(21):2–8,14
He accepted human life, so that he could rise from the dead and live for ever and ever (St Irenaeus)

O Lórd, your stréngth gives jóy to the kíng;*
hów your sáving hélp makes him glád!
You have gránted hím his héart's desíre;*
you háve not refúsed the práyer of his líps.

You cáme to méet him with the bléssings of succéss,*
you have sét on his héad a crówn of pure góld.
He ásked you for lífe and thís you have gíven,*
dáys that will lást from áge to áge.

Your sáving hélp has gíven him glóry.*
You have láid upón him májesty and spléndour,
you have gránted your bléssings to hím for éver.*
You have máde him rejóice with the jóy of your présence.

The kíng has pút his trúst in the Lórd:*
through the mércy of the Most High hé shall stand fírm.
O Lórd, aríse in your stréngth;*
we shall síng and práise your pówer.

Ant. We shall sing and praise your power.
Eastertide: You have assumed your great power, you have begun
your reign, alleluia.

Ant. 3: Lord, you made us a kingdom and priests to serve our God.
Eastertide: May your whole creation serve you, for you spoke and
they came into being, alleluia.

HYMN OF THE REDEEMED   CANTICLE: REV 4:11;5:9,10,12

Worthy are you, our Lord and God,*
to receive glory and honour and power,
for you created all things,*
and by your will they existed and were created.

Worthy are you, O Lord,*
to take the scroll and to open its seals,
for you were slain,†
and by your blood you ransomed men for God*
from every tribe and tongue and people and nation.

You have made us a kingdom and priests to serve our God,*
and we shall reign on earth.

Worthy is the Lamb who was slain,*

to receive power and wealth,
and wisdom and might,*
and honour and glory and blessing.

Ant. Lord, you made us a kingdom and priests to serve our God.
Eastertide: May your whole creation serve you, for you spoke and
they came into being, alleluia.

THROUGH THE YEAR

Scripture Reading   *1 Jn 3:1a,2*
Think of the love that the Father has lavished on us,
by letting us be called God's children;
and that is what we are.
My dear people, we are already the children of God
but what we are to be in the future has not yet been revealed;
we shall be like him
because we shall see him as he really is.

Short Responsory
R̷ Your word, O Lord, will endure for ever. *Repeat* R̷
V̷ Your truth will last from age to age. R̷ Glory be. R̷

Magnificat ant. My spirit exults in the Lord God, my saviour.

Intercessions
Through Christ we are sons of God; in him we see what we shall be
when we come to the Father. With confidence we pray: R̷ Lord, in
your mercy, hear our prayer.
Guide leaders and governments:—give them wisdom and integrity.
R̷
You are the Lord and source of our freedom:—bring those in
captivity of mind or body to the freedom of the children of God. R̷
Give courage and strength to the young.—Help them to choose their
work, and make the right decisions for their way of life. R̷
Give patient tolerance to all who are no longer young;—open the
hearts of the young to accept from them understanding and love. R̷
Receive the departed into your eternal kingdom;—sustain our hope
to reign with you for ever. R̷
Our Father

Concluding Prayer
We give you thanks, Lord God Almighty,
for bringing us safely to the evening of this day;
we humbly ask that the prayer we make with uplifted hands
may be an offering pleasing in your sight.
(We make our prayer) through our Lord.

WEEK 1: WEDNESDAY

Invitatory ant. Let us adore the Lord, for it is he who made us.
Psalm, p 3.

MORNING PRAYER

HYMN

Lord God, your light which dims the stars
Awakes all things,
And all that springs to life in you
Your glory sings.

Your peaceful presence, giving strength,
Is everywhere,
And fallen men may rise again
On wings of prayer.

You are the God whose mercy rests
On all you made;
You gave us Christ, whose love through death
Our ransom paid.

We praise you, Father, with your Son
And Spirit blest,
In whom creation lives and moves,
And finds its rest.

51

PSALMODY

Ant. 1: In your light, God, we see light.
Eastertide: In you, Lord, is the source of life, alleluia.

THE EVIL OF THE SINNER; PSALM 35(36)
THE GOODNESS OF THE LORD
The man who follows me will not walk in darkness, but he will have the light of life for his guide (Jn 8:12)

Sín spéaks to the sínner*
in the dépths of his héart.
There ís no féar of Gód*
befóre his éyes.

He so flátters himsélf in his mínd*
that he knóws not his guílt.
In his móuth are míschief and decéit.*
All wísdom is góne.

He plóts the deféat of góodness*
as he líes on his béd.
He has sét his fóot on evil wáys,*
he clíngs to what is évil.

Your lóve, Lord, réaches to héaven;*
your trúth to the skíes.
Your jústice is líke God's móuntain,*
your júdgments like the déep.

To both mán and béast you give protéction.*
O Lórd, how précious is your lóve.
My Gód, the sóns of mén*
find réfuge in the shélter of your wíngs.

They féast on the ríches of your hóuse;*
they drínk from the stréam of your delíght.
In yóu is the sóurce of lífe*
and ín your líght we see líght.

Keep on lóving thóse who knów you,*
doing jústice for úpright héarts.

Let the fóot of the próud not crúsh me*
nor the hánd of the wícked cast me óut.

Sée how the évil-doers fáll!*
Flung dówn, they shall néver aríse.

Ant. In your light, God, we see light.
Eastertide: In you, Lord, is the source of life, alleluia.

Ant. 2: Lord, you are great, you are glorious, you are wonderfully strong.
Eastertide: You sent forth your Spirit, and they were created, alleluia.

| THE LORD, CREATOR OF THE WORLD, | CANTICLE |
| PROTECTS HIS PEOPLE | JUD 16:2-3A,13-15 |

They began to sing a new song (Rev 5:9)

Begin a song to my God with tambourines,*
sing to my Lord with cymbals.
Raise to him a new psalm;†
exalt him and call upon his name.*
For God is the Lord who crushes wars.

I will sing to my God a new song:†
O Lord, you are great and glorious,*
wonderful in strength, invincible.

Let all your creatures serve you,*
for you spoke, and they were made.
You sent forth your Spirit, and it formed them;*
there is none that can resist your voice.

For the mountains shall be shaken to their foundations with
   the waters;*
at your presence the rocks shall melt like wax,
but to those who fear you*
you will continue to show mercy.

Ant. Lord, you are great, you are glorious, you are wonderfully strong.
Eastertide: You sent forth your Spirit, and they were created, alleluia.

Ant. 3: Cry to God with shouts of joy.
Eastertide: God is king of all the earth; sing praise with all your skill, alleluia.

THE LORD IS THE KING OF ALL   PSALM 46(47)
He is seated at the right hand of the Father, and his kingdom will have no end.

All péoples, cláp your hánds,*
cry to Gód with shóuts of jóy!
For the Lórd, the Most Hígh, we must féar,*
great kíng over áll the éarth.

He subdúes péoples únder us*
and nátions únder our féet.
Our inhéritance, our glóry, is from hím,*
gíven to Jácob out of lóve.

God goes úp with shóuts of jóy;*
the Lord ascénds with trúmpet blást.
Sing práise for Gód, sing práise,*
sing práise to our kíng, sing práise.

God is kíng of áll the éarth,*
Sing práise with áll your skíll.
God is kíng óver the nátions;*
God réigns on his hóly thróne.

The prínces of the péoples are assémbled*
with the péople of Ábraham's Gód.
The rúlers of the éarth belong to Gód,*
to Gód who réigns over áll.

Ant. Cry to God with shouts of joy.
Eastertide: God is king of all the earth; sing praise with all your skill, alleluia.

THROUGH THE YEAR

Scripture Reading   *Tob 4:16-17,19-20*

Do to no one what you would not want done to you. Give your bread to those who are hungry, and your clothes to those who are naked. Ask advice of every wise person. Bless the Lord God in everything; beg him to guide your ways and bring your paths and purposes to their end.

Short Responsory

R⁊ Bend my heart to your will, O God. *Repeat* R⁊
℣ By your word, give me life. R⁊ Glory be. R⁊

Benedictus ant. Show us your mercy, O Lord; remember your holy covenant.

Intercessions

We give thanks to Christ and we praise him because he was not ashamed to call us his brothers. R⁊ Lord Jesus, we are your brothers.
Help us to live the new life of Easter,—so that men may know through us the power of your love. R⁊
Every day is a proof of your love:—As you bring us to this new day, make us new in mind and in heart. R⁊
Teach us to see you present in all men;—help us to recognize you most of all in those who suffer. R⁊
May our lives today be filled with your compassion;—give us the spirit of forgiveness and a generous heart. R⁊
Our Father

Concluding Prayer

God our Saviour,
through the grace of baptism
you made us children of light.
Hear our prayer that we may always walk in that light
and work for truth, as your witnesses before men.
(We make our prayer) through our Lord.

EVENING PRAYER

HYMN

Christ be near at either hand,
Christ behind, before me stand,
Christ with me where'er I go,
Christ around, above, below.

Christ be in my heart and mind,
Christ within my soul enshrined,
Christ control my wayward heart;
Christ abide and ne'er depart.

Christ my life and only way,
Christ my lantern night and day;
Christ be my unchanging friend,
Guide and shepherd to the end.

PSALMODY

Ant. 1: The Lord is my light and my help; whom shall I fear?†
Eastertide: God has exalted him at his own right hand as leader and
Saviour, alleluia.

TRUST IN TIME OF AFFLICTION   PSALM 26(27)
Behold, the place where God dwells among men (Rev 21:3)

I

The Lórd is my líght and my hélp;*
whóm shall I féar?
†The Lórd is the strónghold of my lífe;*
before whóm shall I shrínk?

When évil-dóers draw néar*
to devóur my flésh,
it is théy, my énemies and fóes,*
who stúmble and fáll.

Though an ármy encámp agáinst me*
my héart would not féar.
Though wár break óut agáinst me*
even thén would I trúst.

There is óne thing I ásk of the Lórd,*
for thís I lóng,
to líve in the hóuse of the Lórd,*
all the dáys of my lífe,
to sávour the swéetness of the Lórd,*
to behóld his témple.

For thére he keeps me sáfe in his tént*
in the dáy of évil.
He hídes me in the shélter of his tént,*
on a róck he sets me sáfe.

And nów my héad shall be ráised*
above my fóes who surróund me
and I shall óffer withín his tént†
a sácrifice of jóy.*
I will síng and make músic for the Lórd.

Ant. The Lord is my light and my help; whom shall I fear?
Eastertide: God has exalted him at his own right hand as leader and
Saviour, alleluia.

Ant. 2: It is your face, O Lord, that I seek; hide not your face.
Eastertide: I am sure I shall see the Lord's goodness in the land of the
living, alleluia.

Some stood up and submitted false evidence against Jesus (Mk 14:57)

II

O Lórd, hear my vóice when I cáll;*
have mércy and ánswer.
Of yóu my héart has spóken:*
'Séek his fáce.'

It is your fáce, O Lórd, that I séek;*
híde not your fáce.
Dismíss not your sérvant in ánger;*
yóu have been my hélp.

Dó not abándon or forsáke me,*
O Gód my hélp!
Though fáther and móther forsáke me,*
The Lórd will recéive me.

Instrúct me, Lórd, in your wáy;*
on an éven path léad me.
When they líe in ámbush protéct me*
from my énemy's gréed.
False wítnesses ríse agáinst me,*
bréathing out fúry.

I am súre I shall sée the Lord's góodness*
in the lánd of the líving.
Hope in hím, hold fírm and take héart.*
Hópe in the Lórd!

Ant. It is your face, O Lord, that I seek; hide not your face.
Eastertide: I am sure I shall see the Lord's goodness in the land of the living, alleluia.

Ant. 3: He is the firstborn of all creation; he is supreme over all creatures.
Eastertide: From him, through him and in him are all things that exist: to him be glory for ever, alleluia.

CHRIST IS THE FIRSTBORN OF ALL CREATION,   CANTICLE
THE FIRSTBORN FROM THE DEAD   COL 1:12-20

Let us give thanks to the Father,†
who has qualified us to share*
in the inheritance of the saints in light.

He has delivered us from the dominion of darkness*
and transferred us to the kingdom of his beloved Son,

in whom we have redemption,*
the forgiveness of sins.

He is the image of the invisible God,*
the firstborn of all creation,
for in him all things were created, in heaven and on earth,*
visible and invisible.

All things were created*
through him and for him.
He is before all things,*
and in him all things hold together.

He is the head of the body, the Church;*
he is the beginning,
the firstborn from the dead,*
that in everything he might be pre-eminent.

For in him all the fulness of God was pleased to dwell,*
and through him to reconcile to himself all things,
whether on earth or in heaven,*
making peace by the blood of his cross.

Ant. He is the firstborn of all creation; he is supreme over all creatures.
Eastertide: From him, through him and in him are all things that exist: to him be glory for ever, alleluia.

THROUGH THE YEAR

Scripture Reading   *Jas 1:22,25*
You must do what the word tells you, and not just listen to it and deceive yourselves. But the man who looks steadily at the perfect law of freedom and makes that his habit—not listening and then forgetting, but actively putting it into practice—will be happy in all that he does.

Short Responsory
Ry Redeem me, Lord, and show me your mercy. *Repeat* Ry
Vy Do not cast me away with sinners. Ry Glory be. Ry

Magnificat ant. The Almighty has done great things for me; holy is his name.

Intercessions

The world is ablaze with the glory of God, who cares for his chosen people with infinite love. In the name of the Church we pray:

℟ Lord, show your love to all men.

Be mindful of your Church:—keep her free from evil and make her perfect in your love. ℟

Let all peoples acknowledge that you alone are God, and that Jesus Christ is your Son;—give them the light of faith. ℟

Grant to those around us all that they need,—so that they may know thankfulness and live in peace. ℟

Keep us mindful of those whose work is hard and unrewarded:—may we give every man the respect which is his right. ℟

Give peace to those who have died today;—grant them eternal rest. ℟

Our Father

Concluding Prayer

Lord, support us as we pray,
protect us day and night,
so that we who under your guiding hand
live in a world of change,
may always draw strength from you,
with whom there is no shadow of alteration.
(We make our prayer) through our Lord.

WEEK 1: THURSDAY

Invitatory ant. Come, let us adore the Lord, for he is our God.
Psalm, p 3.

MORNING PRAYER

HYMN

The Father's glory, Christ our light,
With love and mercy comes to span

60

The vast abyss of sin between
The God of holiness and man.

Christ yesterday and Christ today,
For all eternity the same,
The image of our hidden God;
Eternal Wisdom is his name.

He keeps his word from age to age,
Is with us to the end of days,
A cloud by day, a flame by night,
To go before us on his ways.

We bless you, Father, fount of light,
And Christ, your well-beloved Son,
Who with the Spirit dwell in us:
Immortal Trinity in One.

PSALMODY

Ant. 1: Awake, lyre and harp, I will awake the dawn.
Eastertide: O God, arise above the heavens, alleluia.

MORNING PRAYER IN TIME OF AFFLICTION   PSALM 56(57)
This psalm celebrates the passion of Christ (St Augustine)

Have mércy on me, Gód, have mércy*
for in yóu my sóul has taken réfuge.
In the shádow of your wíngs I take réfuge*
till the stórms of destrúction pass bý.

I cáll to Gód the Most Hígh,*
to Gód who has álways been my hélp.
May he sénd from héaven and sáve me†
and sháme thóse who assáil me.*
May Gód send his trúth and his lóve.

My sóul lies dówn among líons,*
who would devóur the sóns of mén.
Their téeth are spéars and árrows,*
their tóngue a shárpened swórd.

O Gód, aríse above the héavens;*
may your glóry shine on eárth!

They láid a snáre for my stéps,*
my sóul was bowed dówn.
They dúg a pít in my páth*
but féll in it themsélves.

My héart is réady, O Gód,†
my héart is réady.*
I will síng, I will síng your práise.

Awáke my sóul,†
awáke lýre and hárp,*
I will awáke the dáwn.

I will thánk you Lórd among the péoples,*
among the nátions I will práise you
for your lóve réaches to the héavens*
and your trúth to the skíes.

O Gód, aríse above the héavens;*
may your glóry shine on eárth!

Ant. Awake, lyre and harp, I will awake the dawn.
Eastertide: O God, arise above the heavens, alleluia.

Ant. 2: Thus says the Lord: my people shall be filled with my good things.
Eastertide: The Lord has ransomed his people, alleluia.

THE JOY OF A LIBERATED PEOPLE   CANTICLE: JER 31:10-14
Jesus had to die to reunite the children of God who had been scattered
(Jn 11:51,52)

O nations, hear the word of the Lord,*
proclaim it to the far-off coasts.
Say: 'He who scattered Israel will gather him*
and guard him as a shepherd guards his flock.'
For the Lord has ransomed Jacob,*
has saved him from an overpowering hand.

They will come and shout for joy on Mount Sion,*
they will stream to the blessings of the Lord,
to the corn, the new wine and the oil,*
to the flocks of sheep and the herds.
Their life will be like a watered garden.*
They will never be weary again.

Then the young girls will rejoice and will dance,*
the men, young and old, will be glad.
I will turn their mourning into joy,*
I will console them, give gladness for grief.
The priests I will again feed with plenty,*
and my people shall be filled with my blessings.

Ant. Thus says the Lord: my people shall be filled with my good things.
Eastertide: The Lord has ransomed his people, alleluia.

Ant. 3: The Lord is great and worthy to be praised in the city of our God.†
Eastertide: God is here, our God for ever and ever, alleluia.

THANKSGIVING FOR THE SALVATION   PSALM 47(48)
  OF GOD'S PEOPLE
He took me to the top of a great mountain, and showed me the holy city of Jerusalem (Rev 21:10)

The Lord is gréat and wórthy to be práised*
in the cíty of our Gód.
†His holy móuntain ríses in béauty,*
the jóy of all the éarth.

Mount Síon, true póle of the éarth,*
the Gréat King's cíty!
Gód, in the mídst of its cítadels,*
has shówn himself its strónghold.

For the kíngs assémbled togéther,*
togéther they advánced.

63

They sáw; at ónce they were astóunded;*
dismáyed, they fled in féar.

A trémbling séized them thére,*
like the pángs of bírth,
By the éast wind yóu have destróyed*
the shíps of Thársis.

As we have héard, só we have séen*
in the cíty of our Gód,
in the cíty of the Lórd of hósts*
which Gód upholds for éver.

O Gód, we pónder your lóve*
withín your témple.
Your práise, O Gód, like your náme*
reaches the énds of the éarth.

With jústice your ríght hand is fílled.*
Mount Síon rejóices;
the péople of Júdah rejóice*
at the síght of your júdgments.

Walk through Síon, wálk all róund it;*
count the númber of its tówers.
Review áll its rámparts,*
exámine its cástles,

that you may téll the néxt generátion*
that súch is our Gód,
our Gód for éver and álways.*
It is hé who léads us.

Ant. The Lord is great and worthy to be praised in the city of our God.
Eastertide: God is here, our God for ever and ever, alleluia.

THROUGH THE YEAR

Scripture Reading   *Is 66:1-2*
Thus says the Lord:
With heaven my throne

and earth my footstool,
what house could you build me,
what place could you make for my rest?
All of this was made by my hand
and all of this is mine—it is the Lord who speaks.
But my eyes are drawn to the man
of humbled and contrite spirit,
who trembles at my word.

Short Responsory

R̸ I called with all my heart; Lord, hear me. *Repeat* R̸
V̸ I will keep your commandments. R̸ Glory be. R̸

Benedictus ant. Let us serve the Lord in holiness, and he will deliver
us from the hands of our enemies.

Intercessions

Let us begin this new day with Christ, thanking him for all he has
brought to us, and asking him to bless us. R̸ Lord accept and bless
our work today.
You offered yourself to the Father on our behalf:—join our offering
with yours. R̸
You are gentle and humble of heart:—teach us to receive others as
you did. R̸
As each day begins, may your light rise in our hearts;—may it
shine forth in charity to the world. R̸
Show your mercy to those who are sick:—may each new day
increase their trust in you. R̸
Our Father

Concluding Prayer

Almighty ever-living God,
we make our prayer to you at morning, noon and evening:
dispel from our hearts the darkness of sin,
and bring us to the true light, Christ your Son,
who lives and reigns with you and the Holy Spirit,
God, for ever and ever.

EVENING PRAYER

HYMN

When God had filled the earth with life
And blessed it, to increase,
Then cattle dwelt with creeping things,
And lion with lamb, at peace.

He gave them vast, untrodden lands,
With plants to be their food;
Then God saw all that he had made
And found it very good.

Praise God the Father of all life,
His Son and Spirit blest,
By whom creation lives and moves,
In whom it comes to rest.

PSALMODY

Ant. 1: O Lord, I cried to you for help and you have healed me. I
will thank you for ever.
Eastertide: You changed my sorrow into joy, alleluia.

THANKSGIVING FOR LIBERATION FROM DEATH   PSALM 29(30)
Christ gives thanks to his Father after his glorious resurrection
(Cassian)

I will práise you, Lórd, yóu have réscued me*
and have nót let my énemies rejóice óver me.

O Lórd, I críed to you for hélp*
and yóu, my Gód, have héaled me.
O Lórd, you have ráised my sóul from the déad,*
restóred me to life from those who sínk into the gráve.

Sing psálms to the Lórd, you who lóve him,*
give thánks to his hóly náme.
His ánger lasts a móment; his fávour all through life.*
At níght there are téars, but jóy comes with dáwn.

66

I sáid to mysélf in my good fórtune:*
'Nóthing will éver distúrb me.'
Your fávour had sét me on a móuntain fástness,*
then you híd your fáce and I was pút to confúsion.

To yóu, Lórd, I críed,*
to my Gód I máde appéal:
'What prófit would my déath be, my góing to the gráve?*
Can dúst give you práise or procláim your trúth?'

The Lórd lístened and had píty.*
The Lórd cáme to my hélp.
For mé you have chánged my móurning into dáncing,*
you remóved my sáckcloth and clóthed me with jóy.
So my sóul sings psálms to you uncéasingly.*
O Lord my Gód, I will thánk you for éver.

Ant. O Lord, I cried to you for help and you have healed me. I will
thank you for ever.
Eastertide: You changed my sorrow into joy, alleluia.

Ant. 2: Happy the man to whom the Lord imputes no guilt.
Eastertide: We are reconciled to God by the death of his Son,
alleluia.

HAPPY IS THE MAN WHOSE OFFENCE IS FORGIVEN   PSALM 31(32)
David says that a man is blessed if God considers him righteous,
irrespective of good deeds (Rom 4:6)

Happy the mán whose offénce is forgíven,*
whose sín is remítted.
O háppy the mán to whom the Lórd†
impútes no guílt,*
in whose spírit is no guíle.

I kept it sécret and my fráme was wásted.*
I gróaned all day lóng
for níght and dáy your hánd*
was héavy upón me.

Indéed, my stréngth was dried úp*
as by the súmmer's héat.

But nów I have acknówledged my síns;*
my guílt I did not híde.
I sáid: 'Í will conféss*
my offénce to the Lórd.'
And yóu, Lórd, have forgíven*
the guílt of my sín.

So let évery good mán pray to yóu*
in the tíme of néed.
The flóods of wáter may reach hígh*
but hím they shall not réach.
Yóu are my híding place, O Lórd;†
you sáve me from distréss.*
You surróund me with críes of delíverance.

Í will instrúct you and téach you*
the wáy you should gó;
Í will gíve you cóunsel*
with my éye upón you.

Be not like hórse and múle, unintélligent,†
needing brídle and bít,*
élse they wíll not appróach you.
Many sórrows has the wícked†
but hé who trústs in the Lórd,*
loving mércy surróunds him.

Rejóice, rejóice in the Lórd,*
exúlt, you júst!
O cóme, ríng out your jóy,*
all you úpright of héart.

Ant. Happy the man to whom the Lord imputes no guilt.
Eastertide: We are reconciled to God by the death of his Son,
alleluia.

Ant. 3: The Lord has given him power and honour and empire, and all peoples will serve him.
Eastertide: Lord, who is your like, majestic in strength and holiness? alleluia.

THE JUDGMENT OF GOD

CANTICLE
REV 11:17-18;12:10B-12A

We give thanks to you, Lord God Almighty,*
who are and who were,
that you have taken your great power*
and begun to reign.

The nations raged,*
but your wrath came,
and the time for the dead to be judged,*
for rewarding your servants, the prophets and saints,
and those who fear your name,*
both small and great.

Now the salvation and the power†
and the kingdom of our God*
and the authority of his Christ have come,
for the accuser of our brethren has been thrown down,*
who accuses them day and night before our God.

And they have conquered him*
by the blood of the Lamb
and by the word of their testimony,*
for they loved not their lives even unto death.
Rejoice, then, O heaven,*
and you that dwell therein.

Ant. The Lord has given him power and honour and empire, and all peoples will serve him.
Eastertide: Lord, who is your like, majestic in strength and holiness? alleluia.

THROUGH THE YEAR

Scripture Reading   *1 Pet 1:6-9*

This is a cause of great joy for you, even though you may for a short time have to bear being plagued by all sorts of trials; so that, when Jesus Christ is revealed, your faith will have been tested and proved like gold—only it is more precious than gold, which is corruptible even though it bears testing by fire—and then you will have praise and glory and honour. You did not see him, yet you love him; and still without seeing him, you are already filled with a joy so glorious that it cannot be described, because you believe; and you are sure of the end to which your faith looks forward, that is, the salvation of your souls.

Short Responsory

R/ The Lord fed us with finest wheat. *Repeat* R/

V/ He filled us with honey from the rock. R/ Glory be. R/

Magnificat ant. The Lord brought down the mighty from their seats, and raised up the lowly.

Intercessions

Let us make our prayer to the God of our salvation because all our hope rests in him. R/ Father, our trust is in you.

Father, you established a covenant with men:—we trust in you, for you are faithful to your word. R/

Send workers into the harvest,—and bring the world to the knowledge and love of you. R/

May the unity of the Church be formed by love and understanding; —gather us together through the gifts of your Holy Spirit. R/

Help men to create a community where justice and peace may flourish:—be with us, lest we labour in vain. R/

Be mindful of the dead, especially those we have known;—have mercy on those who have given us their help. R/

Our Father

Concluding Prayer

Lord God,

you give the moon to illumine the night,

and to dispel the darkness you bring in the light of day:

grant that during this night

we may elude the grasp of Satan
and in the morning rise to give you praise.
(We make our prayer) through our Lord.

WEEK 1: FRIDAY

Invitatory ant. Give thanks to the Lord, for his great love is without
end.
Psalm, p 3.

MORNING PRAYER

HYMN

We bless you, Father, Lord of Life,
To whom all living beings tend,
The source of holiness and grace,
Our first beginning and our end.

We give you thanks, Redeeming Christ,
Who bore our weight of sin and shame;
In dark defeat you conquered sin,
And death by dying, overcame.

Come, Holy Spirit, searching fire,
Whose flame all evil burns away.
Come down to us with light and love,
In silence and in peace to stay.

We praise you, Trinity in One,
Sublime in majesty and might,
Who reign for ever, Lord of all,
In splendour and unending light.

PSALMODY

Ant. 1: Lord, you will be pleased with lawful sacrifice offered on
your altar.

71

Eastertide: Remember me, Lord God, when you come into your kingdom, alleluia.

HAVE MERCY ON ME, GOD PSALM 50(51)
You must be made new in mind and spirit, and put on the new nature of God's creating (Eph 4:23,24)

Have mércy on me, Gód, in your kíndness.*
In your compássion blot óut my offénce.
O wásh me more and móre from my guílt*
and cléanse me fróm my sín.

My offénces trúly I knów them;*
my sín is álways befóre me.
Against yóu, you alóne, have I sínned;*
what is évil in your síght I have dóne.

That you may be jústified whén you give séntence*
and be withóut repróach when you júdge,
O sée, in guílt I was bórn,*
a sínner was Í concéived.

Indéed you love trúth in the héart;*
then in the sécret of my héart teach me wísdom.
O púrify me, thén I shall be cléan;*
O wásh me, I shall be whíter than snów.

Make me héar rejóicing and gládness,*
that the bónes you have crúshed may revíve.
From my síns turn awáy your fáce*
and blót out áll my guílt.

A púre heart creáte for me, O Gód,*
put a stéadfast spírit withín me.
Do not cást me awáy from your présence,*
nor depríve me of your hóly spírit.

Give me agáin the jóy of your hélp;*
with a spírit of férvour sustáin me,
that I may téach transgréssors your wáys*
and sínners may retúrn to yóu.

O réscue me, Gód, my hélper,*
and my tóngue shall ríng out your góodness.
O Lórd, ópen my líps*
and my móuth shall decláre your práise.

For in sácrifice you táke no delíght,*
burnt óffering from mé you would refúse,
my sácrifice a cóntrite spírit.*
A húmbled, contrite héart you will not spúrn.

In your góodness, show fávour to Síon:*
rebuíld the wálls of Jerúsalem.
Thén you will be pléased with lawful sácrifice,*
hólocausts óffered on your áltar.

Ant. Lord, you will be pleased with lawful sacrifice offered on your altar.
Eastertide: Remember me, Lord God, when you come into your kingdom, alleluia.

Ant. 2: All the descendants of Israel shall glory in victory through the Lord.
Eastertide: Truly, God of Israel, the Saviour, you are a God who lies hidden, alleluia.†

ALL THE PEOPLES WILL TURN TO THE LORD CANTICLE
IS 45:15-26

Every knee must bow at the name of Jesus (Phil 2:10)

Truly, God of Israel, the Saviour,*
you are a God who lies hidden.
†They will be put to shame and disgraced,*
all who resist you.
They will take themselves off in dismay,*
the makers of idols.

But Israel is saved by the Lord,*
saved for evermore.
You will never be ashamed or disgraced*
through endless ages.

For this is the word of the Lord,*
the creator of heaven,
the God who made earth and shaped it,*
he who made it firm.
He did not create it in vain,*
he made it to be lived in.

'I am the Lord, there is no other.*
I have not spoken in secret, in some dark place,
I have not said to Jacob's sons*
"Search for me in vain."'

I am the Lord, I speak the truth,
I proclaim what is right.
Assemble, all of you, draw near*
you who have escaped from the nations.

They know nothing, who carry around*
their idols made of wood
and keep on praying to a god*
that cannot save them.

State your case and bring your proofs,*
consult among yourselves.
Who proclaimed this beforehand,*
who foretold it long ago?

Was it not I, the Lord?*
There is no god but me,
a God of justice, a saviour.*
There is none but me.

Turn to me and be saved,*
all the ends of the earth!
For I am God, there is no other;*
by myself I swear it.

It is truth that goes forth from my mouth,*
a word beyond recall.
To me every knee shall bow,*
every tongue shall swear.

They will say: "In the Lord alone*
are victory and power.
And to him will come in dismay*
all who have resisted.
Through the Lord will come victory and glory*
for all Israel's sons." '

Ant. All the descendants of Israel shall glory in victory through the Lord.
Eastertide: Truly, God of Israel, the Saviour, you are a God who lies hidden, alleluia.

Ant. 3: Come before the Lord, singing for joy.
Eastertide: Serve the Lord with joy, alleluia.

When the following psalm has been used at the Invitatory, ps 94, p 371, is said here in place of it.

THE JOY OF THOSE WHO ENTER   PSALM 99(100)
    THE TEMPLE OF THE LORD
The Lord calls all those he has redeemed to sing a hymn of victory
(St Athanasius)

Cry out with jóy to the Lórd, all the éarth.†
Sérve the Lórd with gládness.*
Come befóre him, sínging for jóy.

Know that hé, the Lórd, is Gód.†
He máde us, we belóng to hím,*
we are his péople, the shéep of his flóck.

Gó within his gátes, giving thánks.†
Enter his cóurts with sóngs of práise.*
Give thánks to him and bléss his náme.

Indéed, how góod is the Lórd,†
etérnal his mérciful lóve.*
He is fáithful from áge to áge.   Glory be.

Ant. Come before the Lord, singing for joy.
Eastertide: Serve the Lord with joy, alleluia.

THROUGH THE YEAR

Scripture Reading   *Eph 4:29-32*

Do not use harmful words in talking. Use only helpful words, the kind that build up and provide what is needed, so that what you say will do good to those who hear you. And do not make God's Holy Spirit sad; for the Spirit is God's mark of ownership on you, a guarantee that the Day will come when God will set you free. Get rid of all bitterness, passion, and anger. No more shouting or insults. No more hateful feelings of any sort. Instead, be kind and tender-hearted to one another, and forgive one another, as God has forgiven you in Christ.

Short Responsory

R/ In the morning let me know your love. *Repeat* R/
V/ Make me know the way I should walk. R/ Glory be. R/

Benedictus ant. The Lord has visited his people, he has come to redeem them.

Intercessions

Lord Jesus Christ, we thank you. Through your cross and resurrection you offer freedom and hope to those ready to receive them. R/ Lord, show us your loving-kindness.
We are children of the day:—help us to live in the light of your presence. R/
Guide our thoughts, our words, our actions:—so that what we do today may be pleasing to you. R/
Help us to avoid wrongdoing:—show us your mercy and love. R/
Through your passion and death you have won life for us:—give us the strength of your Holy Spirit. R/
Our Father

Concluding Prayer

Lord God,
you hold out the light of your Word

to those who do not know you.
Strengthen in our hearts the faith you have given us,
so that no trials may quench the fire
your Spirit has kindled within us.
(We make our prayer) through our Lord.

EVENING PRAYER

HYMN

When God made man, he gave him all the earth,
All growing things, with every bird and beast;
Then Adam named them at the Lord's command,
Subdued the greatest of them, and the least.

In his own image God created man,
And when from dust he fashioned Adam's face,
The likeness of his only Son was formed:
His Word incarnate, filled with truth and grace.

To God the Father and to Christ his Son
And blessed Spirit heaven and earth give praise.
Creation with tremendous voice cries out:
All holy is the mighty Lord of days.

PSALMODY

Ant. 1: Lord, heal my soul for I have sinned against you.
Eastertide: Christ made himself poor for our enrichment, alleluia.

PRAYER IN SICKNESS   PSALM 40(41)
One of you will betray me—one who is eating with me (Mk 14:18)

Happy the mán who consíders the póor and the wéak.*
The Lórd will sáve him in the dáy of évil,
will guárd him, give him lífe, make him háppy in the lánd*
and will nót give him úp to the wíll of his fóes.
The Lórd will hélp him on his béd of páin,*
he will bríng him báck from síckness to héalth.

77

As for mé, I said: 'Lórd, have mércy on mé,*
heal my sóul for Í have sínned agáinst you.'
My fóes are spéaking évil agáinst me.*
'How lóng before he díes and his náme be forgótten?'
They cóme to vísit me and spéak empty wórds,*
their héarts full of málice, they spréad it abróad.

My énemies whísper togéther agáinst me.*
They áll weigh úp the évil which is ón me:
'Some déadly thíng has fástened upón him,*
he will nót rise agáin from whére he líes.'
Thus éven my fríend, in whóm I trústed,*
who áte my bréad, has túrned agáinst me.

But yóu, O Lórd, have mércy on mé.*
Let me ríse once móre and Í will repáy them.
By thís I shall knów that yóu are my fríend,*
if my fóes do not shóut in tríumph óver me.
If yóu uphóld me Í shall be unhármed*
and sét in your présence for evermóre.

Bléssed be the Lórd, the Gód of Ísrael*
from áge to áge. Amén. Amén.

Ant. Lord, heal my soul for I have sinned against you.
Eastertide: Christ made himself poor for our enrichment, alleluia.

Ant. 2: The Lord of hosts is with us: the God of Jacob is our
stronghold.
Eastertide: The waters of a river give joy to God's city, alleluia.

GOD IS OUR REFUGE AND STRENGTH   PSALM 45(46)
They will call his name 'Immanuel' which means 'God with us'
(Mt 1:23)

Gód is for ús a réfuge and stréngth,*
a hélper close at hánd, in tíme of distréss:
so wé shall not féar though the éarth should róck,*
though the móuntains fáll into the dépths of the séa,
even thóugh its wáters ráge and fóam,*
even thóugh the móuntains be sháken by its wáves.

The Lórd of hósts is with us:*
the Gód of Jácob is our strónghold.

The wáters of a ríver give jóy to God's cíty,*
the hóly pláce where the Móst High dwélls.
Gód is withín, it cánnot be sháken;*
Gód will hélp it at the dáwning of the dáy.
Nátions are in túmult, kíngdoms are sháken:*
he lífts his vóice, the éarth shrinks awáy.

The Lórd of hósts is with us:*
the Gód of Jácob is our strónghold.

Cóme, consíder the wórks of the Lórd*
the redóubtable déeds he has dóne on the éarth.
He puts an énd to wárs over áll the éarth;†
the bów he bréaks, the spéar he snáps.*
He búrns the shíelds with fíre.
'Be stíll and knów that Í am Gód,*
supréme among the nátions, supréme on the éarth!'

The Lórd of hósts is with us:*
the Gód of Jácob is our strónghold.

Ant. The Lord of hosts is with us: the God of Jacob is our strong-hold.
Eastertide: The waters of a river give joy to God's city, alleluia.

Ant. 3: All the peoples will come and adore you, Lord.
Eastertide: Let us sing to the Lord, great is his triumph, alleluia.

HYMN OF ADORATION   CANTICLE: REV 15:3-4

Great and wonderful are your deeds,*
O Lord God the Almighty!
Just and true are your ways,*
O King of the ages!

Who shall not fear and glorify your name, O Lord?*
For you alone are holy.

All nations shall come and worship you,*
for your judgments have been revealed.

Ant. All the peoples will come and adore you, Lord.
Eastertide: Let us sing to the Lord; great is his triumph, alleluia.

THROUGH THE YEAR

Scripture Reading　　　*Rom 15:1-3*

We who are strong ought to bear with the failings of the weak, and
not to please ourselves; let each of us please his neighbour for his
good, to edify him. For Christ did not please himself; but as it is
written, The reproaches of those who reproached you fell on me.

Short Responsory

Ŗ Christ loved us and has washed away our sins with his blood.
Repeat Ŗ
V̧ He made us a line of kings, priests to serve God. Ŗ Glory be. Ŗ

Magnificat ant. The Lord has come to help us, his servants; he has
remembered his mercy.

Intercessions

God is our loving Father, who cares for us and knows all our needs.
With confidence we pray: Ŗ Father, may we find rest in your love.
Christ, your Son, suffered and died for the Church:—be with all
Christians who are suffering tonight. Ŗ
Bring to the sick your comfort and healing;—strengthen them
through the victory of Calvary. Ŗ
Be near to us, almighty Father,—for you alone can save us from the
evils that threaten us. Ŗ
Strengthen us in the hour of death:—let us know your peace. Ŗ
Bring the dead into your light:— comfort them with your presence. Ŗ
Our Father

Concluding Prayer

Lord God,
teach us the lessons of your Son's Passion,
and so enable us, your people,

to bear the yoke he makes light for us.
(We make our prayer) through our Lord.

WEEK 1: SATURDAY

Invitatory ant. The Lord's is the earth and its fulness: come, let us adore him.
Psalm, p 3.

MORNING PRAYER

HYMN

It were my soul's desire
To see the face of God;
It were my soul's desire
To rest in his abode.

Grant, Lord, my soul's desire,
Deep waves of cleansing sighs,
Grant, Lord, my soul's desire,
From earthly cares to rise.

It were my soul's desire
To imitate my King,
It were my soul's desire
His endless praise to sing.

It were my soul's desire,
When heaven's gate is won,
To find my soul's desire,
Clear shining like the sun.

This still my soul's desire,
Whatever life afford,
To gain my soul's desire
And see thy face, O Lord.

PSALMODY

Ant. 1: My eyes watch for you before dawn.
Eastertide: In your love, give me life, O Lord, alleluia.

PSALM 118(119):145-152 XIX (KOPH)

I cáll with all my héart; Lord, héar me,*
I will kéep your commánds.
I cáll upón you, sáve me*
and Í will do your wíll.

I ríse before dáwn and cry for hélp,*
I hópe in your wórd.
My éyes wátch through the níght*
to pónder your prómise.

In your lóve hear my vóice, O Lórd;*
give me lífe by your decrées.
Those who hárm me unjústly draw néar:*
they are fár from your láw.

But yóu, O Lórd, are clóse:*
your commánds are trúth.
Lóng have I knówn that your wíll*
is estáblished for éver.

Ant. My eyes watch for you before dawn.
Eastertide: In your love, give me life, O Lord, alleluia.

Ant. 2: The Lord is my strength, I will sing his praise; he is my salvation.
Eastertide: For the victors, theirs is the song of God's servant Moses, theirs is the song of the Lamb, alleluia.

HYMN OF VICTORY AFTER CROSSING   CANTICLE
   THE RED SEA   EX 15:1-4A,8-13,17-18
Those who overcame the beast sang the hymn of Moses, the Servant of God (cf Rev 15:2-3)

I will sing to the Lord, glorious his triumph!*
Horse and rider he has thrown into the sea!

82

The Lord is my strength, my song, my salvation.†
This is my God and I extol him,*
my father's God and I give him praise.
The Lord is a warrior!* The Lord is his name.

The chariots of Pharaoh he hurled into the sea.*
At the breath of your anger the waters piled high;
the moving waters stood up like a dam.*
The deeps turned solid in the midst of the sea.

The enemy said: 'I will pursue and overtake them,†
I will divide the plunder, I shall have my will.*
I will draw my sword, my hand shall destroy them.'

You blew with your breath, the sea closed over them.*
They went down like lead into the mighty waters.
Who is like you among the gods, O Lord,†
who is like you, so glorious in holiness,*
spreading fear through your deeds, you who do marvels?

You stretched forth your hand,*
the earth engulfed them;
your love has guided the people you redeemed,*
your power has led them to your holy dwelling-place.

You will lead them and plant them on your mountain,†
the place, O Lord, where you have made your home,*
the sanctuary, Lord, which your hands have made.
The Lord will reign* for ever and ever.

Ant. The Lord is my strength, I will sing his praise; he is my salvation.
Eastertide: For the victors, theirs is the song of God's servant Moses, theirs is the song of the Lamb, alleluia.

Ant. 3: O praise the Lord, all you nations.†
Eastertide: Strong is his love for us, alleluia.

PRAISE TO THE GOD OF MERCY   PSALM 116(117)
I ask the nations to give praise to God for his mercy (Rom 15:8-9)

O práise the Lórd, all you nátions,*

†accláim him all you péoples!

Stróng is his lóve for ús;*
he is fáithful for éver.

Ant. O praise the Lord, all you nations.
Eastertide: Strong is his love for us, alleluia.

THROUGH THE YEAR

Scripture Reading   *2 Pet 1:10-11*

Brothers, you have been called and chosen: work all the harder to justify it by good deeds. If you do all these things there is no danger that you will ever fall away. In this way you will be granted admittance into the eternal kingdom of our Lord and saviour Jesus Christ.

Short Responsory

℟ I called to you, Lord, you are my refuge. *Repeat* ℟
℣ You are all I have in the land of the living. ℟ Glory be. ℟

Benedictus ant. Give your light, Lord, to those who sit in darkness and in the shadow of death.

Intercessions

Christ became man to make us sons of God and he intercedes for us before God our Father. Let us thank him for his loving mercy, and pray: ℟ Open to us the treasures of your love.

You have enlightened us in baptism:—we consecrate our day to you. ℟

Fill us with praise of you today:—may we take your word with us wherever we may go. ℟

Teach us to respond to your word like Mary our Mother:—may your word be fruitful in us. ℟

Give us courage when things go wrong:—strengthen us with faith in you, with hope in your promises and with love of your will. ℟

Our Father

Concluding Prayer

Let the splendour of the resurrection,

light up our hearts and minds, Lord,
scattering the shadows of death,
and bringing us to the radiance of eternity.
(We make our prayer) through our Lord.

WEEK 2: SUNDAY

EVENING PRAYER I

HYMN

Bless'd be the Lord our God!
With joy let heaven ring;
Before his presence let all earth
Its songs of homage bring!
His mighty deeds be told;
His majesty be praised;
To God, enthroned in heav'nly light,
Let every voice be raised!

All that has life and breath,
Give thanks with heartfelt songs!
To him let all creation sing
To whom all praise belongs!
Acclaim the Father's love,
Who gave us God his Son;
Praise too the Spirit, giv'n by both,
With both for ever one!

PSALMODY

ANTIPHON I
Advent: Rejoice and be glad, new Sion. See now how humbly your King, our Saviour, will come to you.
Lent, Sunday 2: Jesus took Peter, James and John the brother of James, and led them up a high mountain where they were alone; and in their presence he was transfigured.

Lent, Palm Sunday: I sat teaching in the Temple day after day and you never laid hands on me. Now you have scourged me and lead me to be crucified.
Eastertide: The man who lives by the truth comes into the light, alleluia.

Through the Year: Your word is a lamp for my steps, Lord, alleluia.†

MEDITATION ON THE WORD OF GOD IN THE LAW

PSALM 118(119):105-112 XIV (NUN)
This is my commandment, that you love each other (Jn 15:12)

Your wórd is a lámp for my stéps*
†and a líght for my páth.
I have swórn and have máde up my mínd*
to obéy your decrées.

Lórd, I am déeply afflícted:*
by your wórd give me life.
Accépt, Lord, the hómage of my líps*
and téach me your decrées.

Though I cárry my life in my hánds,*
I remémber your láw.
Though the wícked trý to ensnáre me*
I do not stráy from your précepts.

Your wíll is my héritage for éver,*
the jóy of my héart.
I sét myself to cárry out your wíll*
in fúlness, for éver.

Ant. Your word is a lamp for my steps, Lord, alleluia.

Ant. Advent: Rejoice and be glad, new Sion. See now how humbly your King, our Saviour, will come to you.
Ant. 2: Strengthen the weary hands: be strong and say, 'Behold. our God will come and he will save us, alleluia.'

Ant. Lent, Sunday 2: Jesus took Peter, James, and John the brother of James, and led them up a high mountain where they were alone; and in their presence he was transfigured.

Ant. 2: His face shone like the sun and his clothes became as white as snow.

Ant. Palm Sunday: I sat teaching in the Temple day after day and you never laid hands on me. Now you have scourged me and lead me to be crucified.

Ant. 2: The Lord God helps me; no insult can wound me.

Ant. Eastertide: The man who lives by the truth comes into the light, alleluia.

Ant. 2: Freed from the pangs of death, the Lord arose from the grave, alleluia.

Ant. 2: O Lord, you will show me the fulness of joy in your presence, alleluia.

THE LORD IS MY PORTION   PSALM 15(16)
God raised up Jesus, freeing him from the pains of death (Acts 2:24)

Presérve me, Gód, I take réfuge in yóu.†
I sáy to the Lórd: 'Yóu are my Gód.*
My háppiness líes in yóu alóne.'

He has pút into my héart a márvellous lóve*
for the fáithful ónes who dwéll in his lánd.
Those who chóose other góds incréase their sórrows.†
Néver will I óffer their ófferings of blóod.*
Néver will I táke their náme upon my líps.

O Lórd, it is yóu who are my pórtion and cúp;*
it is yóu yoursélf who áre my príze.
The lót marked óut for me is mý delíght:*
welcome indéed the héritage that fálls to mé!

I will bléss the Lórd who gíves me cóunsel,*
who éven at níght dirécts my héart.
I kéep the Lórd ever ín my síght:*
since hé is at my ríght hand, Í shall stand fírm.

And so my héart rejóices, my sóul is glád;*
éven my bódy shall rést in sáfety.
For yóu will not léave my sóul among the déad,*
nor lét your belóved knów decáy.

You will shów me the páth of lífe,†
the fúlness of jóy in your présence,*
at your ríght hand háppiness for éver.

Ant. O Lord, you will show me the fulness of joy in your presence, alleluia.

Ant. Advent: Strengthen the weary hands: be strong and say, 'Behold, our God will come and he will save us, alleluia.'
Ant. 3: The Law was given through Moses, grace and truth have come through Jesus Christ.

Ant. Lent, Sunday 2: His face shone like the sun and his clothes became as white as snow.
Ant. 3: Moses and Elijah were speaking of his passion and death, and all he was to fulfil in Jerusalem.

Ant. Lent, Palm Sunday: The Lord God helps me; no insult can wound me.
Ant. 3: The Lord Jesus humbled himself and, in obedience, accepted death, even death on a cross.

Ant. Eastertide: Freed from the pangs of death, the Lord arose from the grave, alleluia.
Ant. 3: Was it not necessary that Christ should suffer thus and so enter into his glory, alleluia?

Ant. 3: Let every creature, in heaven and on earth, bend the knee at the name of Jesus, alleluia.

CHRIST, THE SERVANT OF GOD   CANTICLE: PHIL 2:6-11

Though he was in the form of God,*
Jesus did not count equality with God a thing to be grasped.

He emptied himself,†

88

taking the form of a servant,*
being born in the likeness of men.

And being found in human form,†
he humbled himself and became obedient unto death,*
even death on a cross.

Therefore God has highly exalted him.*
and bestowed on him the name which is above every name,

That at the name of Jesus every knee should bow,*
in heaven and on earth and under the earth,

And every tongue confess that Jesus Christ is Lord,*
to the glory of God the Father.

Ant. Let every creature, in heaven and on earth, bend the knee at
the name of Jesus, alleluia.

Ant. Advent: The Law was given through Moses, grace and truth
have come through Jesus Christ.
Lent, Sunday 2: Moses and Elijah were speaking of his passion and
death, and all he was to fulfil in Jerusalem.
Lent, Palm Sunday: The Lord Jesus humbled himself and, in
obedience, accepted death, even death on a cross.
Eastertide: Was it necessary that Christ should suffer thus and
so enter into his glory, alleluia?

THROUGH THE YEAR

Scripture Reading   *Col 1:3-6a*
May God our Father and the Lord Jesus Christ give you grace and
peace. We always give thanks to God, the Father of our Lord
Jesus Christ, when we pray for you. For we have heard of your faith
in Christ Jesus, and of your love for all God's people. When the
true message, the Good News, first came to you, you heard of the
hope it offers. So your faith and love are based on what you hope
for, which is kept safe for you in heaven. The gospel is bringing
blessings and spreading through the whole world, just as it has
among you.

Short Responsory

R℣ From the rising of the sun to its setting, great is the name of the Lord. *Repeat* R℣

℣ High above the heavens is his glory. R℣ Glory be. R℣

Magnificat antiphon from the Proper of Seasons.

Intercessions

God our Father leads us forward with great love towards the joyful day when we enter his rest. R℣ Our hope is all in you, Lord God.

Father, we pray for N., our Pope, and N., our bishop:—guide them and bless them in their work. R℣

Help the sick to share their sufferings with Christ:—may they know in him the fulness of life and love. R℣

Lord, you found nowhere to lay your head:—make us aware of the needs of the homeless today. R℣

Bless those who work on the land:—may we receive the fruits of the earth with thankfulness. R℣

Father, have mercy on those who have died in the peace of Christ:—receive them into the home you have prepared for them. R℣

Our Father

The concluding prayer from the Proper of Seasons.

Invitatory

Ant. We are the people of the Lord, the flock that is led by his hand: come, let us adore him, alleluia.

Psalm, p 3.

MORNING PRAYER

HYMN

I bind unto myself today
The strong name of the Trinity,
By invocation of the same,
The Three in One, and One in Three.

I bind unto myself today
The power of God to hold and lead,
His eye to watch, his might to stay,
His ear to hearken to my need,

The wisdom of my God to teach,
His hand to guide, his shield to ward;
The word of God to give me speech,
His heavenly host to be my guard.

I bind unto myself the name,
The strong name of the Trinity;
By invocation of the same,
The Three in One, and One in Three,

Of whom all nature hath creation;
Eternal Father, Spirit, Word:
Praise to the Lord of my salvation:
Salvation is of Christ the Lord.

Alternative hymn

All people that on earth do dwell,
Sing to the Lord with cheerful voice;
Him serve with mirth, his praise forth tell,
Come ye before him, and rejoice.

The Lord, ye know, is God indeed;
Without our aid he did us make;
We are his folk, he doth us feed;
And for his sheep he doth us take.

For why, the Lord our God is good:
His mercy is for ever sure;
His truth at all times firmly stood,
And shall from age to age endure.

To Father, Son and Holy Ghost,
The God whom heaven and earth adore,
From men and from the angel-host
Be praise and glory evermore.

PSALMODY

ANTIPHON I

Advent: We have a strong city. The Saviour will set up wall and rampart to guard it. Open the gates, for God is with us, alleluia.

Lent, Sunday 2: The Lord's right hand has triumphed; his right hand raised me up.

Lent, Palm Sunday: The crowds of people, who had gathered for the feastday, called out to the Lord, 'Blessed is he who comes in the name of the Lord. Hosanna in the highest.'

Eastertide: This is the day which was made by the Lord, alleluia.

Through the Year: Blessed is he who comes in the name of the Lord, alleluia.

SONG OF REJOICING IN SALVATION   PSALM 117(118)
This is the stone which was rejected by you builders, but which has become the corner stone (Acts 4:11).

Give thánks to the Lórd for he is góod,*
for his lóve endures for éver.

Let the sóns of Ísrael sáy:*
'His lóve endures for éver.'
Let the sóns of Áaron sáy:*
'His lóve endures for éver.'
Let thóse who fear the Lórd sáy:*
'His lóve endures for éver.'

I cálled to the Lórd in my distréss;*
he ánswered and fréed me.
The Lórd is at my síde; I do not féar.*
What can mán do agáinst me?
The Lórd is at my síde as my hélper:*
I shall look dówn on my fóes.

It is bétter to take réfuge in the Lórd*
than to trúst in mén:
it is bétter to take réfuge in the Lórd*
than to trúst in prínces.

The nátions áll encómpassed me;*
in the Lórd's name I crúshed them.
They cómpassed me, cómpassed me abóut;*
in the Lórd's name I crúshed them.
They cómpassed me abóut like bées;†
they blázed like a fíre among thórns.*
In the Lórd's name I crúshed them.

I was hárd-préssed and was fálling*
but the Lórd came to hélp me.
The Lórd is my stréngth and my sóng;*
hé is my sáviour.
There are shóuts of jóy and víctory*
in the ténts of the júst.

The Lórd's right hánd has tríumphed;*
his ríght hand ráised me.
The Lórd's right hánd has tríumphed;†
I shall not díe, I shall líve*
and recóunt his déeds.
I was púnished, I was púnished by the Lórd,*
but nót doomed to díe.

Ópen to mé the gates of hóliness:*
I will énter and give thánks.
Thís is the Lórd's own gáte*
where the júst may énter.
I will thánk you for yóu have ánswered*
and yóu are my sáviour.

The stóne which the buílders rejécted*
has becóme the córner stone.
Thís is the wórk of the Lórd,*
a márvel in our éyes.
Thís day was máde by the Lórd;*
we rejóice and are glád.

O Lórd, gránt us salvátion;*
O Lórd, grant succéss.

Bléssed in the náme of the Lórd*
is hé who cómes.
We bléss you from the hóuse of the Lórd;*
the Lord Gód is our líght.

Go fórward in procéssion with bránches*
éven to the áltar.
Yóu are my Gód, I thánk you.*
My Gód, I práise you.
Give thánks to the Lórd for he is góod;*
for his lóve endures for éver.

Ant. Blessed is he who comes in the name of the Lord, alleluia.

Ant. Advent: We have a strong city. The Saviour will set up wall and rampart to guard it. Open the gates, for God is with us, alleluia.
Ant. 2: Come to the water all you who thirst: seek the Lord while he may be found, alleluia.

Ant. Lent, Sunday 2: The Lord's right hand has triumphed; his right hand raised me up.
Ant. 2: Let us sing the hymn of the three young men, which they sang in the blazing furnace, blessing the Lord.

Ant. Palm Sunday: The crowds of people, who had gathered for the feastday, called out to the Lord, 'Blessed is he who comes in the name of the Lord. Hosanna in the highest.'
Ant. 2: May we be counted among the faithful, with the angels and with the children. Triumphant over death, we sing with them, 'Hosanna in the highest.'

Ant. Eastertide: This is the day which was made by the Lord, alleluia.
Ant. 2: O Lord, our God, you are blessed in the firmament of heaven, and worthy of praise, alleluia.

Ant. 2: Let us sing a hymn to our God, alleluia.

LET EVERY CREATURE PRAISE THE LORD

The Creator is blessed for ever (Rom 1:25)

You are blest, Lord God of our fathers.*
To you glory and praise for evermore.

Blest your glorious holy name.*
To you glory and praise for evermore.

You are blest in the temple of your glory.*
To you glory and praise for evermore.

You are blest who gaze into the depths.*
To you glory and praise for evermore.

You are blest in the firmament of heaven.*
To you glory and praise for evermore.

You who walk on the wings of the wind:*
To you glory and praise for evermore.

May they bless you, the saints and the angels.*
To you glory and praise for evermore

From the heavens, the earth and the sea,*
To you glory and praise for evermore.

You are blest, Lord God of our fathers.*
To you glory and praise for evermore.

Ant. Let us sing a hymn to our God, alleluia.

Ant. Advent: Come to the water all you who thirst: seek the Lord while he may be found, alleluia.
Ant. 3: Behold, our Lord will come in strength and he will give light to the eyes of his servants, alleluia.

Ant. Lent, Sunday 2: Let us sing the hymn of the three young men, which they sang in the blazing furnace, blessing the Lord.
Ant. 3: Praise the Lord in his mighty heavens.

Ant. Lent, Palm Sunday: May we be counted among the faithful, with the angels and with the children. Triumphant over death, we sing with them, 'Hosanna in the highest.'

Ant. 3: Blessed is he who comes in the name of the Lord; peace in heaven; glory in the highest heavens.

Ant. Eastertide: O Lord, our God, you are blessed in the firmament of heaven, and worthy of praise, alleluia.

Ant. 3: Praise God who sits on the throne; saying 'Amen, Alleluia.'

Ant. 3: Praise the Lord for his surpassing greatness, alleluia.

PRAISE THE LORD   PSALM 150

Sing praise in your spirit, sing praise with your soul, that is: give glory to God in both your soul and your body (Hesychius).

Práise Gód in his hóly pláce,*
práise him in his míghty héavens.
Práise him for his pówerful déeds,*
práise his surpássing gréatness.

O práise him with sóund of trúmpet,*
práise him with lúte and hárp.
Práise him with tímbrel and dánce,*
práise him with stríngs and pípes.

O práise him with resóunding cýmbals,*
práise him with cláshing of cýmbals.
Let éverything that líves and that bréathes*
give práise to the Lórd.

Ant. Praise the Lord for his surpassing greatness, alleluia.

Ant. Advent: Behold, our Lord will come in strength and he will give light to the eyes of his servants, alleluia.
Lent, Sunday 2: Praise the Lord in his mighty heavens.
Lent, Palm Sunday: Blessed is he who comes in the name of the Lord; peace in heaven; glory in the highest heavens.
Eastertide: Praise God who sits on the throne; saying, 'Amen, alleluia.'

THROUGH THE YEAR

Scripture Reading   *Ezek 36:25-27*

I shall pour clean water over you and you will be cleansed; I shall cleanse you of all your defilement and all your idols. I shall give you a new heart, and put a new spirit in you; I shall remove the heart of stone from your bodies and give you a heart of flesh instead. I shall put my spirit in you, and make you keep my laws and sincerely respect my observances.

Short Responsory

R̠ We give thanks to you, O God, and call upon your name. *Repeat* R̠

℣ We recount your wonderful deeds. R̠ Glory be. R̠

Benedictus antiphon from the Proper of Seasons.

Intercessions

Let us thank our Saviour, who came into this world that God might be with us. R̠ We praise you, O Lord, and we thank you.

We welcome you with praise, you are the Daystar, the first fruits from the dead:—let us rise with you to walk in the light of Easter. R̠

Help us on this day of rest to see goodness in all your creatures:— open our eyes and our hearts to your love in the world. R̠

Lord, we meet around your table as your family:—help us to see that our bitterness is forgotten, our discord is resolved, and our sins are forgiven. R̠

We pray for all Christian families:—may your Spirit deepen their unity in faith and love. R̠

Our Father

The concluding prayer from the Proper of Seasons.

EVENING PRAYER II

Holy God, we praise thy name;
Lord of all, we bow before thee!
All on earth thy sceptre own,
All in heaven above adore thee.
Infinite thy vast domain,
Everlasting is thy reign.

Hark! the loud celestial hymn,
Angel choirs above are raising;
Cherubim and seraphim,
In unceasing chorus praising,
Fill the heavens with sweet accord:
Holy, holy, holy, Lord.

Holy Father, holy Son,
Holy Spirit, three we name thee.
While in essence only one
Undivided God we claim thee;
And adoring bend the knee,
While we own the mystery.

Spare thy people, Lord, we pray,
By a thousand snares surrounded;
Keep us without sin today;
Never let us be confounded.
Lo, I put my trust in thee;
Never, Lord, abandon me.

Alternative hymn

Praise, my soul, the King of heaven;
To his feet your tribute bring;
Ransomed, healed, restored, forgiven,
Who like me his praise should sing?
Praise him! Praise him!
Praise him! Praise him!
Praise the everlasting King.

Praise him for his grace and favour,
To our fathers in distress;

Praise him still the same for ever,
Slow to chide and swift to bless,
Praise him! Praise him!
Praise him! Praise him!
Glorious in his faithfulness.

Fatherlike, he tends and spares us;
Well our feeble frame he knows;
In his hand he gently bears us,
Rescues us from all our foes.
Praise him! Praise him!
Praise him! Praise him!
Widely as his mercy flows.

Angels, help us to adore him;
Ye behold him face to face;
Sun and moon bow down before him,
Dwellers all in time and space.
Praise him! Praise him!
Praise him! Praise him!
Praise with us the God of grace.

PSALMODY

ANTIPHON I

Advent: Behold, the Lord will come on the clouds of heaven with great strength, alleluia.

Lent, Sunday 2: The Lord will send forth your sceptre of power with the splendour of the saints.

Lent, Palm Sunday: He was wounded and humbled, but God has raised him up with his own right hand.

Eastertide: He raised Christ from the dead and placed him at his own right hand, in heaven, alleluia.

Through the Year: Christ the Lord is a priest for ever according to the order of Melchizedek, alleluia.

THE MESSIAH IS KING AND PRIEST   PSALM 109(110):1-5,7
He must be king so that he will put all his enemies under his feet
(1 Cor 15:25)

The Lórd's revelátion to my Máster:†
'Sít on my ríght:*
your fóes I will pút beneath your féet.'

The Lórd will wíeld from Síon†
your scéptre of pówer:*
rúle in the mídst of all your fóes.

A prínce from the dáy of your bírth†
on the hóly móuntains;*
from the wómb before the dáwn I begót you.

The Lórd has sworn an óath he will not chánge.†
'You are a príest for éver,*
a príest like Melchízedek of óld.'

The Máster stánding at your ríght hand*
will shatter kíngs in the dáy of his wráth.

He shall drínk from the stréam by the wáyside*
and thérefore he shall líft up his héad.

Ant. Christ the Lord is a priest for ever according to the order of Melchízedek, alleluia.

Ant. Advent: Behold, the Lord will come on the clouds of heaven with great strength, alleluia.
Ant. 2: The Lord will come and will not disappoint us. Wait for him if he seems to delay, for he will surely come, alleluia.

Ant. Lent, Sunday 2: The Lord will send forth your sceptre of power with the splendour of the saints.
Ant. 2: We worship the one God, who made heaven and earth.

Ant. Palm Sunday: He was wounded and humbled, but God has raised him up with his own right hand.
Ant. 2: The blood of Christ purifies us to serve the living God.

Ant. Eastertide: He raised Christ from the dead and placed him at his own right hand, in heaven, alleluia.
Ant. 2: You have been converted from idolatry to the living God, alleluia.

Ant. 2: Our God is in heaven: he has power to do whatever he will, alleluia.

PRAISE OF THE GOD OF TRUTH   PSALM 113B(115)
Turn away from idols and worship the living and true God (1 Thess 1:9)

Not to ús, Lórd, not to ús,*
but to yóur náme give the glóry
for the sáke of your lóve and your trúth,*
lest the héathen say: 'Whére is their Gód?'

But our Gód is ín the héavens;*
he dóes whatéver he wílls.
Their ídols are sílver and góld,*
the wórk of húman hánds.

They have móuths but they cánnot spéak;*
they have éyes but they cánnot sée;
they have éars but they cánnot héar;*
they have nóstrils but they cánnot sméll.

With their hánds they cánnot féel;†
with their féet they cánnot wálk.*
No sóund cómes from their thróats.
Their mákers will cóme to be líke them*
and so will áll who trúst in thém.

Sons of Ísrael, trúst in the Lórd;*
hé is their hélp and their shíeld.
Sons of Áaron, trúst in the Lórd;*
hé is their hélp and their shíeld.

You who féar him, trúst in the Lórd;*
hé is their hélp and their shíeld.
He remémbers us, and hé will bléss us:†
he will bléss the sóns of Ísrael.*
He will bléss the sóns of Áaron.

The Lord will bléss thóse who féar him,*
the líttle no léss than the gréat:
to yóu may the Lórd grant íncrease,*
to yóu and áll your chíldren.

May yóu be bléssed by the Lórd,*
the máker of héaven and éarth.
The héavens belóng to the Lórd*
but the éarth he has gíven to mén.

The déad shall not práise the Lórd,*
nor thóse who go dówn into the sílence.
But wé who líve bless the Lórd*
nów and for éver. Amén.

Ant. Our God is in heaven; he has power to do whatever he will, alleluia.

OUTSIDE LENT

Ant. Advent: The Lord will come and will not disappoint us. Wait for him if he seems to delay, for he will surely come, alleluia.

Ant. 3: The Lord is our judge, the Lord is our King. He will come and make us whole.

Ant. Eastertide: You have been converted from idolatry to the living God, alleluia.

Ant. 3: Alleluia, victory and glory and power belong to our God, alleluia.

Ant. 3: Praise God, all you his servants, both great and small, alleluia.

When chanted, this canticle is sung with Alleluia *as set out below. When recited, it suffices to say* Alleluia *at the beginning and end of each strophe.*

THE MARRIAGE FEAST OF THE LAMB   CANTICLE
                                        CF REV 19:1-2,5-7

Alleluia.

Salvation and glory and power belong to our God,*
(R̥ Alleluia.)
His judgments are true and just.
R̥ Alleluia (alleluia).

Alleluia.
Praise our God, all you his servants,*
(R̥ Alleluia.)
You who fear him, small and great.
R̥ Alleluia (alleluia).

Alleluia.
The Lord our God, the Almighty, reigns,*
(R̥ Alleluia.)
Let us rejoice and exult and give him the glory.
R̥ Alleluia (alleluia).

Alleluia.
The marriage of the Lamb has come,*
(R̥ Alleluia.)
And his bride has made herself ready.
R̥ Alleluia (alleluia).

Ant. Praise God, all you his servants, both great and small, alleluia.

Ant. Advent: The Lord is our judge, the Lord is our King. He will come and make us whole.
Eastertide: Alleluia, victory and glory and power belong to our God, alleluia.

LENT

Ant. Lent, Sunday 2: We worship the one God, who made heaven and earth.
Ant. 3: God did not spare his own Son but gave him up for us all.

Ant. Palm Sunday: The blood of Christ purifies us to serve the living God.
Ant. 3: He carried our sins in his own body on the cross, so that we might die to sin and live for holiness.

103

CHRIST, THE SERVANT OF GOD,
 FREELY ACCEPTS HIS PASSION

CANTICLE
I PET 2:21-24

Christ suffered for you,†
leaving you an example*
that you should follow in his steps.

He committed no sin;*
no guile was found on his lips.
When he was reviled,*
he did not revile in return.

When he suffered,*
he did not threaten;
but he trusted to him*
who judges justly.

He himself bore our sins*
in his body on the tree,
that we might die to sin*
and live to righteousness.

By his wounds you have been healed.

Ant. Lent, Sunday 2: God did not spare his own Son but gave him up for us all.
Palm Sunday: He carried our sins in his own body on the cross, so that we might die to sin and live for holiness.

THROUGH THE YEAR

Scripture Reading *2 Thess 2:13-14*
We feel that we must be continually thanking God for you, brothers whom the Lord loves, because God chose you as first fruits to be saved by the sanctifying Spirit and by faith in the truth. Through the Good News that we brought he called you to this so that you should share the glory of our Lord Jesus Christ.

Short Responsory
R̸ Great is our Lord; great is his might. *Repeat* R̸

℣ His wisdom can never be measured. ℟ Glory be. ℟

Magnificat antiphon from the Proper of Seasons.

Intercessions

Through the gospel, the Lord Jesus calls us to share in his glory.
Let us make our prayer with him to our heavenly Father. ℟ Lord,
in your mercy hear our prayer.

We pray for all nations:—that they may seek the way that leads to
peace; that human rights and freedom may be everywhere respected,
and that the world's resources may be generously shared. ℟

We pray for the Church:—that her leaders may be faithful ministers
of your word, that all her members may be strong in faith and hope
and that you may be recognized in the love she bears to all. ℟

We pray for our families, and the community in which we live:—
that we may find you in them. ℟

We pray for ourselves:—that in the coming week we may serve
others in our work, and find peace when we rest. ℟

We pray for the faithful departed:—that through your mercy they
may rest in peace. ℟

Our Father

The concluding prayer from the Proper of Seasons.

WEEK 2: MONDAY

Invitatory ant. Let us rejoice in the Lord; with songs let us praise
him.
Psalm, p 3.

MORNING PRAYER

HYMN

Come, O Creator Spirit, come,
and make within our hearts your home;

to us your grace eternal give,
who of your breathing move and live.

Our senses with your light inflame,
our hearts to heavenly love reclaim;
our bodies' poor infirmity
with strength perpetual fortify.

Our earthly foe afar repel,
grant us henceforth in peace to dwell;
and so to us, with you for guide,
no ill shall come, no harm betide.

May we by you the Father learn,
and know the Son, and you discern,
who are of both; and thus adore
in perfect faith for evermore.

PSALMODY

Ant. 1: When can I enter and see the face of God?
Holy Week: Jesus said, 'My soul is sorrowful to the point of death.
Wait here and keep awake with me.'
Eastertide: My soul is yearning for you, my God, like a deer that
seeks running streams, alleluia.

THE EXILE'S NOSTALGIA FOR THE LORD'S TEMPLE   PSALM 41(42)
*Let all who are thirsty come; all who want it may have the water of
life* (Rev 22:17)

Líke the déer that yéarns*
for rúnning stréams,
só my sóul is yéarning*
for yóu, my Gód.

My sóul is thírsting for Gód,*
the Gód of my lífe;
whén can I énter and sée*
the fáce of Gód?

My téars have becóme my bréad,*
by níght, by dáy,
as I héar it sáid all the day lóng:*
'Whére is your Gód?'

Thése things will Í remémber*
as I póur out my sóul:
how I would léad the rejóicing crówd*
into the hóuse of Gód,
amid críes of gládness and thanksgíving,*
the thróng wild with jóy.

Whý are you cast dówn, my sóul,*
why gróan withín me?
Hope in Gód; I will práise him stíll,*
my sáviour and my Gód.

My sóul is cast dówn withín me*
as I thínk of yóu,
from the cóuntry of Jórdan and Mount Hérmon,*
from the Híll of Mízar.

Déep is cálling on déep,*
in the róar of wáters:
your tórrents and áll your wáves*
swept óver mé.

By dáy the Lórd will sénd*
his lóving kíndness;
by níght I will síng to hím,*
praise the Gód of my lífe.

I will sáy to Gód, my róck:*
'Whý have you forgótten me?
Whý do Í go móurning*
oppréssed by the fóe?'

With críes that píerce me to the héart,*
my énemies revíle me,
sáying to me áll the day lóng:*
'Whére is your Gód?'

107

Whý are you cast dówn, my sóul,*
why gróan withín me?
Hope in Gód; I will práise him stíll,*
my sáviour and my Gód.

Ant. When can I enter and see the face of God?
Holy Week: Jesus said, 'My soul is sorrowful to the point of death.
Wait here and keep awake with me.'
Eastertide: My soul is yearning for you, my God, like a deer that
seeks running streams, alleluia.

Ant. 2: Show us, Lord, the light of your mercy.
Holy Week: Now sentence is being passed on this world; now the
prince of this world is to be overthrown.
Eastertide: Fill Sion with songs of your praise, Lord, and let the
stories of your great deeds be told, alleluia.

PRAYER FOR THE HOLY CITY OF JERUSALEM　　　　　CANTICLE
　　　　　　　　　　　　　　　　　　　　　　　SIR 36:1-7,13-16
*This is eternal life; to know you the one true God, and Jesus Christ
whom you have sent* (Jn 17:3)

Save us, God of all things,*
strike all the nations with terror;
raise your hand against foreign nations*
that they may see the greatness of your might.

Our sufferings proved your holiness to them;*
let their downfall prove your glory to us.
Let them know, as we ourselves know,*
that there is no other God but you.

Give us signs again, work further wonders,*
clothe your hand, your right arm in glory.

Assemble all the tribes of Jacob,*
as when they first received their inheritance.
Pity the poor people called by your name,*
pity Israel, chosen as your first-born.

Have compassion on the holy city,*
Jerusalem, the place of your rest.
Let Sion ring with your praises,*
let your temple be filled with your glory.

Ant. Show us, Lord, the light of your mercy.
Holy Week: Now sentence is being passed on this world; now the
prince of this world is to be overthrown.
Eastertide: Fill Sion with songs of your praise, Lord, and let the
stories of your great deeds be told, alleluia.

Ant. 3: Blessed are you, Lord, in the vault of heaven.
Holy Week: Jesus leads us in our faith and brings it to perfection;
he endured the cross, disregarding the shamefulness of it, and has
taken his seat at God's right hand.
Eastertide: The glory of God will illumine the city; the Lamb will
be its light, alleluia.

PRAISE FOR THE LORD, CREATOR OF ALL THINGS   PSALM 18(19)A
*The Rising Sun has come to visit us to guide our feet in the way of
peace* (Lk 1:78, 79)

The héavens procláim the glóry of Gód*
and the fírmament shows fórth the wórk of his hánds.
Dáy unto dáy tákes up the stóry*
and níght unto níght makes knówn the méssage.

No spéech, no wórd, no vóice is héard†
yet their spán exténds through áll the eárth,*
their wórds to the útmost bóunds of the wórld.

Thére he has pláced a tént for the sún;†
it comes fórth like a brídegroom cóming from his tént,*
rejóices like a chámpion to rún its cóurse.

At the énd of the ský is the rísing of the sún;†
to the fúrthest énd of the ský is its cóurse.*
There is nóthing concéaled from its búrning héat.

Ant. Blessed are you, Lord, in the vault of heaven.

Holy Week: Jesus leads us in our faith and brings it to perfection; he endured the cross, disregarding the shamefulness of it, and has taken his seat at God's right hand.

Eastertide: The glory of God will illumine the city; the Lamb will be its light, alleluia.

THROUGH THE YEAR

Scripture Reading   *Jer 15:16*

When your words came, I devoured them:
your word was my delight
and the joy of my heart;
for I was called by your name,
Lord, God of Sabaoth.

Short Responsory

Ry Rejoice in the Lord, O you just; for praise is fitting for loyal hearts. *Repeat* Ry
Vy Sing to him a new song. Ry Glory be. Ry

Benedictus ant. Blessed be the Lord, for he has visited us and freed us.

Intercessions

Christ has given us all a share in his priesthood. We offer our prayers and ourselves in union with him. Ry Lord, accept our love and service.

Jesus Christ, you are the eternal priest:—make this morning's offering acceptable to the Father. Ry

Lord, you are love itself:—grant that we may love you. Ry

Give us today the fruits of the Holy Spirit:—make us patient, kind and gentle. Ry

Give us the discernment to know the needs of our neighbours,—and give us the courage to love them as brothers. Ry

Our Father

Concluding Prayer

Almighty Lord and God,

protect us by your power throughout the course of this day,
even as you have enabled us to begin it:
do not let us turn aside to any sin,
but let our every thought, word and deed
aim at doing what is pleasing in your sight.
(We make our prayer) through our Lord.

EVENING PRAYER

HYMN

O Strength and Stay upholding all creation,
Who ever dost thyself unmoved abide,
Yet day by day the light in due gradation
From hour to hour in all its changes guide,

Grant to life's day a calm unclouded ending,
An eve untouched by shadows of decay.
The brightness of a holy death-bed blending
With dawning glories of the eternal day.

Hear us, O Father, gracious and forgiving,
Through Jesus Christ thy co-eternal Word,
Who, with the Holy Ghost, by all things living
Now and to endless ages art adored.

PSALMODY

Ant. 1: You are the fairest of the children of men and graciousness
is poured upon your lips.
Holy Week: He had no beauty, no majesty to draw our eyes, no
grace to make us delight in him.
Easteride: Blessed is he who comes in the name of the Lord, alleluia.

ROYAL WEDDING SONG   PSALM 44(45)
Behold, the bridegroom is coming; go out to meet him (Mt 25:6)

I

My héart overflóws with nóble wórds.†
To the king I must spéak the sóng I have máde,*

111

my tóngue as nímble as the pén of a scríbe.

Yóu are the fáirest of the chíldren of mén†
and gráciousness is póured upón your líps:*
because Gód has bléssed you for évermóre.

O míghty one, gírd your swórd upon your thígh;†
in spléndour and státe, ríde on in tríumph*
for the cáuse of trúth and góodness and ríght.

Take aím with your bów in your dréad right hánd.†
Your árrows are shárp: péoples fall benéath you.*
The fóes of the kíng fall dówn and lose héart.

Your thróne, O Gód, shall endúre for éver.†
A scéptre of jústice is the scéptre of your kíngdom.*
Your lóve is for jústice; your hátred for évil.

Therefore Gód, your Gód, has anóinted yóu†
with the óil of gládness abóve other kíngs:*
your róbes are frágrant with áloes and mýrrh.

From the ívory pálace you are gréeted with músic.†
The dáughters of kíngs are amóng your lóved ones.*
On your ríght stands the quéen in góld of Óphir.

Ant. You are the fairest of the children of men and graciousness is poured upon your lips.
Holy Week: He had no beauty, no majesty to draw our eyes, no grace to make us delight in him.
Eastertide: Blessed is he who comes in the name of the Lord, alleluia.

Ant. 2: Behold, the bridegroom is coming; go out and meet him.
Holy Week: I will grant him very many people as his own, for surrendering himself to death.
Eastertide: Blessed are those who are called to the wedding feast of the Lamb, alleluia.

II

Lísten, O dáughter, give éar to my wórds:*

forgét your own péople and your fáther's hóuse.
Só will the kíng desíre your béauty:*
Hé is your lórd, pay hómage to hím.

And the péople of Týre shall cóme with gífts,*
the ríchest of the péople shall séek your fávour.
The dáughter of the kíng is clóthed with spléndour,*
her róbes embróidered with péarls set in góld.

She is léd to the kíng with her maíden compánions.†
Théy are escórted amid gládness and jóy;*
they páss withín the pálace of the kíng.

Sóns shall be yóurs in pláce of your fáthers:*
you will máke them prínces over áll the éarth.
May this sóng make your náme for éver remémbered.*
May the péoples práise you from áge to áge.

Ant. Behold, the bridegroom is coming; go out and meet him.
Holy Week: I will grant him very many people as his own, for
surrendering himself to death.
Eastertide: Blessed are those who are called to the wedding feast
of the Lamb, alleluia.

Ant. 3: God planned to bring all things together under Christ when
the fulness of time had come.
Holy Week: God has given freely of his goodness to us in his beloved
Son, in whom we gain our freedom through the shedding of his
blood.
Eastertide: From his fulness we have all received, grace upon grace,
alleluia.

GOD, THE SAVIOUR   CANTICLE: EPH 1:3-10
    Blessed be the God and Father*
    of our Lord Jesus Christ,
    who has blessed us in Christ*
    with every spiritual blessing in the heavenly places.

    He chose us in him*
    before the foundation of the world,

that we should be holy*
and blameless before him.

He destined us in love*
to be his sons through Jesus Christ,
according to the purpose of his will,†
to the praise of his glorious grace*
which he freely bestowed on us in the Beloved.

In him we have redemption through his blood,*
the forgiveness of our trespasses,
according to the riches of his grace
which he lavished upon us.

He has made known to us†
in all wisdom and insight*
the mystery of his will,
according to his purpose*
which he set forth in Christ.

His purpose he set forth in Christ,*
as a plan for the fulness of time,
to unite all things in him,*
things in heaven and things on earth.

Ant. God planned to bring all things together under Christ when
the fulness of time had come.

Holy Week: God has given freely of his goodness to us in his
beloved Son, in whom we gain our freedom through the shedding
of his blood.

Eastertide: From his fulness we have all received, grace upon grace,
alleluia.

THROUGH THE YEAR

Scripture Reading   *1 Thess 2:13*
Another reason why we constantly thank God for you is that as
soon as you heard the message that we brought you as God's
message, you accepted it for what it really is, God's message and not
some human thinking; and it is still a living power among you who
believe it.

Short Responsory

R̸ Let my prayer come before you, O Lord. *Repeat* R̸
V̸ Let it rise in your presence like incense. R̸ Glory be. R̸

Magnificat ant. Let my soul proclaim your greatness for ever,
O my God.

Intercessions

Let us give thanks to Christ our Lord who loves and cherishes his
Church. R̸ Be near us, Lord, this evening.
Lord Jesus grant that all men may be saved,—and come to know-
ledge of the truth. R̸
Protect Pope N. and N., our Bishop:—help them, Lord, in your
strength and mercy. R̸
Support those who meet with difficulty and disappointment:—
renew their confidence and sense of purpose. R̸
Christ our loving Lord, in your kindness be with the sick and the
poor, the weak and the dying:—bring them your comfort. R̸
We commend to you all those who, in their lifetime, shared in the
sacred ministry:—let them praise you for ever in heaven. R̸
Our Father

Concluding Prayer

All-powerful God,
since you have given us, your unworthy servants,
the strength to work throughout this day:
accept this evening sacrifice of praise
as we thank you for your gifts.
(We make our prayer) through our Lord.

WEEK 2: TUESDAY

Invitatory ant. A mighty God is the Lord: come, let us adore him.
Psalm, p 3.

MORNING PRAYER

HYMN

Father, we praise you, now the night is over,
active and watchful, stand we all before you;
singing, we offer prayer and meditation: thus we adore you.

Monarch of all things, fit us for your mansions;
banish our weakness, health and wholeness sending;
bring us to heaven, where your saints united joy without ending.

All-holy Father, Son and equal Spirit,
Trinity blessed, send us your salvation;
yours is the glory, gleaming and resounding through all Creation.

PSALMODY

Ant. 1: Lord, send forth your light and your truth.
Holy Week: Lord, plead my cause; from deceitful and cunning men rescue me.
Eastertide: You have come to Mount Sion, and the city of the living God, alleluia.

DESIRE FOR GOD'S TEMPLE   PSALM 42(43)
I, the light, have come into the world (Jn 12:46)

Defénd me, O Gód, and plead my cáuse*
against a gódless nátion.
From decéitful and cúnning mén*
réscue me, O Gód.

Since yóu, O Gód, are my strónghold,*
whý have you rejécted me?
Whý do Í go móurning*
oppréssed by the fóe?

O sénd forth your líght and your trúth;*
let thése be my guíde.

116

Let them bring me to your hóly móuntain*
to the pláce where you dwéll.

And I will cóme to the áltar of Gód,*
the Gód of my jóy.
My redéemer, I will thánk you on the hárp,*
O Gód, my Gód.

Whý are you cast dówn, my sóul,*
why gróan withín me?
Hope in Gód; I will práise him stíll,*
my sáviour and my Gód.

Ant. Lord, send forth your light and your truth.
Holy Week: Lord, plead my cause; from deceitful and cunning men rescue me.
Eastertide: You have come to Mount Sion, and the city of the living God, alleluia.

Ant. 2: Lord, come to our help all the days of our life.
Holy Week: Lord, you have defended the cause of my soul; you have redeemed my life, Lord my God.
Eastertide: Lord, you have kept my soul from destruction, alleluia.

THE ANGUISH OF SICKNESS;   CANTICLE
   THE JOY OF HEALTH   IS 38:10-14,17-20
I was dead, and behold, I am alive and I hold the keys of death (Rev 1:17-18)

I said, In the noontide of my days I must depart;†
I am consigned to the gates of Sheol*
for the rest of my years.

I said, I shall not see the Lord*
in the land of the living;
I shall look upon man no more*
among the inhabitants of the world.

My dwelling is plucked up and removed from me*
like a shepherd's tent;

117

like a weaver I have rolled up my life;*
he cuts me off from the loom.

From day to night you bring me to an end;*
I cry for help until morning;
like a lion he breaks all my bones;*
from day to night you bring me to an end.

Like a swallow or a crane I clamour,*
I moan like a dove.
My eyes are weary with looking upward.*
O Lord, I am oppressed; be my security.

Lo, it was for my welfare*
that I had great bitterness;
but you have held back my life*
from the pit of destruction,
for you have cast all my sins*
behind your back.

For Sheol cannot thank you,*
death cannot praise you;
those who go down to the pit*
cannot hope for your faithfulness.

The living, the living, he thanks you,†
as I do this day;*
the father makes known to the children your faithfulness.

The Lord will save me,*
and we will sing to stringed instruments
all the days of our life,*
at the house of the Lord.

Ant. Lord, come to our help all the days of our life.
Holy Week: Lord, you have defended the cause of my soul; you have redeemed my life, Lord my God.
Eastertide: Lord, you have kept my soul from destruction, alleluia.

Ant. 3: To you our praise is due in Sion, O God.†
Holy Week: My servant, the Just One, will justify many; he will

take their faults on himself.
Eastertide: You care for the earth, you give it water, alleluia.

SOLEMN THANKSGIVING   PSALM 64(65)
Sion is to be understood as the heavenly city (Origen)

To yóu our práise is dúe*
in Síon, O Gód.
†To yóu we páy our vóws,*
you who héar our práyer.

To yóu all flésh will cóme*
with its búrden of sín.
Too héavy for ús, our offénces,*
but you wípe them awáy.

Blessed is hé whom you chóose and cáll*
to dwéll in your cóurts.
We are fílled with the bléssings of your hóuse,*
of your hóly témple.

You kéep your plédge with wónders,*
O Gód our sáviour,
the hópe of áll the éarth*
and of fár distant ísles.

You uphóld the móuntains with your stréngth,*
you are gírded with pówer.
You still the róaring of the séas,†
the róaring of their wáves*
and the túmult of the péoples.

The énds of the éarth stand in áwe*
at the síght of your wónders.
The lánds of súnrise and súnset*
you fíll with your jóy.

You cáre for the éarth, give it wáter,*
you fíll it with ríches.
Your ríver in héaven brims óver†

119

to provide its gráin.*

And thús you províde for the éarth;
You drénch its fúrrows,†
you lével it, sóften it with shówers,*
you bléss its grówth.

You crówn the yéar with your góodness.†
Abúndance flóws in your stéps,*
in the pástures of the wílderness it flóws.

The hílls are gírded with jóy,*
the méadows cóvered with flócks,
the válleys are décked with whéat.*
They shóut for jóy, yes, they síng.

Ant. To you our praise is due in Sion, O God.
Holy Week: My servant, the Just One, will justify many; he will take their faults on himself.
Eastertide: You care for the earth, you give it water, alleluia.

THROUGH THE YEAR

Scripture Reading   *1 Thess 5:4-5*
It is not as if you live in the dark, my brothers, for that Day to overtake you like a thief. No, you are all sons of light and sons of the day: we do not belong to the night or to darkness.

Short Responsory
R̷ Hear my cry, Lord, for I hope in your word. *Repeat* R̷
V̷ I rise before dawn and call for help. R̷ Glory be. R̷

Benedictus ant. Lord, save us from the hands of all who hate us.

Intercessions
Let us bless our Saviour, who by his rising to new life has freed the world from fear. R̷ Lord, lead us to the truth.
Lord Jesus, as this day begins we remember that you are risen,—
and therefore we look to the future with confidence. R̷

We offer you our prayer this morning,—take to yourself our cares, our hopes, and our needs. R⁷

Deepen in us our love for you today,—so that in all things we may find our good, and the good of others. R⁷

Lord Jesus, we pray that through our own troubles, we may learn to feel the sufferings of others;—help us to show them your compassion. R⁷

Our Father

Concluding Prayer

True Light of the world, Lord Jesus Christ,
as you enlighten all men for their salvation,
give us grace, we pray,
to herald your coming
by preparing the ways of justice and of peace.
Who live and reign with the Father and the Holy Spirit,
God, for ever and ever.

EVENING PRAYER

HYMN

Before we end our day, O Lord,
We make this prayer to you:
That you continue in your love
To guard your people here.

Give us this night untroubled rest
And build our strength anew:
Your Splendour driving far away
All darkness of the foe.

Our hearts' desire to love you, Lord,
Watch over while we sleep,
That when the new day dawns on high
We may your praises sing.

All glory be to you, O Christ,
Who saved mankind from death—

121

To share with you the Father's love
And in the Spirit live.

PSALMODY

Ant. 1: You cannot serve both God and wealth.

Holy Week: Insult and terror have been my lot, but the Lord is at my side, a mighty hero.

Eastertide: Look for the things of heaven, not for the things which are upon this earth, alleluia.

THE USELESSNESS OF RICHES   PSALM 48(49)
The rich man will find it very hard to enter the kingdom of heaven (Mt 19:23)

I

Héar this, áll you péoples,*
 give héed, all who dwéll in the wórld,
mén both lów and hígh,*
 rích and póor alíke!

My líps will speak wórds of wísdom.*
 My héart is fúll of ínsight.
I will túrn my mínd to a párable,*
 with the hárp I will sólve my próblem.

Whý should I féar in evil dáys*
 the málice of the fóes who surróund me,
mén who trúst in their wéalth,*
 and bóast of the vástness of their ríches?

For nó man can búy his own ránsom,*
 or pay a príce to Gód for his life.
The ránsom of his sóul is beyónd him.†
He cánnot buy lífe without énd,*
 nor avóid cóming to the gráve.

He knows that wíse men and fóols must both pérish*
 and léave their wéalth to óthers.
Their gráves are their hómes for éver,†
 their dwélling place from áge to áge,*

122

though their námes spread wíde through the lánd.

In his ríches, mán lacks wísdom:*
hé is like the béasts that are destróyed.

Ant. You cannot serve both God and wealth.
Holy Week: Insult and terror have been my lot, but the Lord is at my side, a mighty hero.
Eastertide: Look for the things of heaven, not for the things which are upon this earth, alleluia.

Ant. 2: Store up treasure for yourselves in heaven, says the Lord.
Holy Week: Deliver me, Lord, and set me close to you; let who will raise his hand against me.
Eastertide: The Lord saved my soul from the power of death, alleluia.

II

This is the lót of those who trúst in themsélves,*
who have óthers at their béck and cáll.
Like shéep they are dríven to the gráve,†
where déath shall bé their shépherd*
and the júst shall becóme their rúlers.

With the mórning their óutward show vánishes*
and the gráve becómes their hóme.
But Gód will ránsom me from déath*
and táke my sóul to himsélf.

Then do not féar when a mán grows rích,*
when the glóry of his hóuse incréases.
He takes nóthing with him when he díes,*
his glóry does not fóllow him belów.

Though he fláttered himsélf while he líved:*
'Men will práise me for áll my succéss,'
yet he will gó to jóin his fáthers,*
who will néver see the líght any móre.

In his ríches, mán lacks wísdom:*
hé is like the béasts that are destróyed.

Ant. Store up treasure for yourselves in heaven, says the Lord.
Holy Week: Deliver me, Lord, and set me close to you; let who will raise his hand against me.
Eastertide: The Lord saved my soul from the power of death, alleluia.

Ant. 3: Worthy is the Lamb that was slain, to receive glory and honour.
Holy Week: You were slain, Lord, and with your blood you bought us for God.
Eastertide: Yours, Lord, is the greatness and the power, the glory and the victory, alleluia.

HYMN OF THE REDEEMED   CANTICLE: REV 4:11;5:9,10,12

Worthy are you, our Lord and God,*
to receive glory and honour and power,
for you created all things,*
and by your will they existed and were created.

Worthy are you, O Lord,*
to take the scroll and to open its seals,
for you were slain,†
and by your blood you ransomed men for God*
from every tribe and tongue and people and nation.

You have made us a kingdom and priests to serve our God,*
and we shall reign on earth.
Worthy is the Lamb who was slain,*
to receive power and wealth,
and wisdom and might,*
and honour and glory and blessing.

Ant. Worthy is the Lamb that was slain, to receive glory and honour.
Holy Week: You were slain, Lord, and with your blood you bought us for God.
Eastertide: Yours, Lord, is the greatness and the power, the glory and the victory, alleluia.

Scripture Reading *Rom 3:23–25a*
Since all have sinned and fall short of the glory of God, they are justified by his grace as a gift, through the redemption which is in Christ Jesus, whom God put forward as an expiation by his blood, to be received by faith. This was to show God's righteousness.

Short Responsory
℞ You will give me the fulness of joy in your presence, O Lord.
Repeat ℞
℣ I will find happiness at your right hand for ever. ℞ Glory be. ℞

Magnificat ant. Do great things for us, O Lord, for you are mighty, and Holy is your name.

Intercessions
Christ is the shepherd of his flock: he loves and cares for his people. We turn to him in trust and say: ℞ Lord, we need your care.
Christ our Lord, you are pastor of all the ages,—protect our Bishop, N., and all the pastors of your Church. ℞
Be with those who are persecuted for their faith, and those cut off from the support of the Church:—Good Shepherd, in their pain and isolation may they know your care. ℞
Bring healing to the sick;—give nourishment to the hungry.
We remember those who make our laws and those who apply them:—Lord, give them wisdom and discernment. ℞
Gather the flock for which you laid down your life:—bring home to their Father's house all who have died in your peace. ℞
Our Father

Concluding Prayer
Yours is the day and yours, the night, Lord God:
let the Sun of Justice shine so steadily in our hearts,
that we may come at length
to that light where you dwell eternally.
(We make our prayer) through our Lord.

WEEK 2: WEDNESDAY

Invitatory ant. Cry out with joy to God, all the earth: serve the
Lord with gladness.
Psalm, p 3.

MORNING PRAYER

HYMN

Now that the daylight fills the sky,
we lift our hearts to God on high,
that he, in all we do or say,
would keep us free from harm today;

Would guard our hearts and tongues from strife;
from anger's din would hide our life;
from all ill sights would turn our eyes;
would close our ears from vanities.

Would keep our inmost conscience pure;
our souls from folly would secure;
would bid us check the pride of sense
with due and holy abstinence.

So we, when this new day is gone,
and night in turn is drawing on,
with conscience by the world unstained
shall praise his Name for victory gained.

PSALMODY

Ant. 1: Your ways, O God, are holy. What God is great as our God?
Holy Week: In the day of my distress I sought the Lord with outstretched arms.
Eastertide: The waters saw you. O God; you led your people
through the sea, alleluia.

REMEMBERING THE WORKS OF THE LORD   PSALM 76(77)
We are in difficulties on every side, but never consumed (2 Cor 4:8)

I crý alóud to Gód,*
cry alóud to Gód that he may héar me.

In the dáy of my distréss I sought the Lórd.†
My hánds were raised at níght without céasing;*
my sóul refúsed to be consóled.
I remémbered my Gód and I gróaned.*
I póndered and my spírit fáinted.

You withhéld sléep from my éyes.*
I was tróubled, I cóuld not spéak.
I thóught of the dáys of long agó*
and remémbered the yéars long pást.
At níght I músed within my héart.*
I póndered and my spírit quéstioned.

'Will the Lórd rejéct us for éver?*
Will he shów us his fávour no móre?
Has his lóve vánished for éver?*
Has his prómise cóme to an énd?
Does Gód forgét his mércy*
or in ánger withhóld his compássion?'

I said: 'Thís is what cáuses my gríef;*
that the wáy of the Most Hígh has chánged.'
I remémber the déeds of the Lórd,*
I remémber your wónders of óld,
I múse on áll your wórks*
and pónder your míghty déeds.

Your wáys, O Gód, are hóly.*
What gód is gréat as our Gód?
Yóu are the Gód who works wónders.*
Yóu showed your pówer among the péoples.
Your stróng arm redéemed your péople,*
the sóns of Jácob and Jóseph.

The wáters sáw you, O Gód,†

127

the wáters sáw you and trémbled;*
the dépths were móved with térror.
The clóuds póured down ráin,†
the skíes sent fórth their vóice;*
your árrows fláshed to and fró.

Your thúnder rólled round the ský,*
your fláshes líghted up the wórld.
The éarth was móved and trémbled*
when your wáy léd through the séa,
your páth through the míghty wáters*
and nó one sáw your fóotprints.

You guíded your péople like a flóck*
by the hánd of Móses and Áaron.

Ant. Your ways, O God, are holy. What God is great as our God?
Holy Week: In the day of my distress I sought the Lord with outstretched arms.
Eastertide: The waters saw you. O God; you led your people
through the sea, alleluia.

Ant. 2: My heart exults in the Lord; he humbles and he exalts.
Holy Week: If we have died with Christ, we believe that we shall
also come to life with him.
Eastertide: The Lord gives death and he gives life, alleluia.

THE POOR REJOICE IN THE LORD   CANTICLE
                                                    I SAM 2:1-10

*He put down the mighty from their seats and exalted the lowly; he
filled the hungry with good things* (Lk 1:52-53)

My heart exults in the Lord,*
I find my strength in my God;
my mouth laughs at my enemies*
as I rejoice in your saving help.
There is none like the Lord,†
there is none besides you.*
There is no Rock like our God.

Bring your haughty words to an end,*
let no boasts fall from your lips,
for the Lord is a God who knows all.*
It is he who weighs men's deeds.

The bows of the mighty are broken,*
but the weak are clothed with strength.
Those with plenty must labour for bread,*
but the hungry need work no more.
The childless wife has children now*
but the fruitful wife bears no more.

It is the Lord who gives life and death,*
he brings men to the grave and back;
it is the Lord who gives poverty and riches.*
He brings men low and raises them on high.

He lifts up the lowly from the dust,*
from the ash heap he raises the poor
to set him in the company of princes,*
to give him a glorious throne.

For the pillars of the earth are the Lord's,*
on them he has set the world.
He guards the steps of his faithful,*
but the wicked perish in darkness,
for no man's power gives him victory.*
The enemies of the Lord shall be broken.

The Most High will thunder in the heavens,*
the Lord will judge the ends of the earth.
He will give power to his king*
and exalt the might of his anointed.

Ant. My heart exults in the Lord; he humbles and he exalts.
Holy week: If we have died with Christ, we believe that we shall also
come to life with him.
Eastertide: The Lord gives death and he gives life, alleluia.

Ant. 3: The Lord is king, let earth rejoice.†

Holy Week: God has made Jesus Christ our wisdom and our virtue, our holiness and our freedom.
Eastertide: Light shines forth for the just and joy for the upright of heart, alleluia.

THE GLORY OF THE LORD'S RULE   PSALM 96(97)
This psalm tells of the salvation of the world and of the faith all peoples would have in Christ (St Athanasius)

The Lord is kíng, let éarth rejóice,*
†let áll the cóastlands be glád.
Clóud and dárkness are his ráiment;*
his thróne, jústice and ríght.

A fíre prepáres his páth;*
it búrns up his fóes on every síde.
His líghtnings líght up the wórld,*
the éarth trémbles at the síght.

The móuntains mélt like wáx*
before the Lórd of áll the earth.
The skíes procláim his jústice;*
all péoples sée his glóry.

Let thóse who serve ídols be ashámed,†
those who bóast of their wórthless góds.*
All you spírits, wórship hím.

Síon héars and is glád;†
the péople of Júdah rejóice*
becáuse of your júdgments O Lórd.

For yóu indéed are the Lórd†
most hígh above áll the éarth*
exálted far abóve all spírits.

The Lórd loves thóse who hate évil:†
he guárds the sóuls of his sáints;*
he séts them frée from the wícked.

Líght shines fórth for the júst*

130

and jóy for the úpright of héart.
Rejóice, you júst, in the Lórd;*
give glóry to his hóly náme.

Ant. The Lord is king, let earth rejoice.
Holy Week: God has made Jesus Christ our wisdom and our virtue, our holiness and our freedom.
Eastertide: Light shines forth for the just and joy for the upright of heart, alleluia.

THROUGH THE YEAR

Scripture Reading *Rom 8:35-37*
Who will separate us from the love of Christ? Will affliction, or distress, or persecution, or hunger, or nakedness, or peril, or the sword? Yet in all this we are conquerors, through him who has granted us his love.

Short Responsory
R͡ I will praise the Lord at all times. *Repeat* R͡
V͡ His praise will be always on my lips. R͡ Glory be. R͡

Benedictus ant. Let us serve the Lord in holiness all our days.

Intercessions
Nothing can separate us from the love of Christ, for he promised to be with his Church until the end of time. With confidence in his promise we pray: R͡ Stay with us, Lord Jesus.
In all things we are victorious through your love:—take us into your care today. R͡
Let the love of your Holy Spirit be in our hearts:—so that we may consecrate this day to you. R͡
Help all Christians to answer your call:—may they be salt to the earth, and light to the world. R͡
We pray for all those in industry:—may they work in harmony for justice and for the good of the whole community. R͡
Our Father

Concluding Prayer
Shed your clear light on our hearts, Lord,
so that walking continually in the way of your commandments,
we may never be deceived or misled.
(We make our prayer) through our Lord.

EVENING PRAYER

O Trinity of blessed light,
O unity of princely might,
the fiery sun has gone its way;
shed now within our hearts your ray.

To you our morning song of praise,
to you our evening prayer we raise;
your glory suppliant we adore
for ever and for evermore.

PSALMODY

Ant. 1: We are waiting in hope for the blessings of the glorious coming of our Saviour.
Holy Week: The wicked men said: let us oppress the just man, since his ways are contrary to ours.
Eastertide: Do not let your hearts be troubled; only have faith in me alleluia.

PEACE IN GOD   PSALM 61(62)
May the God of hope fill you with all peace as you believe in him
(Rom 15:13)

In God alóne is my sóul at rést;*
my hélp comes from hím.
He alóne is my róck, my strónghold,*
my fórtress: I stand fírm.

132

How lóng will you áll attack one mán*
to bréak him dówn,
as thóugh he were a tóttering wáll,*
or a túmbling fénce?

Their plán is ónly to destróy:*
they take pléasure in líes.
With their móuth they útter bléssing*
but in their héart they cúrse.

In God alóne be at rést, my sóul;*
for my hópe comes from hím.
He alóne is my róck, my strónghold,*
my fórtress: I stand fírm.

In Gód is my sáfety and glóry,*
the róck of my stréngth.
Take réfuge in Gód all you péople.*
Trúst him at áll times.
Póur out your héarts befóre him*
for Gód is our réfuge.

Cómmon folk are ónly a bréath,*
gréat men an illúsion.
Pláced in the scáles, they ríse;*
they weigh léss than a bréath.

Dó not put your trúst in oppréssion*
nor vain hópes on plúnder.
Dó not set your héart on ríches*
even whén they incréase.

For Gód has sáid only óne thing:*
only twó do I knów:
that to Gód alóne belongs pówer*
and to yóu, Lord, lóve;
and that yóu repáy each mán*
accórding to his déeds.

Ant. We are waiting in hope for the blessings of the glorious coming of our Saviour.

Holy Week: The wicked men said: let us oppress the just man, since
his ways are contrary to ours.
Eastertide: Do not let your hearts be troubled; only have faith in
me, alleluia.

Ant. 2: Let God bless us; let his face shed its light upon us.
Holy Week: He bore the sins of many and interceded for sinners.
Eastertide: Let the peoples praise you, O God; let them rejoice in
your saving help, alleluia.

When the following psalm has been used at the Invitatory, ps. 94,
p 3, is said here in place of it.

ALL THE PEOPLES WILL GIVE PRAISE TO THE LORD   PSALM 66(67)
Let it be known to you that this salvation from God has been sent to
all peoples (Acts 28:28)

O Gód, be grácious and bléss us*
and let your fáce shed its líght upón us.
So will your wáys be knówn upon éarth*
and all nátions learn your sáving hélp.

Let the péoples práise you, O Gód;*
let áll the péoples práise you.

Let the nátions be gládd and exúlt*
for you rúle the wórld with jústice.
With fáirness you rúle the péoples,*
you guíde the nátions on éarth.

Let the péoples práise you, O Gód;*
let áll the péoples práise you.

The éarth has yíelded its frúit*
for Gód, our Gód, has bléssed us.
May Gód still gíve us his bléssing*
till the énds of the éarth revére him.

Let the péoples práise you, O Gód;*
let áll the péoples práise you.

Ant. Let God bless us; let his face shed its light upon us.
Holy Week: He bore the sins of many and interceded for sinners.
Eastertide: Let the peoples praise you, O God; let them rejoice in your saving help, alleluia.

Ant. 3: All things were created in him and he holds all things in being.
Holy Week: In Christ we gain our freedom, the forgiveness of our sins, through the shedding of his blood.
Eastertide: His majesty covers the heavens, the earth is filled with his praise, alleluia.

CHRIST IS THE FIRSTBORN OF ALL CREATION,   CANTICLE
THE FIRSTBORN FROM THE DEAD   COL 1:12-20

Let us give thanks to the Father,†
who has qualified us to share*
in the inheritance of the saints in light.

He has delivered us from the dominion of darkness*
and transferred us to the kingdom of his beloved Son,
in whom we have redemption,*
the forgiveness of sins.

He is the image of the invisible God,*
the firstborn of all creation,
for in him all things were created, in heaven and on earth,*
visible and invisible.

All things were created*
through him and for him.
He is before all things,*
and in him all things hold together.

He is the head of the body, the Church;*
he is the beginning,
the firstborn from the dead,*
that in everything he might be pre-eminent.

For in him all the fulness of God was pleased to dwell,*

135

and through him to reconcile to himself all things,
whether on earth or in heaven,*
making peace by the blood of his cross.

Ant. All things were created in him and he holds all things in being.
Holy Week: In Christ we gain our freedom, the forgiveness of our
sins, through the shedding of his blood.
Eastertide: His majesty covers the heavens, the earth is filled with
his praise, alleluia.

Scripture Reading   *I Pet 5:5b-7*
Wrap yourselves in humility to be servants of each other, because
God refuses the proud and will always favour the humble. Bow
down, then, before the power of God now, and he will raise you
up on the appointed day; unload all your worries on to him, since
he is looking after you.

Short Responsory

R⁷ Guard us, Lord, as the apple of your eye. *Repeat* R⁷
℣ Hide us in the shadow of your wings. R⁷ Glory be. R⁷

Magnificat ant. Show the power of your arm, Lord; put down the
proud and exalt the lowly.

Intercessions
At the end of the day we give thanks to God the Father who re-
conciled the whole universe to himself in Christ. R⁷ Glory to you,
Lord God!
We thank you for the beauty of creation:—may the work of man not
disfigure it, but enhance it to your greater glory. R⁷
We thank you, Father, for all the good things we enjoy:—teach us
to be grateful and to use them well. R⁷
Teach us to seek the things that please you,—then we shall find you
in all that we do. R⁷
Lord, as we journey towards the promised land, feed us with bread
from heaven,—quench our thirst with living water. R⁷
To you, a thousand years are like a single day:—take up those who
have died with hope in you, and waken them into eternity. R⁷
Our Father

Concluding Prayer
Lord God,
whose name is holy
and whose mercy is proclaimed in every generation:
receive your people's prayer,
and let them sing your greatness with never-ending praise.
(We make our prayer) through our Lord.

WEEK 2: THURSDAY

Invitatory ant. Come before the Lord, singing for joy.
Psalm, p 3.

MORNING PRAYER

HYMN

Alone with none but thee, my God,
I journey on my way;
What need I fear, when thou art near,
O King of night and day?
More safe am I within thy hand,
Than if a host did round me stand.

My destined time is fixed by thee,
And death doth know his hour.
Did warriors strong around me throng,
They could not stay his power;
No walls of stone can man defend
When thou thy messenger dost send.

My life I yield to thy decree,
And bow to thy control
In peaceful calm, for from thine arm
No power can wrest my soul.
Could earthly omens e'er appal
A man that heeds the heavenly call!

The child of God can fear no ill,
His chosen dread no foe;
We leave our fate with thee, and wait
Thy bidding when to go.
'Tis not from chance our comfort springs,
Thou art our trust, O King of kings.

PSALMODY

Ant. 1: Lord, rouse up your might and come to our help.
Holy Week: Look, Lord, and answer quickly, for I am in distress.
Eastertide: I am the vine, you are the branches, alleluia.

LORD, COME TO VISIT YOUR VINE PSALM 79(80)
Come, Lord Jesus (Rev 22:20)

O shépherd of Ísrael, héar us,*
you who léad Jóseph's flóck,
shine fórth from your chérubim throne*
upon Éphraim, Bénjamin, Manásseh.
O Lórd, róuse up your míght,*
O Lórd, cóme to our hélp.

Gód of hósts, bríng us báck;*
let your fáce shine on ús and wé shall be sáved.

Lórd God of hósts, how lóng*
will you frówn on your péople's pléa?
You have féd them with téars for their bréad,*
an abúndance of téars for their drínk.
You have máde us the táunt of our néighbours,*
our énemies láugh us to scórn.

Gód of hósts, bríng us báck;*
let your fáce shine on ús and wé shall be sáved.

You bróught a víne out of Égypt;*
to plánt it you dróve out the nátions.
Befóre it you cléared the gróund;*
it took róot and spréad through the lánd.

The móuntains were cóvered with its shádow,*
the cédars of Gód with its bóughs.
It strétched out its bránches to the séa,*
to the Great Ríver it strétched out its shóots.

Then whý have you bróken down its wálls?*
It is plúcked by áll who pass bý.
It is rávaged by the bóar of the fórest,*
devóured by the béasts of the field.

God of hósts, turn agáin, we implóre,*
look dówn from héaven and sée.
Vísit this víne and protéct it,*
the víne your ríght hand has plánted.
Men have búrnt it with fíre and destróyed it.*
May they pérish at the frówn of your fáce.

May your hánd be on the mán you have chósen,*
the mán you have gíven your stréngth.
And we shall néver forsáke you agáin:*
give us lífe that we may cáll upon your náme.

Gód of hósts, bríng us báck;*
let your fáce shine on ús and wé shall be sáved.

Ant. Lord, rouse up your might and come to our help.
Holy Week: Look, Lord, and answer quickly, for I am in distress.
Eastertide: I am the vine, you are the branches, alleluia.

Ant. 2: The Lord has done marvellous things, let them be made known to the whole world.
Holy Week: See now that God is my salvation; I have trust and no fear.
Eastertide: With joy you will draw water from the wells of the Saviour, alleluia.

THE REJOICING OF A REDEEMED PEOPLE   CANTICLE: IS 12:1-6
If any man is thirsty, let him come to me and drink (Jn 7:37)

I thank you Lord, you were angry with me*

139

but your anger has passed and you give me comfort.

Truly, God is my salvation,*
I trust, I shall not fear.
For the Lord is my strength, my song,*
he is my saviour.

With joy you will draw water*
from the wells of salvation.
Give thanks to the Lord, give praise to his name!*
Make his mighty deeds known to the peoples.

Declare the greatness of his name,*
sing a psalm to the Lord!
For he has done glorious deeds;*
make them known to all the earth.

People of Sion, sing and shout for joy*
for great in your midst is the Holy One of Israel.

Ant. The Lord has done marvellous things, let them be made known to the whole world.
Holy Week: See now that God is my salvation; I have trust and no fear.
Eastertide: With joy you will draw water from the wells of the Saviour, alleluia.

Ant. 3: Ring out your joy to God our strength.†
Holy Week: The Lord fed us with finest wheat, he filled us with honey from the rock.
Eastertide: The Lord has fed us with finest wheat, alleluia.

SOLEMN RENEWAL OF THE COVENANT   PSALM 80(81)
Take care that no one among you has a wicked, unbelieving heart (Heb 3:12)

Ring out your jóy to Gód our stréngth,*
†shout in tríumph to the Gód of Jácob.

Raise a sóng and sóund the tímbrel,*
the swéet-sounding hárp and the lúte,
blów the trúmpet at the néw moon,*
when the móon is fúll, on our féast.

For thís is Ísrael's láw,*
a commánd of the Gód of Jácob.
He impósed it as a rúle on Jóseph,*
when he went óut against the lánd of Égypt.

A vóice I did not knów said to mé:*
'I fréed your shóulder from the búrden;
your hánds were fréed from the lóad.*
You cálled in distréss and I sáved you.

I ánswered, concéaled in the stórm cloud,*
at the wáters of Meríbah I tésted you.
Lísten, my péople, to my wárning,*
O Ísrael, if ónly you would héed!

Let there bé no fóreign god amóng you,*
no wórship of an álien gód.
Í am the Lórd your Gód,†
who bróught you from the lánd of Égypt.*
Ópen wide your móuth and I will fíll it.

But my péople did not héed my vóice*
and Ísrael wóuld not óbey,
so I léft them in their stúbbornness of héart*
to fóllow their ówn desígns.

Ó that my péople would héed me,*
that Ísrael would wálk in my wáys!
At ónce I would subdúe their fóes,*
turn my hánd agáinst their énemies.

The Lord's énemies would crínge at their féet*
and their subjéction would lást for éver.
But Ísrael I would féed with finest whéat*
and fíll them with hóney from the róck.'

141

Ant. Ring out your joy to God our strength.
Holy Week: The Lord fed us with finest wheat, he filled us with honey from the rock.
Eastertide: The Lord has fed us with finest wheat, alleluia.

THROUGH THE YEAR

Scripture Reading   *Rom 14:17-19*

The kingdom of God does not mean food and drink but righteousness and peace and joy in the Holy Spirit; he who thus serves Christ is acceptable to God and approved by men. Let us then pursue what makes for peace and for mutual upbuilding.

Short Responsory

R̷ Early in the morning I will think of you, O Lord. *Repeat* R̷
V̷ You have been my help. R̷ Glory be. R̷

Benedictus ant. Give your people knowledge of salvation, Lord, and forgive us our sins.

Intercessions

Blessed be our God and Father: he hears the prayers of his children.
R̷ Lord, hear us.
We thank you, Father, for sending us your Son:—let us keep him before our eyes throughout this day. R̷
Make wisdom our guide,—help us walk in newness of life. R̷
Lord, give us your strength in our weakness:—when we meet problems give us courage to face them. R̷
Direct our thoughts, our words, our actions today,—so that we may know, and do, your will. R̷
Our Father

Concluding Prayer

Lord God, true Light and Creator of light,
grant that faithfully pondering on all that is holy,
we may ever live in the splendour of your presence.
(We make our prayer) through our Lord.

EVENING PRAYER

HYMN

Blest are the pure in heart,
For they shall see our God;
The secret of the Lord is theirs,
Their soul is Christ's abode.

The Lord, who left the heavens,
Our life and peace to bring,
To dwell in lowliness with men,
Their pattern and their King:

Still to the lowly soul
He does himself impart,
And for his dwelling and his throne
Chooses the pure in heart.

Lord, we thy presence seek;
May ours this blessing be;
Give us a pure and lowly heart,
A temple fit for thee.

PSALMODY

Ant. 1: I will make you the light of the nations to bring my salvation to the ends of the earth.

Holy Week: Christ is the First-born from the dead, the Ruler of the kings of the earth. He has made us a kingdom for his God and Father.

Eastertide: God has appointed him to judge all men, both living and dead, alleluia.

THE ROYAL POWER OF THE MESSIAH PSALM 71(72)
They opened their treasures and offered him gifts of gold, frankincense and myrrh (Mt 2:11)

I

O Gód, give your júdgment to the kíng,*

143

to a kíng's son your jústice,
that he may júdge your péople in jústice*
and your póor in right júdgment.

May the móuntains bring forth péace for the péople*
and the hílls, jústice.
May he defénd the póor of the péople†
and save the chíldren of the néedy*
and crúsh the oppréssor.

He shall endúre like the sún and the móon*
from áge to áge.
He shall descénd like ráin on the méadow,*
like ráindrops on the éarth.

In his dáys jústice shall flóurish*
and péace till the móon fails.
He shall rúle from séa to séa,*
from the Great Ríver to earth's bóunds.

Befóre him his énemies shall fáll,*
his fóes lick the dúst.
The kíngs of Thársis and the séa coasts*
shall páy him tríbute.

The kíngs of Shéba and Séba*
shall bríng him gífts.
Before hím all kíngs shall fall próstrate,*
all nátions shall sérve him.

Ant. I will make you the light of the nations to bring my salvation
to the ends of the earth.
Holy Week: Christ is the First-born from the dead, the Ruler of the
kings of the earth. He has made us a kingdom for his God and
Father.
Eastertide: God has appointed him to judge all men, both living
and dead, alleluia.

Ant. 2: The Lord will save the poor; from oppression he will
rescue their lives.

Holy Week: The Lord shall save the poor when they cry and the needy who are helpless.
Eastertide: Every tribe shall be blessed in him, alleluia.

II

For he shall sáve the póor when they crý*
and the néedy who are hélpless.
Hé will have píty on the wéak*
and save the líves of the póor.

From oppréssion he will réscue their líves,*
to hím their blood is déar.
Lóng may he líve,*
may the góld of Shéba be gíven him.
They shall práy for hím without céasing*
and bléss him all the dáy.

May córn be abúndant in the lánd†
to the péaks of the móuntains.*
May its frúit rústle like Lébanon;
may men flóurish in the cíties*
like gráss on the éarth.

May his náme be bléssed for éver*
and endúre like the sún.
Every tríbe shall be bléssed in hím,*
all nátions bless his náme.

Bléssed be the Lórd, God of Ísrael,†
who alóne works wónders, *
ever bléssed his glórious náme.
Let his glóry fill the éarth.*
Amén! Amén!

Ant. The Lord will save the poor; from oppression he will rescue their lives.
Holy Week: The Lord shall save the poor when they cry and the needy who are helpless.
Eastertide: Every tribe shall be blessed in him, alleluia.

Ant. 3: Victory and empire have now been won by our God.
Holy Week: The saints have triumphed by the sacrifice of the Lamb, and by the testimony which they uttered.
Eastertide: Jesus Christ is the same yesterday, today and for ever, alleluia.

THE JUDGMENT OF GOD

CANTICLE
REV 11:17-18;12:10B-12A

We give thanks to you, Lord God Almighty,*
who are and who were,
that you have taken your great power*
and begun to reign.

The nations raged,*
but your wrath came,
and the time for the dead to be judged,*
for rewarding your servants, the prophets and saints,
and those who fear your name,*
both small and great.

Now the salvation and the power†
and the kingdom of our God*
and the authority of his Christ have come,
for the accuser of our brethren has been thrown down,*
who accuses them day and night before our God.

And they have conquered him*
by the blood of the Lamb
and by the word of their testimony,*
for they loved not their lives even unto death.
Rejoice, then, O heaven,*
and you that dwell therein.

Ant. Victory and empire have now been won by our God.
Holy Week: The saints have triumphed by the sacrifice of the Lamb, and by the testimony which they uttered.
Eastertide: Jesus Christ is the same yesterday, today and for ever, alleluia.

Scripture Reading *I Pet 1:22-23*

You have been obedient to the truth and purified your souls until you can love like brothers, in sincerity; let your love for each other be real and from a pure heart—your new birth was not from any mortal seed but from the everlasting word of the living and eternal God.

Short Responsory

℟ The Lord is my shepherd; there is nothing I shall want. *Repeat* ℟
℣ Fresh and green are the pastures where he gives me repose. ℟
Glory be. ℟

Magnificat ant. The Lord has satisfied and filled with good things those who hungered for justice.

Intercessions

Let us lift up our hearts in thankfulness to God our Father, who has blessed us in Christ with every spiritual gift. ℟ Lord, bless your people.

Father, look on the Pope, our bishops, and all Christian leaders:—sustain their faith, their love, and their courage. ℟

Almighty God, we pray for our country:—may it promote justice and brotherhood in the world. ℟

We pray for all who live the Christian life:—Father, look on them with kindness, and see in them the face of your beloved Son. ℟

Remember those who have consecrated themselves to serve you in the religious life:—enrich them in their poverty, love them in their chastity, lighten their hearts in obedience to you. ℟

Give rest to those who have died in Christ:—for with you there is mercy, and fulness of redemption. ℟

Our Father

Concluding Prayer

We beseech your mercy, Lord,
as we offer you this evening praise:
keep our hearts always engaged in meditating on your law,
and grant us the light and reward of eternal life.
(We make our prayer) through our Lord.

WEEK 2: FRIDAY

Invitatory ant. Indeed, how good is the Lord; bless his holy name.
Psalm, p 3.

MORNING PRAYER

HYMN

I am the holy vine,
Which God my Father tends.
Each branch that yields no fruit
My Father cuts away.
Each fruitful branch
He prunes with care
To make it yield
Abundant fruit.

If you abide in me,
I will in you abide.
Each branch to yield its fruit
Must with the vine be one.
So you shall fail
To yield your fruit
If you are not
With me one vine.

I am the fruitful vine,
And you my branches are.
He who abides in me
I will in him abide.
So shall you yield
Much fruit, but none
If you remain
Apart from me.

PSALMODY

Ant. 1: O God, you will not spurn a humbled, contrite heart.

Eastertide: Have courage, my son, your sins are forgiven you, alleluia.

O GOD, HAVE MERCY ON ME   PSALM 50(51)
You must be made new in mind and spirit, and put on the new nature
(Eph 4:23-24)

Have mércy on me, Gód, in your kíndness.*
In your compássion blot óut my offénce.
O wásh me more and móre from my guílt*
and cléanse me fróm my sín.

My offénces trúly I knów them;*
my sín is álways befóre me.
Against yóu, you alóne, have I sínned;*
what is évil in your síght I have dóne.

That you may be jústified whén you give séntence*
and be withóut repróach when you júdge,
O sée, in guílt I was bórn,*
a sínner was Í concéived.

Indéed you love trúth in the héart;*
then in the sécret of my héart teach me wísdom.
O púrify me, thén I shall be cléan;*
O wásh me, I shall be whíter than snów.

Make me héar rejóicing and gládness,*
that the bónes you have crúshed may revíve.
From my síns turn awáy your fáce*
and blót out áll my guílt.

A púre heart creáte for me, O Gód,*
put a stéadfast spírit withín me.
Do not cást me awáy from your présence,*
nor depríve me of your hóly spírit.

Give me agáin the jóy of your hélp;*
with a spírit of férvour sustáin me,
that I may téach transgréssors your wáys*
and sínners may retúrn to yóu.

O réscue me, Gód, my hélper,*
and my tóngue shall ríng out your góodness.
O Lórd, ópen my líps*
and my móuth shall declíre your práise.

For in sácrifice you táke no delíght,*
burnt óffering from mé you would refúse,
my sácrifice, a cóntrite spírit.*
A húmbled, contrite héart you will not spúrn.

In your góodness, show fávour to Síon:*
rebuíld the wálls of Jerúsalem.
Thén you will be pléased with lawful sácrifice,*
hólocausts óffered on your áltar.

Ant. O God, you will not spurn a humbled, contrite heart.
Eastertide: Have courage, my son, your sins are forgiven you,
alleluia.

Ant. 2: In spite of your anger, Lord, have compassion.
Eastertide: Lord, you came with strength to save your people; you
came with your Anointed One, alleluia.

GOD WILL APPEAR IN JUDGMENT   CANTICLE
                                                   HAB 3:2-4,13A,15-19
Lift up your heads, for your redemption is near at hand (Lk 21:28)

Lord, I have heard of your fame,*
I stand in awe at your deeds.
Do them again in our days,†
in our days make them known!*
In spite of your anger, have compassion.

God comes forth from Teman,*
the Holy One comes from Mount Paran.
His splendour covers the sky*
and his glory fills the earth.
His brilliance is like the light,†
rays flash from his hands;*
there his power is hidden.

150

You march out to save your people,*
to save the one you have anointed.
You made a path for your horses in the sea,*
in the raging of the mighty waters.

This I heard and I tremble with terror,*
my lips quiver at the sound.
Weakness invades my bones,*
my steps fail beneath me
yet I calmly wait for the doom*
that will fall upon the people who assail us.

For even though the fig does not blossom,*
nor fruit grow on the vine,
even though the olive crop fail,*
and fields produce no harvest,
even though flocks vanish from the folds*
and stalls stand empty of cattle,

Yet I will rejoice in the Lord*
and exult in God my saviour.
The Lord my God is my strength.†
He makes me leap like the deer,*
he guides me to the high places.

Ant. In spite of your anger, Lord, have compassion.
Eastertide: Lord, you came with strength to save your people;
you came with your Anointed One, alleluia.

Ant. 3: O praise the Lord, Jerusalem.†
Eastertide: Sion, praise your God, for he has established peace in
your land, alleluia.

THE RENEWAL OF JERUSALEM   PSALM 147
Come, and I will show you the bride that the Lamb has chosen (Rev
21:9)

O práise the Lórd, Jerúsalem!*
†Síon, práise your Gód!

151

He has stréngthened the bárs of your gátes,*
he has bléssed the chíldren withín you.
He estáblished péace on your bórders,*
he féeds you with fínest whéat.

He sénds out his wórd to the éarth*
and swíftly rúns his commánd.
He shówers down snów white as wóol,*
he scátters hóar-frost like áshes.

He húrls down háilstones like crúmbs.*
The wáters are frózen at his tóuch;
he sénds forth his wórd and it mélts them:*
at the bréath of his móuth the waters flów.

He mákes his wórd known to Jácob,*
to Ísrael his láws and decrées.
He has not déalt thus with óther nátions;*
he has not táught them hís decrées.

Ant. O praise the Lord, Jerusalem.
Eastertide: Sion, praise your God, for he has established peace in your land, alleluia.

THROUGH THE YEAR

Scripture Reading   *Eph 2:13-16*
Now, in union with Christ Jesus, you who used to be far away have been brought near by the death of Christ. For Christ himself has brought us peace, by making the Jews and Gentiles one people. With his own body he broke down the wall that separated them and kept them enemies. He abolished the Jewish Law, with its commandments and rules, in order to create out of the two races one new people in union with himself, in this way making peace. By his death on the cross Christ destroyed the enmity; by means of the cross he united both races into one body and brought them back to God.

Short Responsory
℟ I call to the Lord, the Most High, for he has been my help.
Repeat ℟

℣ May he send from heaven and save me. ℟ Glory be. ℟

Benedictus ant. Through the loving mercy of our God, the Rising Sun has come to visit us.

Intercessions

Father, we praise you for your Son, our Lord Jesus Christ; through the Holy Spirit he offered himself in sacrifice to you, that we might be delivered from death and selfishness, and be free to live in your peace. ℟ Father, in your will is our peace.

We accept this new day as your gift, Lord;—grant that we may live in newness of life. ℟

You made all things, and keep all things in being;—give us the insight to see your hand at work in them all. ℟

Your Son sealed the new and everlasting covenant in his blood;—help us to live by this covenant and honour it. ℟

As Jesus died on the cross, blood and water flowed from his side;—as we share in the eucharist, pour out your Spirit upon us. ℟

Our Father

Concluding Prayer

Almighty God,
as in this morning prayer we offer you our praise,
grant that, in your kingdom,
together with your saints,
we may praise you with even greater joy.
(We make our prayer) through our Lord.

EVENING PRAYER

HYMN

Day is done, but Love unfailing
Dwells ever here;
Shadows fall, but hope, prevailing,
Calms every fear.

153

Loving Father, none forsaking,
Take our hearts, of Love's own making,
Watch our sleeping, guard our waking,
Be always near!

Dark descends, but Light unending
Shines through our night;
You are with us, ever lending
New strength to sight;
One in love, your truth confessing,
One in hope of heaven's blessing,
May we see, in love's possessing,
Love's endless light!

PSALMODY

Ant. 1: Lord, keep my soul from death, my feet from stumbling.
Eastertide: The Lord saved my soul from the power of death,
alleluia.

THANKSGIVING   PSALM 114(116)
*We must experience many hardships before we can enter the kingdom
of God* (Acts 14:22)

I love the Lórd for hé has héard*
   the crý of my appéal;
for he túrned his éar to mé*
   in the dáy when I cálled him.

They surróunded me, the snáres of déath,†
   with the ánguish of the tómb;*
they cáught me, sórrow and distréss.
I cálled on the Lórd's name.*
   O Lórd my Gód, delíver me!

How grácious is the Lórd, and júst;*
   our Gód has compássion.
The Lórd protécts the simple héarts;*
   I was hélpless so he sáved me.

Turn báck, my sóul, to your rést*
for the Lórd has been góod;
he has képt my sóul from déath,†
my éyes from téars*
and my féet from stúmbling.

I will wálk in the présence of the Lórd*
in the lánd of the líving.

Ant. Lord, keep my soul from death, my feet from stumbling.
Eastertide: The Lord saved my soul from the power of death,
alleluia.

Ant. 2: My help shall come from the Lord who made heaven and
earth.
Eastertide: The Lord protected his people as the apple of his eye,
alleluia.

GOD, THE PROTECTOR OF HIS PEOPLE   PSALM 120(121)
They will never hunger or thirst again; neither the sun or scorching
wind will ever plague them (Rev. 7:16)

I líft up my éyes to the móuntains:*
from whére shall come my hélp?
My hélp shall cóme from the Lórd*
who made héaven and éarth.

May he néver állow you to stúmble!*
Let him sléep not, your guárd.
Nó, he sléeps not nor slúmbers,*
Ísrael's guárd.

The Lórd is your guárd and your sháde;*
at your ríght side he stánds.
By dáy the sún shall not smíte you*
nor the móon in the níght.

The Lórd will guárd you from évil,*
he will guárd your sóul.
The Lord will guárd your góing and cóming*
both nów and for éver.

Ant. My help shall come from the Lord who made heaven and earth.
Eastertide: The Lord protected his people as the apple of his eye, alleluia.

Ant. 3: Your ways are just and true, King of all the ages.
Eastertide: The Lord is my strength and protection, he is my salvation, alleluia.

HYMN OF ADORATION   CANTICLE: REV 15:3-4

Great and wonderful are your deeds,*
O Lord God the Almighty!
Just and true are your ways,*
O King of the ages!

Who shall not fear and glorify your name, O Lord?*
For you alone are holy.
All nations shall come and worship you,*
for your judgments have been revealed.

Ant. Your ways are just and true, King of all the ages.
Eastertide: The Lord is my strength and protection, he is my salvation, alleluia.

THROUGH THE YEAR

Scripture Reading   *1 Cor 2:7-10a*
The hidden wisdom of God which we teach in our mysteries is the wisdom that God predestined to be for our glory before the ages began. It is a wisdom that none of the masters of this age have ever known, or they would not have crucified the Lord of Glory; we teach what scripture calls: the things that no eye has seen and no ear has heard, things beyond the mind of man, all that God has prepared for those who love him. These are the very things that God has revealed to us through the Spirit.

Short Responsory
R℣ Christ died for our sins, that he might offer us to God. *Repeat* R℣
℣ In the body he was put to death, in the spirit he was raised to life.
R℣ Glory be. R℣

Magnificat ant. Remember your mercy, O Lord; according to the promise you made to our fathers.

Intercessions

Christ comforted the widow who had lost her only son: let us pray to him, who will come at the last to wipe away every tear from our eyes. R⁷ Come, Lord Jesus.

Lord Jesus, you consoled especially the poor and troubled:—look with mercy on those in any kind of need. R⁷

The angel brought you the Father's comfort on the eve of your passion:—we pray that your comfort may strengthen those who are dying. R⁷

Let all exiles know your care for them;—may they find their home-lands once more, and come one day in joy to the Father's house. R⁷

Look in love on all whose sins have separated them from you:—reconcile them to yourself and to your Church. R⁷

The dead suffered the pain and loss of human life:—give them the fulness of life and joy in heaven. R⁷

Our Father

Concluding Prayer

Lord God,
the Cross reveals the mystery of your love:
a stumbling block indeed for unbelief,
but the sign of your power and wisdom to us who believe.
Teach us so to contemplate your Son's glorious Passion
that we may always believe and glory in his Cross.
(We make our prayer) through our Lord.

WEEK 2: SATURDAY

Invitatory ant. Let us listen for the voice of the Lord and enter into his peace.
Psalm, p 3.

MORNING PRAYER

Sing, all creation, sing to God in gladness!
Joyously serve him, singing hymns of homage!
Chanting his praises, come before his presence!
Praise the Almighty!

Know that our God is Lord of all the ages!
He is our maker; we are all his creatures,
People he fashioned, sheep he leads to pasture!
Praise the Almighty!

Great in his goodness is the Lord we worship;
Steadfast his kindness, love that knows no ending!
Faithful his word is, changeless, everlasting!
Praise the Almighty!

PSALMODY

Ant. 1: Lord, we proclaim your love in the morning and your truth in the watches of the night.
Eastertide: You have made me glad, O Lord; for the works of your hands I shout with joy, alleluia.

PRAISE OF THE LORD CREATOR   PSALM 91(92)
The deeds of God's only Son are praised (St Athanasius)

It is góod to give thánks to the Lórd*
to make músic to your náme, O Most Hígh,
to procláim your lóve in the mórning*
and your trúth in the wátches of the níght,
on the tén-stringed lýre and the lúte,*
with the múrmuring sóund of the hárp.

Your déeds, O Lórd, have made me glád;*
for the wórk of your hánds I shout with jóy.
O Lórd, how gréat are your wórks!*
How déep are yóur desígns!
The fóolish man cánnot knów this*
and the fóol cánnot understánd.

158

Though the wícked spring úp like gráss*
and áll who do évil thríve:
they are dóomed to be etérnally destróyed.*
But yóu, Lord, are etérnally on hígh.
Sée how your énemies pérish;*
all dóers of évil are scáttered.

To mé you give the wíld-ox's stréngth;*
you anóint me with the púrest óil.
My éyes looked in tríumph on my fóes;*
my éars heard gládly of their fáll.
The júst will flóurish like the pálm-tree*
and grów like a Lébanon cédar.

Plánted in the hóuse of the Lórd*
they will flóurish in the cóurts of our Gód,
stíll bearing frúit when they are óld,*
stíll full of sáp, still gréen,
to procláim that the Lórd is júst.*
In hím, my róck, there is no wróng.

Ant. Lord, we proclaim your love in the morning and your truth in the watches of the night.
Eastertide: You have made me glad, O Lord; for the works of your hands I shout with joy, alleluia.

Ant. 2: Proclaim the greatness of our God.
Eastertide: It is I who give death and life; it is I who strike and also heal, alleluia.

THE DEEDS OF KINDNESS WHICH GOD	CANTICLE
WROUGHT FOR HIS PEOPLE	DEUT 32:1-12

How often have I longed to gather your children as a hen gathers her young under her wings (Mt 23:37)

Listen, O heavens, and I will speak,*
let the earth hear the words on my lips.
May my teaching fall like the rain,*
my speech descend like the dew,

like rain drops on the young green,*
like showers falling on the grass.

For I shall praise the name of the Lord.*
O give glory to this God of ours!
The Rock—his deeds are perfect,*
and all his ways are just,
a faithful God, without deceit,*
a God who is right and just.

Those whom he begot unblemished*
have become crooked, false, perverse.
Is it thus you repay the Lord,*
O senseless and foolish people?
Is he not your father who created you,*
he who made you, on whom you depend?

Remember the days of old,*
consider the years that are past;
ask your father and he will show you,*
ask your elders and they will tell you.

When the Most High gave the nations their heritage*
and disposed men according to his plan,
in fixing the boundaries of the nations*
he thought first of Israel's sons.
For Israel was the Lord's possession,*
Jacob the one he had chosen.

God found him in a wilderness,*
in fearful, desolate wastes;
he surrounded him, he lifted him up,*
he kept him as the apple of his eye.

Like an eagle that watches its nest,*
that hovers over its young,
so he spread his wings; he took him,*
placed him on his outstretched wings.
The Lord alone was his guide*
and no other god was with him.

Ant. Proclaim the greatness of our God.
Eastertide: It is I who give death and life; it is I who strike and also heal, alleluia.

Ant. 3: How great is your name, Lord, through all the earth!
Eastertide: With glory and honour you crowned your Anointed One, alleluia.

THE MAJESTY OF THE LORD, THE DIGNITY OF MAN   PSALM 8
He has put all things under his feet, and appointed him to be head of the whole Church (Eph 1:22)

How gréat is your náme, O Lórd our Gód,*
through áll the éarth!

Your májesty is práised above the héavens;*
on the líps of chíldren and of bábes
you have found práise to fóil your énemy,*
to sílence the fóe and the rébel.

When I see the héavens, the wórk of your hánds,*
The móon and the stárs which you arránged,
what is mán that you should kéep him in mínd,*
mortal mán that you cáre for hím?

Yet you have máde him little léss than a gód;*
with glóry and hónour you crówned him,
gave him pówer over the wórks of your hánd,*
put áll things únder his féet.

Áll of them, shéep and cáttle,*
yes, éven the sávage béasts,
bírds of the aír, and físh*
that máke their wáy through the wáters.

How gréat is your náme, O Lórd our Gód,*
through áll the éarth!

Ant. How great is your name, Lord, through all the earth!
Eastertide: With glory and honour you crowned your Anointed One, alleluia.

THROUGH THE YEAR

Scripture Reading   *Rom 12:14-16a*

Bless those who persecute you; bless and do not curse them. Rejoice with those who rejoice, weep with those who weep. Live in harmony with one another; do not be haughty, but associate with the lowly.

Short Responsory

R℣ When I sing to you my lips shall rejoice. *Repeat* R℣

℣ My tongue shall tell the tale of your justice. R℣ Glory be. R℣

Benedictus ant. Lord, guide our feet into the way of peace.

Intercessions

God the Father has adopted us as brothers of his only Son, and through the ages has stayed with us and kept us in his love. Let us ask him for the needs of the world. R℣ Lord, help us as we work.

We pray for all who plan and build in our cities:—give them respect for every human value. R℣

Pour out your Spirit on artists, craftsmen, and musicians:—may their work bring variety, joy, and inspiration to our lives. R℣

Be with us as the cornerstone of all that we build:—for we can do nothing well without your aid. R℣

You have created us anew in the resurrection of your Son:—give us the strength to create a new life, and a new world. R℣

Our Father

Concluding Prayer

Let us praise you, Lord,
with voice and mind and deed:
and since life itself is your gift,
may all we have and are be yours.
(We make our prayer) through our Lord.

WEEK 3: SUNDAY

EVENING PRAYER I

HYMN

O Light serene of God the Father's glory,
To you, O Christ, we sing,
And with the evening star, at hour of sunset,
Our worship bring.

To Father, Son and God's most Holy Spirit,
Eternal praise is due.
O Christ, who gave your life, the world gives glory
And thanks to you.

PSALMODY

ANTIPHON I
Advent: Rejoice greatly, Jerusalem, for your Saviour will come to you, alleluia.
Lent: Repent and believe the Gospel, says the Lord.
Eastertide: The Lord God is high above the heavens, and from the dust he lifts up the lowly, alleluia.

Through the Year: From the rising of the sun to its setting, great is the name of the Lord.

PRAISED BE THE NAME OF THE LORD   PSALM 112(113)
He put down princes from their thrones and exalted the lowly (Lk 1:52)

Práise, O sérvants of the Lórd,*
práise the náme of the Lórd!
May the náme of the Lórd be bléssed*
both nów and for évermóre!
From the rísing of the sún to its sétting*
práised be the náme of the Lórd!

163

Hígh above all nátions is the Lórd,*
abóve the héavens his glóry.
Whó is like the Lórd, our Gód,*
who has rísen on hígh to his thróne
yet stóops from the héights to look dówn,*
to look dówn upon héaven and éarth?

From the dúst he lífts up the lówly,*
from his mísery he ráises the póor
to sét him in the cómpany of prínces,*
yés, with the prínces of his péople.
To the chíldless wífe he gives a hóme*
and gláddens her héart with chíldren.

Ant. From the rising of the sun to its setting, great is the name of the Lord.

Ant. Advent: Rejoice greatly, Jerusalem, for your Saviour will come to you, alleluia.
Ant. 2: I, the Lord, am coming to deliver you; I am already near and my saving act will not be delayed.

Ant. Lent: Repent and believe the Gospel, says the Lord.
Ant. 2: A thanksgiving sacrifice I make: I will call on the Lord's name.

Ant. Eastertide: The Lord God is high above the heavens and from the dust he lifts up the lowly, alleluia.
Ant. 2: You have loosened my bonds, Lord: a sacrifice of praise I will make to you, alleluia.

Ant. 2: I will take the chalice of salvation, and I will call on the name of the Lord.

THANKSGIVING IN THE TEMPLE   PSALM 115(116)
Through him (Christ), let us offer God an unending sacrifice of praise (Heb 13:15)

I trústed, éven when I sáid:*
'I am sórely afflícted,'

and whén I sáid in my alárm:*
'No mán can be trústed.'

How cán I repáy the Lórd*
for his góodness to mé?
The cúp of salvátion I will ráise;*
I will cáll on the Lórd's name.

My vóws to the Lórd I will fulfíl*
befóre all his péople.
O précious in the éyes of the Lórd*
is the déath of his fáithful.

Your sérvant, Lord, your sérvant am Í;*
you have lóosened my bónds.
A thánksgiving sácrifice I máke:*
I will cáll on the Lórd's name.

My vóws to the Lórd I will fulfíl*
befóre all his péople,
in the córts of the hóuse of the Lórd,*
in your mídst, O Jerúsalem.

Ant. I will take the chalice of salvation, and I will call on the name of the Lord.

Ant. Advent: I, the Lord, am coming to deliver you; I am already near and my saving act will not be delayed.
Ant. 3: Send, Lord, the Lamb, the ruler of the earth, from the Rock of the desert to the mountain of the daughter of Sion.

Ant. Lent: A thanksgiving sacrifice I make: I will call on the Lord's name.
Ant. 3: No one takes my life from me, but I lay it down of my own accord, and I have power to take it up again.

Ant. Eastertide: You have loosened my bonds, Lord: a sacrifice of praise I will make to you, alleluia.
Ant. 3: The Son of God learned to obey through suffering, and he became the source of eternal salvation for all those who obey him, alleluia.

Ant. 3: The Lord Jesus humbled himself, but God exalted him on high for ever.

Though he was in the form of God,*
Jesus did not count equality with God a thing to be grasped.

He emptied himself,†
taking the form of a servant,*
being born in the likeness of men.

And being found in human form,†
he humbled himself and became obedient unto death,*
even death on a cross.

Therefore God has highly exalted him*
and bestowed on him the name which is above every name,

That at the name of Jesus every knee should bow,*
in heaven and on earth and under the earth,

And every tongue confess that Jesus Christ is Lord,*
to the glory of God the Father.

Ant. The Lord Jesus humbled himself, but God exalted him on high for ever.

Ant. Advent: Send, Lord, the Lamb, the ruler of the earth, from the Rock of the desert to the mountain of the daughter of Sion.
Lent: No one takes my life from me, but I lay it down of my own accord, and I have power to take it up again.
Eastertide: The Son of God learned to obey through suffering and he became the source of eternal salvation for all those who obey him, alleluia.

THROUGH THE YEAR

Scripture Reading   *Heb 13:20-21*
I pray that the God of peace, who brought our Lord Jesus back from the dead to become the great Shepherd of the sheep by the

blood that sealed an eternal covenant, may make you ready to do his will in any kind of good action; and turn us all into whatever is acceptable to himself through Jesus Christ, to whom be glory for ever and ever, Amen.

Short Responsory

R℣ How great are your works, O Lord. *Repeat* R℣
℣ In wisdom you have made them all. R℣ Glory be. R℣

Magnificat antiphon from the Proper of Seasons.

Intercessions

Christ our Lord is mindful of all who need him, and does great things for love of them. Let us not be afraid to ask him for all our needs. R℣ Show us your loving kindness.

Lord, we know that the good things we have received today have come as a gift from you:—may we receive them with thankfulness and learn how to give. R℣

Saviour and light of all people, keep missionaries in your special care:—may the light of your Spirit burn strongly in them. R℣

Grant that the world may be filled with the knowledge of your truth;—help us to carry out all you have called us to do. R℣

You healed the sickness and pain of your brothers:—Bring healing and comfort to the spirit of man. R℣

Give rest to the faithful departed;—and bring them to praise you in eternity. R℣

Our Father

The concluding prayer from the Proper of Seasons.

Invitatory

Ant. Come, ring out our joy to the Lord; hail the God who saves us, alleluia.†
Psalm, p 3.

MORNING PRAYER

HYMN

Transcendent God in whom we live,
The Resurrection and the Light,
We sing for you a morning hymn
To end the silence of the night.

When early cock begins to crow
And everything from sleep awakes,
New life and hope spring up again
While out of darkness colour breaks.

Creator of all things that are,
The measure and the end of all,
Forgiving God, forget our sins,
And hear our prayer before we call.

Praise Father, Son and Holy Ghost,
Blest Trinity and source of grace,
Who call us out of nothingness
To find in you our resting-place.

Alternative hymn

Christ is the world's redeemer,
The lover of the pure,
The font of heavenly wisdom,
Our trust and hope secure,
The armour of his soldiers,
The Lord of earth and sky,
Our health while we are living,
Our life when we shall die.

Down in the realm of darkness,
He lay a captive bound,
But at the hour appointed
He rose a victor crowned.
And now, to heaven ascended,
He sits upon a throne,
Whence he had ne'er departed,
His Father's and his own.

All glory to the Father,
The unbegotten One,
All honour be to Jesus,
His sole-begotten Son;
And to the Holy Spirit,
The perfect Trinity,
Let all the worlds give answer,
Amen—so let it be.

PSALMODY

ANTIPHON I

Advent: The Lord will come without delay. He will bring to light what darkness hides and he will reveal himself to all the nations, alleluia.

Lent: Truly your decrees are to be trusted. They are more wondrous than the surgings of the sea.

Eastertide: The Lord is king, with majesty enrobed, alleluia.†

Through the Year: The Lord is wonderful on high, alleluia.

THE SPLENDOUR OF THE LORD CREATOR   PSALM 92(93)
The Lord, our God, the Almighty is king; let us be glad and rejoice and give him praise (Rev 19:6-7)

The Lórd is kíng, with májesty enróbed;†
†the Lórd has róbed himself with míght,*
he has gírded himsélf with pówer.

The wórld you made fírm, not to be móved;†
your thróne has stood fírm from of óld.*
From all etérnity, O Lórd, you áre.

The wáters have lífted up, O Lórd,†
the wáters have lífted up their vóice,*
the wáters have lífted up their thúnder.

Gréater than the róar of mighty wáters,†
more glórious than the súrgings of the séa,*
the Lórd is glórious on hígh.

169

Trúly your decrées are to be trústed.†
Hóliness is fítting to your hóuse,*
O Lórd, until the énd of tíme.

Ant. The Lord is wonderful on high, alleluia.

Ant. *Advent:* The Lord will come without delay. He will bring to light what darkness hides and he will reveal himself to all the nations, alleluia.
Ant. *2:* Every mountain and hill shall be laid low, the rugged places shall be made smooth and the mountain-ranges become a plain. Come, Lord, and do not delay, alleluia.

Ant. *Lent:* Truly your decrees are to be trusted. They are more wondrous than the surgings of the sea.
Ant. *2:* Springs of water, bless the Lord: give glory and eternal praise to him.

Ant. *Eastertide:* The Lord is king, with majesty enrobed, alleluia.
Ant. *2:* The whole creation will be freed and will enjoy the glory and freedom of the children of God, alleluia.

Ant. *2:* May you be praised, Lord, and extolled for ever, alleluia.

LET EVERY CREATURE PRAISE THE LORD　　　　　CANTICLE
　　　　　　　　　　　　　　　　　　　　　　DAN 3:57-88,56
Praise our God, all you his servants (Rev 19:5)

O all you works of the Lord, O bless the Lord.*
To him be highest glory and praise for ever.

And you, angels of the Lord, O bless the Lord.*
To him be highest glory and praise for ever.

And you, the heavens of the Lord, O bless the Lord.*
And you, clouds of the sky, O bless the Lord.
And you, all armies of the Lord, O bless the Lord.*
To him be highest glory and praise for ever.

And you, sun and moon, O bless the Lord.*
And you, the stars of the heavens, O bless the Lord.
And you, showers and rain, O bless the Lord.*
To him be highest glory and praise for ever.

And you, all you breezes and winds, O bless the Lord.*
And you, fire and heat, O bless the Lord.
And you, cold and heat, O bless the Lord.*
To him be highest glory and praise for ever.

And you, showers and dew, O bless the Lord.*
And you, frosts and cold, O bless the Lord.
And you, frost and snow, O bless the Lord.*
To him be highest glory and praise for ever.

And you, night-time and day, O bless the Lord.*
And you, darkness and light, O bless the Lord.
And you, lightning and clouds, O bless the Lord.*
To him be highest glory and praise for ever.

O let the earth bless the Lord.*
To him be highest glory and praise for ever.

And you, mountains and hills, O bless the Lord.*
And you, all plants of the earth, O bless the Lord.
And you, fountains and springs, O bless the Lord.*
To him be highest glory and praise for ever.

And you, rivers and seas, O bless the Lord.*
And you, creatures of the sea, O bless the Lord.
And you, every bird in the sky, O bless the Lord.†
And you, wild beasts and tame, O bless the Lord.*
To him be highest glory and praise for ever.

And you, children of men, O bless the Lord.*
To him be highest glory and praise for ever.

O Israel, bless the Lord. O bless the Lord.*
And you, priests of the Lord, O bless the Lord.
And you, servants of the Lord, O bless the Lord.*
To him be highest glory and praise for ever.

And you, spirits and soul of the just, O bless the Lord.*
And you, holy and humble of heart, O bless the Lord.
Ananias, Azarias, Mizael, O bless the Lord.*
To him be highest glory and praise for ever.

Let us praise the Father, the Son and Holy Spirit:*
To you be highest glory and praise for ever.
May you be blessed, O Lord, in the heavens;*
To you be highest glory and praise for ever.

The Glory be *is omitted after this canticle.*

Ant. May you be praised, Lord, and extolled for ever, alleluia.

Ant. Advent: Every mountain and hill shall be laid low, the rugged places shall be made smooth and the mountain-ranges become a plain. Come, Lord, and do not delay, alleluia.
Ant. 3: I will give salvation to Sion, I will bring my glory to Jerusalem, alleluia.

Ant. Lent: Springs of water, bless the Lord: give glory and eternal praise to him.
Ant. 3: All kings and peoples of the earth, praise God.
Ant. Eastertide: The whole creation will be freed and will enjoy the glory and freedom of the children of God, alleluia.
Ant. 3: The name of the Lord is praised, in heaven and on earth, alleluia.

Ant. 3: Praise the Lord from the heavens, alleluia.†

HYMN OF PRAISE TO THE LORD, THE CREATOR   PSALM 148
*To the One who sits on the throne and to the Lamb, be all praise,
honour, glory and power, for ever and ever (Rev 5:13).*

Práise the Lórd from the héavens,*
†práise him in the héights.
Práise him, all his ángels,*
práise him, áll his hósts.

Práise him, sún and móon,*
práise him, shining stárs.
Práise him, highest héavens*
and the wáters abóve the héavens.

Let them práise the náme of the Lórd.*
He commánded: they were máde.
He fíxed them for éver,*
gave a láw which shall nót pass awáy.

Práise the Lórd from the éarth,*
séa creatures and all óceans,
fire and háil, snow and míst,*
stormy wínds that obéy his wórd;

áll móuntains and hílls,*
all frúit trees and cédars,
béasts, wild and táme,*
réptiles and bírds on the wíng;

áll earth's kíngs and péoples,*
earth's prínces and rúlers;
yóung men and máidens,*
old men togéther with chíldren.

Let them práise the náme of the Lórd*
for he alóne is exálted.
The spléndour of his náme*
réaches beyond héaven and éarth.

He exálts the stréngth of his péople.*
He is the práise of all his sáints,
of the sóns of Ísrael,*
of the péople to whóm he comes clóse.

Ant. Praise the Lord from the heavens, alleluia.

Ant. Advent: I will give salvation to Sion, I will bring my glory to Jerusalem, alleluia.
Lent: All kings and peoples of the earth, praise God.

Eastertide: The name of the Lord is praised, in heaven and on earth, alleluia.

THROUGH THE YEAR

Scripture Reading   *Ezek 37:12b-14*
The Lord God says this: I am now going to open your graves; I mean to raise you from your graves, my people, and lead you back to the soil of Israel. And you will know that I am the Lord, when I open your graves and raise you from your graves, my people. And I shall put my spirit in you, and you will live, and I shall resettle you on your own soil; and you will know that I, the Lord, have said and done this—it is the Lord God who speaks.

Short Responsory
R̷ You are the Christ, the Son of the living God. Have mercy on us. *Repeat* R̷
V̷ You are seated at the right hand of the Father. R̷ Glory be. R̷

Benedictus antiphon from the Proper of Seasons.

Intercessions
We pray to the Father, who sent his Holy Spirit to bring new light to the hearts of us all. R̷ Lord, send us the light of your Spirit.
Blessed are you, the source of all light;—all creation rightly gives you praise. R̷
Through the resurrection of your Son, the world is filled with light:—through the gift of your Spirit, may your light shine out in the Church. R̷
Through your Holy Spirit, the disciples remembered all that Jesus taught them:—pour out your Spirit on the Church that she may be faithful to that teaching. R̷
Light of all the nations, look upon those who live in darkness:—open their hearts to accept you as the one true God. R̷
Our Father

The concluding prayer from the Proper of Seasons.

EVENING PRAYER II

HYMN

In the beginning God created heaven,
The dark and empty earth;
His Spirit moved across the sombre waters
And stirred them with his breath.

Then God created light, and with its coming
The dark was swept away;
The morning came, and then the quiet evening:
The end of God's first day.

To God, the Father of the world, give glory,
With Christ his only Son,
Who with the Spirit govern all creation:
Blest Trinity in One.

Alternative hymn

Praise to the holiest in the height,
And in the depth be praise,
In all his words most wonderful,
Most sure in all his ways.

O loving wisdom of our God!
When all was sin and shame,
A second Adam to the fight
And to the rescue came.

O wisest love! that flesh and blood
Which did in Adam fail,
Should strive afresh against their foe,
Should strive and should prevail.

And that a higher gift than grace
Should flesh and blood refine,
God's presence and his very self,
And essence all divine.

175

O generous love! that he who smote
In man for man the foe,
The double agony in man
For man should undergo.

And in the garden secretly,
And on the cross on high,
Should teach his brethren, and inspire
To suffer and to die.

Praise to the holiest in the height,
And in the depth be praise,
In all his words most wonderful,
Most sure in all his ways.

PSALMODY

ANTIPHON I

Advent: See, the Lord will come. He will sit with princes and he will mount the glorious throne.

Lent: Lord, almighty king, deliver us for the sake of your name. Give us the grace to return to you.

Eastertide: When he had made purification for sin, he sat at the right hand of the Majesty on high, alleluia.

Through the Year: The Lord's revelation to my Master: 'Sit on my right', alleluia.†

THE MESSIAH IS KING AND PRIEST   PSALM 109(110):1-5,7

He must be king so that he will put all his enemies under his feet
(1 Cor 15:25)

The Lórd's revelátion to my Máster:†
'Sít on my ríght:*
†your fóes I will pút beneath your féet.'

The Lórd will wíeld from Síon†
your scéptre of pówer:*
rúle in the mídst of all your fóes.

A prínce from the dáy of your bírth†

on the hóly móuntains;*
from the wómb before the dáwn I begót you.

The Lórd has sworn an óath he will not chánge.†
'You are a príest for éver,*
a príest like Melchízedek of óld.'

The Máster stánding at your ríght hand*
will shatter kíngs in the dáy of his wráth.

He shall drínk from the stréam by the wáyside*
and thérefore he shall líft up his héad.

Ant. The Lord's revelation to my Master: 'Sit on my right', alleluia.

Ant. Advent: See, the Lord will come. He will sit with princes and he will mount the glorious throne.
Ant. 2: The mountains will bring forth joy and the hills justice; for the Lord, the light of the world, comes in strength.

Ant. Lent: Lord, almighty king, deliver us for the sake of your name. Give us the grace to return to you.
Ant. 2: We were ransomed with the precious blood of Christ, the Lamb who is without blemish.

Ant. Eastertide: When he had made purification for sin, he sat at the right hand of the Majesty on high, alleluia.
Ant. 2: The Lord has delivered his people, alleluia.

Ant. 2: The Lord is full of merciful love; he makes us remember his wonders, alleluia.

GREAT ARE THE WORKS OF THE LORD   PSALM 110(111)
How great and wonderful are all your works, Lord God Almighty
(Rev 15:3)

I will thánk the Lórd with all my héart*
in the méeting of the júst and their assémbly.
Gréat are the wórks of the Lórd;*
to be póndered by áll who lóve them.

Majéstic and glórious his wórk,*
his jústice stands fírm for éver.
He mákes us remémber his wónders.*
The Lórd is compássion and lóve.

He gives fóod to thóse who féar him;*
keeps his cóvenant éver in mínd.
He has shówn his míght to his péople*
by gíving them the lánds of the nátions.

His wórks are jústice and trúth:*
his précepts are áll of them súre,
standing fírm for éver and éver:*
they are máde in úprightness and trúth.

He has sént delíverance to his péople†
and estáblished his cóvenant for éver.*
Hóly his náme, to be féared.
To fear the Lórd is the fírst stage of wísdom;†
all who dó so próve themselves wíse.*
His práise shall lást for éver!

Ant. The Lord is full of merciful love; he makes us remember his
wonders, alleluia.

OUTSIDE LENT

Ant. Advent: The mountains will bring forth joy and the hills justice;
for the Lord, the light of the world, comes in strength.
Ant. 3: Let us live justly and honestly while we are awaiting, in
hope, the coming of the Lord.

Ant. Eastertide: The Lord has delivered his people, alleluia.
Ant. 3: Alleluia, the Lord our God is king; let us rejoice and give
glory to him alleluia.

Ant. 3: The Lord our God almighty is king, alleluia.

When chanted, this canticle is sung with Alleluia *as set out below.
When recited, it suffices to say* Alleluia *at the beginning and end of
each strophe.*

THE MARRIAGE FEAST OF THE LAMB

Alleluia.
Salvation and glory and power belong to our God,*
(R⁄ Alleluia.)
His judgments are true and just.
R⁄ Alleluia (alleluia).

Alleluia.
Praise our God, all you his servants,*
(R⁄ Alleluia.)
You who fear him, small and great.
R⁄ Alleluia (alleluia).

Alleluia.
The Lord our God, the Almighty, reigns,*
(R⁄ Alleluia.)
Let us rejoice and exult and give him the glory.
R⁄ Alleluia (alleluia).

Alleluia.
The marriage of the Lamb has come,*
(R⁄ Alleluia.)
And his bride has made herself ready.
R⁄ Alleluia (alleluia).

Ant. The Lord our God almighty is king, alleluia.

Ant. Advent: Let us live justly and honestly while we are awaiting, in hope, the coming of the Lord.
Eastertide: Alleluia, the Lord our God is king; let us rejoice and give glory to him, alleluia.

LENT

Ant. Lent: We were ransomed with the precious blood of Christ, the lamb who is without blemish.
Ant. 3: Ours were the sufferings he bore, ours the sorrows he carried.

CHRIST, THE SERVANT OF GOD,
FREELY ACCEPTS HIS PASSION

CANTICLE

I PET 2:21-24

Christ suffered for you,†
leaving you an example*
that you should follow in his steps.

He committed no sin;*
no guile was found on his lips.
When he was reviled,*
he did not revile in return.

When he suffered,*
he did not threaten;
but he trusted to him*
who judges justly.

He himself bore our sins*
in his body on the tree,
that we might die to sin*
and live to righteousness.

By his wounds you have been healed.

Ant. Ours were the sufferings he bore, ours the sorrows he carried.

THROUGH THE YEAR

Scripture Reading   *1 Pet 1:3-5*
Blessed be God the Father of our Lord Jesus Christ, who in his great mercy has given us a new birth as his sons, by raising Jesus Christ from the dead, so that we have a sure hope and the promise of an inheritance that can never be spoilt or soiled and never fade away, because it is being kept for you in the heavens. Through your faith, God's power will guard you until the salvation which has been prepared is revealed at the end of time.

Short Responsory
R℣ Blessed are you, O Lord, in the vault of heaven. *Repeat* R℣
℣ You are exalted and glorified above all else for ever. R℣ Glory be. R℣

Magnificat antiphon from the Proper of Seasons.

Intercessions

God is ever creative. His love renews all things and is the source of our hope. Let us turn to him in confidence: ℟ Lord, accept our thanks and our prayers.

We give thanks for the order of created things:—you have blessed us with the resources of the earth and the gift of human life. ℟

We give thanks for man's share in your continuing work of creation: —we praise you for your gifts to him of inventive skill and creative vision.

We pray for all the nations of the world:—may those in authority work for peace and goodwill among men. ℟

We pray for all who are homeless today:—we pray for families searching for a place to live, and for refugees driven from their homeland. ℟

Life was your first gift to us:—may those who have died come to its fulness in you. ℟

Our Father

The concluding prayer from the Proper of Seasons.

WEEK 3: MONDAY

Invitatory ant. Let us come before the Lord, giving thanks.
Psalm, p 3.

MORNING PRAYER

HYMN

The day is filled with splendour
When God brings light from light,
And all renewed creation
Rejoices in his sight.

181

The Father gives his children
The wonder of the world
In which his power and glory
Like banners are unfurled.

With every living creature,
Awaking with the day,
We turn to God our Father,
Lift up our hearts and pray:

O Father, Son and Spirit,
Your grace and mercy send,
That we may live to praise you
Today and to the end.

PSALMODY

Ant. 1: They are happy, who dwell in your house, Lord.
17–23 December: Behold, the Lord, the ruler of the kings of the
earth, will come. Happy are those who are ready to meet him.
Eastertide: My heart and my soul ring out their joy to the living
God, alleluia.

LONGING FOR THE TEMPLE OF THE LORD   PSALM 83(84)
*We have no lasting city in this life but we look for one in the life to
come* (Heb 13:14)

How lóvely is your dwélling pláce,*
Lórd, Gód of hósts.

My sóul is lónging and yéarning,*
is yéarning for the córts of the Lórd.
My héart and my sóul ring out their jóy*
to Gód, the líving Gód.

The spárrow hersélf finds a hóme*
and the swállow a nést for her bróod;
she láys her yóung by your áltars,*
Lord of hósts, my kíng and my Gód.

They are háppy, who dwéll in your hóuse,*

182

for éver sínging your práise.
They are háppy, whose stréngth is in yóu,*
in whose héarts are the róads to Síon.

As they gó through the Bítter Válley†
they máke it a pláce of spríngs,*
the áutumn rain cóvers it with bléssings.
They wálk with éver growing stréngth,*
they will sée the God of góds in Síon.

O Lórd God of hósts, hear my práyer,*
give éar, O Gód of Jácob.
Turn your éyes, O Gód, our shíeld,*
lóok on the fáce of your anóinted.

Óne day withín your cóurts*
is bétter than a thóusand elsewhére.
The thréshold of the hóuse of Gód*
I prefér to the dwéllings of the wícked.

For the Lord Gód is a rámpart, a shíeld;*
he will gíve us his fávour and glóry.
The Lórd will not refúse any góod*
to thóse who wálk without bláme.

Lórd, Gód of hósts,*
háppy the mán who trusts in yóu!

Ant. They are happy, who dwell in your house, Lord.
17-23 December: Behold, the Lord, the ruler of the kings of the earth, will come. Happy are those who are ready to meet him.
Eastertide: My heart and my soul ring out their joy to the living God, alleluia.

Ant. 2: Come, let us go up to the mountain of the Lord.
17-23 December: Sing a new song to the Lord: Praise him throughout the world.
Eastertide: Great is the Temple of the Lord; all the nations will go there to worship, alleluia.

THE MOUNTAIN OF THE TEMPLE OF THE LORD   CANTICLE
  TOWERS ABOVE THE MOUNTAINS   IS 2:2-5
All the peoples will come and worship you (Rev 15:4)

It shall come to pass in the latter days†
that the mountain of the house of the Lord*
shall be established as the highest of the mountains,
and shall be raised above the hills;*
and all the nations shall flow to it,

And many peoples shall come, and say:†
'Come, let us go up to the mountain of the Lord,*
to the house of the God of Jacob,
that he may teach us his ways*
and that we may walk in his paths.'
For out of Sion shall go forth the law,*
and the word of the Lord from Jerusalem.

He shall judge between the nations,*
and shall decide for many peoples;
and they shall beat their swords into ploughshares,*
and their spears into pruning hooks;
nation shall not lift up sword against nation,*
neither shall they learn war any more.

O house of Jacob, come,*
let us walk in the light of the Lord.

Ant. Come, let us go up to the mountain of the Lord.
17–23 December: Sing a new song to the Lord: Praise him throughout the world.
Eastertide: Great is the Temple of the Lord; all the nations will go there to worship, alleluia.

Ant. 3: O sing to the Lord, bless his name.
17–23 December: When the Son of Man comes, will he find any faith on earth?
Eastertide: Proclaim to the nations: 'God is king', alleluia.

THE LORD IS KING AND RULER OF ALL THE EARTH   PSALM 95(96)
They were singing a new hymn in front of the throne, in the presence of the Lamb (Cf Rev 14:3)

O síng a new sóng to the Lórd,†
síng to the Lórd all the éarth.*
O síng to the Lórd, bless his náme.

Procláim his hélp day by dáy,†
téll among the nátions his glóry*
and his wónders amóng all the péoples.

The Lord is gréat and wórthy of práise,†
to be féared abóve all góds;*
the góds of the héathens are náught.

It was the Lórd who máde the héavens,†
his are májesty and státe and pówer*
and spléndour in his hóly pláce.

Give the Lórd, you fámilies of péoples,†
give the Lórd glóry and pówer,*
give the Lórd the glóry of his náme.

Bring an óffering and énter his cóurts,†
wórship the Lórd in his témple.*
O éarth, trémble before him.

Procláim to the nátions: 'God is kíng.'†
The wórld he made fírm in its pláce;*
he will júdge the péoples in fáirness.

Let the héavens rejóice and earth be glád,*
let the séa and all withín it thunder práise,
let the lánd and all it béars rejóice,*
all the trées of the wóod shout for jóy

at the présence of the Lórd for he cómes,*
he cómes to rúle the éarth.
With jústice he will rúle the wórld,*
he will júdge the péoples with his trúth.

Ant. O sing to the Lord, bless his name,
17–23 December: When the Son of Man comes, will he find any
faith on earth?
Eastertide: Proclaim to the nations: 'God is king', alleluia.

THROUGH THE YEAR

Scripture Reading   *Jas 2:12-13*
Talk and behave like people who are going to be judged by the law
of freedom, because there will be judgment without mercy for those
who have not been merciful themselves; but the merciful need have
no fear of judgment.

Short Responsory
R/ Blessed be the Lord from age to age. *Repeat* R/
V/ He alone has wrought marvellous works. R/ Glory be. R/

Benedictus ant. Blessed be the Lord, our God.

Intercessions
In the life of his incarnate Son, God has shown us the dignity of
man's labour. With this in mind we pray: R/ Lord, bless our work.
We bless you, Lord, for bringing us to this day;—we thank you
for protecting our lives and giving us what we need. R/
Be with us, Lord, as we take up our daily tasks:—and help us to
remember that it is in your world we live and work. R/
You have called us to serve you responsibly in the world:—help us
to build a just and Christian society. R/
Stay with us and with everyone we meet this day:—let us give your
joy and your peace to the world. R/
Our Father

Concluding Prayer
King of heaven and earth, Lord God,
rule over our hearts and bodies this day.
Sanctify us,
and guide our every thought, word and deed
according to the commandments of your law,

186

so that now and for ever
your grace may free and save us.
(We make our prayer) through our Lord.

EVENING PRAYER

HYMN

Come, praise the Lord, the Almighty, the King of all nations!
Tell forth his fame, O ye peoples, with loud acclamations!
His love is sure;
Faithful his word shall endure,
Steadfast through all generations!

Praise to the Father most gracious, the Lord of creation!
Praise to his Son, the Redeemer who wrought our salvation!
O heav'nly Dove,
Praise to thee, fruit of their love,
Giver of all consolation.

PSALMODY

Ant. 1: Our eyes are turned to the Lord; we look for his mercy.
17–23 December: Behold, the Lord, the ruler of the kings of the earth, will come. Happy are those who are ready to meet him.
Eastertide: The Lord will be your everlasting light; your God will be your glory, alleluia.

THE LORD IS THE HOPE OF HIS PEOPLE PSALM 122(123)
The two blind men cried out, 'Lord, have pity on us, Son of David'
(Mt 20:30)

To you have I lífted up my éyes,*
you who dwéll in the héavens:
my éyes, like the éyes of sláves*
on the hánd of their lórds.

Líke the éyes of a sérvant*
on the hánd of her místress,

so our éyes are on the Lórd our Gód*
till he shów us his mércy.

Have mércy on us, Lórd, have mércy.*
We are fílled with contémpt.
Indéed all too fúll is our sóul†
with the scórn of the rích,*
with the próud man's disdáin.

Ant. Our eyes are turned to the Lord; we look for his mercy.
17–23 December: Behold, the Lord, the ruler of the kings of the
earth, will come. Happy are those who are ready to meet him.
Eastertide: The Lord will be your everlasting light, your God will
be your glory, alleluia.

Ant. 2: Our help is in the name of the Lord, who made heaven and
earth.
17–23 December: Sing a new song to the Lord: praise him throughout the world.
Eastertide: The snare has been broken and we have escaped,
alleluia.

OUR HELP IS IN THE NAME OF THE LORD   PSALM 123 (124)
The Lord said to Paul, 'Do not fear; for I am with you' (Acts 18:9-10)

'If the Lórd had not béen on our síde',*
this is Ísrael's sóng.
'If the Lórd had not béen on our síde*
when mén rose agáinst us,
thén would they have swállowed us alíve*
when their ánger was kíndled.

Thén would the wáters have engúlfed us,*
the tórrent gone óver us;
óver our héad would have swépt*
the ráging wáters.'

Bléssed be the Lórd who did not gíve us*
a préy to their téeth!

Our lífe, like a bírd, has escáped*
from the snáre of the fówler.

Indéed the snáre has been bróken*
and wé have escáped.
Our hélp is in the náme of the Lórd,*
who made héaven and éarth.

Ant. Our help is in the name of the Lord, who made heaven and earth.

17–23 December: Sing a new song to the Lord: praise him throughout the world.

Eastertide: The snare has been broken and we have escaped, alleluia.

Ant. 3: God has chosen us to be his adopted children through his Son.

17–23 December: When the Son of Man comes, will he find any faith on the earth?

Eastertide: When I am lifted up from the earth, I shall draw all men to myself, alleluia.

GOD, THE SAVIOUR   CANTICLE: EPH 1:3-10

Blessed be the God and Father*
of our Lord Jesus Christ,
who has blessed us in Christ*
with every spiritual blessing in the heavenly places.

He chose us in him*
before the foundation of the world,
that we should be holy*
and blameless before him.

He destined us in love*
to be his sons through Jesus Christ,
according to the purpose of his will,†
to the praise of his glorious grace*
which he freely bestowed on us in the Beloved.

In him we have redemption through his blood,*

189

the forgiveness of our trespasses,
according to the riches of his grace*
which he lavished upon us.

He has made known to us†
in all wisdom and insight*
the mystery of his will,
according to his purpose*
which he set forth in Christ.

His purpose he set forth in Christ,*
as a plan for the fulness of time,
to unite all things in him,*
things in heaven and things on earth.

Ant. God has chosen us to be his adopted children through his Son.
17–23 December: When the Son of Man comes, will he find any
faith on the earth?
Eastertide: When I am lifted up from the earth, I shall draw all
men to myself, alleluia.

THROUGH THE YEAR

Scripture Reading   *Jas 4:11-12*
Brothers, do not slander one another. Anyone who slanders a
brother, or condemns him, is speaking against the Law and condemning the Law. But if you condemn the Law, you have stopped
keeping it and become a judge over it. There is only one lawgiver
and he is the only judge and has the power to acquit or to sentence.
Who are you to give a verdict on your neighbour?

Short Responsory

R̰ Heal my soul for I have sinned against you. *Repeat* R̰
℣ I said: 'Lord, have mercy on me.' R̰ Glory be. R̰

Magnificat ant. My soul magnifies the Lord, since God has had
regard for my humble state.

Intercessions
The will of Christ is for all men to be saved. Let us pray that his

will may be done. R⁷ Draw all men to yourself, Lord.

Lord, by your sacrifice on the cross you redeemed us from the slavery of sin:—lead us to the freedom and glory of the sons of God. R⁷

Be with our bishop, N., and all the bishops of your Church:—grant them courage and compassion in their ministry. R⁷

Help those who seek the truth to find it:—let them be consecrated in truth. R⁷

We pray especially for peace in family life, and for those orphaned and widowed:—comfort them in your love. R⁷

May our departed brothers and sisters come to the heavenly city:—there, with the Father and the Holy Spirit, you will reign for ever. R⁷

Our Father

Concluding Prayer

Lord God,
it is our bounden duty to proclaim you as the Light
with whom there is no alteration or shadow of change:
enlighten our darkness as we reach the close of this day,
and in your mercy forgive us our sins.
(We make our prayer) through our Lord.

WEEK 3: TUESDAY

Invitatory ant. The Lord is a great king: come, let us adore him.
Psalm, p 3.

MORNING PRAYER

HYMN

O Christ, the Light of heaven
And of the world true Light,
You come in all your radiance
To cleave the web of night.

May what is false within us
Before your truth give way.
That we may live untroubled,
With quiet hearts this day.

May steadfast faith sustain us,
And hope made firm in you;
The love that we have wasted,
O God of love, renew.

Blest Trinity we praise you
In whom our quest will cease;
Keep us with you for ever
In happiness and peace.

PSALMODY

Ant. 1: Lord, you blessed your land; you forgave the guilt of your people.

17–23 December: The Lord will come from his holy place: he will come to save his people.

Eastertide: You will restore our life again, Lord, and your people will rejoice in you, alleluia.

OUR SALVATION IS AT HAND   PSALM 84(85)
When our Saviour came on earth God blessed his land (Origen)

O Lórd, you once fávoured your lánd*
and revíved the fórtunes of Jácob,
you forgáve the guílt of your péople*
and cóvered áll their síns.
You avérted áll your ráge,*
you cálmed the héat of your ánger.

Revíve us now, Gód, our hélper!*
Put an énd to your gríevance agáinst us.
Will you be ángry with ús for éver,*
will your ánger néver céase?

Will you nót restóre again our lífe*
that your péople may rejóice in yóu?
Let us sée, O Lórd, your mércy*
and gíve us your sáving hélp.

I will héar what the Lord Gód has to sáy,*
a vóice that spéaks of péace,
péace for his péople and his fríends*
and those who túrn to hím in their héarts.
His help is néar for thóse who féar him*
and his glóry will dwéll in our lánd.

Mércy and faíthfulness have mét;*
jústice and péace have embráced.
Fáithfulness shall spríng from the éarth*
and jústice look dówn from héaven.

The Lórd will máke us prósper*
and our éarth shall yíeld its frúit.
Jústice shall márch befóre him*
and péace shall fóllow his stéps.

Ant. Lord, you blessed your land; you forgave the guilt of your people.
17–23 December: The Lord will come from his holy place: he will come to save his people.
Eastertide: You will restore our life again, Lord, and your people will rejoice in you, alleluia.

Ant. 2: At night my soul longs for you; I watch for you at daybreak.
17–23 December: We have a strong city, Sion. The Saviour will set up wall and rampart to guard it. Open the gates, for God is with us, alleluia.
Eastertide: We put our trust in the Lord and he gave us peace, alleluia.

HYMN AFTER VICTORY OVER THE ENEMY   CANTICLE
IS 26:1-4,7-9,12

The city walls stood on twelve foundation stones (cf. Rev 21:14)

We have a strong city;*
he sets up salvation as walls and bulwarks.
Open the gates*
that the righteous nation which keeps faith may enter in.

You keep him in perfect peace,†
whose mind is stayed on you,*
because he trusts in you.
Trust in the Lord for ever,*
for the Lord God is an everlasting rock.

The way of the righteous is level;*
you make smooth the path of the righteous.
In the path of your judgments, O Lord,*
we wait for you.

My soul yearns for you in the night,*
my spirit within me earnestly seeks you;
for when your judgments are in the earth,*
the inhabitants of the world learn righteousness.

O Lord, you will ordain peace for us;*
you have wrought for us all our works.

Ant. At night my soul longs for you; I watch for you at daybreak.
17–23 December: We have a strong city, Sion. The Saviour will set
up wall and rampart to guard it. Open the gates, for God is with
us, alleluia.
Eastertide: We put our trust in the Lord and he gave us peace,
alleluia.

Ant. 3: Lord, let your face shed its light upon us.
17–23 December: Let us know your way on earth, Lord: let all the
peoples know your saving power.
Eastertide: The earth has yielded its fruit; let the nations be glad
and exult, alleluia.

When the following psalm has been used at the Invitatory ps 94, p 371, is said here in place of it.

ALL THE PEOPLES WILL GIVE PRAISE TO THE LORD   PSALM 66(67)
Let it be known to you that this salvation from God has been sent to all peoples (Acts 28:28)

> O Gód, be grácious and bléss us*
> and let your fáce shed its líght upón us.
> So will your wáys be knówn upon éarth*
> and all nátions learn your sáving hélp.
>
> Let the péoples práise you, O Gód;*
> let áll the péoples práise you.
>
> Let the nátions be glád and exúlt*
> for you rúle the wórld with jústice.
> With fáirness you rúle the péoples,*
> you guíde the nátions on éarth.
>
> Let the péoples práise you, O Gód;*
> let áll the péoples práise you.
>
> The éarth has yíelded its frúit*
> for Gód, our Gód, has bléssed us.
> May Gód still gíve us his bléssing*
> till the énds of the éarth revére him.
>
> Let the péoples práise you, O Gód;*
> let áll the péoples práise you.

Ant. Lord, let your face shed its light upon us.
17–23 December: Let us know your way on earth, Lord: let all the peoples know your saving power.
Eastertide: The earth has yielded its fruit; let the nations be glad and exult, alleluia.

THROUGH THE YEAR

Scripture Reading   *1 Jn 4:14-15*
We ourselves saw and we testify
that the Father sent his Son

as saviour of the world.
If anyone acknowledges that Jesus is the Son of God,
God lives in him, and he in God.

Short Responsory

R̷ My helper is my God; I will place my trust in him. *Repeat* R̷
V̷ He is my refuge; he sets me free. R̷ Glory be. R̷

Benedictus ant. The Lord has raised up a mighty saviour for us, as he
promised through the lips of his prophets.

Intercessions

By shedding his blood for us, Christ gathered together a new people
from every corner of the earth. Let us pray to him: R̷ Christ, be
mindful of your people.
Christ, our king and redeemer:—help us to know your power and
your love. R̷
Christ, our hope and courage:—sustain us throughout the day. R̷
Christ, our refuge and strength:—fight with us against our weakness. R̷
Christ, our joy and solace:—stay with the poor and lonely. R̷
Our Father

Concluding Prayer

Almighty God,
to whom this world with all its goodness and beauty belongs,
give us grace joyfully to begin this day in your name,
and to fill it with an active love for you and our neighbour.
(We make our prayer) through our Lord.

EVENING PRAYER

HYMN

O Strength and Stay, upholding all creation,
Who ever dost thyself unmoved abide,

Yet day by day the light in due gradation
From hour to hour in all its changes guide,

Grant to life's day a calm unclouded ending,
An eve untouched by shadows of decay,
The brightness of a holy death-bed blending
With dawning glories of the eternal day.

Hear us, O Father, gracious and forgiving,
Through Jesus Christ thy co-eternal Word,
Who, with the Holy Ghost, by all things living
Now and to endless ages art adored.

PSALMODY

Ant. 1: The Lord surrounds his people.
17–23 December: The Lord will come from his holy place: he will come to save his people.
Eastertide: Peace be with you, it is I; do not be afraid, alleluia.

THE LORD, THE PROTECTOR OF HIS PEOPLE   PSALM 124(125)
Peace to the Israel of God (Gal 6:16)

Thóse who put their trúst in the Lórd†
are like Mount Síon, that cánnot be sháken,*
that stánds for éver.

Jerúsalem! The móuntains surróund her,†
so the Lórd surróunds his péople*
both nów and for éver.

For the scéptre of the wícked shall not rést*
over the lánd of the júst
for féar that the hánds of the júst*
should túrn to évil.

Do góod, Lord, to thóse who are góod,*
to the úpright of héart;
but the cróoked and thóse who do évil,†
drive them awáy!*

On Ísrael, péace!

197

Ant. The Lord surrounds his people.
17–23 December: The Lord will come from his holy place: he will come to save his people.
Eastertide: Peace be with you, it is I; do not be afraid, alleluia.

Ant. 2: Unless you become like little children you will not enter the kingdom of heaven.
17–23 December: We have a strong city, Sion. The Saviour will set up wall and rampart to guard it. Open the gates, for God is with us, alleluia.
Eastertide: O Israel, hope in the Lord, alleluia.

CHILDLIKE CONFIDENCE IN THE LORD   PSALM 130(131)
Learn from me, for I am gentle and humble in heart (Mt 11:29)

> O Lórd, my héart is not próud*
> nor háughty my éyes.
> I have not góne after things too gréat*
> nor márvels beyónd me.

> Trúly I have sét my sóul*
> in sílence and péace.
> As a child has rést in its mother's árms,*
> even só my sóul.

> O Ísrael, hópe in the Lórd*
> both nów and for éver.

Ant. Unless you become like little children you will not enter the kingdom of heaven.
17–23 December: We have a strong city, Sion. The Saviour will set up wall and rampart to guard it. Open the gates, for God is with us, alleluia.
Eastertide: O Israel, hope in the Lord, alleluia.

Ant. 3: Lord, you made us a kingdom and priests to serve our God.
17–23 December: Let us know your way on earth, Lord: let all the peoples know your saving power.
Eastertide: May your whole creation serve you; for you spoke and they came into being, alleluia.

HYMN OF THE REDEEMED   CANTICLE: REV 4:11;5:9,10,12

Worthy are you, our Lord and God,*
to receive glory and honour and power,
for you created all things,*
and by your will they existed and were created.

Worthy are you, O Lord,*
to take the scroll and to open its seals,
for you were slain,†
and by your blood you ransomed men for God*
from every tribe and tongue and people and nation.

You have made us a kingdom and priests to serve our God,*
and we shall reign on earth.

Worthy is the Lamb who was slain,*
to receive power and wealth,
and wisdom and might,*
and honour and glory and blessing.

Ant. Lord, you made us a kingdom and priests to serve our God.
17–23 December: Let us know your way on earth, Lord: let all the
peoples know your saving power.
Eastertide: May your whole creation serve you; for you spoke and
they came into being, alleluia.

THROUGH THE YEAR

Scripture Reading   *Rom 12:9–12*
Let love be genuine; hate what is evil, hold fast to what is good;
love one another with brotherly affection; outdo one another in
showing honour. Never flag in zeal, be aglow with the Spirit, serve
the Lord. Rejoice in your hope, be patient in tribulation, be constant
in prayer.

Short Responsory
℟ Your word, O Lord, will endure for ever. *Repeat* ℟
℣ Your truth will last from age to age. ℟ Glory be. ℟

Magnificat ant. My spirit exults in the Lord God, my saviour.

Intercessions

God has established his people in hope. Nothing can break the confidence of those who love him. Let us proclaim: ℟ Father, our trust is in you.

We give you thanks, Lord God,—for you have made man rich in all wisdom and insight. ℟

Lord God, you know the hearts of all rulers:—may they work for the good of the people they govern. ℟

Lord, you empower mankind to glorify this world with art:—make our work live with vision and true hope. ℟

You do not allow us to be tempted beyond our limits:—strengthen the weak, raise up the fallen. ℟

Father, you have promised men a share in your Son's resurrection on the last day:—remember those who have gone before us on the path to eternal life. ℟

Our Father

Concluding Prayer

Let our evening prayer rise up before your throne of mercy, Lord, and let your blessing come down upon us:
so that now and for ever
your grace may help and save us.
(We make our prayer) through our Lord.

WEEK 3: WEDNESDAY

Invitatory ant. Let us adore the Lord, for it is he who made us.
Psalm, p 3.

MORNING PRAYER

HYMN

Lord God, your light which dims the stars
Awakes all things,
And all that springs to life in you
Your glory sings.

200

Your peaceful presence, giving strength,
Is everywhere,
And fallen men may rise again
On wings of prayer.

You are the God whose mercy rests
On all you made;
You gave us Christ, whose love through death
Our ransom paid.

We praise you, Father, with your Son
And Spirit blest.
In whom creation lives and moves,
And finds its rest.

PSALMODY

Ant. 1: Give joy to your servant, Lord, for to you I lift up my soul.
17–23 December: The Lord who is all-powerful will come from Sion
to save his people.
Eastertide: All the nations shall come to adore you, O Lord, alleluia.

PRAYER OF A POOR MAN IN DISTRESS   PSALM 85(86)
Blessed be God who comforts us in all our sorrows (2 Cor 1:3-4)

Turn your éar, O Lórd, and give ánswer*
for Í am póor and néedy.
Preserve my lífe, for Í am fáithful:*
save the sérvant who trústs in yóu.

You are my Gód, have mércy on me, Lórd,*
for I crý to you áll the day lóng.
Give jóy to your sérvant, O Lórd,*
for to yóu I líft up my sóul.

O Lórd, you are góod and forgíving,*
full of lóve to áll who cáll.
Give héed, O Lórd, to my práyer*
and atténd to the sóund of my vóice.

In the dáy of distréss I will cáll*
and súrely yóu will replý.
Among the góds there is nóne like you, O Lórd;*
nor wórk to compáre with yoúrs.

All the nátions shall cóme to adóre you*
and glórify your náme, O Lórd:
for you are gréat and do márvellous déeds,*
yóu who alóne are Gód.

Shów me, Lórd, your wáy†
so that Í may wálk in your trúth.*
Guide my héart to féar your náme.

I will práise you, Lord my Gód, with all my héart
and glórify your náme for éver;*
for your lóve to mé has been gréat:
you have sáved me from the dépths of the gráve.

The próud have rísen agáinst me;†
rúthless men séek my life:*
to yóu they páy no héed.

But yóu, God of mércy and compássion,*
slów to ánger, O Lórd,
abóunding in lóve and trúth,*
túrn and take píty on mé.

O gíve your stréngth to your sérvant*
and sáve your hándmaid's són.
Shów me a sígn of your fávour†
that my fóes may sée to their sháme*
that you consóle me and gíve me your hélp.

Ant. Give joy to your servant, Lord, for to you I lift up my soul.
17–23 December: The Lord who is all-powerful will come from
Sion to save his people.
Eastertide: All the nations shall come to adore you, O Lord,
alleluia.

Ant. 2: Blessed is the man who walks in justice and speaks what is true.

17–23 December: About Sion I will not be silent until her Holy One shines forth like light.

Eastertide: Our eyes will see the king in his splendour, alleluia.

GOD WILL RULE WITH JUSTICE   CANTICLE: IS 33:13-16

The promise that was made is for you and your children and for all those who are far away (Acts 2:39)

Hear, you who are far off,*
what I have done;
and you who are near,*
acknowledge my might.

The sinners in Sion are afraid;*
trembling has seized the godless:
'Who among us can dwell with the devouring fire?*
Who among us can dwell with everlasting burnings?'

He who walks righteously and speaks uprightly,†
who despises the gain of oppressions,*
who shakes his hands lest they hold a bribe,
who stops his ears from hearing of bloodshed*
and shuts his eyes from looking upon evil,

He will dwell on the heights;*
his place of defence will be the fortresses of rocks;
his bread will be given him,*
his water will be sure.

Ant. Blessed is the man who walks in justice and speaks what is true.

17–23 December: About Sion I will not be silent until her Holy One shines forth like light.

Eastertide: Our eyes will see the king in his splendour, alleluia.

Ant. 3: Acclaim the King, the Lord.

17–23 December: The Spirit of the Lord is upon me. He sent me to bring the Good News to the poor.

Eastertide: All men will see the salvation of our God, alleluia.

THE LORD IS VICTOR AND A JUST RULER PSALM 97(98)
This psalm tells of the first coming of the Lord and of the faith of all peoples (St Athanasius)

Síng a new sóng to the Lórd*
for hé has worked wónders.
His ríght hand and his hóly árm*
have bróught salvátion.

The Lórd has made knówn his salvátion;*
has shown his jústice to the nátions.
He has remémbered his trúth and lóve*
for the hóuse of Ísrael.

All the énds of the éarth have séen*
the salvátion of our Gód.
Shóut to the Lórd all the éarth,*
ríng out your jóy.

Sing psálms to the Lórd with the hárp*
with the sóund of músic.
With trúmpets and the sóund of the hórn*
acclaim the Kíng, the Lórd.

Let the séa and all withín it, thúnder;*
the wórld, and all its péoples.
Let the rívers cláp their hánds*
and the hílls ring out their jóy.

Rejóice at the présence of the Lórd,*
for he comes to rúle the éarth.
He will rúle the wórld with jústice*
and the péoples with fáirness.

Ant. Acclaim the King, the Lord.
17–23 December: The Spirit of the Lord is upon me. He sent me to bring the Good News to the poor.
Eastertide: All men will see the salvation of our God, alleluia.

Scripture Reading   *Job 1:21;2:10b*
Naked I came from my mother's womb,
naked I shall return.
The Lord gave, the Lord has taken back.
Blessed be the name of the Lord!
If we take happiness from God's hand, must we not take sorrow too?

Short Responsory
R̷ Bend my heart to your will, O God. *Repeat* R̷
V̷ By your word, give me life. R̷ Glory be. R̷

Benedictus ant. Show us your mercy, O Lord; remember your holy
covenant.

Intercessions
God is love: he who dwells in love dwells in God, and God in him.
In Jesus Christ we see how God loves us. Let us renew our faith
in his love: R̷ Lord Jesus, you loved us and gave yourself for us.
You have given us life and light this morning:—let us give thanks
for such great gifts. R̷
You are sole master of the future:—keep us from despair and the
fear of what is to come. R̷
Love has no ambition to seek anything for itself:—strengthen our
will to give up selfishness today. R̷
May your love in us overcome all things:—let there be no limit to
our faith, our hope, and our endurance. R̷
Our Father

Concluding Prayer
Lord God,
in your wisdom you created us,
by your providence you rule us:
penetrate our inmost being with your holy light,
so that our way of life
may always be one of faithful service to you.
(We make our prayer) through our Lord.

EVENING PRAYER

HYMN

Christ be near at either hand,
Christ behind, before me stand
Christ with me where e'er I go,
Christ around, above, below.

Christ be in my heart and mind,
Christ within my soul enshrined,
Christ control my wayward heart;
Christ abide and ne'er depart.

Christ my life and only way,
Christ my lantern night and day;
Christ be my unchanging friend,
Guide and shepherd to the end.

PSALMODY

Ant. 1: Those who were sowing in tears, will sing when they reap.
17-23 December: The Lord who is all-powerful will come from
Sion to save his people.
Eastertide: Your sorrow will turn to joy, alleluia.

JOY AND HOPE IN GOD   PSALM 125(126)
Just as you are sharing in our sufferings, so also will you share our
consolations (2 Cor 1:7)

When the Lórd delivered Síon from bóndage,*
It séemed like a dréam.
Thén was our móuth filled with láughter,*
on our líps there were sóngs.

The héathens themsélves said: 'What márvels*
the Lórd worked for thém!'
What márvels the Lórd worked for ús!*
Indéed we were glád.

206

Delíver us, O Lórd, from our bóndage*
as stréams in dry lánd.
Thóse who are sówing in téars*
will síng when they réap.

They go óut, they go óut, full of téars,*
carrying séed for the sówing:
they come báck, they come báck, full of sóng,*
cárrying their shéaves.

Ant. Those who were sowing in tears, will sing when they reap.
17–23 December: The Lord who is all-powerful will come from Sion
to save his people.
Eastertide: Your sorrow will turn to joy, alleluia.

Ant. 2: The Lord will build a house for us; he will watch over our
city.
17–23 December: About Sion I will not be silent until her Holy
One shines forth like light.
Eastertide: Whether we live or whether we die, we belong to the
Lord, alleluia.

SUCCESS DEPENDS ON THE LORD'S BLESSING   PSALM 126(127)
You are God's building (1 Cor 3:9)

If the Lórd does not búild the hóuse,*
in váin do its búilders lábour;
if the Lórd does not wátch over the cíty,*
in váin does the wátchman keep vígil.

In váin is your éarlier rísing,*
your góing láter to rést,
you who tóil for the bréad you éat:*
when he pours gífts on his belóved while they slúmber.

Truly sóns are a gíft from the Lórd,*
a bléssing, the frúit of the wómb.
Indéed the sóns of yóuth*
are like árrows in the hánd of a wárrior.

Ó the háppiness of the mán*
who has fílled his quíver with these árrows!
Hé will have no cáuse for sháme*
when he dispútes with his fóes in the gáteways.

Ant. The Lord will build a house for us; he will watch over our city.
17–23 December: About Sion I will not be silent until her Holy
One shines forth like light.
Eastertide: Whether we live or whether we die, we belong to the
Lord, alleluia.

Ant. 3: He is the first-born of all creation; he is supreme over all
creatures.
17–23 December: The Spirit of the Lord is upon me. He sent me to
bring the Good News to the poor.
Eastertide: From him, through him and in him are all things that
exist: to him be glory for ever, alleluia.

CHRIST IS THE FIRST-BORN OF ALL CREATION   CANTICLE
THE FIRST-BORN FROM THE DEAD   COL 1:12-20

Let us give thanks to the Father,†
who has qualified us to share*
in the inheritance of the saints in light.

He has delivered us from the dominion of darkness*
and transferred us to the kingdom of his beloved Son,
in whom we have redemption,*
the forgiveness of sins.

He is the image of the invisible God,*
the first-born of all creation,
for in him all things were created, in heaven and on earth,*
visible and invisible.

All things were created*
through him and for him.
He is before all things,*
and in him all things hold together.

He is the head of the body, the Church;*
he is the beginning,
the first-born from the dead,*
that in everything he might be pre-eminent.

For in him all the fulness of God was pleased to dwell,*
and through him to reconcile to himself all things,
whether on earth or in heaven,*
making peace by the blood of his cross.

Ant. He is the first-born of all creation; he is supreme over all creatures.
17–23 December: The Spirit of the Lord is upon me. He sent me to bring the Good News to the poor.
Eastertide: From him, through him and in him are all things that exist: to him be glory for ever, alleluia.

THROUGH THE YEAR

Scripture Reading   *Eph 3:20-21*
To him who is able to do so much more than we can ever ask for, or even think of, by means of the power working in us: to God be the glory in the church and in Christ Jesus, for all time, for ever and ever! Amen.

Short Responsory
R̲ Redeem me, Lord, and show me your mercy. *Repeat* R̲
V̲ Do not cast me away with sinners. R̲ Glory be. R̲

Magnificat ant. The Almighty has done great things for me; Holy is his name.

Intercessions
I may have faith strong enough to move mountains: but if I have no love, I am nothing. With this in mind we pray: R̲ Lord, grant us your love.
Lord, sustain us as we build and grow towards you:—increase our faith as we work. R̲
We are assailed by doubts, and weighed down by uncertainties,—

release our hearts, to journey towards you with hope. ℟ Lord, grant us your love.

Love keeps no score of wrong, and does not gloat over evil:—help us to delight in the truth, and rejoice in your gifts to others. ℟

Confirm the pilgrim Church in the faith of the apostles:—help us to encourage each other, sharing our gifts. ℟

Bring those who have died in your peace to that knowledge which fulfils faith and answers hope,—grant them the fulness of your love. ℟

Our Father

Concluding Prayer

Let your people's cry come into your loving presence, Lord.
Forgive them their sins,
so that by your grace they may be devoted to your service,
and rest secure under your protecting hand.
(We make our prayer) through our Lord.

WEEK 3: THURSDAY

Invitatory ant. Come, let us adore the Lord, for he is our God.
Psalm, p 3.

MORNING PRAYER

HYMN

The Father's glory, Christ our light,
With love and mercy comes to span
The vast abyss of sin between
The God of holiness and man.

Christ yesterday and Christ today,
For all eternity the same,
The image of our hidden God;
Eternal Wisdom is his name.

He keeps his word from age to age,
Is with us to the end of days,
A cloud by day, a flame by night,
To go before us on his ways.

We bless you, Father, fount of light,
And Christ, your well-beloved Son,
Who with the Spirit dwell in us:
Immortal Trinity in One.

PSALMODY

Ant. 1: Glorious things are told of you, O city of God.

17–23 December: I look to you, Lord, for help; come and save me,
Lord, for I seek refuge in you.

Eastertide: We will dance and sing; you are the source of our life
and our joy, city of God, alleluia.

JERUSALEM, MOTHER OF ALL NATIONS   PSALM 86(87)
The Jerusalem which is above is free and is our mother (Gal 4:26)

On the hóly móuntain is his cíty*
chérished by the Lórd.
The Lórd prefers the gátes of Síon*
to áll Jacob's dwéllings.
Of yóu are told glórious thíngs,*
O cíty of Gód!

'Bábylon and Égypt I will cóunt*
among thóse who knów me;
Philístia, Týre, Ethiópia,*
thése will be her chíldren
and Síon shall be cálled "Móther"*
for áll shall be her chíldren.'

It is hé, the Lórd Most Hígh,*
who gives éach his pláce.
In his régister of péoples he wrítes:*
'Thése are her chíldren'
and while they dánce they will síng:*
'In yóu all find their hóme.'

Ant. Glorious things are told of you, O city of God.

17–23 December: I look to you, Lord, for help; come and save me, Lord, for I seek refuge in you.

Eastertide: We will dance and sing; you are the source of our life and our joy, city of God, alleluia.

Ant. 2: The Lord is coming in power; the prize of his victory is with him.

17–23 December: Lord, give those who wait for you their reward, and let your prophets be found worthy of belief.

Eastertide: He will tend his flock like a shepherd and carry them in his arms, alleluia.

THE GOOD SHEPHERD:	CANTICLE
GOD MOST-HIGH AND ALL WISE	IS 40:10-17

Behold, I come quickly, and my reward is with me (Rev 22:12)

Behold, the Lord God comes with might,*
and his arm rules for him;
behold, his reward is with him,*
and his recompense before him.

He will feed his flock like a shepherd,*
he will gather the lambs in his arms,
he will carry them in his bosom,*
and gently lead those that are with young.

Who has measured the waters in the hollow of his hand*
and marked off the heavens with a span,
enclosed the dust of the earth in a measure†
and weighed the mountains in scales*
and the hills in a balance?

Who has directed the Spirit of the Lord,*
or as his counsellor has instructed him?
Whom did he consult for his enlightenment,*
and who taught him the path of justice,
taught him knowledge,*
and showed him the way of understanding?

Behold, the nations are like a drop from a bucket,*
and are accounted as the dust on the scales;
behold, he takes up the isles*
like fine dust.

Lebanon would not suffice for fuel,*
nor are its beasts enough for a burnt offering.
All the nations are as nothing before him,*
they are accounted by him as less than nothing and emptiness.

Ant. The Lord is coming in power; the prize of his victory is with him.
17–23 December: Lord, give those who wait for you their reward,
and let your prophets be found worthy of belief.
Eastertide: He will tend his flock like a shepherd and carry them in
his arms, alleluia.

Ant. 3: Exalt the Lord our God; bow down before his holy mountain.
17–23 December: Turn to us, Lord, and make no delay in coming to
your servants.
Eastertide: The Lord is great in Sion; he is supreme above all
peoples, alleluia.

THE LORD OUR GOD IS HOLY   PSALM 98(99)
You are higher than Cherubim; you changed the bad state of the
earth, when you came in a nature like ours (St Athanasius)

The Lórd is kíng; the péoples trémble.†
He is thróned on the chérubim; the eárth quákes.*
The Lórd is gréat in Síon.

Hé is supréme over áll the péoples.†
Let them práise his náme, so térrible and gréat.*
He is hóly, fúll of pówer.

Yóu are a kíng who lóves what is ríght;†
you have estáblished équity, jústice and ríght;*
yóu have estáblished them in Jácob.

Exált the Lórd our Gód;†
bow dówn before Síon, his fóotstool.*
Hé the Lórd is hóly.

Amóng his príests were Áaron and Móses,†
among thóse who invóked his náme was Sámuel.*
They invóked the Lórd and he ánswered.

To thém he spóke in the píllar of clóud.†
They díd his wíll; they képt the láw,*
which hé, the Lórd, had gíven.

O Lórd our Gód, you ánswered thém.†
For thém yóu were a Gód who forgíves;*
yet you púnished áll their offénces.
Exált the Lórd our Gód;†
bow dówn before his hóly móuntain*
for the Lórd our Gód is hóly.

Ant. Exalt the Lord our God; bow down before his holy mountain.
17-23 December: Turn to us, Lord and make no delay in coming
to your servants.
Eastertide: The Lord is great in Sion; he is supreme above all
peoples, alleluia.

THROUGH THE YEAR

Scripture Reading *I Pet 4:10-11*
Each one of you has received a special grace, so, like good stewards
responsible for all these different graces of God, put yourselves at
the service of others. If you are a speaker, speak in words which
seem to come from God; if you are a helper, help as though every
action was done at God's orders; so that in everything God may
receive the glory through Jesus Christ.

Short Responsory
R̥ I called with all my heart; Lord, hear me. *Repeat* R̥
℣ I will keep your commandments. R̥ Glory be. R̥

Benedictus ant. Let us serve the Lord in holiness, and he will deliver
us from the hands of our enemies.

214

Intercessions

We adore and praise our God who reigns above the heavens. He is the Lord of all things and before him all creation is as nothing.
Ry We adore you, our Lord and God.

Eternal Father, it is by your gift that we praise you:—the wonder of our making is only surpassed by the splendour and joy of our coming to life in Christ. Ry

Lord, be with us as we start a new day:—move our hearts to seek you and our wills to serve you. Ry

Deepen our awareness of your presence:—teach us reverence and love for all that you made. Ry

To know you is to love those you created:—let our lives and our work be of service to our brothers. Ry

Our Father

Concluding Prayer

Almighty, ever-living God,
shed the light of your glory
on the peoples who are living in the shadow of death,
as you did long ago,
when our Lord Jesus Christ, the Sun of Justice,
came among us from on high.
(We make our prayer) through our Lord.

EVENING PRAYER

HYMN

When God had filled the earth with life
And blessed it, to increase,
Then cattle dwelt with creeping things,
And lion with lamb, at peace.

He gave them vast, untrodden lands,
With plants to be their food;
Then God saw all that he had made
And found it very good.

Praise God the Father for all life,
His Son and Spirit blest,
By whom creation lives and moves,
In whom it comes to rest.

PSALMODY

Ant. 1: Your faithful shall ring out their joy as they enter your dwelling place, Lord.
17–23 December: I look to you, Lord, for help; come and save me, Lord, for I seek refuge in you.
Eastertide: The Lord God gave him the throne of David, his father, alleluia.

THE PROMISE OF GOD   PSALM 131(132)
   TO THE HOUSE OF DAVID
The Lord God will give him the throne of David, his father (Lk 1:32)

I

O Lórd, remémber Dávid*
and áll the many hárdships he endúred,
the óath he swóre to the Lórd,*
his vów to the Stróng One of Jácob.

'I will not énter the hóuse where I líve*
nor gó to the béd where I rést.
I will gíve no sléep to my éyes*
to my éyelids I will gíve no slúmber
till I fínd a pláce for the Lórd,*
a dwélling for the Stróng One of Jácob.'

At Éphrata we héard of the árk;*
we fóund it in the pláins of Yearím.
'Let us gó to the pláce of his dwélling;*
let us gó to knéel at his fóotstool.'

Go up, Lórd, to the pláce of your rést,*
yóu and the árk of your stréngth.
Your príests shall be clóthed with hóliness:*
your fáithful shall ríng out their jóy.

216

For the sáke of Dávid your sérvant*
dó not rejéct your anóinted.

Ant. Your faithful shall ring out their joy as they enter your dwelling place, Lord.
17–23 December: I look to you, Lord, for help; come and save me, Lord, for I seek refuge in you.
Eastertide: The Lord God gave him the throne of David, his father, alleluia.

Ant. 2: The Lord has chosen Sion as his dwelling place.
17–23 December: Lord, give those who wait for you their reward, and let your prophets be found worthy of belief.
Eastertide: Jesus Christ is the only Ruler over all, the King of kings and Lord of lords, alleluia.

II

The Lórd swore an óath to Dávid;*
he wíll not go báck on his wórd:
'A són, the frúit of your bódy,*
will I sét upón your thróne.

If they kéep my cóvenant in trúth*
and my láws that Í have táught them,
their sóns álso shall rúle*
on your thróne from áge to áge.'

For the Lórd has chósen Síon;*
he has desíred it fór his dwélling:
'Thís is my résting-place for éver,*
hére have I chósen to líve.

I will gréatly bléss her próduce,*
I will fíll her póor with bréad.
I will clóthe her príests with salvátion*
and her fáithful shall ríng out their jóy.

Thére David's stóck will flówer:*
I will prepáre a lámp for my anóinted.
I will cóver his énemies with sháme*
but on hím my crówn shall shíne.'

Glory be.

217

Ant. The Lord has chosen Sion as his dwelling place.
17–23 December: Lord, give those who wait for you their reward, and let your prophets be found worthy of belief.
Eastertide: Jesus Christ is the only Ruler over all, the King of kings and Lord of lords, alleluia.

Ant. 3: The Lord has given him power and honour and empire and all peoples will serve him.
17–23 December: Turn to us, Lord, and make no delay in coming to your servants.
Eastertide: Lord, who is your like, majestic in strength and holiness, alleluia?

THE JUDGMENT OF GOD   CANTICLE
                                                REV 11:17-18;12:10B-12A

We give thanks to you, Lord God Almighty,*
who are and who were,
that you have taken your great power*
and begun to reign.

The nations raged,*
but your wrath came,
and the time for the dead to be judged,*
for rewarding your servants, the prophets and saints,
and those who fear your name,*
both small and great.

Now the salvation and the power†
and the kingdom of our God*
and the authority of his Christ have come,
for the accuser of our brethren has been thrown down,*
who accuses them day and night before our God.

And they have conquered him*
by the blood of the Lamb
and by the word of their testimony,*
for they loved not their lives even unto death.
Rejoice, then, O heaven*
and you that dwell therein.

218

Ant. The Lord has given him power and honour and empire and all peoples will serve him.

7-23 December: Turn to us, Lord, and make no delay in coming to our servants.

Eastertide: Lord, who is your like, majestic in strength and holiness, alleluia?

THROUGH THE YEAR

Scripture Reading   *1 Pet 3:8-9*

You should all agree among yourselves and be sympathetic; love the brothers, have compassion and be modest and humble. Never pay back one wrong with another, or an angry word with another one; instead, pay back with a blessing. That is what you are called to do, so that you inherit a blessing yourself.

Short Responsory

R̷ The Lord fed us with finest wheat. *Repeat* R̷

V̷ He filled us with honey from the rock. R̷ Glory be. R̷

Magnificat ant. The Lord brought down the mighty from their seats, and raised up the lowly.

Intercessions

Christ is the high priest of his people: it is in him that we come together to make our prayer to the Father of us all. R̷ Father, put new hearts within us.

We thank you for calling us into the Church:—bless us with constant faith, and make it a source of life for others. R̷

Lord, bless N., our Pope:—we pray that his faith may not fail, and that he may strengthen his brothers. R̷

Turn sinners back to you:—grant us a humble and contrite heart. R̷

Your Son knew what it was to be excluded from his homeland.—Be mindful of those who must live far from their family and country. R̷

Give eternal rest to the dead:—bring the whole Church together in heaven. R̷

Our Father

Concluding Prayer
We offer you, Lord, our thanksgiving
at the close of this day:
in your mercy forgive the faults we have committed through
   human frailty.
(We make our prayer) through our Lord.

WEEK 3: FRIDAY

Invitatory ant. Give thanks to the Lord, for his great love is without
end.
Psalm, p 3.

MORNING PRAYER

HYMN

We bless you, Father, Lord of Life,
To whom all living beings tend,
The source of holiness and grace,
Our first beginning and our end.

We give you thanks, Redeeming Christ,
Who bore our weight of sin and shame;
In dark defeat you conquered sin,
And death, by dying, overcame.

Come, Holy Spirit, searching fire,
Whose flame all evil burns away.
Come down to us with light and love,
In silence and in peace to stay.

We praise you, Trinity in One,
Sublime in majesty and might,
Who reign for ever, Lord of all,
In splendour and unending light.

PSALMODY

Ant. 1: Against you alone have I sinned; Lord, have mercy on me.
17–23 December: The one who is to rule will come from Sion: 'The Lord, Immanuel' is his great name.
Eastertide: O Lord, wash me more and more from my guilt, alleluia.

O GOD, HAVE MERCY ON ME   PSALM 50(51)
You must be made new in mind and spirit, and put on the new nature
(Eph 4:23-24)

Have mércy on me, Gód, in your kíndness.*
In your compássion blot óut my offénce.
O wásh me more and móre from my guílt*
and cléanse me fróm my sín.

My offénces trúly I knów them;*
my sín is álways befóre me.
Against yóu, you alóne, have I sínned;*
what is évil in your síght I have dóne.

That you may be jústified whén you give séntence*
and be withóut repróach when you júdge,
O sée, in guílt I was bórn,*
a sínner was Í concéived.

Indéed you love trúth in the héart;*
then in the sécret of my héart teach me wísdom.
O púrify me, thén I shall be cléan;*
O wásh me, I shall be whíter than snów.

Make me héar rejóicing and gládness,*
that the bónes you have crúshed may revíve.
From my síns turn awáy your fáce*
and blót out áll my guílt.

A púre heart creáte for me, O Gód,*
put a stéadfast spírit withín me.
Do not cást me awáy from your présence,*
nor depríve me of your hóly spírit.

221

Give me agáin the jóy of your hélp;*
with a spírit of férvour sustáin me,
that I may téach transgréssors your wáys*
and sínners may retúrn to yóu.

O réscue me, Gód, my hélper,*
and my tóngue shall ríng out your góodness.
O Lórd, ópen my líps*
and my móuth shall decláre your práise.

For in sácrifice you táke no delíght,*
burnt óffering from mé you would refúse,
my sácrifice, a cóntrite spírit.*
A húmbled, contrite héart you will not spúrn.

In your góodness, show fávour to Síon:*
rebuíld the wálls of Jerúsalem.
Thén you will be pléased with lawful sácrifice,*
hólocausts óffered on your áltar.

Ant. Against you alone have I sinned; Lord, have mercy on me.
17–23 December: The one who is to rule will come from Sion: 'The Lord, Immanuel' is his great name.
Eastertide: O Lord, wash me more and more from my guilt, alleluia.

Ant. 2: We know our offences, Lord; we have sinned against you.
17–23 December: Stand steadfast. You will see the helping power of the Lord.
Eastertide: Christ bore our sins in his own body on the cross, alleluia.

LAMENT OF THE PEOPLE IN TIME   CANTICLE
OF FAMINE AND WAR   JER 14:17-21
The kingdom of God is at hand. Repent, and believe in the gospel
(Mk 1:15)

Let my eyes run down with tears night and day,*
and let them not cease,
for the virgin daughter of my people is smitten with a
     great wound,*

with a very grievous blow.

If I go out into the field,*
behold, those slain by the sword!
And if I enter the city,*
behold, the diseases of famine!
For both prophet and priest ply their trade through the land,*
and have no knowledge.

Have you utterly rejected Judah?
Does your soul loathe Sion?
Why have you smitten us*
so that there is no healing for us?

We looked for peace,*
but no good came;
for a time of healing,*
but behold, terror.

We acknowledge our wickedness, O Lord,†
and the iniquity of our fathers,*
for we have sinned against you.
Do not spurn us, for your name's sake,†
do not dishonour your glorious throne;*
remember and do not break your covenant with us.

Ant. We know our offences, Lord; we have sinned against you.
17-23 December: Stand steadfast. You will see the helping power
of the Lord.
Eastertide: Christ bore our sins in his own body on the cross,
alleluia.

Ant. 3: The Lord is God; we are his people, the sheep of his flock.
17-23 December: I look to the Lord; I will await the God who
saves me.
Eastertide: Come before the Lord, singing for joy, alleluia.

*When the following psalm has been used at the Invitatory, ps 94, p 3,
is said here in place of it.*

223

THE JOY OF THOSE WHO ENTER   PSALM 99(100)
    THE TEMPLE OF THE LORD
The Lord calls all those he has redeemed to sing a hymn of victory
(St Athanasius)

Cry out with jóy to the Lórd, all the éarth.†
Sérve the Lórd with gládness.*
Come befóre him, sínging for jóy.

Know that hé, the Lórd, is Gód.†
He máde us, we belóng to hím,*
we are his péople, the shéep of his flóck.

Gó within his gátes, giving thánks.†
Enter his córts with sóngs of práise.*
Give thánks to him and bléss his náme.

Indéed, how góod is the Lórd,†
etérnal his mérciful lóve.*
He is fáithful from áge to áge.

Ant. The Lord is God; we are his people, the sheep of his flock.
17–23 December: I look to the Lord; I will await the God who saves
me.
Eastertide: Come before the Lord, singing for joy, alleluia.

THROUGH THE YEAR

Scripture Reading   *2 Cor 12:9b-10*
I am most happy, then, to be proud of my weaknesses, in order to
feel the protection of Christ's power over me. I am content with
weaknesses, insults, hardships, persecutions, and difficulties for
Christ's sake. For when I am weak, then I am strong.

Short Responsory
R̹ In the morning let me know your love. *Repeat* R̹
V̹ Make me know the way I should walk. R̹ Glory be. R̹

Benedictus ant. The Lord has visited his people, he has come to
redeem them.

Intercessions

We have a high priest, able to sympathize with us in our weakness, one who, because of his likeness to us, has been tempted in every way, but did not sin. Let us pray to him: R7 Show us your mercy and compassion.

Lord, for the joy which lay in the future, you willingly went to the cross:—make us share your death, that we may also share your joy. R7

Lord, you said 'Let any man who thirsts come to me and drink':—give your Spirit now to those who thirst for you. R7

You sent your disciples to preach the gospel to every nation:—bless those men and women who devote their lives to preaching the gospel today. R7

Help those in pain to know that the Father cares for them—for he loves them as he loves his own Son. R7

Our Father

Concluding Prayer

Almighty Father,
let your light so penetrate our minds,
that walking by your commandments
we may always follow you, our leader and guide.
(We make our prayer) through our Lord.

EVENING PRAYER

HYMN

When God made man, he gave him all the earth,
All growing things, with every bird and beast;
Then Adam named them at the Lord's command,
Subdued the greatest of them, and the least.

In his own image God created man,
And when from dust he fashioned Adam's face,
The likeness of his only Son was formed:
His Word incarnate, filled with truth and grace.

To God the Father and to Christ his Son
And blessèd Spirit heav'n and earth give praise.
Creation with tremendous voice cries out:
All holy is the mighty Lord of days.

PSALMODY

Ant. 1: The Lord is great; our God is high above all gods.

17–23 December: The one who is to rule will come from Sion:
'The Lord, Immanuel' is his great name.

Eastertide: I, the Lord, am your Saviour, I am your Redeemer,
alleluia.

PRAISE FOR THE LORD   PSALM 134(135)
WHO DOES MARVELLOUS THINGS

*You are a chosen race. Sing the praises of the one who called you out
of darkness into his wonderful light* (1 Pet 2:9)

I

Práise the náme of the Lórd,*
práise him, sérvants of the Lórd,
who stánd in the hóuse of the Lórd*
in the cóurts of the hóuse of our Gód.

Praise the Lórd for the Lórd is góod.*
Sing a psálm to his náme for he is lóving.
For the Lórd has chosen Jácob for himsélf*
and Ísrael for his ówn posséssion.

For I knów the Lórd is gréat,*
that our Lórd is high above all góds.
The Lórd does whatéver he wílls,*
in héaven, on éarth, in the séas.

He summons clóuds from the énds of the éarth;†
makes líghtning prodúce the ráin;*
from his tréasuries he sénds forth the wínd.

The fírst-born of the Egýptians he smóte,*
of mán and béast alíke.
Sígns and wónders he wórked†

in the mídst of your lánd, O Égypt,*
against Pháraoh and áll his sérvants.

Nátions in their gréatness he strúck*
and kíngs in their spléndour he sléw.
Síhon, kíng of the Ámorites,†
Óg, the kíng of Báshan,*
and áll the kíngdoms of Cánaan.
He let Ísrael inhérit their lánd;*
on his péople their lánd he bestówed.

Ant. The Lord is great; our God is high above all gods.

17–23 December: The one who is to rule will come from Sion: 'The Lord, Immanuel' is his great name.

Eastertide: I, the Lord, am your Saviour, I am your Redeemer, alleluia.

Ant. 2: Sons of Israel, bless the Lord! Sing a psalm to his name, for he is loving.

17–23 December: Stand steadfast. You will see the helping power of the Lord.

Eastertide: Blessed is the kingdom of our father David which has come among us, alleluia.

II

Lórd, your náme stands for éver,*
unforgótten from áge to áge:
for the Lórd does jústice for his péople;*
the Lórd takes píty on his sérvants.

Pagan ídols are sílver and góld,*
the wórk of húman hánds.
They have móuths but they cánnot spéak;*
they have éyes but they cánnot sée.

They have éars but they cánnot héar;*
there is néver a bréath on their líps.
Their mákers will come to bé like thém*
and so will áll who trúst in thém!

227

Sons of Ísrael, bléss the Lórd!*
Sons of Áaron, bléss the Lórd!
Sons of Lévi, bléss the Lórd!*
You who féar him, bléss the Lórd!

From Síon may the Lórd be bléssed,*
hé who dwélls in Jerúsalem!

Ant. Sons of Israel, bless the Lord! Sing a psalm to his name, for he is loving.

17–23 December: Stand steadfast. You will see the helping power of the Lord.

Eastertide: Blessed is the kingdom of our father David which has come among us, alleluia.

Ant. 3: All peoples will come and adore you, Lord.

17–23 December: I look to the Lord; I will await the God who saves me.

Eastertide: Let us sing to the Lord; great is his triumph, alleluia.

HYMN OF ADORATION   CANTICLE: REV 15:3-4

Great and wonderful are your deeds.*
O Lord God the Almighty!
Just and true are your ways,*
O King of the ages†

Who shall not fear and glorify your name, O Lord?*
For you alone are holy.
All nations shall come and worship you,*
for your judgments have been revealed.

Ant. All peoples will come and adore you, Lord.

17–23 December: I look to the Lord; I will await the God who saves me.

Eastertide: Let us sing to the Lord; great is his triumph, alleluia.

THROUGH THE YEAR

Scripture Reading   *Jas 1:2-4*
My brothers! Consider yourselves fortunate when all kinds of

trials come your way, because you know that when your faith succeeds in facing such trials, the result is the ability to endure. Be sure that your endurance carries you all the way, without failing, so that you may be perfect and complete, lacking nothing.

Short Responsory

R̷ Christ loved us and has washed away our sins with his blood.
Repeat R̷
V̷ He made us a line of kings, priests to serve God. R̷ Glory be. R̷

Magnificat ant. The Lord has come to help us, his servants; he has remembered his mercy.

Intercessions

Father, Christ prayed that we be forgiven through his passion. As you accepted him, accept his prayer for all sinners. R̷ Father, into your hands I commend my spirit.
Through his beloved disciple, Jesus gave us Mary to be our mother;
—with her we pray to you for all her children. R̷
Father, heed the anguish of those who cry out to you with your Son:—'My God, my God, why have you forsaken me?' R̷
Help us to hear the cry, 'I thirst';—help us to see your Son, even in the least of his brothers. R̷
To the man dying with him, Jesus said, 'Truly I say to you, this day you will be with me in Paradise.'—Father, let those words be heard again by those who die tonight. R̷
We pray for those who have gone before us, signed with the sign of the cross:—may they rise with Christ in power when his voice resounds again through the universe: 'It is consummated.' R̷
Our Father

Concluding Prayer

Holy Father and Lord,
you willed that Christ your Son
should be the price of our salvation.
Give us grace so to live,
that through sharing his sufferings
we may be strengthened by the power of his resurrection,

who lives and reigns with you and the Holy Spirit,
God, for ever and ever.

WEEK 3: SATURDAY

Invitatory ant. The Lord's is the earth and its fulness: come, let
us adore him.
Psalm, p 3.

MORNING PRAYER

HYMN

It were my soul's desire
To see the face of God;
It were my soul's desire
To rest in his abode.

Grant, Lord, my soul's desire,
Deep waves of cleansing sighs,
Grant, Lord, my soul's desire,
From earthly cares to rise.

It were my soul's desire
To imitate my King,
It were my soul's desire
His endless praise to sing.

It were my soul's desire,
When heaven's gate is won,
To find my soul's desire,
Clear shining like the sun.

This still my soul's desire,
Whatever life afford,
To gain my soul's desire
And see thy face, O Lord.

PSALMODY

Ant. 1: You, O Lord, are close: your ways are truth.

17–23 December: God will come from Lebanon and his splendour is like the light.

Eastertide: The words I have spoken to you are spirit and they are life, alleluia.

PSALM 118(119):145-152 XIX(KOPH)

I cáll with all my héart; Lord, héar me,*
I will kéep your commánds.
I cáll upón you, sáve me*
and Í will do your wíll.

I ríse before dáwn and cry for hélp,*
I hópe in your wórd.
My éyes wátch through the níght*
to pónder your prómise.

In your lóve hear my vóice, O Lórd;*
give me lífe by your decrées.
Those who hárm me unjústly draw néar:*
they are fár from your láw.

But yóu, O Lórd, are clóse:*
your commánds are trúth.
Lóng have I knówn that your wíll*
is estáblished for éver.

Ant. You, O Lord, are close: your ways are truth.

17–23 December: God will come from Lebanon and his splendour is like the light.

Eastertide: The words I have spoken to you are spirit and they are life, alleluia.

Ant. 2: Lord, let your wisdom be with me to help me and to work with me.

17–23 December: Send the Holy One, like the dew, you heavens, and let the clouds rain down. Let the earth open for the Saviour to spring forth.

Eastertide: Lord, you have set up your temple and altar on your holy mountain, alleluia.

O LORD, GIVE ME WISDOM   CANTICLE: WIS 9:1-6,9-11
I myself will give you an eloquence and a wisdom that none of your opponents will be able to resist (Lk 21:15)

O God of my fathers and Lord of mercy,*
who have made all things by your word,
and by your wisdom have formed man*
to have dominion over the creatures you have made,
and rule the world in holiness and righteousness,*
and pronounce judgment in uprightness of soul,
give me the wisdom that sits by your throne,*
and do not reject me from among your servants.

For I am your slave*
and the son of your maidservant,
a man who is weak and short-lived,*
with little understanding of judgment and laws;
for even if one is perfect among the sons of men,†
yet without the wisdom that comes from you*
he will be regarded as nothing.

With you is wisdom, who knows your works*
and was present when you made the world,
and who understands what is pleasing in your sight*
and what is right according to your commandments.

Send her forth from the holy heavens,*
and from the throne of your glory send her,
that she may be with me and toil,*
and that I may learn what is pleasing to you;
for she knows and understands all things,†
and she will guide me wisely in my actions*
and guard me with her glory.

Ant. Lord, let your wisdom be with me to help me and to work with me.

17–23 December: Send the Holy One, like the dew, you heavens, and let the clouds rain down. Let the earth open for the Saviour to spring forth.

Eastertide: Lord, you have set up your temple and altar on your holy mountain, alleluia.

Ant. 3: The truth of the Lord will stand firm for ever.

17–23 December: Israel, be ready to meet the Lord, for he is coming.

Eastertide: I am the Way, the Truth and the Life, alleluia.

PRAISE TO THE GOD OF MERCIFUL LOVE PSALM 116(117)
I ask the nations to give praise to God for his mercy (Rom 15:8-9)

> O práise the Lórd, all you nátions,*
> accláim him all you péoples!
>
> Stróng is his lóve for ús;*
> he is fáithful for éver.

Ant. The truth of the Lord will stand firm for ever.

17–23 December: Israel, be ready to meet the Lord, for he is coming.

Eastertide: I am the Way, the Truth and the Life, alleluia.

THROUGH THE YEAR

Scripture Reading *Phil 2:14-15*
Do everything without complaining or arguing, so that you may be innocent and pure, as God's perfect children who live in a world of corrupt and sinful people. You must shine among them like stars lighting up the sky.

Short Responsory
R̰ I called to you, Lord, you are my refuge. *Repeat* R̰
V̰ You are all I have in the land of the living. R̰ Glory be. R̰

Benedictus ant. Give your light, Lord, to those who sit in darkness and in the shadow of death.

Intercessions

From all eternity God chose Mary to be Mother of Christ. Therefore she is above all other creatures both in heaven and on earth.
With her we proclaim: R℣ My soul glorifies the Lord.

Father, your Son Jesus gave his mother to the Church, a perfect
example of faith:—may we accept your word in faith, as she did. R℣

Mary listened to your voice, and brought your Word into the world:
—by answering your call, may we too bring your Son to men. R℣

You strengthened Mary to stand at the foot of the cross and filled
her with joy at the resurrection:—by her intercession, lighten our
sorrow and reinforce our hope. R℣

Our Father

Concluding Prayer

Lord God,
source and origin of our salvation,
make our lives here on earth so proclaim your glory,
that we may praise you without ceasing in heaven.
(We make our prayer) through our Lord.

WEEK 4: SUNDAY

EVENING PRAYER I

HYMN

Bless'd be the Lord our God!
With joy let heaven ring;
Before his presence let all earth
Its songs of homage bring!
His mighty deeds be told;
His majesty be praised;

To God, enthroned in heav'nly light,
Let every voice be raised!
All that has life and breath,

Give thanks with heartfelt songs!
To him let all creation sing
To whom all praise belongs!
Acclaim the Father's love,
Who gave us God his Son;
Praise too the Spirit, giv'n by both,
With both for ever one!

PSALMODY

ANTIPHON I

Advent: See, the One Desired by all the peoples will come, and the house of the Lord will be filled with glory, alleluia.

Lent: Let us enter God's house with rejoicing.

Eastertide: May the peace of Christ reign in your hearts, alleluia.

Through the Year: Pray for the peace of Jerusalem.

THE HOLY CITY OF JERUSALEM   PSALM 121(122)
You have come to Mount Zion and the city of the living God, the heavenly Jerusalem (Heb 12:22)

I rejoiced when I héard them sáy:*
'Let us gó to God's hóuse.'
And nów our féet are stánding*
within your gátes, O Jerúsalem.

Jerúsalem is búilt as a cíty*
stróngly compáct.
It is thére that the tríbes go úp,*
the tríbes of the Lórd.

For Ísrael's láw it ís,*
there to práise the Lord's náme.
Thére were set the thrónes of júdgment*
of the hóuse of Dávid.

For the péace of Jerúsalem práy:*
'Péace be to your hómes!
May péace réign in your wálls,*
in your pálaces, péace!'

235

For lóve of my bréthren and fríends*
I say: 'Péace upon yóu!'
For lóve of the hóuse of the Lórd*
I will ásk for your góod.

Ant. Pray for the peace of Jerusalem.

Ant. Advent: See, the One Desired by all the peoples will come, and
the house of the Lord will be filled with glory, alleluia.
Ant. 2: Come, Lord, do not delay; release your people Israel from
their bonds.

Ant. Lent: Let us enter God's house with rejoicing.
Ant. 2: Sleepers, awake; rise from the dead; and Christ will give you
light.

Ant. Eastertide: May the peace of Christ reign in your hearts,
alleluia.
Ant. 2: In your blood, you redeemed us for God, alleluia.

Ant. 2: From the morning watch even until night my soul is longing
for the Lord.

OUT OF THE DEPTHS I CRY   PSALM 129(130)
He will save his people from their sins (Mt 1:21)

Out of the dépths I crý to you, O Lórd,*
Lórd, hear my vóice!
O lét your éars be atténtive*
to the vóice of my pléading.

If you, O Lórd, should márk our guílt,*
Lórd, who would survíve?
But with yóu is fóund forgíveness:*
for thís we revére you.

My sóul is wáiting for the Lórd,*
I cóunt on his wórd.
My sóul is lónging for the Lórd*
more than wátchman for dáybreak.

Let the wátchman cóunt on dáybreak*
and Ísrael on the Lórd.

Becáuse with the Lórd there is mércy*
and fúlness of redémption,
Ísrael indéed he will redéem*
from áll its iníquity.

Ant. From the morning watch even until night my soul is longing for the Lord.

Ant. Advent: Come, Lord, do not delay; release your people Israel from their bonds.

Ant. 3: Behold, now the appointed time has come for God to send his Son into the world.

Ant. Lent: Sleepers, awake, rise from the dead; and Christ will give you light.

Ant. 3: God loved us so much that he was generous with his mercy: when we were dead through our sins, he brought us to life in Christ.

Ant. Eastertide: In your blood, you redeemed us for God, alleluia.

Ant. 3: Was it not necessary that Christ should suffer thus and so enter into his glory, alleluia?

Ant. 3: Let every creature, in heaven and on earth, bend the knee at the name of Jesus.

CHRIST, THE SERVANT OF GOD   CANTICLE: PHIL 2:6-11

Though he was in the form of God,*
Jesus did not count equality with God a thing to be grasped.

He emptied himself,†
taking the form of a servant,*
being born in the likeness of men.

And being found in human form†
he humbled himself and became obedient unto death,*
even death on a cross.

Therefore God has highly exalted him*
and bestowed on him the name which is above every name,

That at the name of Jesus every knee should bow,*
in heaven and on earth and under the earth,

And every tongue confess that Jesus Christ is Lord,*
to the glory of God the Father.

Ant. Let every creature, in heaven and on earth, bend the knee at the name of Jesus.

Ant. Advent: Behold, now the appointed time has come for God to send his Son into the world.
Lent: God loved us so much that he was generous with his mercy: when we were dead through our sins, he brought us to life in Christ.
Eastertide: Was it not necessary that Christ should suffer thus and so enter into his glory, alleluia?

THROUGH THE YEAR

Scripture Reading   *2 Pet 1:19-20*
So we are even more confident of the message proclaimed by the prophets. You will do well to pay attention to it, because it is like a lamp shining in a dark place, until the Day dawns and the light of the morning star shines in your hearts. Above all else, however, remember this: no one can explain, by himself, a prophecy in the Scriptures. For no prophetic message ever came from the will of man, but men were carried along by the Holy Spirit as they spoke the message that came from God.

Short Responsory
R⁊ From the rising of the sun to its setting, great is the name of the Lord. *Repeat* R⁊
℣ High above the heavens is his glory. R⁊ Glory be. R⁊

Magnificat antiphon from the Proper of Seasons.

Intercessions

Let us pray to Christ, who, of his fulness, gives his brothers love in return for love. ℟ Lord Jesus, hear our prayer.

Firstborn from the dead, you have cleansed us of our sins by your blood.—Lead us to understand what you have done for us. ℟

You have called us to be heralds of the good news:—help us to enter the depths of its message and to make it our own. ℟

King of peace, guide the actions of those who govern:—may your Spirit move them to care for those whom society rejects. ℟

Guide the steps of those who are oppressed, those persecuted for race, colour, or religion:—let their dignity be respected, and their rights upheld. ℟

Welcome all who have died in your peace;—bring them to everlasting life with our Lady and all the saints. ℟

Our Father.

The concluding prayer from the Proper of Seasons.

Invitatory

Ant. We are the people of the Lord, the flock that is led by his hand: come, let us adore him, alleluia.
Psalm, p 3.

MORNING PRAYER

HYMN

I bind unto myself today
The strong name of the Trinity,
By invocation of the same,
The Three in One, and One in Three.

I bind unto myself today
The power of God to hold and lead,
His eye to watch, his might to stay,
His ear to hearken to my need,

The wisdom of my God to teach,
His hand to guide, his shield to ward;
The word of God to give me speech,
His heavenly host to be my guard.

I bind unto myself the name,
The strong name of the Trinity;
By invocation of the same,
The Three in One, and One in Three,
Of whom all nature hath creation;
Eternal Father, Spirit, Word:
Praise to the Lord of my salvation:
Salvation is of Christ the Lord.

Alternative hymn

All people that on earth do dwell,
Sing to the Lord with cheerful voice;
Him serve with mirth, his praise forth tell,
Come ye before him, and rejoice.

The Lord, ye know, is God indeed;
Without our aid he did us make;
We are his folk, he doth us feed;
And for his sheep he doth us take.

For why, the Lord our God is good:
His mercy is for ever sure;
His truth at all times firmly stood,
And shall from age to age endure.

To Father, Son and Holy Ghost,
The God whom heaven and earth adore,
From men and from the angel-host
Be praise and glory evermore.

PSALMODY

ANTIPHON I
Advent: Sound the trumpet in Sion for the Lord is near: see, he will come to save us, alleluia.
Lent: You are my God, I thank you. My God, I praise you.

Eastertide: I shall not die, I shall live and recount the deeds of the Lord, alleluia.

Through the Year: Give thanks to the Lord, for his great love is without end, alleluia.

SONG OF REJOICING IN SALVATION   PSALM 117(118)
This is the stone which was rejected by you builders, but which has become the cornerstone (Acts 4:11)

Give thánks to the Lórd for he is góod,*
for his lóve endures for éver.

Let the sóns of Ísrael sáy:*
'His lóve endures for éver.'
Let the sóns of Áaron sáy:*
'His lóve endures for éver.'
Let thóse who fear the Lórd sáy:*
'His lóve endures for éver.'

I cálled to the Lórd in my distréss;*
he ánswered and fréed me.
The Lórd is at my síde; I do not féar.*
What can mán do agáinst me?
The Lórd is at my síde as my hélper:*
I shall look dówn on my fóes.

It is bétter to take réfuge in the Lórd*
than to trúst in mén:
it is bétter to take réfuge in the Lórd*
than to trúst in prínces.

The nátions áll encómpassed me;*
in the Lórd's name I crúshed them.
They cómpassed me, cómpassed me abóut;*
in the Lórd's name I crúshed them.
They cómpassed me abóut like bées;†
they blázed like a fíre among thórns.*
In the Lórd's name I crúshed them.

I was hárd-préssed and was fálling*
but the Lórd came to hélp me.
The Lórd is my stréngth and my sóng;*
hé is my sáviour.
There are shóuts of jóy and víctory*
in the ténts of the júst.

The Lórd's right hánd has tríumphed;*
his ríght hand ráised me.
The Lórd's right hánd has tríumphed;†
I shall not díe, I shall líve*
and recóunt his déeds.
I was púnished, I was púnished by the Lórd,*
but nót doomed to díe.

Ópen to mé the gates of hóliness:*
I will énter and give thánks.
Thís is the Lórd's own gáte*
where the júst may énter.
I will thánk you for yóu have ánswered*
and yóu are my sáviour.

The stóne which the búilders rejécted*
has becóme the córner stone.
Thís is the wórk of the Lórd,*
a márvel in our éyes.
Thís day was máde by the Lórd;*
we rejóice and are glád.

O Lórd, gránt us salvátion;*
O Lórd, grant succéss.
Bléssed in the náme of the Lórd*
is hé who cómes.
We bléss you from the hóuse of the Lórd;*
the Lord Gód is our líght.

Go fórward in procéssion with bránches*
éven to the áltar.
Yóu are my Gód, I thánk you.*
My Gód, I práise you.

Give thánks to the Lórd for he is góod;*
for his lóve endures for éver.

Ant. Give thanks to the Lord, for his great love is without end, alleluia.

Ant. Advent: Sound the trumpet in Sion for the Lord is near: see, he will come to save us, alleluia.

Ant. 2: The Lord comes! Go to meet him and say: Great is his reign, and his kingdom will have no end. He is God, the Strong One, the Ruler of the world, the Prince of peace, alleluia.

Ant. Lent: You are my God, I thank you. My God, I praise you.

Ant. 2: Lord, you can deliver us from the hand of the one who is stronger than we are; save us, Lord, our God.

Ant. Eastertide: I shall not die, I shall live and recount the deeds of the Lord, alleluia.

Ant. 2: Blessed be your glorious and holy name, alleluia.

Ant. 2: Alleluia, all works of the Lord bless the Lord, alleluia.

LET EVERY CREATURE PRAISE THE LORD   CANTICLE
DAN 3:52-57

The Creator is blessed for ever (Rom 1:25)

You are blest, Lord God of our fathers.*
To you glory and praise for evermore.

Blest your glorious holy name.*
To you glory and praise for evermore.

You are blest in the temple of your glory.*
To you glory and praise for evermore.

You are blest who gaze into the depths.*
To you glory and praise for evermore.

You are blest in the firmament of heaven.*
To you glory and praise for evermore.

You who walk on the wings of the wind:*
To you glory and praise for evermore.

May they bless you, the saints and the angels.*
To you glory and praise for evermore.

From the heavens, the earth and the sea,*
To you glory and praise for evermore.

You are blest, Lord God of our fathers.*
To you glory and praise for evermore.

Ant. Alleluia, all works of the Lord bless the Lord, alleluia.

Ant. Advent: The Lord comes! Go to meet him and say: Great is his reign, and his kingdom will have no end. He is God, the Strong One, the Ruler of the world, the Prince of peace, alleluia.
Ant. 3: Your all-powerful Word, Lord, will come from the royal throne, alleluia.

Ant. Lent: Lord, you can deliver us from the hand of the one who is stronger than we are; save us, Lord, our God.
Ant. 3: Praise God in his wonderful works.

Ant. Eastertide: Blessed be your glorious and holy name, alleluia.
Ant. 3: Tell the greatness of our God. The works of God are perfect; and all his ways are right, alleluia.

Ant. 3: Let everything that breathes give praise to the Lord, alleiuia.

PRAISE THE LORD   PSALM 150
Sing praise in your spirit, sing praise with your soul, that is: give glory to God in both your soul and your body (Hesychius)

Práise Gód in his hóly pláce,*
práise him in his míghty héavens.
Práise him for his pówerful déeds,*
práise his surpássing gréatness.

O práise him with sóund of trúmpet,*
práise him with lúte and hárp.
Práise him with tímbrel and dánce,*
práise him with stríngs and pípes.

O práise him with resóunding cýmbals,*
práise him with cláshing of cýmbals.
Let éverything that líves and that bréathes*
give práise to the Lórd.

Ant. Let everything that breathes give praise to the Lord, alleluia.

Ant. Advent: Your all-powerful Word, Lord, will come from the royal throne, alleluia.
Lent: Praise God in his wonderful works.
Eastertide: Tell the greatness of our God. The works of God are perfect; and all his ways are right, alleluia.

THROUGH THE YEAR

Scripture Reading   *2 Tim 2:8,11-13*
Remember the Good News that I carry, 'Jesus Christ is risen from the dead, sprung from the race of David.'
Here is a saying that you can rely on:
If we have died with him, then we shall live with him.
If we hold firm, then we shall reign with him.
If we disown him, then he will disown us.
We may be unfaithful, but he is always faithful,
for he cannot disown his own self.

Short Responsory
Ry̆ We give thanks to you, O God, and call upon your name.
Repeat Ry̆
y̆ We recount your wonderful deeds. Ry̆ Glory be. Ry̆

Benedictus antiphon from the Proper of Seasons.

Intercessions
To the only God, our Saviour, through Jesus Christ our Lord, be glory, majesty, dominion, and authority, before all time, now, and for ever. Ry̆ We praise you, O God: we acknowledge you to be the Lord.
We bless you, Lord, creator of the universe: we were sinners, in

245

need of your grace:—yet now you have called us to live in knowledge and service of you. ℟ We praise you, O God: we acknowledge you to be the Lord.

Your Son has shown us the way.—As we follow in his steps, may
we never wander from the path that leads to life. ℟

We celebrate today the resurrection of your Son:—in suffering and
in gladness, may it bring us deep joy. ℟

O Lord, give us the spirit of prayer and praise:—let us always and
everywhere give you thanks. ℟

Our Father

The concluding prayer from the Proper of Seasons.

EVENING PRAYER II

HYMN

Holy God, we praise thy name;
Lord of all, we bow before thee!
All on earth thy sceptre own,
All in heaven above adore thee.
Infinite thy vast domain,
Everlasting is thy reign.

Hark! the loud celestial hymn,
Angel choirs above are raising;
Cherubim and seraphim,
In unceasing chorus praising,
Fill the heavens with sweet accord:
Holy, holy, holy, Lord.

Holy Father, holy Son,
Holy Spirit, three we name thee.
While in essence only one
Undivided God we claim thee;
And adoring bend the knee,
While we own the mystery.

Spare thy people, Lord, we pray,
By a thousand snares surrounded;
Keep us without sin today;
Never let us be confounded,
Lo, I put my trust in thee;
Never, Lord, abandon me.

Alternative hymn

Praise, my soul, the King of heaven;
To his feet your tribute bring;
Ransomed, healed, restored, forgiven,
Who like me his praise should sing?
Praise him! Praise him!
Praise him! Praise him!
Praise the everlasting King.

Praise him for his grace and favour,
To our fathers in distress;
Praise him still the same for ever,
Slow to chide and swift to bless,
Praise him! Praise him!
Praise him! Praise him!
Glorious in his faithfulness.

Fatherlike, he tends and spares us;
Well our feeble frame he knows;
In his hands he gently bears us,
Rescues us from all our foes.
Praise him! Praise him!
Praise him! Praise him!
Widely as his mercy flows.

Angels, help us to adore him;
Ye behold him face to face;
Sun and moon bow down before him,
Dwellers all in time and space.
Praise him! Praise him!
Praise him! Praise him!
Praise with us the God of grace.

PSALMODY

ANTIPHON 1

Advent: See, how splendid is he who comes to save the peoples.
Lent: God has appointed him to judge everyone, living and dead.
Eastertide: You must look for the things of heaven, where Christ is, sitting at God's right hand, alleluia.

Through the Year: In holy splendour I begot you before the dawn, alleluia.

THE MESSIAH IS KING AND PRIEST   PSALM 109(110):1-5,7
He must be king so that he will put all his enemies under his feet
(1 Cor 15:25)

The Lórd's revelátion to my Máster:†
'Sít on my ríght:*
your fóes I will pút beneath your féet.'

The Lórd will wíeld from Síon†
your scéptre of pówer:*
rúle in the mídst of all your fóes.

A prínce from the dáy of your bírth†
on the hóly móuntains;*
from the wómb before the dáwn I begót you.

The Lórd has sworn an óath he will not chánge.†
'You are a príest for éver,*
a príest like Melchízedek of óld.'

The Máster stánding at your ríght hand*
will shatter kíngs in the dáy of his wráth.

He shall drínk from the stréam by the wáyside*
and thérefore he shall líft up his héad.

Ant. In holy splendour I begot you before the dawn, alleluia.

Ant. Advent: See, how splendid is he who comes to save the peoples.
Ant. 2: The rugged places shall be made smooth and the mountain-ranges shall become plains. Come, Lord, and do not delay, alleluia.

Ant. Lent: God has appointed him to judge everyone, living and dead.

Ant. 2: Happy is the man to whom the Lord shows mercy; he will never waver.

Ant. Eastertide: You must look for the things of heaven where Christ is, sitting at God's right hand, alleluia.

Ant. 2: He has risen as a light in the darkness, for the upright of heart, alleluia.

Ant. 2: Blessed are those who hunger and thirst for justice, for they shall have their fill.

THE HAPPINESS OF A JUST MAN   PSALM 111(112)
Be like children of the light; for the fruits of the light are seen in
complete goodness and right living and truth (Eph 5:8-9)

Happy the mán who féars the Lórd,*
who tákes delíght in all his commánds.
His sóns will be pówerful on éarth;*
the chíldren of the úpright are bléssed.

Ríches and wéalth are in his hóuse;*
his jústice stands fírm for éver.
He is a líght in the dárkness for the úpright:*
he is génerous, mérciful and júst.

The góod man takes píty and lénds,*
he condúcts his affáirs with hónour.
The júst man will néver wáver:*
hé will be remémbered for éver.

He has no féar of évil néws;*
with a fírm heart he trústs in the Lórd.
With a stéadfast héart he will not féar;*
he will sée the dównfall of his fóes.

Open-hánded, he gíves to the póor;†
his jústice stands fírm for éver.*
His héad will be ráised in glóry.

The wicked man sées and is ángry,†
grinds his téeth and fádes awáy;*
the desíre of the wícked leads to dóom.

Ant. Blessed are those who hunger and thirst for justice, for they
shall have their fill.

OUTSIDE LENT

Ant. Advent: The rugged places shall be made smooth and the
mountain-ranges shall become plains. Come, Lord, and do not
delay, alleluia.

Ant. 3: Great will be his reign and peace will be everlasting, alleluia.

Ant. Eastertide: He has risen as a light in the darkness for the
upright of heart, alleluia.

Ant. 3: Alleluia, victory and glory and power to our God, alleluia.

Ant. 3: Praise God, all you his servants, both great and small,
alleluia.

*When chanted, this canticle is sung with Alleluia as set out below.
When recited, it suffices to say Alleluia at the beginning and end of
each strophe.*

THE MARRIAGE FEAST OF THE LAMB   CANCITLE
                                                    CF REV 19:1-2,5-7

Alleluia.
Salvation and glory and power belong to our God,*
(R℣ Alleluia.)
His judgments are true and just.
R℣ Alleluia (alleluia).

Alleluia.
Praise our God, all you his servants,*
(R℣ Alleluia.)
You who fear him, small and great.
R℣ Alleluia (alleluia).

Alleluia.
The Lord our God, the Almighty, reigns,*
(R⁷ Alleluia.)
Let us rejoice and exult and give him the glory.
R⁷ Alleluia (alleluia).

Alleluia.
The marriage of the Lamb has come,*
(R⁷ Alleluia.)
And his bride has made herself ready.
R⁷ Alleluia (alleluia).

Ant. Praise God, all you his servants, both great and small, alleluia.

Ant. Advent: Great will be his reign and peace will be everlasting, alleluia.
Eastertide: Alleluia, victory and glory and power to our God, alleluia.

LENT

Ant. Happy is the man to whom the Lord shows mercy; he will never waver.
Ant. 3: God fulfilled what he had foretold in the words of all the prophets: that Christ would suffer.

CHRIST, THE SERVANT OF GOD,	CANTICLE
FREELY ACCEPTS HIS PASSION	I PET 2:21-24

Christ suffered for you,†
leaving you an example*
that you should follow in his steps.

He committed no sin;*
no guile was found on his lips.
When he was reviled,*
he did not revile in return.

When he suffered,*
he did not threaten;

251

but he trusted to him*
who judges justly.

He himself bore our sins*
in his body on the tree,
that we might die to sin*
and live to righteousness.

By his wounds you have been healed.

Ant. God fulfilled what he had foretold in the words of all the
prophets: that Christ would suffer.

THROUGH THE YEAR

Scripture Reading   *Heb 12:22-24*
What you have come to is Mount Zion and the city of the living
God, the heavenly Jerusalem where the millions of angels have
gathered for the festival, with the whole Church in which everyone
is a 'first-born son' and a citizen of heaven. You have come to God
himself, the supreme judge, and been placed with spirits of the saints
who have been made perfect; and to Jesus, the mediator who brings
a new covenant and a blood for purification which pleads more
insistently than Abel's.

Short Responsory
℟ Great is our Lord; great is his might. *Repeat* ℟
℣ His wisdom can never be measured. ℟ Glory be. ℟

Magnificat antiphon from the Proper of Seasons.

Intercessions
In the Church, God has made known to us his hidden purpose:
to make all things one in Christ. Let us pray that his will may be
done. ℟ Father, unite all things in Christ.
We give you thanks for the presence and power of your Spirit in the
Church:—give us the will to search for unity, and inspire us to pray
and work together. ℟
We give you thanks for all whose work proclaims your love:—
help us to serve the communities in whose life we share. ℟

Father, care for all who serve in the Church as ministers of your word and sacraments:—may they bring your whole family to the unity for which Christ prayed. R̥

Your people have known the ravages of war and hatred:— grant that they may know the peace left by your Son. R̥

Fulfil the hopes of those who sleep in your peace:—bring them to that final resurrection when you will be all in all. R̥

Our Father

The concluding prayer from the Proper of Seasons.

WEEK 4: MONDAY

Invitatory ant. Let us rejoice in the Lord; with songs let us praise him. *Psalm, p 3.*

MORNING PRAYER

HYMN

Come, O Creator Spirit, come,
and make within our hearts your home;
to us your grace eternal give,
who of your breathing move and live.

Our senses with your light inflame,
our hearts to heavenly love reclaim;
our bodies' poor infirmity
with strength perpetual fortify.

Our earthly foe afar repel,
grant us henceforth in peace to dwell;
and so to us, with you for guide,
no ill shall come, no harm betide.

May we by you the Father learn,
and know the Son, and you discern,

who are of both; and thus adore
in perfect faith for evermore.

PSALMODY

Ant. 1: In the morning, Lord, you fill us with your love.

17–23 December: Behold, the Lord, the ruler of the kings of the
earth, will come. Happy are those who are ready to meet him.

Eastertide: Let the splendour of the Lord, our God, be upon us,
alleluia.

LET THE SPLENDOUR OF THE LORD   PSALM 89(90)
   COME UPON US

*With the Lord one day is like a thousand years, and a thousand years
is like a day* (2 Pet 3:8)

O Lórd, you have béen our réfuge*
from óne generátion to the néxt.
Befóre the móuntains were bórn†
or the éarth or the wórld brought fórth,*
you are Gód, without begínning or énd.

You túrn men báck into dúst*
and say: 'Go báck, sóns of mén.'
To yóur eyes a thóusand yéars†
are like yésterday, cóme and góne,*
no móre than a wátch in the níght.

You swéep men awáy like a dréam,*
like gráss which springs úp in the mórning.
In the mórning it springs úp and flówers:*
by évening it wíthers and fádes.

So wé are destróyed in your ánger*
strúck with térror in your fúry.
Our gúilt lies ópen befóre you;*
our sécrets in the líght of your fáce.

All our dáys pass awáy in your ánger.*
Our lífe is óver like a sígh.
Our spán is séventy yéars*

254

or éighty for thóse who are stróng.

And most of thése are émptiness and páin.*
They pass swíftly and wé are góne.
Who understánds the pówer of your ánger*
and féars the stréngth of your fúry?

Make us knów the shórtness of our lífe*
that we may gáin wísdom of héart.
Lord, relént! Is your ánger for éver?*
Show píty tó your sérvants.

In the mórning, fill us with your lóve;*
we shall exúlt and rejóice all our dáys.
Give us jóy to bálance our afflíction*
for the yéars when we knéw misfórtune.

Show fórth your wórk to your sérvants;*
let your glóry shíne on their chíldren.
Let the fávour of the Lórd be upón us:†
give succéss to the wórk of our hánds,*
give succéss to the wórk of our hánds.

Ant. In the morning, Lord, you fill us with your love.

17–23 December: Behold, the Lord, the ruler of the kings of the earth, will come. Happy are those who are ready to meet him.
Eastertide: Let the splendour of the Lord, our God, be upon us, alleluia.

Ant. 2: Let the praise of the Lord resound from the ends of the earth.
17–23 December: Sing to the Lord a new song, his praise to the end of the earth.†
Eastertide: I will turn darkness into light before them, alleluia.

HYMN TO GOD, THE VICTOR AND SAVIOUR   CANTICLE
IS 42:10-16
They were singing a new hymn before the throne of God (Rev 14:3)

Sing to the Lord a new song,*
his praise to the end of the earth!

255

†Let the sea roar and all that fills it,*
the coastlands and their inhabitants;
let the desert and its cities lift up their voice,*
the villages that Kedar inhabits.

Let the inhabitants of Sela sing for joy,*
let them shout from the top of the mountains.
Let them give glory to the Lord,*
and declare his praise in the coastlands.

The Lord goes forth like a mighty man,*
like a man of war he stirs up his fury;
he cries out, he shouts aloud,*
he shows himself mighty against his foes.

For a long time I have held my peace,*
I have kept still and restrained myself;
now I will cry out like a woman in travail,*
I will gasp and pant.

I will lay waste mountains and hills,*
and dry up all their herbage;
I will turn the rivers into islands,*
and dry up the pools.

And I will lead the blind*
in a way that they know not;
in paths that they have not known*
I will guide them.
I will turn the darkness before them into light,*
the rough places into level ground.

Ant. Let the praise of the Lord resound from the ends of the earth.

17–23 December: Sing to the Lord a new song, his praise to the end of the earth.

Eastertide: I will turn darkness into light before them, alleluia.

Ant. 3: Praise the name of the Lord, you who stand in the house of the Lord.

17–23 December: When the Son of Man comes, will he find any faith on earth?

Eastertide: The Lord has power to do whatever he will, alleluia.

PRAISE FOR THE LORD,
WHO DOES MARVELLOUS THINGS

PSALM 134(135):1-12

You are a chosen race. Sing the praises of the one who called you out of darkness into his wonderful light (Cf 1 Pet 2:9)

Práise the náme of the Lórd,*
práise him, sérvants of the Lórd,
who stánd in the hóuse of the Lórd*
in the cóurts of the hóuse of our Gód.

Praise the Lórd for the Lórd is góod.*
Sing a psálm to his náme for he is lóving.
For the Lórd has chosen Jácob for himsélf*
and Ísrael for his ówn posséssion.

For I knów the Lórd is gréat,*
that our Lórd is hígh above all góds.
The Lórd does whatéver he wílls,*
in héaven, on éarth, in the séas.

He summons clóuds from the énds of the éarth;†
makes líghtning prodúce the ráin;*
from his tréasuries he sénds forth the wínd.

The fírst-born of the Egýptians he smóte,*
of mán and béast alíke.
Sígns and wónders he wórked†
in the mídst of your lánd, O Égypt,*
against Pháraoh and áll his sérvants.

Nátions in their gréatness he strúck*
and kíngs in their spléndour he sléw:
Síhon, kíng of the Ámorites,†
Óg, the kíng of Báshan,*
and áll the kíngdoms of Cánaan.
He let Ísrael inhérit their lánd;*
on his péople their lánd he bestówed.

Ant. Praise the name of the Lord, you who stand in the house of the Lord.

17–23 December: When the Son of Man comes, will he find any faith on earth?

Eastertide: The Lord has power to do whatever he will, alleluia.

THROUGH THE YEAR

Scripture Reading   *Jud 8:21b-23*

Remember that our fathers were put to the test to prove their love of God. Remember how our father Abraham was tested and became the friend of God after many trials and tribulations. The same was true of Isaac, Jacob, Moses, and all those who met with God's favour. They remained steadfast in the face of tribulations of every kind.

Short Responsory

R7 Rejoice in the Lord, O you just; for praise is fitting for loyal hearts. *Repeat* R7

V Sing to him a new song. R7 Glory be. R7

Benedictus ant. Blessed be the Lord, for he has visited us and freed us.

Intercessions

Almighty Father, the heavens cannot hold your greatness: yet through your Son we have learned to say: R7 Father, may your kingdom come!

We praise you as your children;—may your name be kept holy in the hearts of all mankind. R7

Help us to live in the hope of heaven today:—make us ready to do your will on earth. R7

Give us this day the courage to forgive others:—as you forgive us our trespasses. R7

Father, be with us in all our trials:—do not allow us to fall away from you. R7

Our Father

Concluding Prayer

Lord God,
who entrusted the earth to men

to till it and care for it,
and made the sun to serve their needs:
give us grace this day to work faithfully for your glory
and for our neighbours' good.
(We make our prayer) through our Lord.

EVENING PRAYER

HYMN

We praise you, Father, for your gift
Of dusk and nightfall over earth,
Foreshadowing the mystery
Of death that leads to endless day.

Within your hands we rest secure;
In quiet sleep our strength renew;
Yet give your people hearts that wake
In love to you, unsleeping Lord.

Your glory may we ever seek
In rest, as in activity,
Until its fulness is revealed,
O Source of life, O Trinity.

PSALMODY

Ant. 1: Give thanks to the Lord, for his great love is without end.
17–23 December: Behold, the Lord, the ruler of the kings of the earth, will come. Happy are those who are ready to meet him.
Eastertide: Anyone who is in Christ is a new creature, alleluia.

PASCHAL HYMN   PSALM 135(136)
To tell of the works of the Lord is to give praise (Cassiodorus)

I

O give thánks to the Lórd for he is góod,*
   for his lóve endúres for éver.
Give thánks to the Gód of góds,*

259

for his lóve endúres for éver.
Give thánks to the Lórd of lórds,*
for his lóve endúres for éver;

who alóne has wrought márvellous wórks,*
for his lóve endúres for éver;
whose wísdom it wás made the skíes,*
for his lóve endúres for éver;
who fíxed the earth fírmly on the séas,*
for his lóve endúres for éver.

It was hé who máde the great líghts,*
for his lóve endúres for éver,
the sún to rúle in the dáy,*
for his lóve endúres for éver,
the móon and stárs in the níght,*
for his lóve endúres for éver.

Ant. Give thanks to the Lord, for his great love is without end.
17–23 December: Behold, the Lord, the ruler of the kings of the earth, will come. Happy are those who are ready to meet him.
Eastertide: Anyone who is in Christ is a new creature, alleluia.

Ant. 2: Great and wonderful are your works, Lord God Almighty.
17–23 December: Sing a new song to the Lord; Praise him throughout the world.
Eastertide: Let us love God, then, since he loved us first, alleluia.

II

The first-bórn of the Egýptians he smóte,*
for his lóve endúres for éver.
He brought Ísrael óut from their mídst,*
for his lóve endúres for éver;
arm outstrétched, with pówer in his hánd,*
for his lóve endúres for éver.

He divíded the Réd Sea in twó,*
for his lóve endúres for éver;
he made Ísrael páss through the mídst,*

260

for his lóve endúres for éver;
he flung Pháraoh and his fórce in the séa,*
for his lóve endúres for éver.

Through the désert his péople he léd,*
for his lóve endúres for éver.
Nátions in their gréatness he strúck,*
for his lóve endúres for éver.
Kíngs in their spléndour he sléw,*
for his lóve endúres for éver.

Síhon, kíng of the Ámorites,*
for his lóve endúres for éver;
and Óg, the kíng of Báshan,*
for his lóve endúres for éver.

He let Ísrael inhérit their lánd,*
for his lóve endúres for éver.
On his sérvant their lánd he bestówed,*
for his lóve endúres for éver.
He remémbered ús in our distréss,*
for his lóve endúres for éver.

And he snátched us awáy from our fóes,*
for his lóve endúres for éver.
He gives fóod to áll living thíngs,*
for his lóve endúres for éver.
To the Gód of héaven give thánks,*
for his lóve endúres for éver.

Ant. Great and wonderful are your works, Lord God Almighty.
17–23 December: Sing a new song to the Lord: Praise him throughout the world.
Eastertide: Let us love God, then, since he loved us first, alleluia.

Ant. 3: God planned to bring all things together under Christ when the fulness of time had come.
17–23 December: When the Son of Man comes, will he find any faith on earth?
Eastertide: From his fulness we have all received, grace upon grace, alleluia.

GOD, THE SAVIOUR   CANTICLE: EPH 1:3-10

Blessed be the God and Father*
of our Lord Jesus Christ,
who has blessed us in Christ*
with every spiritual blessing in the heavenly places.

He chose us in him*
before the foundation of the world,
that we should be holy*
and blameless before him.

He destined us in love*
to be his sons through Jesus Christ,
according to the purpose of his will,†
to the praise of his glorious grace*
which he freely bestowed on us in the Beloved.

In him we have redemption through his blood,*
the forgiveness of our trespasses,
according to the riches of his grace*
which he lavished upon us.

He has made known to us†
in all wisdom and insight*
the mystery of his will,
according to his purpose*
which he set forth in Christ.

His purpose he set forth in Christ,*
as a plan for the fulness of time,
to unite all things in him,*
things in heaven and things on earth.

Ant. God planned to bring all things together under Christ when the
fulness of time had come.

17–23 December: When the Son of Man comes, will he find any
faith on earth?

Eastertide: From his fulness we have all received, grace upon grace,
alleluia.

262

THROUGH THE YEAR

Scripture Reading   *I Thess 3:12-13*

May the Lord be generous in increasing your love and make you love one another and the whole human race as much as we love you. And may he so confirm your hearts in holiness that you may be blameless in the sight of our God and Father when our Lord Jesus Christ comes with all his saints.

Short Responsory

R/ Let my prayer come before you, O Lord. *Repeat* R/
V/ Let it rise in your presence like incense. R/ Glory be. R/

Magnificat ant. Let my soul proclaim your greatness for ever, O my God.

Intercessions

Let us pray to God who never deserts those who trust in him.
R/ Lord, in your mercy, hear our prayer.
Pour out your Spirit on the Church;—let men see in her the greatness of your loving kindness. R/
Be with the priests and ministers of your Church:—what they preach to others, may they practise in their lives. R/
Teach us to understand one another more deeply:—by your presence free us from prejudice and fear. R/
Give married couples constancy and mutual understanding:—may their difficulties help to deepen the love they have for each other. R/
Pardon the sins of all our departed brothers and sisters:—may they enjoy new life in the company of your saints. R/
Our Father

Concluding Prayer

Stay with us, Lord Jesus, as evening falls:
be our companion on our way.
In your mercy inflame our hearts and raise our hope,
so that, in union with our brethren,
we may recognize you in the scriptures,
and in the breaking of Bread.
Who live and reign with the Father and the Holy Spirit,
God, for ever and ever.

WEEK 4: TUESDAY

Invitatory ant: A mighty God is the Lord: come, let us adore him.
Psalm, p 3.

MORNING PRAYER

HYMN

Father, we praise you, now the night is over,
active and watchful, stand we all before you;
singing, we offer prayer and meditation: thus we adore you.

Monarch of all things, fit us for your mansions;
banish our weakness, health and wholeness sending;
bring us to heaven, where your saints united joy without ending.

All-holy Father, Son and equal Spirit,
Trinity blessed, send us your salvation;
yours is the glory, gleaming and resounding through all creation.

PSALMODY

Ant. 1: I will sing to you, O Lord, and I will walk in the way of perfection.

17–23 December: The Lord will come from his holy place: he will come to save his people.

Eastertide: The man who does the will of my Father will enter the kingdom of heaven, alleluia.

DECLARATION OF A JUST RULER   PSALM 100(101)
If you love me, keep my commandments (Jn 14:15)

My sóng is of mércy and jústice;*
I síng to you, O Lórd.
I will wálk in the wáy of perféction.*
O whén, Lord, will you cóme?

I will wálk with blámeless héart*
within my hóuse;

264

I will not sét befóre my éyes*
whatéver is báse.

I will háte the wáys of the cróoked;*
they sháll not be my fríends.
The false-héarted must kéep far awáy;*
the wícked I disówn.

The man who slánders his néighbour in sécret*
I will bríng to sílence.
The mán of proud lóoks and haughty héart*
I will néver endúre.

I lóok to the fáithful in the lánd*
that they may dwéll with mé.
He who wálks in the wáy of perféction*
shall bé my fríend.

No mán who práctises decéit*
shall líve within my hóuse.
No mán who utters líes shall stánd*
befóre my éyes.

Mórning by mórning I will sílence*
all the wícked in the lánd,
upróoting from the cíty of the Lórd*
áll who do évil.

Ant. I will sing to you, O Lord, and I will walk in the way of perfection.

17–23 December: The Lord will come from his holy place: he will come to save his people.
Eastertide: The man who does the will of my Father will enter the kingdom of heaven, alleluia.

Ant. 2: O Lord, do not withdraw your favour from us.
17–23 December: We have a strong city, Sion. The Saviour will set up wall and rampart to guard it. Open the gates, for God is with us, alleluia.
Eastertide: O Lord, let all the peoples see your loving mercy towards us, alleluia.

THE PRAYER OF AZARIAH IN THE FURNACE CANTICLE

DAN 3:3,4,6,11-18

Repent and turn to God, that your sins may be wiped out (Acts 3:19)

Blessed are you, O Lord, God of our fathers,†
and worthy of praise,*
and your name is glorified for ever.

You are just*
in all that you have done to us,
for we have sinned†
and lawlessly departed from you,*
and have sinned in all things.

For your name's sake†
do not give us up utterly,*
and do not break your covenant.

Do not withdraw your mercy from us*
for the sake of Abraham your beloved,
and for the sake of Isaac your servant*
and Israel your holy one, to whom you promised
to make their descendants as many as the stars of heaven*
and as the sand on the shore of the sea.

For we, O Lord, have become fewer than any nation,†
and are brought low this day in all the world*
because of our sins;
and at this time there is no prince, or prophet, or leader,*
no burnt offering, or sacrifice, or oblation, or incense,
no place to make an offering before you*
or to find mercy.

Yet with a contrite heart and a humble spirit*
may we be accepted,
as though it were with burnt offerings of rams and bulls*
and with tens of thousands of fat lambs.

Such may our sacrifice be in your sight this day,*
and may we wholly follow you,
for there will be no shame*

for those who trust in you.

And now with all our heart we follow you,*
we fear you and seek your face.

Ant. O Lord, do not withdraw your favour from us.

17–23 December: We have a strong city, Sion. The Saviour will set up wall and rampart to guard it. Open the gates, for God is with us, alleluia.

Eastertide: O Lord, let all the peoples see your loving mercy towards us, alleluia.

Ant. 3: I will sing a new song to you, O God.

17–23 December: Let us know your way on earth, Lord: let all the peoples know your saving power.

Eastertide: The Lord is my refuge and my saviour, alleluia.

FOR VICTORY AND PEACE   PSALM 143(144):1-10
I can do all things with the help of the One who gives me strength
(Phil 4:13)

Bléssed be the Lórd, my róck†
who tráins my árms for báttle,*
who prepáres my hánds for wár.

Hé is my lóve, my fórtress;*
hé is my strónghold, my sáviour,
my shíeld, my pláce of réfuge.*
He brings péoples únder my rúle.

Lórd, what is mán that you cáre for him,*
mortal mán, that you kéep him in mínd;
mán, who is mérely a bréath*
whose life fádes like a shádow?

Lówer your héavens and come dówn;*
touch the móuntains; wréathe them in smóke.
Flash your líghtnings; róut the fóe,*
shoot your árrows and pút them to flíght.

267

Reach dówn from héaven and sáve me;†
draw me óut from the míghty wáters,*
from the hánds of álien fóes
whose móuths are fílled with líes,*
whose hánds are ráised in pérjury.

To you, O Gód, will I síng a new sóng;*
I will pláy on the tén-stringed hárp
to yóu who give kíngs their víctory,*
who set Dávid your sérvant frée.

Ant. I will sing a new song to you, O God.

17–23 December: Let us know your way on earth, Lord: let all the peoples know your saving power.

Eastertide: The Lord is my refuge and my saviour, alleluia.

THROUGH THE YEAR

Scripture Reading   Is 55:1

Oh, come to the water all you who are thirsty;
though you have no money, come!
Buy corn without money, and eat,
and, at no cost, wine and milk.

Short Responsory

R⁷ Hear my cry, Lord, for I hope in your word. *Repeat* R⁷
V⁷ I rise before dawn and call for help. R⁷ Glory be. R⁷

Benedictus ant. Lord, save us from the hands of all who hate us.

Intercessions

Our sufferings bring acceptance, acceptance brings hope: and our hope will not deceive us, for the Spirit has been poured into our hearts. It is through the same Spirit that we pray: R⁷ Stay with us, Lord, on our journey.

Help us to realize that our troubles are slight and short-lived;—they are as nothing compared with the joy we shall have when we reach our home with you. R⁷

Come to the lonely, the unloved, those without friends;—show

268

them your love, and help them to care for their brothers and sisters.
R⁷
Take away our pride, temper our anger:—may we follow you in
your gentleness: may you make us humble of heart. R⁷
Give us the fulness of your Spirit, the Spirit of sonship:—make our
love for each other generous and sincere. R⁷
Our Father

Concluding Prayer
Increase in us, Lord, your gift of faith,
so that the praise we offer you
may ever yield its fruit from heaven.
(We make our prayer) through our Lord.

EVENING PRAYER

HYMN
Before we end our day, O Lord,
We make this prayer to you:
That you continue in your love
To guard your people here.

Give us this night untroubled rest
and build our strength anew:
Your Splendour driving far away
All darkness of the foe.

Our hearts' desire to love you, Lord,
Watch over while we sleep,
That when the new day dawns on high
We may your praises sing.

All glory be to you, O Christ,
Who saved mankind from death—
To share with you the Father's love
And in the Spirit live.

PSALMODY

Ant. 1: If I forget you, Jerusalem, let my right hand wither!
17–23 December: The Lord will come from his holy place: he will come to save his people.
Eastertide: Sing to us one of the songs of Sion, alleluia.

BY THE RIVERS OF BABYLON   PSALM 136(137):1-6
This bodily captivity of the people must be understood as pointing to their spiritual captivity (St Hilary)

By the rívers of Bábylon†
thére we sat and wépt,*
remémbering Síon;
on the póplars that gréw there*
we húng up our hárps.

For it was thére that they ásked us,†
our cáptors, for sóngs,*
our oppréssors, for jóy.
'Síng to us,' they sáid,*
'one of Síon's sóngs.'

O hów could we síng†
the sóng of the Lórd*
on álien sóil?
If I forgét you, Jerúsalem,*
let my right hand wíther!

O lét my tóngue†
cléave to my móuth*
if I remémber you nót,
if I príze not Jerúsalem*
abóve all my jóys!

Ant. If I forget you, Jerusalem, let my right hand wither!
17–23 December: The Lord will come from his holy place: he will come to save his people.
Eastertide: Sing to us one of the songs of Sion, alleluia.

Ant. 2: Before the angels I will bless you, my God.
17–23 December: We have a strong city, Sion. The Saviour will set up wall and rampart to guard it. Open the gates, for God is with us, alleluia.
Eastertide: In the midst of affliction you have given me life, alleluia.

THANKSGIVING   PSALM 137(138)
The kings of the earth will bring glory and honour to the holy city
(cf Rev 21:24)

I thánk you, Lórd, with all my héart,*
you have héard the wórds of my móuth.
In the présence of the ángels I will bléss you.*
I will adóre before your hóly témple.

I thánk you for your fáithfulness and lóve*
which excél all we éver knew of yóu.
On the dáy I cálled, you ánswered;*
you incréased the stréngth of my sóul.

Áll earth's kíngs shall thánk you*
when they héar the wórds of your móuth.
They shall síng of the Lórd's wáys:*
'How gréat is the glóry of the Lórd!'

The Lord is hígh yet he lóoks on the lówly*
and the háughty he knóws from afár.
Though I wálk in the mídst of afflíction*
you give me life and frustráte my fóes.

You strétch out your hánd and sáve me,*
your hánd will do áll things for mé.
Your lóve, O Lórd, is etérnal,*
discárd not the wórk of your hánds.

Ant. Before the angels I will bless you, my God.
17–23 December: We have a strong city, Sion. The Saviour will set up wall and rampart to guard it. Open the gates, for God is with us, alleluia.
Eastertide: In the midst of affliction you have given me life, alleluia.

Ant. 3: Worthy is the Lamb that was slain, to receive glory and honour.

17–23 December: Let us know your way on earth, Lord: let all the peoples know your saving power.

Eastertide: Yours, Lord, is the greatness and the power, the glory and the victory, alleluia.

HYMN OF THE REDEEMED   CANTICLE: REV 4:11;5:9,10,12

Worthy are you, our Lord and God,*
to receive glory and honour and power,
for you created all things,*
and by your will they existed and were created.

Worthy are you, O Lord,*
to take the scroll and to open its seals,
for you were slain,†
and by your blood you ransomed men for God*
from every tribe and tongue and people and nation.

You have made us a kingdom and priests to serve our God,*
and we shall reign on earth.
Worthy is the Lamb who was slain,*
to receive power and wealth,
and wisdom and might,*
and honour and glory and blessing.

Ant. Worthy is the Lamb that was slain, to receive glory and honour.

17–23 December: Let us know your way on earth, Lord: let all the peoples know your saving power.

Eastertide: Yours, Lord, is the greatness and the power, the glory and the victory, alleluia.

THROUGH THE YEAR

Scripture Reading   *Col 3:16*
Christ's message, in all its richness, must live in your hearts. Teach and instruct each other with all wisdom. Sing psalms, hymns, and sacred songs; sing to God, with thanksgiving in your hearts.

Short Responsory

℟ You will give me the fulness of joy in your presence, O Lord.
Repeat ℟
℣ I will find happiness at your right hand for ever. ℟ Glory be. ℟

Magnificat ant. Do great things for us, O Lord, for you are mighty, and Holy is your name.

Intercessions

Christ taught us to set our hearts on the Kingdom of God, and on its justice. In that Kingdom all that we need will be given to us. Until then, let us pray: ℟ Your Kingdom come, O Lord.

Blessed are those who know their need of God:—lead us to seek your face in purity of heart. ℟

Blessed are those who work for no reward, those who suffer for what is right:—comfort them with your presence, lighten their burden. ℟

Blessed are the gentle, those who show mercy, and forgive;—they shall know your forgiveness at the end of time. ℟

Blessed are the peacemakers, those who reconcile conflict and hate:—they are indeed the sons of God. ℟

Bring consolation to all who mourn the dead:—may they share the blessed hope of all who have died in the peace of Christ. ℟

Our Father

Concluding Prayer

As we pray before you, Lord,
we ask you, in your mercy, for the grace
always to ponder in our hearts
what we proclaim with our lips.
(We make our prayer) through our Lord.

WEEK 4: WEDNESDAY

Invitatory ant. Cry out with joy to God all the earth: serve the Lord with gladness.
Psalm, p 3.

MORNING PRAYER

HYMN

Now that the daylight fills the sky,
we lift our hearts to God on high,
that he, in all we do or say,
would keep us free from harm today;

Would guard our hearts and tongues from strife;
from anger's din would hide our life;
from all ill sights would turn our eyes;
would close our ears from vanities;

Would keep our inmost conscience pure;
our souls from folly would secure;
would bid us check the pride of sense
with due and holy abstinence.

So we, when this new day is gone,
and night in turn is drawing on,
with conscience by the world unstained
shall praise his Name for victory gained.

PSALMODY

Ant. 1: My heart is ready, O God, my heart is ready.†
17–22 December: The Lord who is all powerful will come from Sion
to save his people.
Eastertide: O God, arise above the heavens, alleluia.

PRAISE FOR GOD AND PRAYER FOR HELP   PSALM 107(108)
*Since the Son of God has been exalted above the heavens, his glory
is preached over all the earth* (Arnobius)

My héart is réady, O Gód;*
†I will síng, síng your práise.
Awáke, my sóul;†
awáke, lýre and hárp.*
I will awáke the dáwn.

I will thánk you, Lórd, among the péoples,*
among the nátions I will práise you,
for your lóve réaches to the héavens*
and your trúth to the skíes.
O Gód, aríse above the héavens;*
may your glóry shine on eárth!

O cóme and delíver your fríends;*
hélp with your ríght hand and replý.
From his hóly place Gód has made this prómise:†
'I will tríumph and divíde the land of Shéchem;*
I will méasure out the válley of Súccoth.

Gílead is míne and Manásseh.†
Éphraim I táke for my hélmet,*
Júdah for my commánder's stáff.
Móab I will úse for my wáshbowl,†
on Édom I will plánt my shóe.*
Over the Phílistines I will shóut in tríumph.'

But who will léad me to cónquer the fórtress?*
Who will bríng me face to fáce with Édom?
Will you útterly rejéct us, O Gód,*
and no lónger márch with our ármies?

Give us hélp agáinst the fóe:*
for the hélp of mán is váin.
With Gód wé shall do brávely*
and hé will trámple down our fóes.

Ant. My heart is ready, O God, my heart is ready.

17–23 December: The Lord who is all-powerful will come from Sion to save his people.

Eastertide: O God, arise above the heavens, alleluia.

Ant. 2: The Lord has clothed me in a garment of justice and salvation.

17–23 December: About Sion I will not be silent until her Holy One shines forth like light.

Eastertide: The Lord will make justice and praise spring up in the sight of the nations, alleluia.

THE PROPHET REJOICES IN THE NEW JERUSALEM

CANTICLE
IS 61:10-62:5

I saw the holy city, the new Jerusalem, as beautiful as a bride prepared to meet her husband (Rev 21:2)

I will greatly rejoice in the Lord,*
my soul shall exult in my God;
for he has clothed me with the garments of salvation,*
he has covered me with the robe of righteousness,
as a bridegroom decks himself with a garland,*
and as a bride adorns herself with her jewels.

For as the earth brings forth its shoots,*
and as a garden causes what is sown in it to spring up,
so the Lord God will cause righteousness and praise*
to spring forth before all the nations.

For Sion's sake I will not keep silent,*
and for Jerusalem's sake I will not rest
until her vindication goes forth as brightness,*
and her salvation as a burning torch.

The nations shall see your vindication,*
and all the kings your glory;
and you shall be called by a new name*
which the mouth of the Lord will give.

You shall be a crown of beauty*
in the hand of the Lord,
and a royal diadem*
in the hand of your God.

You shall no more be termed Forsaken,*
and your land shall no more be termed Desolate;
but you shall be called My delight in her,*
and your land Married;
for the Lord delights in you,*
and your land shall be married.

For as a young man marries a virgin,*
so shall your sons marry you,

276

and as the bridegroom rejoices over the bride,*
so shall your God rejoice over you.

Ant. The Lord has clothed me in a garment of justice and salvation.
17-23 December: About Sion I will not be silent until her Holy One shines forth like light.
Eastertide: The Lord will make justice and praise spring up in the sight of the nations, alleluia.

Ant. 3: I will praise my God all my days.
17-23 December: The Spirit of the Lord is upon me. He sent me to bring the Good News to the poor.
Eastertide: The Lord will reign for ever; he is your God, O Sion, alleluia.

THE HAPPINESS OF THOSE   PSALM 145(146)
  WHO PUT THEIR TRUST IN THE LORD
Let us praise the Lord all our days, that is, in all our conduct
(Arnobius)

My sóul, give práise to the Lórd;†
I will práise the Lórd all my dáys,*
make músic to my Gód while I líve.

Pút no trúst in prínces,*
in mortal mén in whóm there is no hélp.
Take their bréath, they retúrn to cláy*
and their pláns that dáy come to nóthing.

He is háppy who is hélped by Jacob's Gód,*
whose hópe is in the Lórd his Gód,
who alóne made héaven and éarth,*
the séas and áll they contáin.

It is hé who keeps fáith for éver,*
who is júst to thóse who are oppréssed.
It is hé who gives bréad to the húngry,*
the Lórd, who sets prísoners frée,

the Lórd who gives síght to the blínd,*

277

who ráises up thóse who are bowed dówn,
the Lórd, who protécts the stránger*
and uphólds the wídow and órphan.

It is the Lórd who lóves the júst*
but thwárts the páth of the wícked.
The Lórd will réign for éver,*
Sion's Gód, from áge to áge.

Ant. I will praise my God all my days.
17–23 December: The Spirit of the Lord is upon me. He sent me to
bring the Good News to the poor.
Eastertide: The Lord will reign for ever; he is your God, O Sion,
alleluia.

THROUGH THE YEAR

Scripture Reading   *Deut 4:39-40a*
Understand this today and take it to heart: the Lord is God indeed,
in heaven above as on earth beneath, he and no other. Keep his
laws and commandments as I give them to you today.

Short Responsory

R̸ I will praise the Lord at all times. *Repeat* R̸
V̸ His praise will be always on my lips. R̸ Glory be. R̸

Benedictus ant. Let us serve the Lord in holiness all our days.

Intercessions
Praise be to the God and Father of our Lord Jesus Christ. In his
great mercy, he gave us new birth into a living hope by his Son's
resurrection from the dead. To him we pray: R̸ Father, give us
your strength.
Turn our eyes to Jesus Christ your Son.—May he lead us in our
faith and bring it to perfection. R̸
We pray for cheerfulness and a generous heart;—may we bring
joy to our homes, to our work, and to all whom we meet. R̸
We pray for all who are working today;—be with them at home and
in the city, in the factory and in the fields. R̸

We pray for those who have no work;—we pray for the disabled
and the sick, for those who cannot find work, and for those who
are retired. R̷

Our Father

Concluding Prayer

Remember, Lord, your solemn covenant,
renewed and consecrated by the blood of the Lamb,
so that your people may obtain forgiveness for their sins,
and a continued growth in grace.
(We make our prayer) through our Lord.

EVENING PRAYER

HYMN

O Trinity of blessed light
O unity of princely might,
the fiery sun has gone its way;
shed now within our hearts your ray.

To you our morning song of praise,
to you our evening prayer we raise;
your glory suppliant we adore
for ever and for evermore.

PSALMODY

Ant. 1: How wonderful is this knowledge of yours that you have
shown me, Lord.

17–23 December: The Lord who is all-powerful will come from
Sion to save his people.

Eastertide: Night will be as clear as the day, alleluia.

THE LORD SEES ALL THINGS   PSALM 138(139):1-18,23-24
*Who could ever know the mind of the Lord? Who could ever be his
counsellor?* (Rom 11:34)

I

O Lórd, you séarch me and you knów me,†

279

you knów my résting and my rísing,*
you discérn my púrpose from afár.
You márk when I wálk or lie dówn,*
all my wáys lie ópen to yóu.

Before éver a wórd is on my tóngue *
you knów it, O Lórd, through and thróugh.
Behínd and befóre you besíege me,*
your hánd ever láid upón me.
Too wónderful for mé, this knówledge,*
too hígh, beyónd my réach.

O whére can I gó from your spírit,*
or whére can I flée from your fáce?
If I clímb the héavens, you are thére.*
If I líe in the gráve, you are thére.

If I táke the wíngs of the dáwn*
and dwéll at the séa's furthest énd,
even thére your hánd would léad me,*
your ríght hand would hóld me fást.

If I sáy: 'Let the dárkness híde me*
and the líght aróund me be níght,'
even dárkness is not dárk for yóu*
and the níght is as cléar as the dáy.

Ant. How wonderful is this knowledge of yours that you have shown me, Lord.
17–23 December: The Lord who is all-powerful will come from Sion to save his people.
Eastertide: Night will be as clear as the day, alleluia.

Ant. 2: I am the Lord, who test the mind and heart; I give each man what his conduct deserves.
17–23 December: About Sion I will not be silent until her Holy One shines forth like light.
Eastertide: I know my sheep, and they know me, alleluia.

280

II

For it was yóu who creáted my béing,*
knit me togéther in my móther's wómb.
I thánk you for the wónder of my béing,*
for the wónders of áll your creátion.

Alréady you knéw my sóul,*
my bódy held no sécret from yóu
when Í was being fáshioned in sécret*
and móulded in the dépths of the éarth.

Your éyes saw áll my áctions,*
they were áll of them wrítten in your bóok;
every óne of my dáys was decréed*
before óne of them cáme into béing.

To mé, how mystérious your thóughts,*
the súm of them nót to be númbered!
If I cóunt them, they are móre than the sánd;*
to fínish, I must be etérnal, like yóu.

O séarch me, Gód, and know my héart.*
O tést me and knów my thóughts.
See that I fóllow not the wróng páth*
and léad me in the páth of life etérnal.

Ant. I am the Lord, who test the mind and heart; I give each man
what his conduct deserves.
17–23 December: About Sion I will not be silent until her Holy
One shines forth like light.
Eastertide: I know my sheep, and they know me, alleluia.

Ant. 3: All things were created in him, and he holds all things in
being.
17–23 December: The Spirit of the Lord is upon me. He sênt me to
bring the Good News to the poor.
Eastertide: His majesty covers the heavens, the earth is filled with
his praise, alleluia.

CHRIST IS THE FIRST-BORN OF ALL CREATION,
THE FIRST-BORN FROM THE DEAD

CANTICLE
COL 1:12-20

Let us give thanks to the Father,†
who has qualified us to share*
in the inheritance of the saints in light.

He has delivered us from the dominion of darkness*
and transferred us to the kingdom of his beloved Son,
in whom we have redemption,*
the forgiveness of sins.

He is the image of the invisible God,*
the first-born of all creation,
for in him all things were created, in heaven and on earth,*
visible and invisible.

All things were created*
through him and for him.
He is before all things,*
and in him all things hold together.

He is the head of the body, the Church;*
he is the beginning,
the first-born from the dead,*
that in everything he might be pre-eminent.

For in him all the fulness of God was pleased to dwell,*
and through him to reconcile to himself all things,
whether on earth or in heaven,*
making peace by the blood of his cross.

Ant. All things were created in him, and he holds all things in being.
17–23 December: The Spirit of the Lord is upon me. He sent me to
bring the Good News to the poor.
Eastertide: His majesty covers the heavens, the earth is filled with
his praise, alleluia.

THROUGH THE YEAR

Scripture Reading   *1 Jn 2:3-6*
We can be sure that we know God

only by keeping his commandments.
Anyone who says, 'I know him',
and does not keep his commandments,
is a liar,
refusing to admit the truth.
But when anyone does obey what he has said,
God's love comes to perfection in him.
We can be sure that we are in God
only when the one who claims to be living in him
is living the same kind of life as Christ lived.

Short Responsory

R℣ Guard us, Lord, as the apple of your eye. *Repeat* R℣
℣ Hide us in the shadow of your wings. R℣ Glory be. R℣

Magnificat ant. Show the power of your arm, Lord; put down the proud and exalt the lowly.

Intercessions

Let us ask the Father, from whom every family in heaven and on earth takes its name, to send the Spirit of his Son into our hearts as we pray: R℣ Lord, in your mercy, hear our prayer.
O Lord, the creator and redeemer of all mankind, we humbly pray for all men of every race in every kind of need:—make your ways known to them, and reveal your salvation to all nations. R℣
May the whole Church be guided and governed by your Holy Spirit;—let all who call themselves Christians be led into the way of truth and hold the faith in unity of spirit. R℣
We commend to your fatherly goodness all who are afflicted or distressed;—comfort and relieve them according to their needs, and grant them the love and consolation of your Spirit. R℣
Father, give a place of life and rest to those who have died in your peace:—may we share with them in the glory of Jesus Christ, who died to save us all. R℣
Our Father

Concluding Prayer

Remember your people, Lord, and show them mercy:

as you satisfy the hungry with food from heaven,
enrich our poverty from your abundance.
(We make our prayer) through our Lord.

WEEK 4: THURSDAY

Invitatory ant. Come before the Lord, singing for joy.
Psalm, p 3.

MORNING PRAYER

HYMN

Alone with none but thee, my God,
I journey on my way;
What need I fear, when thou art near,
O King of night and day?
More safe am I within thy hand,
Than if a host did round me stand.

My destined time is fixed by thee,
And Death doth know his hour.
Did warriors strong around me throng,
They could not stay his power;
No walls of stone can man defend
When thou thy messenger dost send.

My life I yield to thy decree,
And bow to thy control
In peaceful calm, for from thine arm
No power can wrest my soul.
Could earthly omens e'er appal
A man that heeds the heavenly call!

The child of God can fear no ill,
His chosen dread no foe;

284

We leave our fate with thee, and wait
Thy bidding when to go.
'Tis not from chance our comfort springs,
Thou art our trust, O King of kings.

PSALMODY

Ant. 1: In the morning let me know your love, O Lord.

17–23 December: I look to you, Lord, for help; come and save me,
Lord, for I seek refuge in you.

Eastertide: For your name's sake, Lord, give me life, alleluia.

PRAYER IN DESOLATION   PSALM 142(143):1-11

*A man is made righteous not by obedience to the Law, but by faith
in Jesus Christ* (Gal 2:16)

Lórd, lísten to my práyer:†
túrn your éar to my appéal.*
You are fáithful, you are júst; give ánswer.
Do not cáll your sérvant to júdgment*
for nó one is júst in your síght.

The enémy pursúes my sóul;*
he has crúshed my life to the gróund;
he has máde me dwéll in dárkness*
like the déad, lóng forgótten.
Thérefore my spírit fáils;*
my héart is númb withín me.

I remémber the dáys that are pást:*
I pónder áll your wórks.
I múse on what your hánd has wróught†
and to yóu I strétch out my hánds.*
Like a párched land my sóul thirsts for yóu.

Lórd, make háste and ánswer;*
for my spírit fáils withín me.
Dó not híde your fáce*
lest I becóme like thóse in the gráve.

In the mórning let me knów your lóve*
for I pút my trúst in yóu.
Make me knów the wáy I should wálk:*
to yóu I lift up my sóul.

Réscue me, Lórd, from my énemies;*
I have fléd to yóu for réfuge.
Téach me to dó your wíll*
for yóu, O Lórd, are my Gód.
Let yóur good spírit guíde me*
in wáys that are lével and smóoth.

For your náme's sake, Lórd, save my lífe;*
in your jústice save my sóul from distréss.

Ant. In the morning let me know your love, O Lord.
17–23 December: I look to you, Lord, for help; come and save me,
Lord, for I seek refuge in you.
Eastertide: For your name's sake, Lord, give me life, alleluia.

Ant. 2: The Lord will send peace flowing like a river upon Jerusalem.
17–23 December: Lord, give those who wait for you their reward,
and let your prophets be found worthy of belief.
Eastertide: I will see you again, and then your hearts will be filled
with joy, alleluia.

CONSOLATION AND JOY   CANTICLE
IN THE HOLY CITY   IS 66:10-14A
The Jerusalem which is above is free and is our mother (Gal 4:26)

Rejoice with Jerusalem, and be glad for her,*
all you who love her;
rejoice with her in joy,*
all you who mourn over her,

That you may suck and be satisfied*
with her consoling breasts,
that you may drink deeply with delight*
from the abundance of her glory.

For thus says the Lord:†
Behold, I will extend prosperity to her like a river,*
and the wealth of the nations like an overflowing stream;
and you shall suck, you shall be carried upon her hip,*
and dandled upon her knees.

As one whom his mother comforts,†
so I will comfort you;*
you shall be comforted in Jerusalem.
You shall see, and your heart shall rejoice;*
your bones shall flourish like the grass.

Ant. The Lord will send peace flowing like a river upon Jerusalem.
17–23 December: Lord, give those who wait for you their reward,
and let your prophets be found worthy of belief.
Eastertide: I will see you again, and then your hearts will be filled
with joy, alleluia.

Ant. 3: To our God be joyful praise.
17–23 December: Turn to us, Lord, and make no delay in coming to
your servants.
Eastertide: The Lord builds up Jerusalem, he heals the broken-
hearted, alleluia.

THE POWER AND GOODNESS OF THE LORD   PSALM 146(147)
You, O God, we worship; you, O Lord, we adore

Praise the Lórd for hé is góod;†
sing to our Gód for hé is lóving:*
to hím our práise is dúe.

The Lórd buílds up Jerúsalem*
and bríngs back Ísrael's éxiles,
he héals the bróken-héarted,*
he bínds up áll their wóunds.
He fíxes the númber of the stárs;*
he cálls each óne by its náme.

Our Lórd is gréat and almíghty;*

287

his wísdom can néver be méasured.
The Lórd ráises the lówly;*
he húmbles the wícked to the dúst.
O síng to the Lórd, giving thánks;*
sing psálms to our Gód with the hárp.

He cóvers the héavens with clóuds;*
he prepáres the ráin for the éarth,
making móuntains spróut with gráss*
and with plánts to sérve man's néeds.
He provídes the béasts with their fóod*
and young rávens that cáll upón him.

His delíght is nót in hórses*
nor his pléasure in wárriors' stréngth.
The Lórd delights in thóse who revére him,*
in thóse who wáit for his lóve.

Ant. To our God be joyful praise.
17–23 December: Turn to us, Lord, and make no delay in coming to
your servants.
Eastertide: The Lord builds up Jerusalem, he heals the broken-
hearted, alleluia.

THROUGH THE YEAR

Scripture Reading   *Rom 8:18-21*
I consider that the sufferings of this present time are not worth
comparing with the glory that is to be revealed to us. For the
creation waits with eager longing for the revealing of the sons of
God; for the creation was subjected to futility, not of its own will
but by the will of him who subjected it in hope; because the creation
itself will be set free from its bondage to decay and obtain the
glorious liberty of the children of God.

Short Responsory
R/ Early in the morning I will think of you, O Lord. *Repeat* R/
V/ You have been my help. R/ Glory be. R/

Benedictus ant. Give your people knowledge of salvation, Lord, and
forgive us our sins.

Intercessions

It is the Father's will that men should see him in the face of his beloved Son. Let us honour him as we say: ℟ Hallowed be your name.

Christ greeted us with good news:—may the world hear it through us, and find hope. ℟

We praise and thank you, Lord of heaven and earth;—you are the hope and joy of men in every age. ℟

May Christ's coming transform the Church;—and renew its youth and vigour in the service of men. ℟

We pray for Christians who suffer for their belief:—sustain them in their hope. ℟

Our Father

Concluding Prayer

Grant us, Lord, a true knowledge of salvation,
so that, freed from fear and from the power of our foes,
we may serve you faithfully,
all the days of our life.
(We make our prayer) through our Lord.

EVENING PRAYER

HYMN

Blest are the pure in heart,
For they shall see our God;
The secret of the Lord is theirs,
Their soul is Christ's abode.

The Lord, who left the heavens,
Our life and peace to bring,
To dwell in lowliness with men,
Their pattern and their King:

Still to the lowly soul
He does himself impart,
And for his dwelling and his throne
Chooses the pure in heart.

Lord, we thy presence seek;
May ours this blessing be;
Give us a pure and lowly heart,
A temple fit for thee.

PSALMODY

Ant. 1: The Lord is my love and my refuge; in him I place my trust
17–23 December: I look to you, Lord, for help; come and save me,
Lord, for I seek refuge in you.
Eastertide: The Lord is my stronghold and my saviour, alleluia.

FOR VICTORY AND PEACE   PSALM 143(144)
*His arms are well trained for battle, since he has overcome the world,
for he says, 'I have overcome the world'* (St Hilary)

I

Bléssed be the Lórd, my róck†
who tráins my árms for báttle,*
who prepáres my hánds for wár.

Hé is my lóve, my fórtress;*
hé is my strónghold, my sáviour,
my shíeld, my pláce of réfuge.*
He brings péoples únder my rúle.

Lórd, what is mán that you cáre for him,*
mortal mán, that you kéep him in mínd;
mán, who is mérely a bréath*
whose life fádes like a shádow?

Lówer your héavens and come dówn;*
touch the móuntains; wréathe them in smóke.
Flash your líghtnings; róut the fóe,*
shoot your árrows and pút them to flíght.

Reach dówn from héaven and sáve me;†
draw me óut from the míghty wáters,*
from the hánds of álien fócs
whose móuths are fílled with líes,*
whose hánds are ráised in pérjury.

290

Ant. The Lord is my love and my refuge; in him I place my trust.

17–23 December: I look to you, Lord, for help; come and save me, Lord, for I seek refuge in you.

Eastertide: The Lord is my stronghold and my saviour, alleluia.

Ant. 2: Blessed the people whose God is the Lord.

17–23 December: Lord, give those who wait for you their reward, and let your prophets be found worthy of belief.

Eastretide: Thanks be to God, who has given us the victory through our Lord, Jesus Christ, alleluia.

II

To you, O Gód, will I síng a new sóng;*
I will pláy on the tén-stringed hárp
to yóu who give kíngs their víctory,*
who set Dávid your sérvant frée.

You set him frée from the évil swórd;*
you réscued him from álien fóes
whose móuths were fílled with líes,*
whose hánds were ráised in pérjury.

Let our sóns then flóurish like sáplings*
grown táll and stróng from their yóuth:
our dáughters gráceful as cólumns,*
adórned as thóugh for a pálace.

Let our bárns be fílled to overflówing*
with cróps of évery kínd;
our shéep incréasing by thóusands,†
mýriads of shéep in our fíelds,*
our cáttle héavy with yóung,

no rúined wáll, no éxile,*
no sóund of wéeping in our stréets.
Háppy the péople with such bléssings;*
happy the péople whose Gód is the Lórd.

Ant. Blessed the people whose God is the Lord.

17–23 December: Lord, give those who wait for you their reward,

and let your prophets be found worthy of belief.
Eastertide: Thanks be to God, who has given us the victory through
our Lord, Jesus Christ, alleluia.

Ant. 3: Victory and empire have now been won by our God.
17–23 December: Turn to us, Lord, and make no delay in coming to
your servants.
Eastertide: Jesus Christ is the same yesterday, today and for ever,
alleluia.

THE JUDGMENT OF GOD

CANTICLE
REV 11:17-18;12:10B-12A

We give thanks to you, Lord God Almighty,*
who are and who were,
that you have taken your great power*
and begun to reign.

The nations raged,*
but your wrath came,
and the time for the dead to be judged,*
for rewarding your servants, the prophets and saints,
and those who fear your name,*
both small and great.

Now the salvation and the power†
and the kingdom of our God *
and the authority of his Christ have come,
for the accuser of our brethren has been thrown down,*
who accuses them day and night before our God.

And they have conquered him*
by the blood of the Lamb
and by the word of their testimony,*
for they loved not their lives even unto death.
Rejoice, then, O heaven,*
and you that dwell therein.

Ant. Victory and empire have now been won by our God.

292

17–23 December: Turn to us, Lord, and make no delay in coming to your servants.

Eastertide: Jesus Christ is the same yesterday, today and for ever, alleluia.

THROUGH THE YEAR

Scripture Reading   *Cf Col 1:23*

You must, of course, continue faithful on a sure and firm foundation, and not allow yourselves to be shaken from the hope you gained when you heard the gospel which has been preached to everybody in the world.

Short Responsory

℟ The Lord is my shepherd; there is nothing I shall want. *Repeat* ℟
℣ Fresh and green are the pastures where he gives me repose. ℟
Glory be. ℟

Magnificat ant. The Lord has satisfied and filled with good things those who hungered for justice.

Intercessions

The light shines out in the darkness and the darkness cannot overcome it. Let us thank our Lord for bringing his light to our lives.
℟ Lord Jesus Christ, you are our light.

Word of God, you have brought the light of eternity to the darkened world:—may it open the minds and hearts of all the children of the Church. ℟

Show your care for all who dedicate their lives to the service of others:—may your grace inspire their actions and sustain them to the end. ℟

Lord, you healed the paralytic and forgave him his sins:—pardon all our guilt, and heal the wounds of our sins. ℟

Men follow the light to new knowledge and discovery:—may they use your gifts to serve the whole human family, and so give glory to you. ℟

Lead the dead from darkness into your own wonderful light;—in your mercy show them the radiance of your glory. ℟

Our Father

293

Concluding Prayer
Listen favourably to our evening prayer, Lord,
and grant that as we follow your Son's example,
we may, by perseverance, yield a harvest of good works.
(We make our prayer) through our Lord.

WEEK 4: FRIDAY

Invitatory ant. Indeed, how good is the Lord; bless his holy name.
Psalm, p 3.

MORNING PRAYER

HYMN

I am the holy vine,
Which God my Father tends.
Each branch that yields no fruit
My Father cuts away.
Each fruitful branch
He prunes with care
To make it yield
Abundant fruit.

If you abide in me,
I will in you abide,
Each branch to yield its fruit
Must with the vine be one.
So you shall fail
To yield your fruit
If you are not
With me one vine.

I am the fruitful vine,
And you my branches are.
He who abides in me
I will in him abide.

294

So shall you yield
Much fruit, but none
If you remain
Apart from me.

PSALMODY

Int. 1: A pure heart create for me, O God, put a steadfast spirit within me.

7-23 December: The one who is to rule will come from Sion: 'The Lord, Immanuel' is his great name.

Eastertide: Christ gave himself up for us as a fragrant offering and a sacrifice to God, alleluia.

O GOD, HAVE MERCY ON ME   PSALM 50(51)
You must be made new in mind and spirit, and put on the new nature (Eph 4:23-24)

Have mércy on me, Gód, in your kíndness.*
In your compássion blot óut my offénce.
O wásh me more and móre from my guílt*
and cléanse me fróm my sín.

My offénces trúly I knów them;*
my sín is álways befóre me.
Against yóu, you alóne, have I sínned;*
what is évil in your síght I have dóne.

That you may be jústified whén you give séntence*
and be withóut repróach when you júdge,
O sée, in guílt I was bórn,*
a sínner was Í concéived.

Indéed you love trúth in the héart;*
then in the sécret of my héart teach me wísdom.
O púrify me, thén I shall be cléan;*
O wásh me, I shall be whíter than snów.

Make me héar rejóicing and gládness,*
that the bónes you have crúshed may revíve.

295

From my síns turn awáy your fáce*
and blót out áll my guílt.

A púre heart creáte for me, O Gód,*
put a stéadfast spírit withín me.
Do not cást me awáy from your présence,*
nor depríve me of your hóly spírit.

Give me agáin the jóy of your hélp;*
with a spírit of férvour sustáin me,
that I may téach transgréssors your wáys*
and sínners may retúrn to yóu.

O réscue me, Gód, my hélper,*
and my tóngue shall ríng out your góodness.
O Lórd, ópen my líps*
and my móuth shall decláre your práise.

For in sácrifice you táke no delíght,*
burnt óffering from mé you would refúse,
my sácrifice, a cóntrite spírit.*
A húmbled, contrite héart you will not spúrn.

In your góodness, show fávour to Síon:*
rebuíld the wálls of Jerúsalem.
Thén you will be pléased with lawful sácrifice,*
hólocausts óffered on your áltar.

Ant. A pure heart create for me, O God, put a steadfast spirit within me.

17–23 December: The one who is to rule will come from Sion: 'The Lord, Immanuel' is his great name.

Eastertide: Christ gave himself up for us as a fragrant offering and a sacrifice to God, alleluia.

Ant. 2: Rejoice, O Jerusalem, since through you all men will be gathered together to the Lord.

17–23 December: Stand steadfast. You will see the helping power of the Lord.

Eastertide: Jerusalem, city of God, you will be radiant with light, alleluia.

THANKSGIVING FROM A LIBERATED PEOPLE   CANTICLE
                                                        TOB 13:8-11,13-15

*He showed me the holy city of Jerusalem and it had all the radiant
glory of God (Rev 21:10-11)*

Let all men speak,*
and give God thanks in Jerusalem.
O Jerusalem, the holy city,†
he will afflict you for the deeds of your sons,*
but again he will show mercy to the sons of the righteous.

Give thanks worthily to the Lord,†
and praise the King of the ages,*
that his tent may be raised for you again with joy.

May he cheer those within you who are captives,†
and love those within you who are distressed,*
to all generations for ever.

Many nations will come from afar*
to the name of the Lord God,
bearing gifts in their hands,*
gifts for the King of heaven.
Generations of generations*
will give you joyful praise.

Rejoice and be glad*
for the sons of the righteous,
for they will be gathered together,*
and will praise the Lord of the righteous.

How blessed are those who love you!*
They will rejoice in your peace.
Blessed are those who grieved*
over all your afflictions,
for they will rejoice for you upon seeing all your glory,†
and they will be made glad for ever.*

Let my soul praise God the great King!

Ant. Rejoice, O Jerusalem, since through you all men will b⌐
gathered together to the Lord.

17-23 December: Stand steadfast. You will see the helping power o⌐
the Lord.

Eastertide: Jerusalem, city of God, you will be radiant with light
alleluia.

Ant. 3: Sion, praise your God, who has sent out his word to the
earth.

17-23 December: I look to the Lord; I will await the God who saves
me.

Eastertide: I saw the new Jerusalem, coming down from heaven,
alleluia.

THE RENEWAL OF JERUSALEM   PSALM 147
Come, and I will show you the bride that the Lamb has married
(Rev 21:9)

O práise the Lórd, Jerúsalem!*
Síon, práise your Gód!

He has stréngthened the bárs of your gátes,*
he has bléssed the chíldren withín you.
He estáblished péace on your bórders,*
he féeds you with fínest whéat.

He sénds out his wórd to the éarth*
and swíftly rúns his commánd.
He shówers down snów white as wóol,*
he scátters hóar-frost like áshes.

He húrls down háilstones like crúmbs.*
The wáters are frózen at his tóuch;
he sénds forth his wórd and it mélts them:*
at the bréath of his móuth the waters flów.

He mákes his wórd known to Jácob,*
to Ísrael his láws and decrées.
He has not déalt thus with óther nátions;*
he has not táught them hís decrées.

Ant. Sion, praise your God, who has sent out his word to the earth.

17–23 December: I look to the Lord; I will await the God who saves me.

Eastertide: I saw the new Jerusalem, coming down from heaven, alleluia.

THROUGH THE YEAR

Scripture Reading   *Gal 2:19b-20*

With Christ I hang upon the cross, and yet I am alive; or rather, not I; it is Christ that lives in me. True, I am living, here and now, this mortal life; but my real life is the faith I have in the Son of God, who loved me, and gave himself for me.

Short Responsory

R̸ I call to the Lord, the Most High, for he has been my help. *Repeat* R̸

V̸ May he send from heaven and save me. R̸ Glory be. R̸

Benedictus ant. Through the loving mercy of our God, the Rising Sun has come to visit us.

Intercessions

Christ is the image of the unseen God, the first-born of all creation, and the first to be born from the dead. All things are to be reconciled through him because he made peace by his death on the cross. We pray to him: R̸ Lord Jesus, come to us today.

We have been baptized into your death:—may we be cleansed of greed and envy, and clothed in the strength and gentleness of your love. R̸

We have been sealed with the Holy Spirit who has been given to us; —confirm us in your service, and help us to bear witness to you in the society in which we live. R̸

Before you suffered, you longed to eat the passover with your disciples:—as we take part in your eucharist, may we share in your resurrection. R̸

You continue to work in your faithful people:—create through them a new world where injustice and destruction will give way to growth, freedom and hope. R̸

Our Father

Concluding Prayer
Lord God,
bestow a full measure of your grace on us
who are gathered here in prayer.
As you work within us
to keep us in the path of your commandments,
may we receive consolation in this present life
and eternal joys in the next.
(We make our prayer) through our Lord.

EVENING PRAYER

HYMN

Day is done, but Love unfailing
Dwells ever here;
Shadows fall, but hope, prevailing,
Calms every fear.
Loving Father, none forsaking,
Take our hearts, of Love's own making,
Watch our sleeping, guard our waking,
Be always near!

Dark descends, but Light unending
Shines through our night;
You are with us, ever lending
New strength to sight;
One in love, your truth confessing,
One in hope of heaven's blessing,
May we see, in love's possessing,
Love's endless light!

PSALMODY

Ant. 1: I will bless you day after day and tell of your wonderful
deeds, O Lord.
17–23 December: The one who is to rule will come from Sion: 'The
Lord, Immanuel' is his great name.

Eastertide: God so loved the world that he gave his only Son, alleluia.

PRAISE OF GOD'S MAJESTY PSALM 144(145)
You, O Lord, are the One who was and who is, the Just One (Rev 16:5)

I

I will give you glóry, O Gód my Kíng,*
I will bléss your náme for éver.

I will bléss you dáy after dáy*
and práise your náme for éver.
The Lord is gréat, híghly to be práised,*
his gréatness cánnot be méasured.

Age to áge shall procláim your wórks,*
shall decláre your míghty déeds,
shall spéak of your spléndour and glóry,*
tell the tále of your wónderful wórks.

They will spéak of your térrible déeds,*
recóunt your gréatness and míght.
They will recáll your abúndant góodness;*
age to áge shall ríng out your jústice.

The Lord is kínd and fúll of compássion,*
slow to ánger, abóunding in lóve.
How góod is the Lord to áll,*
compássionate to áll his créatures.

All your créatures shall thánk you, O Lórd,*
and your fríends shall repéat their bléssing.
They shall spéak of the glóry of your réign*
and decláre your míght, O Gód,

to make knówn to mén your mighty déeds*
and the glórious spléndour of your réign.
Yóurs is an éverlasting kíngdom;*
your rúle lasts from áge to áge.

(Glory be)

Ant. I will bless you day after day and tell of your wonderful deeds, O Lord.

17–23 December: The one who is to rule will come from Sion: 'The Lord, Immanuel' is his great name.

Eastertide: God so loved the world that he gave his only Son, alleluia.

Ant. 2: The eyes of all creatures look to you, Lord; you are close to all who call upon you.

17–23 December: Stand steadfast. You will see the helping power of the Lord.

Eastertide: To the eternal King, the undying, invisible and only God, be all honour and glory, alleluia.

II

The Lord is fáithful in áll his wórds*
and lóving in áll his déeds.
The Lórd suppórts all who fáll*
and ráises áll who are bowed dówn.

The éyes of all créatures look to yóu*
and you gíve them their fóod in due tíme.
You ópen wíde your hánd,*
grant the desíres of áll who líve.

The Lord is júst in áll his wáys*
and lóving in áll his déeds.
He is clóse to áll who cáll him,*
who cáll on hím from their héarts.

He gránts the desíres of those who féar him,*
he héars their crý and he sáves them.
The Lórd protécts all who lóve him;*
but the wícked he will útterly destróy.

Let me spéak the práise of the Lórd,†
let all mankínd bléss his holy náme*
for éver, for áges unénding.

Ant. The eyes of all creatures look to you, Lord; you are close to all who call upon you.

17–23 December: Stand steadfast. You will see the helping power of the Lord.

Eastertide: To the eternal King, the undying, invisible and only God, be all honour and glory, alleluia.

Ant. 3: Your ways are just and true, King of all the ages.

17–23 December: I look to the Lord; I will await the God who saves me.

Eastertide: The Lord is my strength and protection, he is my salvation, alleluia.

HYMN OF ADORATION   CANTICLE: REV 15:3-4

> Great and wonderful are your deeds,*
> O Lord God the Almighty!
> Just and true are your ways,*
> O King of the ages!
>
> Who shall not fear and glorify your name, O Lord?*
> For you alone are holy.
> All nations shall come and worship you,*
> for your judgments have been revealed.

Ant. Your ways are just and true, King of all the ages.

17–23 December: I look to the Lord; I will await the God who saves me.

Eastertide: The Lord is my strength and protection, he is my salvation, alleluia.

THROUGH THE YEAR

Scripture Reading   *Rom 8:1-2*
There is now no condemnation for those who are in Christ Jesus. For the law of the Spirit of life in Christ Jesus has set me free from the law of sin and death.

Short Responsory

R̸ Christ died for our sins, that he might offer us to God. *Repeat* R̸
V̸ In the body he was put to death, in the spirit he was raised to life.
R̸ Glory be. R̸

Magnificat ant. Remember your mercy, O Lord; according to the promise you made to our fathers.

Intercessions

God's love for us was revealed when God sent into the world his only Son so that we might have life through him. We are able to love God because he loved us first. And so we pray: R̸ Lord, help us to love you and to love one another.

Jesus forgave the penitent woman her sins because she had loved much;—may we too know his healing touch and love you with all our hearts. R̸

You look with compassion on the humble and contrite of heart:—in your goodness, turn our hearts to you and help us to do what we know to be right. R̸

We acknowledge the suffering we have caused to others:—we ask forgiveness for our neglect and indifference. R̸

We ask you to remember tonight those who are in great difficulty: give new heart to those who have lost their faith in man and in God, to those who seek the truth but cannot find it. R̸

Remember all those who put their hope in you while they lived:—through the passion and death of your Son, grant them the remission of all their sins. R̸

Our Father

Concluding Prayer

God of power and mercy,
who willed that Christ your Son should suffer for the salvation of all
   the world,
grant that your people may strive to offer themselves to you as a
   living sacrifice,
and may be filled with the fulness of your love.
(We make our prayer) through our Lord.

WEEK 4: SATURDAY

Invitatory ant. Let us listen for the voice of the Lord and enter into his peace.
Psalm, p 3.

MORNING PRAYER

HYMN

Sing, all creation, sing to God in gladness!
Joyously serve him, singing hymns of homage!
Chanting his praises, come before his presence!
    Praise the Almighty!

Know that our God is Lord of all the ages!
He is our maker; we are all his creatures,
People he fashioned, sheep he leads to pasture!
    Praise the Almighty!

Great in his goodness is the Lord we worship;
Steadfast his kindness, love that knows no ending!
Faithful his word is, changeless, everlasting!
    Praise the Almighty!

PSALMODY

Ant. 1: It is good to make music to your name, O Most High, to proclaim your love in the morning.
24 December: You, Bethlehem, will not be least among the towns of Juda: for the leader who will rule my people Israel will come from you.
Eastertide: O Lord, how great are your works, alleluia.

PRAISE OF THE LORD, CREATOR   PSALM 91(92)
The deeds of God's only Son are praised (St Athanasius)

It is góod to give thánks to the Lórd*

to make músic to your náme, O Most Hígh,
to procláim your lóve in the mórning*
and your trúth in the wátches of the níght,
on the tén-stringed lýre and the lúte,*
with the múrmuring sóund of the hárp.

Your déeds, O Lórd, have made me glád;*
for the wórk of your hánds I shout with jóy.
O Lórd, how gréat are your wórks!*
How déep are yóur desígns!
The fóolish man cánnot knów this*
and the fóol cánnot understánd.

Though the wícked spring úp like gráss*
and áll who do évil thríve,
they are dóomed to be etérnally destróyed.*
But yóu, Lord, are etérnally on hígh.
Sée how your énemies pérish;*
all dóers of évil are scáttered.

To mé you give the wíld-ox's stréngth;*
you anóint me with the púrest óil.
My éyes looked in tríumph on my fóes;*
my éars heard gládly of their fáll.
The júst will flóurish like the pálm-tree*
and grów like a Lébanon cédar.

Plánted in the hóuse of the Lórd*
they will flóurish in the cóurts of our Gód,
still bearing frúit when they are óld,*
still full of sáp, still gréen,
to procláim that the Lórd is júst.*
In hím, my róck, there is no wróng.

Ant. It is good to make music to your name, O Most High, to proclaim your love in the morning.
24 December: You, Bethlehem, will not be least among the towns of Juda: for the leader who will rule my people Israel will come from you.
Eastertide: O Lord, how great are your works, alleluia.

Ant. 2: I will give you a new heart, and put a new spirit in you.
24 December: Lift up your heads for your redemption is at hand.
Eastertide: I will pour purifying water over you, alleluia.

THE LORD WILL GIVE HIS PEOPLE NEW LIFE CANTICLE
EZEK 36:24-28

They shall be his people, and he will be their God; his name is God-with-them (Rev 21:3)

I will take you from the nations,†
and gather you from all the countries,*
and bring you into your own land.

I will sprinkle clean water upon you,†
and you shall be clean from all your uncleannesses,*
and from all your idols I will cleanse you.

A new heart I will give you,*
and a new spirit I will put within you;
and I will take out of your flesh the heart of stone*
and give you a heart of flesh.

And I will put my spirit within you,†
and cause you to walk in my statutes*
and be careful to observe my ordinances.

You shall dwell in the land*
which I gave to your fathers;
and you shall be my people,*
and I will be your God.

Ant. I will give you a new heart, and put a new spirit in you.
24 December: Lift up your heads for your redemption is at hand.
Eastertide: I will pour purifying water over you, alleluia.

Ant. 3: On the lips of children and of babes you have found praise, Lord.
24 December: Tomorrow your salvation will be with you, says the Lord, God almighty.

307

Eastertide: All things are yours, and you are Christ's and Christ is God's, alleluia.

THE MAJESTY OF GOD, THE DIGNITY OF MAN   PSALM 8
He has put all things under his feet, and appointed him to be head of the whole Church (Eph 1:22)

How gréat is your náme, O Lórd our Gód,*
through áll the éarth!

Your májesty is práised above the héavens;*
on the líps of chíldren and of bábes
you have found práise to fóil your énemy,*
to sílence the fóe and the rébel.

When I see the héavens, the wórk of your hánds,*
the móon and the stárs which you arránged,
what is mán that you should kéep him in mínd,*
mortal mán that you cáre for hím?

Yet you have máde him little léss than a gód;*
with glóry and hónour you crówned him,
gave him pówer over the wórks of your hánd,*
put áll things únder his féet.

Áll of them, shéep and cáttle,*
yes, éven the sávage béasts,
bírds of the aír, and físh*
that máke their wáy through the wáters.

How gréat is your náme, O Lórd our Gód,*
through áll the éarth!

Ant. On the lips of children and of babes you have found praise, Lord.
24 December: Tomorrow your salvation will be with you, says the Lord, God almighty.
Eastertide: All things are yours, and you are Christ's and Christ is God's, alleluia.

Scripture Reading   *2 Pet 3:13-14*

What we are waiting for is what he promised: the new heavens and new earth, the place where righteousness will be at home. So then, my friends, while you are waiting, do your best to live lives without spot or stain so that he will find you at peace. Think of our Lord's patience as your opportunity to be saved.

Short Responsory

Ry When I sing to you my lips shall rejoice. *Repeat* Ry

Vy My tongue shall tell the tale of your justice. Ry Glory be. Ry

Benedictus ant. Lord, guide our feet into the way of peace.

Intercessions

God's gift was not a spirit of timidity, but the Spirit of power and love, and self-control. With complete confidence we pray: Ry Father, send us your Spirit.

Praise be to God, the Father of our Lord Jesus Christ:—in Christ you have given us every spiritual blessing. Ry

By the power of the Holy Spirit, Mary brought Christ into the world:—through the Church, may Christ be born again today in the hearts of men. Ry

Father, may your Spirit lead us forward out of solitude:—may he lead us to open the eyes of the blind, to proclaim the Word of light, to reap together the harvest of life. Ry

Let our striving for your kingdom not fall short through selfishness or fear:—may the universe be alive with the Spirit, and our homes be the pledge of a world redeemed. Ry

Our Father

Concluding Prayer

All-powerful, eternal God,
splendour of true light and never-ending day:
at this return of the morning hour
chase away the night of sin,
and fill our minds with the glory of your coming.
(We make our prayer) through our Lord.

NIGHT PRAYER

HYMNS FOR NIGHT PRAYER

109 Christ, the true light of us, true morn,
Dispersing far the shades of night,
Light whereof every light is born,
Pledge of the beatific light,

Thou all the night our guardian be
Whose watch no sleep or slumber knows;
Thou be our peace, that stayed on thee
Through darkness we may find repose.

Sleep then our eyes, but never sleep
The watchful heaven-directed heart,
And may thy hand in safety keep
The servants whose desire thou art.

Look on us, thou, and at our side
Our foes and thine repulse afar;
Through every ill the faithful guide
Who in thy blood redeemèd are.

While soul within the body clings,
Body and soul defend us, Lord,
Sure in the shadow of thy wings,
Kept in thy lasting watch and ward.

8TH CENTURY
TR W. H. SHEWRING

110 Now it is evening; time to cease from labour,
Father, according to thy will and pleasure,
Through the night-season, have thy faithful people
Safe in thy keeping.

Far from our dwellings drive the evil spirits;
Under the shadow of thy wings protect us;
Be thou our guardian through the hours of darkness,
Strong to defend us.

310

Call we, ere sleeping, on the name of Jesus;
Rise we at day-break, strong to serve thee better;
Order our doings, well begun and ended,
All to thy glory.

Fountain of goodness, bless the sick and needy;
Visit the captive, solace the afflicted;
Shelter the stranger, feed your starving children;
Strengthen the dying.

Father, who neither slumberest nor sleepest,
Thou, to whom darkness is as clear as noonday,
Have us this night-time, for the sake of Jesus,
Safe in thy keeping.

P. HERBERT D. 1571
TR G. R. WOODWARD 1848–1934
AND COMPILERS OF *The BBC Hymn Book*

III Lead, kindly Light, amid the encircling gloom,
Lead thou me on;
The night is dark, and I am far from home,
Lead thou me on.
Keep thou my feet; I do not ask to see
The distant scene; one step enough for me.

I was not ever thus, nor prayed that thou
Shouldst lead me on;
I loved to choose and see my path; but now
Lead thou me on.
I loved the garish day, and, spite of fears,
Pride ruled my will: remember not past years.

So long thy power hath blest me, sure it still
Will lead me on
O'er moor and fen, o'er crag and torrent, till
The night is gone,
And with the morn those Angel faces smile,
Which I have loved long since, and lost awhile.

J. H. NEWMAN 1801–90

112 Abide with me; fast falls the eventide;
   The darkness deepens; Lord, with me abide;
   When other helpers fail, and comforts flee,
   Help of the helpless, O abide with me.

   Swift to its close ebbs out life's little day:
   Earth's joys grow dim, its glories pass away;
   Change and decay in all around I see;
   O thou who changest not, abide with me.

   Hold thou thy Cross before my closing eyes;
   Shine through the gloom, and point me to the skies;
   Heaven's morning breaks, and earth's vain shadows flee;
   In life, in death, O Lord, abide with me.

H. F. LYTE 1793–1847

113 The day thou gavest, Lord, is ended.
   The darkness falls at thy behest,
   To thee our morning hymns ascended,
   Thy praise shall sanctify our rest.

   We thank thee that thy Church unsleeping,
   While earth rolls onward into light,
   Through all the world her watch is keeping,
   And rests not now by day or night.

   As over continent and island
   The dawn leads on another day,
   The voice of prayer is never silent,
   Nor dies the strain of praise away.

   The sun that bids us rest is waking
   Our brethren 'neath the western sky,
   And hour by hour fresh lips are making
   Thy wondrous doings heard on high.

   So be it, Lord, thy throne shall never,
   Like earth's proud empires, pass away;
   Thy kingdom stands, and grows for ever,
   Till all thy creatures own thy sway.

J. ELLERTON 1826–93

114 Now thank we all our God,
With heart and hands and voices,
Who wondrous things hath done,
In whom his world rejoices;
Who from our mother's arms
Hath blessed us on our way
With countless gifts of love,
And still is ours today.

O may this bounteous God
Through all our life be near us,
With ever joyful hearts
And blessèd peace to cheer us;
And keep us in his grace,
And guide us when perplexed,
And free us from all ills
In this world and the next.

All praise and thanks to God
The Father now be given,
The Son, and him who reigns
With them in highest heaven,
The one eternal God,
Whom earth and heaven adore;
For thus it was, is now,
And shall be evermore.

M. RINKART 1586–1649
TR C. WINKWORTH 1829–78

313

115 Lord of all hopefulness, Lord of all joy,
　　Whose trust, ever childlike, no care could destroy,
　　Be there at our waking, and give us, we pray,
　　Your bliss in our hearts, Lord, at the break of the day.

　　Lord of all eagerness, Lord of all faith,
　　Whose strong hands were skilled at the plane and the lathe
　　Be there at our labours, and give us, we pray,
　　Your strength in our hearts, Lord, at the noon of the day.

　　Lord of all kindliness, Lord of all grace,
　　Your hands swift to welcome, your arms to embrace,
　　Be there at our homing, and give us, we pray,
　　Your love in our hearts, Lord, at the eve of the day.

　　Lord of all gentleness, Lord of all calm,
　　Whose voice is contentment, whose presence is balm,
　　Be there at our sleeping, and give us, we pray,
　　Your peace in our hearts, Lord, at the end of the day.

JAN STRUTHER 1901-53

116 Sweet Saviour, bless us e'er we go,
　　Thy word into our minds instil,
　　And make our lukewarm hearts to glow
　　With lowly love and fervent will.
　　Through life's long day and death's dark night,
　　O gentle Jesus, be our light.

　　The day is done, its hours have run,
　　And thou hast taken count of all,
　　The scanty triumphs grace hath won,
　　The broken vow, the frequent fall.
　　Through life's long day and death's dark night,
　　O gentle Jesus, be our light.

　　For all we love, the poor, the sad,
　　The sinful,—unto thee we call;
　　O let thy mercy make us glad;
　　Thou art our Jesus and our All.
　　Through life's long day and death's dark night,
　　O gentle Jesus, be our light.　　　　　　F. W. FABER 1814-63

FINAL ANTHEMS
TO THE BLESSED VIRGIN MARY

117 Alma Redemptóris Mater, quae pérvia caeli
Porta manes, et stella maris, succúrre cadénti,
Surgere qui curat, pópulo: tu quae genuísti,
Natúra miránte, tuum sanctum Genitórem,
Virgo prius ac postérius, Gabriélis ab ore
Sumens illud Ave, peccatórum miserére.

118 Mother of Christ! hear thou thy people's cry,
Star of the deep, and portal of the sky!
Mother of him who thee from nothing made,
Sinking we strive, and call to thee for aid:
Oh, by that joy which Gabriel brought to thee,
Thou Virgin first and last, let us thy mercy see.

119 Ave Regína caelórum!
Ave, Dómina angelórum;
Salve radix, salve porta
Ex qua mundo lux est orta.
Gaude, Virgo gloriósa,
Super omnes speciósa.
Vale, O valde decóra!
Et pro nobis Christum exóra.

120 Hail, Queen of Heaven, beyond compare,
To whom the angels homage pay;
Hail, Root of Jesse, Gate of Light,
That opened for the world's new Day.

Rejoice, O Virgin unsurpassed,
In whom our ransom was begun,
For all your loving children pray
To Christ, our Saviour, and your Son.

STANBROOK ABBEY

315

121 Regína caeli, laetáre! allelúia.
Quia quem meruísti portáre, allelúia.
Resurréxit sicut dixit; allelúia.
Ora pro nobis Deum; allelúia.

122 Joy fill your heart, O Queen most high, alleluia!
Your Son who in the tomb did lie, alleluia!
Has risen as he did prophesy, alleluia!
Pray for us, Mother, when we die, alleluia!
Alleluia, alleluia, alleluia!

JAMES QUINN SJ

or

123 Queen of heaven, rejoice, alleluia!
for he whom you were worthy to bear, alleluia!
has risen as he said, alleluia!
Pray for us to God, alleluia!

124 Salve, Regína, Mater misericórdiae;
vita, dulcédo, et spes nostra, salve.
Ad te clamámus, éxsules fílii Hevae,
ad te suspirámus, geméntes et flentes
in hac lacrimárum valle.
Eia, ergo, advocáta nostra, illos tuos
misericórdes óculos ad nos convérte;
et Iesum, benedíctum fructum ventris tui,
nobis post hoc exílium osténde.
O clemens, O pia, O dulcis Virgo María.

125 Hail, our Queen and Mother blest!
Joy when all was sadness,
Life and hope you gave mankind,
Mother of our gladness!
Children of the sinful Eve,
Sinless-Eve, befriend us,
Exiled in this vale of tears:
Strength and comfort send us!

316

Pray for us, O Patroness,
Be our consolation!
Lead us home to see your Son,
Jesus, our salvation!
Gracious are you, full of grace,
Loving as none other,
Joy of heaven and joy of earth,
Mary, God's own Mother!

126 O sanctíssima, O piíssima,
Dulcis virgo María!
Mater amáta, intemeráta,
Ora, ora pro nobis.

Tu solácium et refúgium,
Virgo, mater María!
Quidquid optamus, per te sperámus;
Ora, ora pro nobis.

Ecce débiles, perquam flébiles,
Salva nos, O María!
Tolle languóres, sana dolóres,
Ora, ora pro nobis.

Virgo réspice, Mater, ádspice,
Audi nos, O María.
Tu medicínam portas divínam,
Ora, ora pro nobis.

Tua gáudia et suspíria
Iuvent nos, O María!
In te sperámus, ad te clamámus,
Ora, ora pro nobis.

317

127 O most holy one, O most pitiful, O sweet Virgin Mary!
Mother best beloved, Mother undefiled, pray for us!

Thou art our comfort, and our refuge, Virgin Mother Mary!
All that we long for, through thee we hope for; Pray for us!

See how weak we are, lost in tears; save us, O Mary!
Lighten our anguish; soothe our sorrows; pray for us!

Virgin, turn and look; Mother behold us; hear us, O Mary!
Thou art the bearer of health divine; pray for us!

May thy joys and thy sorrows be our help, O Mary!
In thee we hope; to thee we cry; pray for us!

NIGHT PRAYER

AFTER EVENING PRAYER I OF SUNDAYS AND SOLEMNITIES

℣ O God, come to our aid . . .

Here an examination of conscience is commended. In a common celebration this may be inserted in a penitential act using the formulas given in the Missal.

Hymn

A hymn suitable to the Hour is here said.
A selection of such hymns, nos. 109–116 is given above, pp 310 ff.

PSALMODY

Ant. 1: Lord, have mercy and hear me.
Eastertide: Alleluia, alleluia, alleluia.

THANKSGIVING   PSALM 4
The Lord raised him from the dead and made him worthy of all admiration (St Augustine)

When I cáll, ánswer me, O Gód of jústice;*
from ánguish you reléased me, have mércy and héar me!

O mén, how lóng will your héarts be clósed,*
will you lóve what is fútile and séek what is fálse?

It is the Lórd who grants fávours to thóse whom he lóves;*
the Lórd héars me whenéver I cáll him.

Fear him; do not sín: pónder on your béd and be stíll.*
Make jústice your sácrifice and trúst in the Lórd.

'What can bríng us háppiness?' mány sáy.*
Let the líght of your fáce shíne on us, O Lórd.

You have pút into my héart a gréater jóy*
than théy have from abúndance of córn and new wíne.

319

I will líe down in péace and sléep comes at ónce*
for yóu alone, Lórd, make me dwéll in sáfety.

Ant. Lord, have mercy and hear me.
Ant. 2: Bless the Lord through the night.

EVENING PRAYER IN THE TEMPLE   PSALM 133(134)
*Praise our God, all you his servants, and all who revere him, both great
and small* (Rev 19:5)

O cóme, bléss the Lórd,*
all yóu who sérve the Lórd,
who stánd in the hóuse of the Lórd,*
in the cóurts of the hóuse of our Gód.

Lift up your hánds to the hóly pláce*
and bléss the Lórd through the níght.

May the Lórd bléss you from Síon,*
he who máde both héaven and éarth.

Ant. Bless the Lord through the night.
Eastertide: Alleluia, alleluia, alleluia.

Scripture Reading   *Deut 6:4-7*
Hear, O Israel: the Lord our God is one Lord; and you shall love
the Lord your God with all your heart, and with all your soul, and
with all your might. And these words which I command you this
day shall be upon your heart; and you shall teach them diligently
to your children, and shall talk of them when you sit in your house,
and when you walk by the way, and when you lie down, and when
you rise.

Short Responsory
Outside Eastertide
R̲ Into your hands, Lord, I commend my spirit. *Repeat* R̲
V̲ You have redeemed us, Lord God of truth. R̲ Glory be. R̲

Easter Octave
This is the day which was made by the Lord: let us rejoice and be glad, alleluia.

Eastertide
℟ Into your hands, Lord, I commend my spirit, alleluia, alleluia.
Repeat ℟
℣ You have redeemed us, Lord God of truth. ℟ Glory be. ℟

Ant. Save us, Lord, while we are awake; protect us while we sleep; that we may keep watch with Christ and rest with him in peace (alleluia).

NUNC DIMITTIS   CANTICLE: LK 2:29-32
Christ is the light of the nations and the glory of Israel

At last, all-powerful Master,†
you give leave to your servant*
to go in peace, according to your promise.

For my eyes have seen your salvation*
Which you have prepared for all nations,
the light to enlighten the Gentiles*
and give glory to Israel, your people.

Ant. Save us, Lord, while we are awake; protect us while we sleep; that we may keep watch with Christ and rest with him in peace (alleluia).

Concluding Prayer
Sundays and Easter Octave
Come to visit us, Lord, this night,
so that by your strength we may rise at daybreak
to rejoice in the resurrection of Christ, your Son,
who lives and reigns for ever and ever.

Solemnities which do not occur on a Sunday
Visit this house, we pray you, Lord:
drive far away from it all the snares of the enemy.
May your holy angels stay here and guard us in peace,
and let your blessing be always upon us.
Through Christ our Lord.

Blessing
The Lord grant us a quiet night and a perfect end. ℟ Amen.

This concludes the Hour even in recitation on one's own.
Anthem to the Blessed Virgin, see pp 315 ff.

AFTER EVENING PRAYER II OF SUNDAYS AND SOLEMNITIES

All as above except the following.

PSALMODY

Ant. He will conceal you with his wings; you will not fear the terror of the night.
Eastertide: Alleluia, alleluia, alleluia.

IN THE SHELTER OF THE MOST HIGH   PSALM 90(91)
Behold, I have given you power to tread underfoot serpents and
scorpions (Lk 10:19)

He who dwélls in the shélter of the Most Hígh*
and abídes in the sháde of the Almíghty
sáys to the Lórd: 'My réfuge,*
my strónghold, my Gód in whom I trúst!'

It is hé who will frée you from the snáre*
of the fówler who séeks to destróy you;
hé will concéal you with his pínions*
and únder his wíngs you will find réfuge.

You will not féar the térror of the níght*
nor the árrow that flíes by dáy,

nor the plágue that prówls in the dárkness*
nor the scóurge that lays wáste at nóon.

A thóusand may fáll at your síde,*
tén thousand fáll at your ríght,
yóu, it will néver appróach;*
his fáithfulness is búckler and shíeld.

Your éyes have ónly to lóok*
to sée how the wícked are repáid,
yóu who have sáid: 'Lórd, my réfuge!'*
and have máde the Most Hígh your dwélling.

Upon yóu no évil shall fáll,*
no plágue appróach where you dwéll.
For yóu has he commánded his ángels,*
to kéep you in áll your wáys.

They shall béar you upón their hánds*
lest you stríke your fóot against a stóne.
On the líon and the víper you will tréad*
and trámple the young líon and the drágon.

Since he clíngs to me in lóve, I will frée him;*
protéct him for he knóws my náme.
When he cálls I shall ánswer: 'I am wíth you.'*
I will sáve him in distréss and give him glóry.

With léngth of life I will contént him;*
I shall lét him see my sáving pówer.

Ant. He will conceal you with his wings; you will not fear the terror
of the night.
Eastertide: Alleluia, alleluia, alleluia.

Scripture Reading   *Rev 22:4-5*
They will see the Lord face to face, and his name will be written on
their foreheads. It will never be night again and they will not need
lamplight or sunlight, because the Lord God will be shining on them.
They will reign for ever and ever.

Short Responsory
Outside Eastertide
℟ Into your hands, Lord, I commend my spirit. *Repeat* ℟
℣ You have redeemed us, Lord God of truth. ℟ Glory be. ℟

Easter Triduum
Christ humbled himself for us, and, in obedience, accepted death,
(*Good Friday, add:*) even death on a cross.
(*Holy Saturday, add further:*) Therefore God raised him to the
heights and gave him the name which is above all other names.

Easter Octave
This is the day which was made by the Lord: let us rejoice and be
glad, alleluia.

Eastertide
℟ Into your hands, Lord, I commend my spirit, alleluia, alleluia.
Repeat ℟
℣ You have redeemed us, Lord God of truth. ℟ Glory be. ℟

Ant. Save us, Lord, while we are awake; protect us while we sleep;
that we may keep watch with Christ and rest with him in peace
(alleluia).

NUNC DIMITTIS   CANTICLE: LK 2:29-32
Christ is the light of the nations and the glory of Israel

At last, all-powerful Master,†
you give leave to your servant*
to go in peace, according to your promise.

For my eyes have seen your salvation*
Which you have prepared for all nations,
the light to enlighten the Gentiles*
and give glory to Israel, your people.

Ant. Save us, Lord, while we are awake; protect us while we sleep,
that we may keep watch with Christ and rest with him in peace
(alleluia).

Concluding Prayer
Sundays and Easter Octave
God our Father,
as we have celebrated today the mystery of the Lord's resurrection,
grant our humble prayer:
free us from all harm
that we may sleep in peace
and rise in joy to sing your praise.
Through Christ our Lord.

Easter Triduum and Solemnities which do not fall on Sundays
Visit this house, we pray you, Lord:
drive far away from it all the snares of the enemy.
May your holy angels stay here and guard us in peace,
and let your blessing be always upon us.
Through Christ our Lord.

Blessing
The Lord grant us a quiet night and a perfect end. ℟ Amen.

¶ *On Weekdays either the following series of Night Prayers or one
of the two given for Sundays may be used.*

MONDAY

All as above, pp 319 ff, except for the following

PSALMODY

Ant. You, Lord God, are slow to anger, abounding in love.
Eastertide: Alleluia, alleluia, alleluia.

PRAYER OF A POOR MAN IN DISTRESS   PSALM 85(86)
Blessed be God who comforts us in all our sorrows (2 Cor 1:3-4)

Turn your éar, O Lórd, and give ánswer*
for Í am póor and néedy.
Preserve my lífe, for Í am fáithful:*
save the sérvant who trústs in yóu.

You are my Gód, have mércy on me, Lórd,*
for I crý to you áll the day lóng.
Give jóy to your sérvant, O Lórd,*
for to yóu I líft up my sóul.

O Lórd, you are góod and forgíving,*
full of lóve to áll who cáll.
Give héed, O Lórd, to my práyer*
and atténd to the sóund of my vóice.

In the dáy of distréss I will cáll*
and súrely yóu will replý.
Among the góds there is nóne like you, O Lórd;*
nor wórk to compáre with yóurs.

All the nátions shall cóme to adóre you*
and glórify your náme, O Lórd:
for you are gréat and do márvellous déeds,*
yóu who alóne are Gód.

Shów me, Lórd, your wáy†
so that Í may wálk in your trúth.*
Guide my héart to féar your náme.

I will práise you, Lord my Gód, with all my héart*
and glórify your náme for éver;
for your lóve to mé has been gréat:*
you have sáved me from the dépths of the gráve.

The próud have rísen agáinst me;†
rúthless men séek my lífe:*
to yóu they páy no héed.

But yóu, God of mércy and compássion,*
slów to ánger, O Lórd,
abóunding in lóve and trúth,*
túrn and take píty on mé.

O gíve your stréngth to your sérvant*
and sáve your hándmaid's són.
Shów me a sígn of your fávour†
that my fóes may sée to their sháme*
that you consóle me and gíve me your hélp.

Ant. You, Lord God, are slow to anger, abounding in love.
Eastertide: Alleluia, alleluia, alleluia.

Scripture Reading   *1 Thess 5:9-10*

God chose us to possess salvation through our Lord Jesus Christ,
who died for us in order that we might live together with him,
whether we are alive or dead when he comes.

Short Responsory

Outside Eastertide

℟ Into your hands, Lord, I commend my spirit. *Repeat* ℟
℣ You have redeemed us, Lord God of truth. ℟ Glory be. ℟

Eastertide

℟ Into your hands, Lord, I commend my spirit, alleluia, alleluia.
Repeat ℟
℣ You have redeemed us, Lord God of truth. ℟ Glory be. ℟

Ant. Save us, Lord, while we are awake; protect us while we sleep;
that we may keep watch with Christ and rest with him in peace
(alleluia).

NUNC DIMITTIS   CANTICLE: LK 2:29-32
Christ is the light of the nations and the glory of Israel.

At last, all-powerful Master,†
    you give leave to your servant*
to go in peace, according to your promise.

For my eyes have seen your salvation*
    which you have prepared for all nations,
the light to enlighten the Gentiles*
    and give glory to Israel, your people.

Ant. Save us, Lord, while we are awake; protect us while we sleep;
that we may keep watch with Christ and rest with him in peace
(alleluia).

Concluding Prayer

Lord, give our bodies restful sleep;
and let the work we have done today
be sown for an eternal harvest.
Through Christ our Lord.

Blessing

The Lord grant us a quiet night and a perfect end. ℟ Amen.

TUESDAY

All as above, pp 319 ff, except for the following.

PSALMODY

Ant. Do not hide your face from me, for in you have I put my trust.
Eastertide: Alleluia, alleluia, alleluia.

PRAYER IN DESOLATION   PSALM 142(143):1–11
*A man is made righteous not by obedience to the Law, but by faith in
Jesus Christ* (Gal 2:16)

Lórd, lísten to my práyer:†
túrn your éar to my appéal.*
You are fáithful, you are júst; give ánswer.
Do not cáll your sérvant to júdgment*
for nó one is júst in your síght.

The énemy pursúes my sóul;*
he has crúshed my life to the gróund;
he has máde me dwéll in dárkness*
like the déad, lóng forgótten.
Thérefore my spírit fáils;*
my héart is númb withín me.

I remémber the dáys that are pást:*
I pónder áll your wórks.
I múse on what your hánd has wróught†
and to yóu I strétch out my hánds.*
Like a párched land my sóul thirsts for yóu.

328

Lórd, make háste and ánswer;*
for my spírit fáils withín me.
Dó not híde your fáce*
lest I becóme like thóse in the gráve.

In the mórning let me knów your lóve*
for I pút my trúst in yóu.
Make me knów the wáy I should wálk:*
to yóu I líft up my sóul.

Réscue me, Lórd, from my énemies;*
I have fléd to yóu for réfuge.
Téach me to dó your will*
for yóu, O Lórd, are my Gód.
Let yóur good spírit guíde me*
in wáys that are lével and smóoth.

For your náme's sake, Lórd, save my lífe;*
in your jústice save my sóul from distréss.

Ant. Do not hide your face from me, for in you have I put my trust.
Eastertide: Alleluia, alleluia, alleluia.

Scripture Reading   *I Pet 5:8-9*
Be calm but vigilant, because your enemy the devil is prowling
round like a roaring lion, looking for someone to eat. Stand up to
him, strong in faith.

Short Responsory
Outside Eastertide
R⁊ Into your hands, Lord, I commend my spirit. *Repeat* R⁊
℣ You have redeemed us, Lord God of truth. R⁊ Glory be. R⁊

Eastertide
R⁊ Into your hands, Lord, I commend my spirit, alleluia, alleluia.
Repeat R⁊
℣ You have redeemed us, Lord God of truth. R⁊ Glory be. R⁊

Ant. Save us, Lord, while we are awake; protect us while we sleep;
that we may keep watch with Christ and rest with him in peace
(alleluia).

329

NUNC DIMITTIS   CANTICLE: LK 2:29-32
Christ is the light of the nations and the glory of Israel

At last, all-powerful Master,†
you give leave to your servant*
to go in peace, according to your promise.

For my eyes have seen your salvation*
which you have prepared for all nations,
the light to enlighten the Gentiles*
and give glory to Israel, your people.

Ant. Save us, Lord, while we are awake; protect us while we sleep;
that we may keep watch with Christ and rest with him in peace
(alleluia).

Concluding Prayer
In your mercy, Lord,
dispel the darkness of this night.
Let your household so sleep in peace,
that at the dawn of a new day,
they may, with joy, waken in your name.
Through Christ our Lord.

Blessing
The Lord grant us a quiet night and a perfect end. R⁷ Amen.

WEDNESDAY

All as above pp 319 ff, except for the following.

PSALMODY

Ant. 1: O God, be my protector and my refuge.
Eastertide: Alleluia, alleluia, alleluia

CONFIDENT PRAYER IN DISTRESS   PSALM 30(31):1-6
Father, into your hands I commend my spirit (Lk 23:46)

In yóu, O Lórd, I take réfuge.*

Let me néver be pút to sháme.
In your jústice, sét me frée,
héar me and spéedily réscue me.

Be a róck of réfuge fór me,*
a míghty strónghold to sáve me,
for yóu are my róck, my strónghold.*
For your náme's sake, léad me and gúide me.

Reléase me from the snáres they have hídden*
for yóu are my réfuge, Lórd.
Into your hánds I comménd my spírit.*
It is yóu who will redéem me, Lórd.

Ant. O God, be my protector and my refuge.
Ant. 2: Out of the depths I cry to you, O Lord.†

OUT OF THE DEPTHS I CRY　　　　　　　PSALM 129(130)
He will save his people from their sins (Mt 1:21)

Out of the dépths I crý to you, O Lórd,*
†Lórd, hear my vóice!
O lét your éars be atténtive*
to the vóice of my pléading.

If you, O Lórd, should márk our guílt,*
Lórd, who would survíve?
But with yóu is fóund forgíveness:*
for thís we revére you.

My sóul is wáiting for the Lórd,*
I cóunt on his wórd.
My sóul is lónging for the Lórd*
more than wátchman for dáybreak.
Let the wátchman cóunt on dáybreak*
and Ísrael on the Lórd.

Becáuse with the Lórd there is mércy*
and fúlness of redémption,
Ísrael indéed he will redéem*
from áll its iníquity.　　　　　　　　　Glory be.

Ant. Out of the depths I cry to you, O Lord.
Eastertide: Alleluia, alleluia, alleluia.

Scripture Reading   *Eph 4:26-27*

Do not let resentment lead you into sin; the sunset must not find you still angry. Do not give the devil his opportunity.

Short Responsory

Outside Eastertide
R℣ Into your hands, Lord, I commend my spirit. *Repeat* R℣
℣ You have redeemed us, Lord God of truth. R℣ Glory be. R℣

Eastertide
R℣ Into your hands, Lord, I commend my spirit, alleluia, alleluia.
Repeat R℣
℣ You have redeemed us, Lord God of truth. R℣ Glory be. R℣

Ant. Save us, Lord, while we are awake; protect us while we sleep; that we may keep watch with Christ and rest with him in peace (alleluia).

NUNC DIMITTIS   CANTICLE: LK 2:29-32
Christ is the light of the nations and the glory of Israel

At last, all-powerful Master,†
you give leave to your servant*
to go in peace, according to your promise.

For my eyes have seen your salvation*
which you have prepared for all nations,
the light to enlighten the Gentiles*
and give glory to Israel, your people.

Ant. Save us, Lord, while we are awake; protect us while we sleep; that we may keep watch with Christ and rest with him in peace (alleluia).

Concluding Prayer
Lord Jesus Christ,
meek and humble of heart,
you offer to those who follow you
a yoke that is good to bear,
a burden that is light.
Accept, we beg you, our prayer and work of this day,
and grant us the rest we need
that we may be ever more willing to serve you,
who live and reign for ever and ever.

Blessing
The Lord grant us a quiet night and a perfect end. ℟ Amen.

THURSDAY

All as above, pp 319 ff, except for the following.

PSALMODY

Ant. My body shall rest in safety.
Eastertide: Alleluia, alleluia, alleluia.

THE LORD IS MY PORTION   PSALM 15(16)
God raised up Jesus, freeing him from the pains of death (Acts 2:24)

Presérve me, Gód, I take réfuge in yóu.†
I sáy to the Lórd: 'Yóu are my Gód.*
My háppiness líes in yóu alóne.'

He has pút into my héart a márvellous lóve*
for the fáithful ónes who dwéll in his lánd.
Those who chóose other góds incréase their sórrows.†
Néver will I óffer their ófferings of blóod.*
Néver will I táke their náme upon my líps.

O Lórd, it is yóu who are my pórtion and cúp;*
it is yóu yoursélf who áre my príze.
The lót marked óut for me is mý delíght:*
welcome indéed the héritage that fálls to mé!

333

I will bléss the Lórd who gíves me cóunsel,*
whc éven at níght dirécts my héart.
I kéep the Lórd ever ín my síght:*
since hé is at my ríght hand, Í shall stand fírm.

And so my héart rejóices, my sóul is glád;*
éven my bódy shall rést in sáfety.
For yóu will not léave my sóul among the déad,*
nor lét your belóved knów decáy.

You will shów me the páth of life,†
the fúlness of jóy in your présence,*
at your ríght hand háppiness for éver.

Ant. My body shall rest in safety.
Eastertide: Alleluia, alleluia, alleluia.

Scripture Reading   *1 Thess 5:23*
May the God who gives us peace make you completely his, and keep
your whole being, spirit, soul, and body, free from all fault, at the
coming of our Lord Jesus Christ.

Short Responsory
Outside Eastertide
R̷ Into your hands, Lord, I commend my spirit. *Repeat* R̷
V̷ You have redeemed us, Lord God of truth. R̷ Glory be. R̷

Eastertide
R̷ Into your hands, Lord, I commend my spirit, alleluia, alleluia.
Repeat R̷
V̷ You have redeemed us, Lord God of truth. R̷ Glory be. R̷

Ant. Save us, Lord, while we are awake; protect us while we sleep;
that we may keep watch with Christ and rest with him in peace
(alleluia).

NUNC DIMITTIS   CANTICLE: LK 2:29-32
Christ is the light of the nations and the glory of Israel

At last, all-powerful Master,†

you give leave to your servant*
to go in peace, according to your promise.

For my eyes have seen your salvation*
which you have prepared for all nations,
the light to enlighten the Gentiles*
and give glory to Israel, your people.

Ant. Save us, Lord, while we are awake; protect us while we sleep;
that we may keep watch with Christ and rest with him in peace
(alleluia).

Concluding Prayer

Lord our God,
restore us again by the repose of sleep
after the fatigue of our daily work:
so that, continually renewed by your help,
we may serve you in body and soul.
Through Christ our Lord.

Blessing

The Lord grant us a quiet night and a perfect end. R̷ Amen.

FRIDAY

All as above, pp 319 ff, except for the following.

PSALMODY

Ant. Lord my God, I call for help by day; I cry at night before you.†
Eastertide: Alleluia, alleluia, alleluia.

PRAYER OF ONE WHO IS GRAVELY ILL   PSALM 87(88)
This is your hour; this is the reign of darkness (Lk 22:53)

Lord my Gód, I call for hélp by dáy;*
I crý at níght befóre you.
†Let my práyer cóme into your présence.*
O túrn your éar to my crý.

For my sóul is fílled with évils;*
my lífe is on the brínk of the gráve.
I am réckoned as óne in the tómb:*
I have réached the énd of my stréngth,

like óne alóne among the déad;*
like the sláin lýing in their gráves;
like thóse you remémber no móre,*
cut óff, as they áre, from your hánd.

You have láid me in the dépths of the tómb,*
in pláces that are dárk, in the dépths.
Your ánger weighs dówn upón me:*
I am drówned benéath your wáves.

You have táken awáy my fríends*
and máde me háteful in their síght
Imprísoned, I cánnot escápe;*
my éyes are súnken with gríef.

I cáll to you, Lórd, all the day lóng;*
to yóu I strétch out my hánds.
Will you wórk your wónders for the déad?*
Will the shádes stánd and práise you?

Will your lóve be tóld in the gráve*
or your fáithfulness amóng the déad?
Will your wónders be knówn in the dárk*
or your jústice in the lánd of oblívion?

As for mé, Lord, I cáll to you for hélp:*
in the mórning my práyer comes befóre you.
Lórd, whý do you rejéct me?*
Whý do you híde your fáce?

Wrétched, close to déath from my yóuth,*
I have bórne your tríals; I am númb.
Your fúry has swépt down upón me;*
your térrors have útterly destróyed me.

They surróund me all the dáy like a flóod,*
they assáil me áll togéther.

336

Friend and néighbour you have táken awáy:*
my óne compánion is dárkness.

Ant. Lord my God, I call for help by day; I cry at night before you.
Eastertide: Alleluia, alleluia, alleluia.

Scripture Reading   *Jer 14:9*
Lord, you are in our midst, we are called by your name. Do not
desert us, O Lord our God.

Short Responsory
Outside Eastertide
R℣ Into your hands, Lord, I commend my spirit. *Repeat* R℣
℣ You have redeemed us, Lord God of truth. R℣ Glory be. R℣

Eastertide
R℣ Into your hands, Lord, I commend my spirit, alleluia, alleluia.
Repeat R℣
℣ You have redeemed us, Lord God of truth. R℣ Glory be. R℣

Ant. Save us, Lord, while we are awake; protect us while we sleep;
that we may keep watch with Christ and rest with him in peace
(alleluia).

NUNC DIMITTIS   CANTICLE: LK 2:29-32
Christ is the light of the nations and the glory of Israel

At last, all-powerful Master,†
you give leave to your servant*
to go in peace, according to your promise.

For my eyes have seen your salvation*
which you have prepared for all nations,
the light to enlighten the Gentiles*
and give glory to Israel, your people.

Ant. Save us, Lord, while we are awake; protect us while we sleep;
that we may keep watch with Christ and rest with him in peace
(alleluia).

Concluding Prayer

Give us grace, almighty God,
so to unite ourselves in faith with your only Son,
who underwent death and lay buried in the tomb
that we may rise again in newness of life with him,
who lives and reigns for ever and ever.

Blessing

The Lord grant us a quiet night and a perfect end. ℟ Amen.

THE PROPER OF SEASONS

A selection of texts is given in the pages that follow to enable the user to advert to the season of the year. For the full variety of seasonal texts offered by the Liturgy of the Hours, see The Divine Office, Daily Prayer, *or* Morning and Evening Prayer.

   Unless otherwise indicated, the psalmody is as given in the Four Week Psalter. A hymn suitable to the season and to the time of day should be chosen.

SEASON OF ADVENT
SUNDAYS OF ADVENT

EVENING PRAYER I

Hymn for Advent.

PSALMODY

Psalms and canticle with proper antiphons as in the psalter for the relevant week.

Scripture Reading   *1 Thess 5:23-24*

May the God who gives us peace make you completely his, and keep your whole being, spirit, soul, and body, free from all fault, at the coming of our Lord Jesus Christ. He who calls you will do it, for he is faithful!

Short Responsory

R̥ Show us, Lord, your steadfast love. *Repeat* R̥
V̥ And grant us your salvation. R̥ Show us, Lord . . .
Glory be to the Father and to the Son and to the Holy Spirit. R̥
Show us, Lord . . .

Magnificat Antiphon

See the name of the Lord comes from afar. His splendour fills the whole world.

Intercessions

The Son of God is coming with great power: all mankind shall see his face and be reborn.—R̥ Come, Lord Jesus: do not delay!
You will bring us wisdom, fresh understanding and new vision.—R̥
You will bring us good news, and power which will transform our lives.—R̥
You will bring us truth, showing us the way to our Father.—R̥
Born of a woman, you will open in our flesh the way to eternal life and joy.—R̥

Our Father

Concluding Prayer
Grant, almighty Father,
that when Christ comes again
we may go out to meet him,
bearing the harvest of good works
achieved by your grace.
We pray that he will receive us into the company of the saints and
call us into the kingdom of heaven.
(We make our prayer) through our Lord Jesus Christ your Son,
who lives and reigns with you and the Holy Spirit,
God, for ever and ever. R̃ Amen.

Invitatory
Ant. Let us adore the Lord, the king who is to come.

Ps 94, p. 3.

MORNING PRAYER

Scripture Reading   *Rom 13:11-12*
It is full time now for you to wake from sleep. For salvation is nearer
to us now than when we first believed; the night is far gone, the day
is at hand. Let us then cast off the works of darkness and put on the
armour of light.

Short Responsory
R̃ Christ, Son of the living God, have mercy on us. *Repeat* R̃
Ṽ You are coming into the world. R̃
Glory be to the Father and to the Son and to the Holy Spirit. R̃

Benedictus Antiphon
The Holy Spirit will come upon you, Mary. Do not be afraid, for
you will bear in your womb the Son of God, alleluia.

Intercessions

Father, you have given us the grace of looking forward to the coming of your Son: ℟ Send us your loving kindness.

Bring us to life, Lord:—may we be the servants found watching when the Master returns. ℟

Send your Son to those who wait in hope:—let no man search for you in vain. ℟

Bless us as we work:—give us faith until the end, when your Son will come in glory. ℟

Father, we praise you for the presence of the Spirit in our lives, —making men and women bearers of your message and your purpose. ℟

Our Father

Concluding Prayer

Grant, almighty Father,
that when Christ comes again
we may go out to meet him,
bearing the harvest of good works
achieved by your grace.
We pray that he will receive us into the company of the saints
and call us into the kingdom of heaven.
(We make our prayer) through our Lord.

EVENING PRAYER II

Scripture Reading   *Phil 4:4-5*

Rejoice in the Lord always; again I will say, Rejoice. Let all men know your forbearance. The Lord is at hand.

Short Responsory

℟ Show us, Lord, your steadfast love. *Repeat* ℟
℣ And grant us your salvation. ℟ Glory be. ℟

Magnificat Antiphon

Do not be afraid, Mary, for you have found favour with God. Behold, you will conceive and bear a son, alleluia.

Intercessions

We pray to our Lord, who is the way, the truth, and the life.
R̸ Come, and remain with us, Lord.

Gabriel announced your coming to the Virgin Mary:—Son of the Most High, come to claim your kingdom. R̸

John the Baptist rejoiced to see your day:—come, bring us your salvation. R̸

Simeon acknowledged you, Light of the World:—bring your light to all men of goodwill. R̸

We look for you as watchmen look for the dawn:—you are the sun that will wake the dead to new life. R̸ Come, and remain with us, Lord.

Our Father

The concluding Prayer as at Morning Prayer.

MONDAYS OF ADVENT

Invitatory ant. Let us adore the Lord, the king who is to come.

Ps 94, p 3.

MORNING PRAYER

Hymn for Advent.

Scripture Reading *Is 2:3*

'Come, let us go up to the mountain of the Lord, to the house of the God of Jacob; that he may teach us his ways and that we may walk in his paths.' For out of Zion shall go forth the law, and the word of the Lord from Jerusalem.

Short Responsory

R̸ The glory of the Lord will shine on you, Jerusalem. Like the sun he will rise over you. *Repeat* R̸

Ᵽ His glory will appear in your midst. R̸ Glory be. R̸

Benedictus Antiphon

Lift up your eyes, Jerusalem, and see the power of the king. Behold, the Saviour comes. He will free you from your bonds.

Intercessions

As we take up again our daily work, we turn to Christ and ask for his blessing. ℟ Come, Lord Jesus!

Christ, you are the Daystar, powerfully dispelling our darkness:
—awaken our faith from sleep. ℟

Reveal your presence in the world—through the lives of Christian men and women. ℟

Come to create a new world,—where justice and peace may find a home. ℟

End the long night of our pride,—and make us humble of heart. ℟
Our Father

Concluding Prayer

Give us the grace, Lord,
to be ever on the watch for Christ, your Son.
When he comes and knocks at our door,
let him find us alert in prayer,
joyfully proclaiming his glory.
(We make our prayer) through our Lord.

EVENING PRAYER

Hymn for Advent.

Scripture Reading   *Phil 3:20b-21*

It is to heaven that we look expectantly for the coming of our Lord Jesus Christ to save us; he will form this humbled body of ours anew, moulding it into the image of his glorified body, so effective is his power to make all things obey him.

Short Responsory

℟ Come to us and save us, Lord, God almighty. *Repeat* ℟
℣ Let your face smile on us and we shall be safe. ℟ Glory be. ℟

Magnificat Antiphon

The angel of the Lord brought the good news to Mary and she
conceived by the power of the Holy Spirit, alleluia.

Intercessions

As we make our evening prayer, we acknowledge the times when we
have preferred darkness before true light. R/ Lord, that we may see!

You came, as man, into this world:—free us from the darkness of
its sin. R/

Forgive us the hatred and envy that cloud our vision—give us a
generous spirit. R/

You come to us through those who share our lives—open our hearts
to recognize you. R/

Lord, do not forget our brothers,—who in all ages have hoped to see
your light. R/

Our Father

The concluding prayer as at Morning Prayer.

TUESDAYS OF ADVENT

Invitatory ant. Let us adore the Lord, the king who is to come.

MORNING PRAYER

Hymn for Advent.

Scripture Reading   *Gen 49:10*

Juda shall not want a branch from his stem, a prince drawn from his
stock, until the day when he comes who is to be sent to us, he, the
hope of the nations.

Short Responsory

R/ The glory of the Lord will shine on you, Jerusalem. Like the sun
he will rise over you. *Repeat* R/

V/ His glory will appear in your midst. R/ Glory be. R/

Benedictus Antiphon

A shoot shall spring from the stock of Jesse: the whole world shall be filled with the glory of the Lord and all flesh shall see the saving power of God.

Intercessions

It is time for us to wake from our sleep: the day of our salvation is near. R⁷ Lord, may your kingdom come!

Help us to show our repentance—by a new way of living. R⁷

Prepare us for the coming of your Word—by opening our hearts to receive him. R⁷

Help us to overcome our pride,—and raise us from the depths of our weakness. R⁷

Throw down the walls of hatred between nations;—clear the way for those who work for peace. R⁷

Our Father

Concluding Prayer

Take pity on our distress, Lord God:
show us your love.
May the coming of your Son strengthen us
and cleanse us from all trace of sin.
(We make our prayer) through our Lord.

EVENING PRAYER

Hymn for Advent.

Scripture Reading *Cf 1 Cor 1:7b-9*

You wait expectantly for our Lord Jesus Christ to reveal himself. He will keep you firm to the end, without reproach on the Day of our Lord Jesus. It is God himself who called you to share in the life of his Son.

Short Responsory

R⁷ Come to us and save us, Lord God almighty. *Repeat* R⁷

℣ Let your face smile on us and we shall be safe. R⁷ Glory be. R⁷

Magnificat Antiphon

Seek the Lord while he may be found, call upon him while he is near, alleluia.

Intercessions

The Lord God said: 'I shall look for the lost one, bring back the stray, bandage the wounded and make the weak strong.' R/ Lord our God, come to save us.

Lord God, you made us and sustain us with your love:—help us to recognize that you are in our midst. R/

You are close to each one of us:—open our hearts to love you. R/

We pray for those who find their lives a burden too heavy to bear —Lord, be their strength and their hope. R/

You are Life, and the enemy of death:—rescue us and all the faithful departed from eternal darkness. R/

Our Father

The concluding prayer as at Morning Prayer.

WEDNESDAYS OF ADVENT

Invitatory ant. Let us adore the Lord, the king who is to come.

MORNING PRAYER

Hymn for Advent.

Scripture Reading　　　　*Is 7:14b-15*

The maiden is with child and will soon give birth to a son whom she will call Immanuel. On curds and honey will he feed until he knows how to refuse evil and choose good.

Short Responsory

R/ The glory of the Lord will shine on you, Jerusalem. Like the sun he will rise over you. *Repeat* R/

V/ His glory will appear in your midst. R/ Glory be. R/

Benedictus Antiphon

There is one coming who is more powerful than I am. I am not fit to undo the strap of his sandals.

Intercessions

The Word of God has chosen to live among us: let us thank him and give him praise: R̷ Come, Lord Jesus!

Bring justice to those bowed down with suffering:—defend the poor and the powerless. R̷

Prince of Peace, turn our jealousies into love,—teach us to forgive rather than give way to anger. R̷

When you come to judge the world,—may we stand before you without fear. R̷

You stand in our midst unknown:—help us to find you in the poor and the troubled. R̷

Our Father

Concluding Prayer

Prepare our hearts, Lord,
by the power of your grace.
When Christ comes,
may he find us worthy
to receive from his hand the bread of heaven
at the feast of eternal life.
(We make our prayer) through our Lord.

EVENING PRAYER

Hymn for Advent.

Scripture Reading   *1 Cor 4:5*

There must be no passing of premature judgment. Leave that until the Lord comes: he will light up all that is hidden in the dark and reveal the secret intentions of men's hearts. Then will be the time for each one to have whatever praise he deserves, from God.

Short Responsory

R/ Come to us and save us, Lord God almighty. *Repeat* R/
V/ Let your face smile on us and we shall be safe. R/ Glory be. R/

Magnificat Antiphon

The law will go forth from Sion, and the word of the Lord from Jerusalem.

Intercessions

Let us pray to God the Father who is Lord and Ruler of all. R/ Come and visit your people!

Come as the shepherd to tend your flock;—gather all men into the unity of the Church. R/

Lord, remember all the sons of Abraham,—all who await your promise in faith. R/

We pray for those who seek to escape from life;—Lord, give them hope to live by and courage to persevere. R/

Remember those who have died;—show them the glory your Son has gained for them. R/

Our Father

The concluding prayer as at Morning Prayer.

THURSDAYS OF ADVENT

Invitatory ant. Let us adore the Lord, the king who is to come.

MORNING PRAYER

Hymn for Advent.

Scripture Reading   *Is 45:8*

Rain righteousness, you heavens, let the skies above pour down; let the earth open to receive it, that it may bear the fruit of salvation with righteousness in blossom at its side.

Short Responsory

℟ The glory of the Lord will shine on you, Jerusalem. Like the sun he will rise over you. *Repeat* ℟

℣ His glory will appear in your midst. ℟ Glory be. ℟

Benedictus Antiphon

I will wait for the Lord who saves me. I will hope in him, for he is coming, alleluia.

Intercessions

Let the heavens open, and the skies rain down the just one; let the earth bring forth Christ, who is the wisdom and power of God. ℟ Be near us, Lord, today.

Lord Jesus Christ, you have called us into your kingdom:—may we enter in, and live according to your call. ℟

The world does not know you:—show yourself, in our midst, to all our brothers. ℟

We thank you, Lord, for all that we have:—move us to give of our plenty to those who have little. ℟

We look for your coming, Lord Jesus:—when you knock, may we be found watching in prayer and rejoicing in praise. ℟

Our Father

Concluding Prayer

Show forth your power, Lord, and come.
Come in your great strength and help us.
Be merciful and forgiving,
and hasten the salvation which only our sins delay.
(We make our prayer) through our Lord.

EVENING PRAYER

Hymn for Advent.

Scripture Reading   *Jas 5:7-8,9b*

Be patient, then, my brothers, until the Lord comes. See how the farmer is patient as he waits for his land to produce precious crops. He waits patiently for the autumn and spring rains. And you also

must be patient! Keep your hopes high, for the day of the Lord'
coming is near. The Judge is near, ready to come in!

Short Responsory

R? Come to us and save us, Lord God almighty. *Repeat* R?
V? Let your face smile on us and we shall be safe. R? Glory be. R?

Magnificat Antiphon

You are the most blessed of all women, and blessed is the fruit o
your womb.

Intercessions

Let us pray to Christ, the great light promised by the prophets to
those dwelling in the shadow of death: R? Come, Lord Jesus!

You enlighten all men—open the hearts of your people to a wider
world. R?

Son of God, in you we see the Father—come to reveal to us what
true love means. R?

Christ Jesus, you come to us as man—may the welcome we give you
make us sons of God. R?

You open the gates of liberty and life—bring the dead into everlasting freedom. R?

Our Father

The concluding prayer as at Morning Prayer.

FRIDAYS OF ADVENT

Invitatory ant. Let us adore the Lord, the king who is to come.

MORNING PRAYER

Hymn for Advent.

Scripture Reading   *Jer 30:21,22*
A ruler shall appear, one of themselves,

a governor shall arise from their own number.
I will myself bring him near and so he shall approach me, says the
     Lord.
So you shall be my people,
and I will be your God.

Short Responsory

Ry The glory of the Lord will shine on you, Jerusalem. Like the sun
he will rise over you. *Repeat* Ry
℣ His glory will appear in your midst. Ry Glory be. Ry

Benedictus Antiphon

Behold the one who is both God and man: He comes forth from the
stock of David and sits on the throne, alleluia.

Intercessions

It was the Father's will that men should see him in the face of his
beloved Son. Ry Hallowed be your name!
Christ greeted us with good news:—may the world hear it through
us, and find hope. Ry
We praise and thank you, Lord of heaven and earth:—the hope and
joy of men in every age. Ry
May Christ's coming transform the Church,—renewing its youth
and vigour in the service of men. Ry
We pray for Christians who suffer for their beliefs:—sustain them
in their hope. Ry
Our Father

Concluding Prayer

Call forth your power, Lord;
come and save us from the judgment
that threatens us by reason of our sins.
Come, and set us free.
(We make our prayer) through our Lord.

EVENING PRAYER

Hymn for Advent.

Scripture Reading   *2 Pet 3:8b-9*

There is no difference in the Lord's sight between one day and a thousand years; to him, the two are the same. The Lord is not slow to do what he has promised, as some think. Instead, he is patient with you, because he does not want anyone to be destroyed, but wants all to turn away from their sins.

Short Responsory

R/ Come to us and save us, Lord God almighty. *Repeat* R/

V/ Let your face smile on us and we shall be safe. R/ Glory be. R/

Magnificat Antiphon

Out of Egypt I have called my son. He will come and save his people.

Intercessions:

As we prepare to celebrate the birth of Christ, we pray that the Church may come to birth again in our times. R/ Be born in us, Lord.

Lord Jesus, born of Mary,—come again into our world. R/

Help us to show compassion and respect for the mentally ill,—since we are all children of God. R/

Through the Church's proclamation of your coming,—bring light to those who search for truth. R/

You were born to die for our sins:—at our death may we be born into your life. R/

Our Father

The concluding prayer as at Morning Prayer.

354

SATURDAYS OF ADVENT

Invitatory ant. Let us adore the Lord, the king who is to come.

MORNING PRAYER

Hymn for Advent.

Scripture Reading   *Is 11:1-2*

A shoot shall grow from the stock of Jesse, and a branch shall spring from his roots. The spirit of the Lord shall rest upon him, a spirit of wisdom and understanding, a spirit of counsel and power, a spirit of knowledge and the fear of the Lord.

Short Responsory

R̂ The glory of the Lord will shine on you, Jerusalem. Like the sun he will rise over you. *Repeat* R̂

V̂ His glory will appear in your midst. R̂ Glory be. R̂

Benedictus Antiphon

Do not be afraid, Sion: behold, your God will come, alleluia.

Intercessions:

The Lord, our God, is coming: let us put aside fear, and look forward to the future with courage. R̂ Your kingdom come!

Lord, you make all things and renew them:—all creation displays your work. R̂

You have given us dominion over the earth;—may our work have a share of your creative power. R̂

We pray for those who work for the relief of suffering in others;—may they also know comfort and understanding. R̂ Your kingdom come!

As we rest from our work at the end of the week,—restore our strength and give us time to know you. R̂

Our Father

Concluding Prayer
Lord, to free man from his sinful state
you sent your only Son into this world.
Grant to us who in faith and love wait for his coming
your gift of grace
and the reward of true freedom.
(We make our prayer) through our Lord.

SEASON OF CHRISTMAS

Christmas Day
THE NATIVITY OF
OUR LORD JESUS CHRIST

Solemnity

EVENING PRAYER I

Hymn

A noble flow'r of Juda from tender roots has sprung,
A rose from stem of Jesse, as prophets long had sung,
A blossom fair and bright,
That in the midst of winter will change to dawn our night.

The rose of grace and beauty of which Isaiah sings
Is Mary, virgin mother, and Christ the flow'r she brings.
By God's divine decree
She bore our loving Saviour, who died to set us free.

To Mary, dearest Mother, with fervent hearts we pray:
Grant that your tender infant will cast our sins away,
And guide us with his love
That we shall ever serve him, and live with him above.

PSALMODY

Ant. 1: The King of Peace has shown himself in glory: all the peoples desire to see him.

PSALM 112(113)

Práise, O sérvants of the Lórd,*
práise the náme of the Lórd!
May the náme of the Lórd be bléssed*
both nów and for évermóre!
From the rísing of the sún to its sétting*
práised be the náme of the Lórd!

357

High above all nátions is the Lórd,*
abóve the héavens his glóry.
Whó is like the Lórd, our Gód,*
who has rísen on hígh to his thróne
yet stóops from the héights to look dówn,*
to look dówn upon héaven and éarth?

From the dúst he lífts up the lówly,*
from his mísery he ráises the póor
to sét him in the cómpany of prínces,*
yés, with the prínces of his péople.
To the chíldless wífe he gives a hóme*
and gláddens her héart with chíldren.

Ant. The King of Peace has shown himself in glory: all the peoples
desire to see him.
Ant. 2: He sends out his word to the earth and swiftly runs his
command.

PSALM 147

O práise the Lórd, Jerúsalem!*
Síon, práise your Gód!

He has stréngthened the bárs of your gátes,*
he has bléssed the children withín you.
He estáblished péace on your bórders,*
he féeds you with fínest whéat.

He sénds out his wórd to the éarth*
and swíftly rúns his commánd.
He shówers down snów white as wóol,*
he scátters hóar-frost like áshes.

He húrls down háilstones like crúmbs.*
The wáters are frózen at his tóuch;
he sénds forth his wórd and it mélts them:*
at the bréath of his móuth the waters flów.

He mákes his wórd known to Jácob,*
to Ísrael his láws and decrées.

358

He has not déalt thus with óther nátions;*
he has not táught them hís decrées.

Ant. He sends out his word to the earth and swiftly runs his command.

Ant. 3: The Word of God, born of the Father before time began, humbled himself today for us and became man.

CANTICLE: PHIL 2:6-11

Though he was in the form of God,*
Jesus did not count equality with God a thing to be grasped.

He emptied himself,†
taking the form of a servant,*
being born in the likeness of men.

And being found in human form,†
he humbled himself and became obedient unto death,*
even death on a cross.

Therefore God has highly exalted him*
and bestowed on him the name which is above every name,

That at the name of Jesus every knee should bow,*
in heaven and on earth and under the earth.

And every tongue confess that Jesus Christ is Lord,*
to the glory of God the Father.

Ant. The Word of God, born of the Father before time began, humbled himself today for us and became man.

Scripture Reading   *Gal 4:4-5*

When the appointed time came, God sent his Son, born of a woman,
—born a subject of the Law, to redeem the subjects of the Law and
to enable us to be adopted as sons.

Short Responsory

℟ Today you know that the Lord will come. *Repeat* ℟
℣ In the morning you will see his glory. ℟ Glory be. ℟

Magnificat ant. When the sun rises in the heavens you will see the king of kings. He comes forth from the Father like a bridegroom coming in splendour from his wedding chamber.

Intercessions

Let us turn in prayer to Christ who emptied himself to assume the condition of a slave. He was tempted in every way that we are, but did not sin. Ry Save us through your birth.

Coming into our world, Lord Jesus, you open the new age which the prophets foretold.—In every age, may the Church come again to new birth. Ry

You took on our human weakness.—Be the eyes of the blind, the strength of the weak, the friend of the lonely. Ry

Lord, you were born among the poor:—show them your love. Ry

Your birth brings eternal life within man's reach;—comfort the dying with hope of new life in heaven. Ry

Gather the departed to yourself;—and make them radiant in your glory. Ry

Our Father

Concluding Prayer

Fill us with confidence, Lord God,
when your Only-begotten Son comes as our judge.
We welcome him with joy as our redeemer;
year by year renew that joy
as we await the fulfilment of our redemption
by Jesus Christ our Lord, your Son,
who lives and reigns with you and the Holy Spirit,
God, for ever and ever.

¶ *Night Prayer is said only by those who do not attend the Office of Readings and Midnight Mass.*

Invitatory

Ant. Christ has been born for us: come, let us adore him.

¶ *Morning Prayer should not regularly be said immediately after Midnight Mass, but in the morning.*

MORNING PRAYER

Hymn

Afar from where the sun doth rise
To lands beneath the western skies,
Homage to Christ our King we pay,
Born of a Virgin's womb this day.

Blessed Creator, thou didst take
A servant's likeness for our sake,
And didst in flesh our flesh restore
To bid thy creature live once more.

Chaste was the womb where thou didst dwell,
Of heavenly grace the hidden cell;
Nor might the blessed Maid proclaim
Whence her dread Guest in secret came.

Down from on high God came to rest
His glory in a sinless breast;
Obedience at his word believed,
And virgin innocence conceived.

Ere long, that holy Child she bore
By Gabriel's message named before,
Whom, yet unborn, with eager pride,
The swift forerunner prophesied.

Fast doth he sleep, where straw doth spread
A humble manger for his bed;
A Mother's milk that strength renewed
Which gives the birds of heaven their food.

Glory to God, the angels cry;
Earth hears the echo from on high;
Mankind's true Shepherd and its Lord
By shepherd hearts is first adored.

PSALMODY

Ant. 1: Shepherds, tell us whom you have seen. Who has appeared
on earth? We have seen the newborn child and we have heard the
choirs of angels praising the Lord, alleluia.

Psalms and canticle of Sunday, Week 1.

Ant. 2: The angel said to the shepherds, 'I bring you news of great joy. Today the Saviour of the world has been born to you, alleluia

Ant. 3: Today a child is born to us. His name will be called 'Might God', alleluia.

Scripture Reading   *Heb 1:1-2*
When in former times God spoke to our forefathers, he spoke i fragmentary and varied fashion through the prophets. But in this th final age he has spoken to us in the Son whom he has made heir t the whole universe, and through whom he created all orders o existence.

Short Responsory
R⁊ The Lord has made known our salvation, alleluia, alleluia.
Repeat R⁊
V⁊ He has revealed his saving power. R⁊ Glory be. R⁊

Benedictus ant. Glory be to God on high, and on earth peace among his chosen people, alleluia.

Intercessions
God our Father, this morning we eagerly greet the birth of Jesus our brother and Saviour. He is the Daystar from on high, the light bearer who brings the dawn to us, who wait patiently for his coming
R⁊ Glory to God in the highest, and on earth peace among men.
Father, bless on this holy day the Church all over the world.—May she light afresh in men's hearts the lamps of hope and peace. R⁊
Your Son has come to us in the fulness of time:—let those who wait for him recognize his coming. R⁊
His birth bound heaven to earth in harmony and peace.—Establish that same peace among nations and men of today. R⁊
With Mary and Joseph we rejoice in the birth of Jesus.—May we welcome Christ as they did. R⁊
Our Father

Concluding Prayer

Almighty God,
your incarnate Word fills us
with the new light he brought to men.
Let the light of faith in our hearts
shine through all that we do and say.
(We make our prayer) through our Lord.

EVENING PRAYER II

Hymn

Christ, whose blood for all men streamed,
Light, that shone ere morning beamed,
God and God's eternal Son,
Ever with the Father one;

Splendour of the Father's light,
Star of hope for ever bright,
Hearken to the prayers that flow
From thy servants here below.

Lord, remember that in love
Thou didst leave thy throne above,
Man's frail nature to assume
In the holy Virgin's womb.

Now thy Church, each circling year,
Celebrates that love so dear;
Love that brought thee here alone,
For the guilty to atone.

Let not earth alone rejoice,
Seas and skies unite their voice
In a new song, to the morn
When the Lord of life was born.

Virgin-born, to thee be praise,
Now and through eternal days;
Father, equal praise to thee,
With the Spirit, ever be.

PSALMODY

Ant. 1: All authority and dominion are yours on the day of your strength; you are resplendent in holiness. From the womb before the dawn I begot you.

PSALM 109(110):1-5,7

The Lórd's revelátion to my Máster:†
'Sít on my ríght:*
your fóes I will pút beneath your féet.'

The Lórd will wíeld from Síon†
your scéptre of pówer:*
rúle in the mídst of all your fóes.

A prínce from the dáy of your bírth†
on the hóly móuntains;*
from the wómb before the dáwn I begót you.

The Lórd has sworn an óath he will not chánge.†
'You are a príest for éver,*
a príest like Melchízedek of óld.'

The Máster stánding at your ríght hand*
will shatter kíngs in the dáy of his wráth.

He shall drínk from the stréam by the wáyside*
and thérefore he shall líft up his héad.

Ant. All authority and dominion are yours on the day of your strength; you are resplendent in holiness. From the womb before the dawn I begot you.

Ant. 2: With the Lord there is unfailing love. Great is his power to set men free.

PSALM 129(130)

Out of the dépths I crý to you, O Lórd,*
Lórd, hear my vóice!
O lét your éars be atténtive*
to the vóice of my pléading.

If you, O Lórd, should márk our guílt,*
Lórd, who would survíve?
But with yóu is fóund forgíveness:*
for thís we revére you.

My sóul is wáiting for the Lórd,*
I cóunt on his wórd.
My sóul is lónging for the Lórd*
more than wátchman for dáybreak.
Let the wátchman cóunt on dáybreak*
and Ísrael on the Lórd.

Becáuse with the Lórd there is mércy*
and fúlness of redémption,
Ísrael indéed he will redéem*
from áll its iníquity.

Ant. With the Lord there is unfailing love. Great is his power to set men free.

Ant. 3: The Word was God in the beginning and before all time; today he is born to us, the Saviour of the world.

CANTICLE: COL 1:12-20

Let us give thanks to the Father,†
who has qualified us to share*
in the inheritance of the saints in light.

He has delivered us from the dominion of darkness*
and transferred us to the kingdom of his beloved Son,
in whom we have redemption,*
the forgiveness of sins.

He is the image of the invisible God,*
the first-born of all creation,
for in him all things were created, in heaven and on earth,*
visible and invisible.

All things were created*
through him and for him.
He is before all things,*
and in him all things hold together.

365

He is the head of the body, the Church;*
he is the beginning,
the first-born from the dead,*
that in everything he might be pre-eminent,

For in him all the fulness of God was pleased to dwell,*
and through him to reconcile to himself all things,
whether on earth or in heaven,*
making peace by the blood of his cross.

Ant. The Word was God in the beginning and before all time; today
he is born to us, the Saviour of the world.

Scripture Reading   *1 Jn 1:1-3*

Something which has existed since the beginning,
that we have heard,
and we have seen with our own eyes;
that we have watched
and touched with our hands:
the Word, who is life—
this is our subject.
That life was made visible:
we saw it and we are giving our testimony,
telling you of the eternal life
which was with the Father
and has been made visible to us.
What we have seen and heard
we are telling you
so that you too may be in union with us,
as we are in union
with the Father
and with his Son Jesus Christ.

Short Responsory

R̸ The Word became flesh, alleluia, alleluia. *Repeat* R̸
V̸ And he lived among us. R̸ Glory be. R̸

Magnificat ant. Today Christ is born, today the Saviour has appeared; today the angels sing on earth, the archangels rejoice; today
upright men shout out for joy: Glory be to God on high, alleluia.

Intercessions

Today the angels' message rings through the world. Gathered together in prayer, we rejoice in the birth of our brother, the Saviour of us all. R7 Lord Jesus, your birth is our peace.

May our lives express what we celebrate at Christmas:—may its mystery enrich your Church this year. R7

We join the shepherds in adoring you,—we kneel before you, holy child of Bethlehem. R7

We pray for the shepherds of your Church:—be close to them as they proclaim your birth to mankind. R7

As we travel on this earthly pilgrimage, may your light shine in our hearts,—and may we see your glory, born in our midst. R7

Word of the Father, you became man for us and raised us to a new life.—May the dead share with us in the new birth which Christmas proclaims. R7

Our Father

Concluding Prayer

God, our Father,
our human nature is the wonderful work of your hands,
made still more wonderful by your work of redemption.
Your Son took to himself our manhood,
grant us a share in the godhead of Jesus Christ,
who lives and reigns with you and the Holy Spirit,
God, for ever and ever.

Sunday within the Octave of Christmas
FEAST OF THE HOLY FAMILY

Psalter: Week 1

EVENING PRAYER I
(Only on a Saturday)

Magnificat ant. The boy Jesus stayed behind in Jerusalem without his parents knowing it. They thought he was with the other pilgrims and they sought him among their relations and friends.

The concluding prayer as at Morning Prayer.

MORNING PRAYER

Benedictus ant. Lord, let the example of your holy family enlighten our minds; set our feet on the way of peace.

Concluding Prayer
God, our Father,
in the Holy Family of Nazareth
you have given us the true model of a Christian home.
Grant that by following Jesus, Mary, and Joseph
in their love for each other and in the example of their family life
we may come to your home of peace and joy.
(We make our prayer) through our Lord.

EVENING PRAYER

Magnificat ant. 'Son, why have you treated us like this? Your father and I have been looking for you anxiously.' 'Why were you looking for me? Did you not know that I was bound to be where my Father is?'

The concluding prayer as at Morning Prayer.

WEEKDAYS
DURING THE CHRISTMAS SEASON

Invitatory ant. Christ has been born for us: come, let us adore him.

MORNING PRAYER

Hymn, antiphons, psalms and canticle from Christmas Day, pp 361 ff.

Scripture Reading   *Is 9:6*
To us a child is born, to us a son is given; and the government will be upon his shoulder, and his name will be called 'Wonderful Counsellor, Mighty God, Everlasting Father, Prince of Peace.'

Short Responsory

R℣ The Lord has made known our salvation, alleluia, alleluia.

Repeat R℣

℣ He has revealed his saving power. R℣ Glory be. R℣

Benedictus ant. At the birth of the Lord the choir of angels chanted: Praise be to our God, who sits on the throne, and to the Lamb.

Intercessions

Let us pray to Christ in whom all things are restored by the Father's will. R℣ Most loving Son of God, hear our prayer.

Son of God, in the fulness of time you became a man:—share with us your love for everyone. R℣

You emptied yourself to enrich us with your glory:—make us selfless ministers of your gospel. R℣

You brought light into the darkness of our lives:—guide all our actions in the ways of virtue, justice and peace. R℣

May our hearts be disposed to hear your word—and so be able to do good for ourselves and for our fellow-men. R℣

Our Father

Concluding Prayer

Almighty God and Father,

the human birth of your Only-begotten Son

was the beginning of new life.

May he set us free from the tyranny of sin.

(We make our prayer) through our Lord.

EVENING PRAYER

Hymn, antiphons, psalms and canticle from Evening Prayer II of Christmas Day, pp 363 ff.

Scripture Reading   *2 Pet 1:3-4*

By his divine power, Christ has given us all the things that we need for life and for true devotion, bringing us to know God himself, who has called us by his own glory and goodness. In making these gifts, he has given us the guarantee of something very great and wonderful to come: through them you will be able to share the divine nature and to escape corruption in a world that is sunk in vice.

Short Responsory

R⁷ The Word became flesh, alleluia, alleluia. *Repeat* R⁷

V⁷ And he lived among us. R⁷ Glory be. R⁷

Magnificat ant. We glorify you, Mother of God; for Christ was born of you. Keep safe from harm all those who honour you.

Intercessions

Let us acclaim Christ with joy, for out of Bethlehem, in the land of Judah, came a leader who guides his holy people. R⁷ May your grace be with us, Lord.

Christ, our Saviour, speak to those who have not heard your name, —draw all men to yourself. R⁷

Lord, gather all nations into your Church—that the family of man may become the people of God. R⁷

King of kings, direct the minds and hearts of rulers;—guide them to work justly for peace on earth. R⁷

Give faith to those who live in doubt—and hope to those who live in fear. R⁷

Console the sad, comfort those who are in their last agony;—lead them to be refreshed at the spring of your grace. R⁷

Our Father

The concluding prayer as at Morning Prayer.

1 January
Octave Day of Christmas

SOLEMNITY OF MARY, MOTHER OF GOD

EVENING PRAYER I

Magnificat ant. God loved us so much that he sent his own Son in a mortal nature like ours: he was born of a woman, he was born subject to the Law, alleluia.

The concluding prayer as at Morning Prayer.

MORNING PRAYER

Benedictus ant. Today a wonderful mystery is announced: something new has taken place; God has become man; he remained what he was and has become that which he was not: and though the two natures remain distinct, he is one.

Concluding Prayer
God, our Father,
since you gave mankind a saviour through blessed Mary,
virgin and mother,
grant that we may feel the power of her intercession
when she pleads for us with Jesus Christ, your Son,
the author of life,
who lives and reigns with you and the Holy Spirit,
God, for ever and ever.

EVENING PRAYER II

Magnificat ant. Blessed is the womb that bore you, Christ, and blessed are the breasts that suckled you, for you are the Lord and Saviour of the world, alleluia.

The concluding prayer as at Morning Prayer.

THE EPIPHANY OF THE LORD

Solemnity

EVENING PRAYER I

Magnificat ant. The Magi saw the star and said to one another: This is the sign of the great King; let us go and seek him; let us offer him gifts: gold, frankincense and myrrh.

The concluding prayer as at Morning Prayer.

MORNING PRAYER

Benedictus ant. Today the Church has been joined to her heavenly bridegroom, since Christ has purified her of her sins in the river Jordan: the Magi hasten to the royal wedding and offer gifts: the wedding guests rejoice since Christ has changed water into wine, alleluia.

Concluding Prayer
On this day, Lord God,
by a guiding star you revealed your Only-begotten Son
to all the peoples of the world.
Lead us from the faith by which we know you now
to the vision of your glory, face to face.
(We make our prayer) through our Lord.

EVENING PRAYER II

Magnificat ant. Three wonders mark this day we celebrate: today the star led the Magi to the manger; today water was changed into wine at the marriage feast; today Christ desired to be baptized by John in the river Jordan to bring us salvation, alleluia.

The concluding prayer as at Morning Prayer.

Sunday After 6 January
THE BAPTISM OF THE LORD

Feast

If the Sunday is 7 or 8 January, the Feast of the Baptism is omitted.

EVENING PRAYER I

Magnificat ant. The Saviour came to be baptized. He, the second Adam, renewed our corrupted nature by the waters of baptism, and he clothed us with a garment which can never perish.

The concluding prayer as at Morning Prayer.

MORNING PRAYER

Benedictus ant. Christ is baptized and the whole world is made holy; he wipes out the debt of our sins; we will all be purified by water and the Holy Spirit.

Concluding Prayer
Almighty, ever-living God,
when Christ was baptized in the river Jordan
the Holy Spirit came upon him
and your voice proclaimed from heaven 'This is my beloved Son.'
Grant that we,
who by water and the Holy Spirit are your adopted children,
may continue steadfast in your love.
(We make our prayer) through our Lord.

EVENING PRAYER II

Magnificat ant. Jesus Christ has loved us and has purified us from our sins in his blood. He has made us a kingdom and priesthood for God and his Father. To him be glory and kingly power for ever.

The concluding prayer as at Morning Prayer.

SEASON OF LENT
SUNDAYS OF LENT

EVENING PRAYER I

Hymn for Lent.

PSALMODY

Psalms and canticle with proper antiphons as in the psalter for the relevant week.

Scripture Reading   *2 Cor 6:1-4a*
We urge this appeal upon you: you have received the grace of God; do not let it go for nothing. God's own words are: In the hour of my favour I gave heed to you, on the day of deliverance I came to your aid. The hour of favour has now come; now, I say, has the day of deliverance dawned. In order that our service may not be brought into discredit, we avoid giving offence in anything. As God's servants, we try to recommend ourselves in all circumstances.

Short Responsory
R7 Hear us, Lord, and have mercy, for we have sinned against you.
Repeat R7
V Listen, Christ, to the prayers of those who cry to you. R7 Glory be.
R7

Magnificat Antiphon
Man cannot live on bread alone but by every word that comes from the mouth of God.

Intercessions
Let us give glory to Christ the Lord. He is our master, our example and our brother. R7 Lord, give life to your people.
Lord Jesus, you became a man like us in every way, but did not sin;
—may we open our lives to others, share their laughter and tears, and grow day by day in love. R7

Let us serve you in the hungry and give you to eat;—let us see you in the thirsty and give you to drink. R̷

You raised up Lazarus from the dead;—call sinners from their living death to faith and repentance. R̷

May we live up to the example of Mary and the saints;—may we follow you more perfectly in everything. R̷

Let the dead rise in your glory,—let them rejoice for ever in your love. R̷

Our Father

Concluding Prayer

Through our annual Lenten observance, Lord,
deepen our understanding of the mystery of Christ
and make it a reality in the conduct of our lives.
(We make our prayer) through our Lord.

Invitatory

Antiphon of Lent.

MORNING PRAYER

Hymn for Lent.
Psalms and canticle with proper antiphons as in the psalter.

Scripture Reading   *Cf Neh 8:8,10*

This day is holy to the Lord your God; do not mourn or weep. For this day is holy to our Lord; and do not be grieved, for the joy of the Lord is your strength.

Short Responsory

R̷ Christ, Son of the living God, have mercy on us. *Repeat* R̷
V̷ You were wounded because of our sins. R̷ Glory be. R̷

Benedictus Antiphon

Jesus was led by the Spirit into the desert, to be tempted by the devil. He fasted for forty days and forty nights, after which he was hungry.

Intercessions

Let us bless our Redeemer, who has brought us to this day of salvation. R℘ Lord, create a new spirit within us.

Christ, our life, we were buried with you in baptism to rise from the dead;—lead us this day along the new path of life. R℘

You went everywhere, Lord, doing good for everyone;—help us to care for the common good of all. R℘

Help us to work with other people to build the earthly city;—but never let us lose sight of your heavenly kingdom. R℘

Healer of souls and bodies, mend our broken lives;—let us receive all the blessings of your holiness. R℘

Our Father

Concluding Prayer

Through our annual Lenten observance, Lord,
deepen our understanding of the mystery of Christ
and make it a reality in the conduct of our lives.
(We make our prayer) through our Lord.

EVENING PRAYER II

Hymn for Lent.
Psalms and canticle with proper antiphons as in the psalter.

Scripture Reading   *1 Cor 9:24-25*

All the runners at the stadium are trying to win, but only one of them gets the prize. You must run in the same way, meaning to win. All the fighters at the games go into strict training; they do this just to win a wreath that will wither away, but we do it for a wreath that will never wither.

Short Responsory

R℘ Hear us, Lord, and have mercy, for we have sinned against you.
Repeat R℘
℣ Listen, Christ, to the prayers of those who cry to you. R℘ Glory be.
R℘

Magnificat Antiphon

Keep watch over us, eternal Saviour. Do not let the cunning tempter overcome us, for you have become our helper at all times.

Intercessions

God the Father has chosen for himself a people, who are born again, not from any mortal seed but from his everlasting Word. Let us praise his name and turn to him in prayer. ℟ Lord, have mercy on your people.

Merciful God, hear our prayers for all your people;—may they hunger more for your word than for any human food. ℟

Teach us to love sincerely the people of our nation and of every race on earth;—may we work for their peace and welfare. ℟

Strengthen those who will be reborn in baptism;—make them living stones in the temple of your Spirit. ℟

May the dying go forward in hope to meet Christ, their judge;—may they see your face and be happy for ever. ℟

Our Father

The concluding prayer as at Morning Prayer.

MONDAYS OF LENT

Invitatory antiphon of Lent.

MORNING PRAYER

Hymn for Lent.
Psalms and canticle with the antiphons as in the psalter.

Scripture Reading   *Ex 19:4-6a*

You have seen how I bore you on eagles' wings and brought you to myself. Now therefore, if you will obey my voice and keep my covenant, you shall be my own possession among all peoples; for all the earth is mine, and you shall be to me a kingdom of priests and a holy nation.

Short Responsory

R̷ It is he who will free me from the snare of the hunters. *Repeat* R̷
V̷ And from the evil word. R̷ Glory be. R̷

Benedictus Antiphon

Come, you blessed of my Father, inherit the kingdom prepared for you from the foundation of the world.

Intercessions

Blessed be Jesus, our Saviour. Through his death he has opened up for us the way of salvation. Let us pray: R̷ Direct your people, Lord, in the path of true life.

Merciful God, in baptism you gave us a life that is new;—may we ever grow in your likeness. R̷

Let us bring joy this day to those who are in need;—and draw us nearer to you through the help we give them. R̷

Help us to do what is right and good;—let us seek you always with all our heart. R̷

Forgive us for the times we have hurt other people, and failed to preserve the unity of your family;—Lord, have mercy on us. R̷

Our Father

Concluding Prayer

Turn our hearts back to you, God our Saviour;
form us by your heavenly teaching,
so that we may truly profit by our Lenten observance.
(We make our prayer) through our Lord.

EVENING PRAYER

Hymn for Lent.
Psalms and canticle with the antiphons as in the psalter.

Scripture Reading   *Rom 12:1-2*

My brothers, I implore you by God's mercy to offer your very selves to him: a living sacrifice, dedicated and fit for his acceptance, the worship offered by mind and heart. Adapt yourselves no longer to the pattern of this present world, but let your minds be remade and your whole nature thus transformed. Then you will be able to discern the will of God, and to know what is good, acceptable, and perfect.

Short Responsory

R̸ I said: 'Lord, have mercy on me.' *Repeat* R̸

V̸ 'Heal my soul for I have sinned against you.' R̸ Glory be. R̸

Magnificat Antiphon

Anything you did for the least of these who are mine, you did for me, says the Lord.

Intercessions

Let us call on the name of the Lord Jesus, who saves his people from their sins. R̸ Jesus, Son of David, have mercy on us.

Christ our Lord, you gave yourself up for the Church to make her holy;—renew her once more through the spirit of repentance. R̸

Good master, let young people discover that way of life which you have planned for each one of them;—may they be faithful to your grace and fulfil your will for them. R̸

Give hope to the sick and make them well again;—help us to comfort and take care of them. R̸

In baptism you made us sons of the Father;—may we live for you now and always. R̸

Grant to the faithful departed peace and glory;—let us reign with them one day in your heavenly kingdom. R̸

Our Father

The concluding prayer as at Morning Prayer.

TUESDAYS OF LENT

Invitatory antiphon of Lent.

MORNING PRAYER

Hymn for Lent.

Scripture Reading　　　*Joel 2:12-13*

Come back to me with all your hearts, fasting, weeping, mourning.
Let your hearts be broken not your garments torn; turn to the
Lord your God again, for he is all tenderness and compassion, slow
to anger, rich in graciousness, and ready to relent.

Short Responsory

Ry It is he who will free me from the snare of the hunters. *Repeat* Ry
Vy And from the evil word. Ry Glory be. Ry

Benedictus Antiphon

Lord, teach us to pray, as John taught his disciples.

Intercessions

Let us bless Christ, who is our bread from heaven. Ry Christ, bread
of life, strengthen us.

Lord, give us a share in the bread of the eucharist,—fill us with the
blessings of your paschal sacrifice. Ry Christ, bread of life, strengthen
us.

May we take your word to our hearts in faith and obedience;—yield
a harvest in us through our perseverance. Ry

Make us eager to fulfil your plan for the world—that the Church
may spread the great message of peace. Ry

We have sinned, Lord, we have sinned;—take away our guilt by
your saving grace. Ry

Our Father

Concluding Prayer

Look with favour on your family, Lord,
and as at this time we restrain the desires of the body
may our hearts burn with love of you.
(We make our prayer) through our Lord.

EVENING PRAYER

Hymn for Lent.

Scripture Reading   *Jas 2:14,17,18b*

What does it profit, my brethren, if a man says he has faith but has not works? Can his faith save him? So faith by itself, if it has no works, is dead. Show me your faith apart from your works, and I by my works will show you my faith.

Short Responsory

R̷ I said: 'Lord, have mercy on me.' *Repeat* R̷

V̷ 'Heal my soul for I have sinned against you.' R̷ Glory be. R̷

Magnificat Antiphon

When you pray, go into your room and shut the door and pray to your Father there.

Intercessions

Let us pray earnestly to Christ the Lord. He tells us to watch and pray that we may not fall into temptation. R̷ Hear us, Lord, and have mercy.

Lord Jesus, you promised to be with those who are gathered in your name;—keep us united with you as we pray to the Father in the Holy Spirit. R̷

Cleanse your Church from every stain of sin;—make her alive with hope and the power of the Spirit. R̷

Help us to care for our neighbour and show your love for men;—through us let the light of your salvation shine in the world. R̷

Let your peace spread to the ends of the earth;—let men see in every place the signs of your presence. R̷

Bring the dead to everlasting happiness;—let glory and immortal life be theirs. R̷

Our Father

The concluding prayer as at Morning Prayer.

WEDNESDAYS OF LENT

Invitatory antiphon of Lent.

MORNING PRAYER

Hymn for Lent.

Scripture Reading   *Deut 7:6,8-9*

The Lord your God has chosen you to be a people for his own possession, out of all the peoples that are on the face of the earth. It is because the Lord loves you, and is keeping the oath which he swore to your fathers, that the Lord has brought you out with a mighty hand, and redeemed you from the house of bondage, from the hand of Pharaoh king of Egypt. Know therefore that the Lord your God is God, the faithful God who keeps covenant and steadfast love with those who love him and keep his commandments, to a thousand generations.

Short Responsory

℟ It is he who will free me from the snare of the hunters. *Repeat* ℟
℣ And from the evil word. ℟ Glory be. ℟

Benedictus Antiphon

A wicked, godless generation asks for a sign; and the only sign that will be given it is the sign of the prophet Jonah.

Intercessions

Blessed be Christ our Saviour. In him we become a new creation, the old order passes and all things are renewed. Let us pray in living hope. ℟ Renew us, Lord, in your Spirit.

You promised us, Lord, a new heaven and a new earth;—renew us in your Spirit, that we may come to the new Jerusalem and rejoice in you for ever. ℟

Let us work with you to fill the world with your Spirit;—let us perfect our earthly city in justice, charity and peace. ℟

Grant that we may put aside our apathy;—help us to recognize with joy the power you have given us. ℟

Set us free from all evil;—show us in the confusion of our lives the things that really matter. ℟
Our Father

Concluding Prayer
Look with favour on our Lenten observance, Lord,
and while we subdue our bodies by self-denial,
renew our spirit with the grace that prompts us to good works.
(We make our prayer) through our Lord.

EVENING PRAYER

Hymn for Lent.

Scripture Reading   *Phil 2:12b-15a*
Keep on working, with fear and trembling, to complete your salvation, for God is always at work in you to make you willing and able to obey his own purpose. Do everything without complaining or arguing, that you may be innocent and pure, as God's perfect children.

Short Responsory
℟ I said: 'Lord, have mercy on me.' *Repeat* ℟
℣ 'Heal my soul for I have sinned against you.' ℟ Glory be. ℟

Magnificat Antiphon
As Jonah spent three days and three nights inside the whale, so will the Son of Man be inside the heart of the earth.

or

The man who keeps the commandments of God and teaches them to others will be considered great in the kingdom of heaven.

Intercessions
God our Father knows all the needs of his people, but he wants us to give first place to his kingdom. Let us proclaim his greatness in our prayer. ℟ May your kingdom come in all its justice.
Holy Father, you gave us Christ as the shepherd of our souls;—may

your people always have priests who care for them with his great love. R̷ — May your kingdom come in all its justice.

Grant that Christians will prove brothers to the sick;—show them the features of your Son in the faces of those who suffer. R̷

Help those who do not believe in the gospel to come into your Church;—build it up in love to manifest your goodness everywhere. R̷

Father, we know that we are sinners;—grant us your forgiveness and reconcile us with your Church. R̷

May the dead enter eternal life,—may they abide with you for ever. R̷

Our Father

The concluding prayer as at Morning Prayer.

THURSDAYS OF LENT

Invitatory antiphon of Lent.

MORNING PRAYER

Hymn for Lent.

Scripture Reading   *Cf 1 Kings 8:51-53a*

We are your people, Lord, and your heritage. Let your eyes be open to the supplication of your servant and to the supplication of your people Israel, giving ear to us whenever we call to you. For you separated us from among all the people of the earth to be your heritage.

Short Responsory

R̷ It is he who will free me from the snare of the hunters. *Repeat* R̷

℣ And from the evil word. R̷ Glory be. R̷

Benedictus Antiphon

If you, evil though you are, know how to give good gifts to your children, how much more will your Father who is in heaven give good things to those who ask him.

Intercessions

We give praise to Christ our Lord, the radiant light of the world. He guides our steps in a path of light and we no longer live in darkness. Let us turn to him in confident prayer. R7 May your word light up our way.

Christ, our Saviour, may we grow today in your likeness,—may we gain through the second Adam what was lost by the first. R7

May your word take flesh in our lives and your truth shine forth in our actions;—may your love burn brightly within us. R7

Teach us to work for the good of all, whether the time is right or not; —make your Church a welcome light for the whole human family. R7

May we always treasure your friendship and come to know its depth;—may we atone for the sins against your wisdom and love. R7

Our Father

Concluding Prayer

In your bounty, Lord,
give us the Spirit
who alone can teach us to think and do what is right,
so that we, who without you cannot exist,
may live in loving obedience to your will.
(We make our prayer) through our Lord.

EVENING PRAYER

Hymn for Lent.

Scripture Reading   *Jas 4:7-8,10*

Be God's true subjects; stand firm against the devil, and he will run away from you; come close to God, and he will come close to you. You that are sinners must wash your hands clean, you that are in two minds must purify the intention of your hearts. Humble yourselves before the Lord, and he will exalt you.

Short Responsory

R̷ I said: 'Lord, have mercy on me.' *Repeat* R̷
V̷ 'Heal my soul for I have sinned against you.' R̷ Glory be. R̷

Magnificat Antiphon

Ask, and it will be given to you; seek, and you will find; knock, and the door will be open to you.

Intercessions

Let us pray to Christ the Lord, who gave us the new commandment to love one another. R̷ Lord, may your people grow in love.
Good master, teach us to love you in our fellow men,—teach us to serve you in our brothers. R̷
You interceded with the Father for those who nailed you to the cross;—help us to love our enemies and pray for those who injure us. R̷ Lord, may your people grow in love.
Through the mystery of your body and blood deepen our courage and faith,—strengthen the weak, comfort the sorrowful and fill the dying with new hope. R̷
Light of the world, you gave sight to the man born blind;—enlighten men in baptism through the washing in water and the word of life. R̷
Grant to the dead your everlasting love;—count us among the chosen of God. R̷
Our Father

The concluding prayer as at Morning Prayer.

FRIDAYS OF LENT

Invitatory antiphon of Lent.

MORNING PRAYER

Hymn for Lent.

Scripture Reading   *Is 53:11b-12*

By his sufferings shall my servant justify many, taking their faults
on himself. Hence, I will grant whole hordes for his tribute, he shall
divide the spoil with the mighty, for surrendering himself to death,
and letting himself be taken for a sinner, while he was bearing the
faults of many and praying all the time for sinners.

Short Responsory

R̷ It is he who will free me from the snare of the hunters. *Repeat* R̷
V̷ And from the evil word. R̷ Glory be. R̷

Benedictus Antiphon

If your virtue does not surpass that of the scribes and Pharisees, you
will never enter the kingdom of heaven.

Intercessions

We give thanks to Christ the Lord, who died on the cross that we
might live. Let us pray to him with all our heart. R̷ Lord Jesus, may
your death bring us to life.

Master and Saviour, you have taught us by your life and renewed us
by your passion;—do not allow us to grow used to sin. R̷

You call on us to feed the hungry;—let us deny ourselves some food
this day to help our brothers in their need. R̷

May we accept from your hands this day of Lent:—may we make it
yours by deeds of love. R̷

End the rebellion within our hearts;—make us generous and willing
to share. R̷

Our Father

Concluding Prayer

Bend our wills, Lord, so that by this Lenten observance
we may fit ourselves to celebrate the Easter festival;
and as we have all undertaken to subdue the body,
may we all be renewed in spirit.
(We make our prayer) through our Lord.

EVENING PRAYER

Hymn for Lent.

Scripture Reading   *Jas 5:16,19-20*

Confess your sins to one another, and pray for one another, and then you will be healed. My brothers, if one of your number should stray from the truth and another succeed in bringing him back, be sure of this: any man who brings a sinner back from his crooked ways will be rescuing his soul from death and cancelling innumerable sins.

Short Responsory

R̸ I said: 'Lord, have mercy on me.' *Repeat* R̸

V̸ 'Heal my soul for I have sinned against you.' R̸ Glory be. R̸

Magnificat Antiphon

If you are offering your gift at the altar and there remember that your brother has something against you, leave your offering there before the altar, go and be reconciled with your brother first, and then come and present your offering.

Intercessions

Let us pray to the Lord Jesus, who sanctified his people by his own blood. R̸ Lord, have mercy on your people.

Christ our Redeemer, through your suffering help us to mortify our bodies and stand firm in every trial;—may we be ready to celebrate your rising from the dead. R̸

As prophets of God's kingdom may Christians make you known throughout the world,—and may they confirm their message by lives of faith, hope and love. R̸

Lord, give strength to the afflicted;—and give us the will to do everything to help and comfort them. R̸

Teach the faithful to be united with your passion in times of trouble and distress;—let the power of your salvation shine forth in their lives. R̸

Lord, giver of life, remember those who have died;—grant them the glory of your resurrection. R̸

Our Father

The concluding prayer as at Morning Prayer.

SATURDAYS OF LENT

Invitatory antiphon of Lent.

MORNING PRAYER

Hymn for Lent.

Scripture Reading   *Is 1:16-18*
Wash, make yourselves clean, take your wrong-doing out of my
sight. Cease to do evil. Learn to do good, search for justice, help the
oppressed, be just to the orphan, plead for the widow. Come now,
let us talk this over, says the Lord: though your sins are like scarlet,
they shall be white as snow; though they are red as crimson, they
shall be like wool.

Short Responsory
R̷ It is he who will free me from the snare of the hunters. *Repeat* R̷
V̷ And from the evil word. R̷ Glory be. R̷

Benedictus Antiphon
Pray for those who persecute you and for those who treat you badly;
in this way you will be sons of your Father in heaven, says the Lord.

Intercessions
Christ the Lord has made men into a new creation. He gives them a
new birth in the waters of baptism and nourishes them with his word
and his body. Let us glorify him in our prayer. R̷ Renew us, Lord,
by your grace.
Jesus, you are gentle and humble in spirit;—grant us something of
your pity, something of your kindness and something of your
patience towards all men. R̷
Teach us to be neighbours to the sad and the needy;—let us imitate
you, the good Samaritan. R̷
May the Blessed Virgin, your Mother, intercede for religious women;

—through her prayers may they serve you in the Church ever more perfectly. R⁊ Renew us, Lord, by your grace.

Grant us the gift of your mercy,—pardon our sins and save us from punishment. R⁊

Our Father

Concluding Prayer

Turn our hearts to yourself, eternal Father,
so that, always seeking the one thing necessary
and devoting ourselves to works of charity,
we may worship you in spirit and in truth.
(We make our prayer) through our Lord.

HOLY WEEK

PALM SUNDAY OF THE PASSION OF THE LORD

Psalter: Week 2

EVENING PRAYER I

Hymn for Holy Week.
Psalms and canticle with proper antiphons as in the psalter.

Scripture Reading   *1 Pet 1:18-21*
Remember the ransom that was paid to free you from the useless way of life your ancestors handed down was not paid in anything corruptible, neither in silver nor gold, but in the precious blood of a lamb without spot or stain, namely Christ; who, though known since before the world was made, has been revealed only in our time, the end of the ages, for your sake. Through him you now have faith in God, who raised him from the dead and gave him glory for that very reason—so that you would have faith and hope in God.

Short Responsory

℟ We worship you, Christ, and we bless you. *Repeat* ℟
℣ By your cross you have redeemed the world. ℟ Glory be. ℟

Magnificat ant. Hail, Son of David, our king and redeemer of the world! The prophets foretold that you would come and save us.

Intercessions

As his passion drew near, Christ looked on Jerusalem and wept, because it did not recognize that God's salvation had come. Let us pray in faith and repentance. ℟ Lord, have mercy on your people.
Lord, you longed to gather the children of Jerusalem as a hen gathers her chicks under her wings;—help all men to recognize that their moment of salvation has come. ℟
Do not abandon your faithful, even when they desert you;—restore us to yourself, Lord Jesus, and we shall be restored. ℟
Through your suffering help us to mortify our bodies—that we may

be ready to celebrate your rising from the dead. ℟ Lord, have mercy on your people.

You are reigning now in the glory of the Father;—remember those who have died today. ℟

Our Father

Concluding Prayer

Almighty, ever-living God,
you gave our Saviour the command
to become man and undergo the cross,
as an example of humility for all men to follow.
We have the lessons of his sufferings;
give us also the fellowship of his resurrection.
(We make our prayer) through our Lord.

Invitatory

Ant. Christ the Lord was tempted and suffered for us. Come, let us adore him.

MORNING PRAYER

Hymn for Holy Week.
Psalms and canticle with proper antiphons as in the psalter.

Scripture Reading   *Zech 9:9*

Rejoice, rejoice, daughter of Zion, shout aloud, daughter of Jerusalem; for see, your king is coming to you, his cause won, his victory gained.

Short Responsory

℟ You have redeemed us, Lord, by your blood. *Repeat* ℟
℣ From every tribe and tongue and people and nation. ℟ Glory be.
℟

Benedictus ant. With waving palm branches let us adore the Lord as he comes; let us go to meet him with hymns and songs, rejoicing and singing: Blessed be the Lord.

Intercessions

Let us adore Christ the Lord. When he entered Jerusalem, the crowds proclaimed him Messiah and king. ℟ Blessed is he who comes in the name of the Lord.

Hosanna to you, the Son of David, the king of ages;—hosanna to you in your triumph over death and hell. ℟

You went up to Jerusalem to endure the passion and enter into glory;—lead your Church into the paschal feast of eternal life. ℟

You made your cross the tree of life;—share your victory with all the baptized. ℟

You came to save sinners;—bring into your kingdom all who believe, hope and love. ℟

Our Father

Concluding Prayer

Almighty, ever-living God,
you gave our Saviour the command
to become man and undergo the cross,
as an example of humility for all men to follow.
We have the lessons of his sufferings:
give us also the fellowship of his resurrection.
(We make our prayer), through our Lord.

EVENING PRAYER II

Hymn for Holy Week.
Psalms and canticle with proper antiphons as in the psalter.

Scripture Reading   *Acts 13:26-30a*

My brothers, it is to us that this message of salvation has been sent! For the people who live in Jerusalem and their leaders did not know that he is the Saviour, nor did they understand the words of the prophets that are read every Sabbath day. Yet they made the prophets' words come true by condemning Jesus. And even though they could find no reason to pass the death sentence on him, they asked Pilate to have him put to death. And after they had done everything that the Scriptures say about him, they took him down from the cross and placed him in a grave. But God raised him from the dead.

Short Responsory

Ry We worship you, Christ, and we bless you. *Repeat* Ry

Vy By your cross you have redeemed the world. Ry Glory be. Ry

Magnificat ant. It is written: 'I will strike the shepherd down and the sheep of his flock will be scattered.' But after my resurrection I will go before you into Galilee; there you will see me, said the Lord.

Intercessions

Let us pray humbly to the Saviour of all men. He went up to Jerusalem to endure the passion and enter into his glory. Ry Sanctify the people you redeemed by your blood.

Christ our Redeemer, let us share in your passion by works of penance;—let us attain the glory of your resurrection. Ry

Grant us the protection of your Mother, the comforter of the afflicted;—help us to extend to others the consolation you have given us. Ry

Take care of those we have discouraged and those we have wronged; —help us to learn from our sufferings so that justice and love may prevail in the end. Ry

You humbled yourself even to accepting death, death on a cross; —grant to your servants obedience and patience. Ry

Share with the dead your bodily glory;—let us rejoice one day with them in the fellowship of the saints. Ry

Our Father

The concluding prayer as at Morning Prayer.

EASTER TRIDUUM

HOLY THURSDAY

EVENING PRAYER

Evening Prayer is said only by those who do not attend the Evening Mass of the Lord's Supper.

Hymn for Holy Week.
Psalms and canticle with proper antiphons as in the psalter Thursday, Week 2.

Scripture Reading *Heb 13:12-13*
Jesus suffered outside the gate to sanctify the people with his own blood. Let us go to him, then, outside the camp, and share his degradation. For there is no eternal city for us in this life but we look for one in the life to come. Through him let us offer God an unending sacrifice of praise, a verbal sacrifice that is offered every time we acknowledge his name.

In place of the short responsory the following antiphon is said:
Ant. Christ humbled himself for us, and, in obedience, accepted death.

Magnificat ant. As they were eating, Jesus took bread, and when he had said the blessing he broke it and gave it to his disciples.

Intercessions
Let us adore our Saviour, who at the Last Supper, on the night he was betrayed, entrusted to the Church the memorial of his death and resurrection to be celebrated throughout the ages. Confident that he will hear us, we pray: ℟ Sanctify the people whom you redeemed by your blood.
Christ, our Redeemer, let us share in your passion by works of penance;—let us attain the glory of your resurrection. ℟
Grant us the protection of your Mother, the comforter of the afflicted;—may we bring to others the consolation you have given us. ℟

395

Unite the faithful to your passion in times of trouble and distress
—let the power of your salvation shine forth in their lives. ℟ Sanctify
the people whom you redeemed by your blood.
You humbled yourself even to accepting death, death on a cross;—
grant to your servants obedience and patience. ℟
Share with the dead your bodily glory;—let us rejoice one day
with them in the fellowship of the saints. ℟
Our Father

Concluding Prayer
Lord God,
since for your glory and our salvation,
you willed Christ your Son to be the eternal High Priest:
grant that the people he gained for you by his blood,
may be strengthened by his cross and resurrection
when they take part in his memorial sacrifice.
(We make our prayer) through our Lord.

¶ *Night Prayer as given for After Evening Prayer II of Sundays,
pp 322 ff. In place of the short responsory the following antiphon is
said:*

Ant. Christ humbled himself for us, and, in obedience, accepted
death.

GOOD FRIDAY

Invitatory ant. Christ, the Son of God, redeemed us with his blood.
Come, let us adore him.
Psalm, p 3.

MORNING PRAYER

Hymn
Gall he drinks; his strength subduing,
Reed and thorn and nail and spear
Plot his gentle frame's undoing;
Blood and water thence appear,

With their cleansing tide renewing
Earth and sea and starry sphere.

Hail, true cross, of beauty rarest,
King of all the forest trees;
Leaf and flower and fruit thou bearest
Medicine for a world's disease;
Fairest wood, and iron fairest—
Yet more fair, who hung on these.

Bend thy branches down to meet him,
Bend that stubborn heart of thine;
Let thy native force, to greet him,
All its ruggedness resign;
Gently let thy wood entreat him,
Royal sufferer, and divine.

Victim of our race, he deignéd
On thy arms to lay his head;
Thou the ark, whose refuge gainéd,
Sinful man no more may dread;
Ark, whose planks are deeply stainéd
With the blood the Lamb hath shed.

Honour, glory, might and merit
To the eternal Trinity,
Father, Son and Holy Spirit,
Throned in heaven co-equally;
All that doth the world inherit,
Praise one God in Persons three.

PSALMODY

Ant. 1: God did not spare his own Son, but gave him up for us all.

PSALM 50(51)

Have mércy on me, Gód, in your kíndness.*
In your compássion blot óut my offénce.
O wásh me more and móre from my guílt*
and cléanse me fróm my sín.

My offénces trúly I knów them;*
my sín is álways befóre me.
Against yóu, you alóne, have I sínned;*
what is évil in your síght I have dóne.

That you may be jústified whén you give séntence*
and be withóut repróach when you júdge,
O sée, in guílt I was bórn,*
a sínner was Í concéived.

Indéed you love trúth in the héart;*
then in the sécret of my héart teach me wísdom.
O púrify me, thén I shall be cléan;*
O wásh me, I shall be whíter than snów.

Make me héar rejóicing and gládness,*
that the bónes you have crúshed may revíve.
From my síns turn awáy your fáce*
and blót out áll my guílt.

A púre heart creáte for me, O Gód,*
put a stéadfast spírit withín me.
Do not cást me awáy from your présence,*
nor depríve me of your hóly spírit.

Give me agáin the jóy of your hélp;*
with a spírit of férvour sustáin me,
that I may téach transgréssors your wáys*
and sínners may retúrn to yóu.

O réscue me, Gód, my hélper,*
and my tóngue shall ríng out your góodness.
O Lórd, ópen my líps*
and my móuth shall decláre your práise.

For in sácrifice you táke no delíght,*
burnt óffering from mé you would refúse,
my sácrifice, a cóntrite spírit.*
A húmbled, contrite héart you will not spúrn.

In your góodness, show fávour to Síon:*
rebuíld the wálls of Jerúsalem.

Thén you will be pléased with lawful sácrifice,*
hólocausts óffered on your áltar.

Ant. God did not spare his own Son, but gave him up for us all.
Ant. 2: Jesus Christ showed his love for us and freed us from our sins with his life's blood.

CANTICLE: HAB 3:2-4,13A,16-19

Lord, I have heard of your fame,*
I stand in awe at your deeds.
Do them again in our days,†
in our days make them known!*
In spite of your anger, have compassion.

God comes forth from Teman,*
the Holy One comes from Mount Paran.
His splendour covers the sky*
and his glory fills the earth.
His brilliance is like the light,†
rays flash from his hands;*
there his power is hidden.

You march out to save your people,*
to save the one you have anointed.
You make a path for your horses in the sea,*
in the raging of the mighty waters.

This I heard and I tremble with terror,
my lips quiver at the sound.
Weakness invades my bones,*
my steps fail beneath me,
yet I calmly wait for the doom*
that will fall upon the people who assail us.

For even though the fig does not blossom,*
nor fruit grow on the vine,
even though the olive crop fail,*
and fields produce no harvest,
even though flocks vanish from the folds*
and stalls stand empty of cattle,

Yet I will rejoice in the Lord*
and exult in God my saviour.
The Lord my God is my strength.†
He makes me leap like the deer,*
he guides me to the high places.

Ant. Jesus Christ showed his love for us and freed us from our sins
with his life's blood.
Ant. 3: We venerate your cross, Lord; we praise and glorify your
holy resurrection: because of the tree joy has come into the whole
world.

PSALM 147

O práise the Lórd, Jerúsalem!*
Síon, práise your Gód!

He has stréngthened the bárs of your gátes,*
he has bléssed the chíldren withín you.
He estáblished péace on your bórders,*
he féeds you with fínest whéat.

He sénds out his wórd to the éarth*
and swíftly rúns his commánd.
He shówers down snów white as wóol,*
he scátters hóar-frost like áshes.

He húrls down háilstones like crúmbs.*
The wáters are frózen at his tóuch;
he sénds forth his wórd and it mélts them:*
at the bréath of his móuth the waters flów.

He mákes his wórd known to Jácob,*
to Ísrael his láws and decrées.
He has not déalt thus with óther nátions;*
he has not táught them hís decrées.

Ant. We venerate your cross, Lord; we praise and glorify your holy
resurrection: because of the tree joy has come into the whole world.

Scripture Reading   *Is 52:13-15*

See, my servant will prosper, he shall be lifted up, exalted, rise to great heights. As the crowds were appalled on seeing him—so disfigured did he look that he seemed no longer human—so will the crowds be astonished at him and kings stand speechless before him; for they shall see something never told and witness something never heard before.

In place of the short responsory the following antiphon is said:
Ant. Christ humbled himself for us, and, in obedience, accepted death, even death on a cross.

Benedictus ant. Over his head was placed the charge against him: 'This is Jesus, the Nazarene, the King of the Jews.'

Intercessions

Let us pray to our Redeemer, who suffered for us, was buried, and rose from the dead. ℟ Lord, have mercy on us.
Lord and master, for us you became obedient even to death;—keep us faithful to God's will in the darkness of our lives. ℟
Jesus, our life, by dying on the cross you destroyed hell and death;—grant that we may die with you and rise with you in glory. ℟
Christ, our king, you were the scorn of the people, a worm not a man;—teach us to tread your path of humility. ℟
Jesus, our Saviour, you laid down your life for your friends;—let us love one another as you have loved us. ℟
Jesus, our hope, you stretched out your hands on the cross to embrace all ages of men;—gather all God's scattered children into the kingdom of salvation. ℟
Our Father

Concluding Prayer

Be mindful, Lord, of this your family,
for whose sake our Lord Jesus Christ, when betrayed,
did not hesitate to yield himself into his enemies' hands,
and undergo the agony of the cross:
he who lives and reigns with you and the Holy Spirit,
God, for ever and ever.

EASTER SUNDAY
Eastertide Begins

MORNING PRAYER

Today the Invitatory is always said at the beginning of Morning Prayer.
Invitatory ant. The Lord has truly risen, alleluia.
Psalm, p 3.

Hymn

Bring, all ye dear-bought nations, bring, alleluia,
Your richest praises to your King, alleluia,
That spotless Lamb, who more than due, alleluia,
Paid for his sheep, and those sheep you, alleluia.
Alleluia, alleluia, alleluia.

That guiltless Son, who bought your peace, alleluia,
And made his Father's anger cease, alleluia.
Then, Life and Death together fought, alleluia,
Each to a strange extreme were brought, alleluia.
Alleluia, alleluia, alleluia.

We, Lord, with faithful hearts and voice, alleluia,
On this thy rising day rejoice, alleluia.
O thou, whose power o'ercame the grave, alleluia,
By grace and love us sinners save, alleluia.
Alleluia, alleluia, alleluia.

Ant. 1: Christ has risen; he is the light of his people, whom he has redeemed with his blood, alleluia.

Psalms and canticle of Sunday, Week 1.

Ant. 2: Christ, our Redeemer, has risen from the tomb: let us sing a hymn to the Lord, our God, alleluia.

Ant. 3: Alleluia, the Lord has risen as he promised, alleluia.

Scripture Reading *Acts 10:40-43*

God raised Jesus from death on the third day and caused him to appear. He was not seen by all the people, but only by us who are the witnesses that God had already chosen. We ate and drank with him after God raised him from death. And he commanded us to preach the gospel to the people, and to testify that he is the one whom God has appointed Judge of the living and the dead. All the prophets spoke about him, saying that everyone who believes in him will have his sins forgiven through the power of his name.

In place of the short responsory the following antiphon is said:
Ant. This is the day which was made by the Lord: let us rejoice and be glad, alleluia.

Benedictus ant. Very early on the Sunday morning, just after the sun had risen, they came to the tomb, alleluia.

Intercessions

Let us pray to Christ, the author of life. God raised him from the dead, and he himself will raise us to life by his own power. ℟ Christ, our life, save us.

Christ, you are the light that drives out darkness and draws men to holiness;—let us make this day a living hymn of praise. ℟

Lord, you followed the way of suffering, even to the cross;—grant that we may die with you and come to life with you. ℟

Our master and our brother, you have made us a kingdom of priests to serve God our Father;—let us offer you with joy the sacrifice of praise. ℟

King of glory, we look forward to the day of your coming,—then we shall see your face and share in your splendour. ℟

Our Father

Concluding Prayer

On this day, Lord God,
you opened for us the way to eternal life
through your only Son's victory over death.
Grant that as we celebrate the feast of his resurrection
we may be renewed by your Holy Spirit

and rise again in the light of life.
(We make our prayer) through our Lord.

The concluding invitation: Go in the peace of Christ, alleluia, alleluia.
℟ Thanks be to God, alleluia, alleluia.

¶ *This concluding invitation is used at Morning and Evening Prayer
for the whole Easter Octave.*

EVENING PRAYER

Hymn for Easter Day.

PSALMODY

Ant. 1: Mary Magdalen came with the other Mary to see the tomb
where the Lord had been laid, alleluia.

PSALM 109(110):1-5,7

The Lórd's revelátion to my Máster:†
'Sít on my ríght:*
your fóes I will pút beneath your féet.'

The Lórd will wíeld from Síon†
your scéptre of pówer:*
rúle in the mídst of all your fóes.

A prínce from the dáy of your bírth†
on the hóly móuntains;*
from the wómb before the dáwn I begót you.

The Lórd has sworn an óath he will not chánge.†
'You are a príest for éver,*
a príest like Melchízedek of óld.'

The Máster stánding at your ríght hand*
will shatter kíngs in the dáy of his wráth.

He shall drínk from the stréam by the wáyside*
and thérefore he shall líft up his héad.   Glory be.

Ant. Mary Magdalen came with the other Mary to see the tomb
where the Lord had been laid, alleluia.

Ant. 2: Come and see where the Lord was laid, alleluia.

PSALM 113A(114)

When Ísrael came fórth from Égypt,*
Jacob's sóns from an álien péople,
Júdah becáme the Lord's témple,*
Ísrael becáme his kíngdom.

The séa fléd at the síght:*
the Jórdan turned báck on its cóurse,
the móuntains léapt like ráms*
and the hílls like yéarling shéep.

Whý was it, séa, that you fléd,*
that you túrned back, Jórdan, on your cóurse?
Móuntains, that you léapt like ráms,*
hílls, like yéarling shéep?

Trémble, O éarth, before the Lórd,*
in the présence of the Gód of Jácob,
who túrns the róck into a póol*
and flínt into a spríng of wáter.

Ant. Come and see where the Lord was laid, alleluia.

Ant. 3: Jesus said, 'Go, and tell my brothers that they are to leave for
Galilee; they will see me there.' Alleluia.

When chanted, this canticle is sung with Alleluia *as set out below; when
recited it suffices to say* Alleluia *at the beginning and end of each
strophe.*

CANTICLE: REV 19:1,5-7

Alleluia.
Salvation and glory and power belong to our God,*
(℟ Alleluia.)
His judgments are true and just.
℟ Alleluia (alleluia).

Alleluia.
Praise our God, all you his servants,*
(R̷ Alleluia.)
you who fear him, small and great.
R̷ Alleluia (alleluia).

Alleluia.
The Lord our God, the Almighty, reigns.*
(R̷ Alleluia.)
Let us rejoice and exult and give him the glory.
R̷ Alleluia (alleluia).

Alleluia.
The marriage of the Lamb has come,*
(R̷ Alleluia.)
and his bride has made herself ready.
R̷ Alleluia (alleluia).

Ant. Jesus said, 'Go, and tell my brothers that they are to leave for Galilee; they will see me there.' Alleluia.

Scripture Reading   *Heb 10:12-14*
Christ has offered one single sacrifice for sins, and then taken his place for ever at the right hand of God, where he is now waiting until his enemies are made into a footstool for him. By virtue of that one single offering he has achieved the eternal perfection of all whom he is sanctifying.

In place of the short responsory the following antiphon is said:
Ant. This is the day which was made by the Lord: let us rejoice and be glad, alleluia.

Magnificat ant. On the evening of that Sunday, when the disciples were gathered behind locked doors, Jesus came and stood among them. He said to them, 'Peace be with you, alleluia.'

Intercessions
Let us pray with joy to Christ the Lord. He rose from the dead and is living now to intercede for us. R̷ Victorious king, hear us.
Christ, you are the light of the world and the salvation of nations;

—set us on fire with your Spirit as we proclaim the wonder of your resurrection. R℣

Let Israel recognize in you the Messiah it has longed for;—fill all men with the knowledge of your glory. R℣

Keep us united in the communion of saints;—may we find rest with them, when life's work is done. R℣

You have overcome death, the last enemy of man;—destroy everything in us that is at enmity with God. R℣

Christ, our Saviour, you became obedient to death, but God raised you to the heights;—receive our brothers into the kingdom of your glory. R℣

Our Father

Concluding Prayer
On this day, Lord God,
you opened for us the way to eternal life
through your only Son's victory over death.
Grant that as we celebrate the feast of his resurrection
we may be renewed by your Holy Spirit
and rise again in the light of life.
(We make our prayer) through our Lord.

Concluding invitation: Go in the peace of Christ, alleluia, alleluia.
R℣ Thanks be to God, alleluia, alleluia.

During the Easter Octave and on Low Sunday, Morning Prayer and Evening Prayer of Easter Sunday may be used.

NIGHT PRAYER

During Eastertide, psalms are said or sung under the following single antiphon:
Ant. Alleluia, alleluia, alleluia.

During the Easter Octave either form of Night Prayer for Sundays, pp 319 ff, or pp 322 ff, is used daily, and in place of the short responsory, the following antiphon is said:

Ant. This is the day which was made by the Lord: let us rejoice and be glad, alleluia.

SUNDAYS
OF THE EASTER SEASON

Sundays 3 and 7: Psalter Week .
Sunday 4: Psalter Week .
Sunday 5: Psalter Week .
Sunday 6: Psalter Week .

EVENING PRAYER I

Hymn for Eastertide.
Psalms and canticle with proper antiphons as in the psalter.

Scripture Reading   *1 Pet 2:9-10*
You are a chosen race, a royal priesthood, a consecrated nation, a
people set apart to sing the praises of God who called you out o
darkness into his wonderful light. Once you were not a people at all
and now you are the people of God; once you were outside the
mercy and now you have been given mercy.

Short Responsory
R﹀ The disciples rejoiced, alleluia, alleluia. *Repeat* R﹀
℣ They saw the Lord. R﹀ Glory be. R﹀

Magnificat Antiphon
Stay with us, Lord, for evening is approaching and the day is almos
over, alleluia.

Intercessions
Let us pray to Christ, our life and our resurrection. R﹀ Son of the
living God, protect your people.
We pray for your Catholic Church;—may she reveal among the
nations your kingdom of justice and holiness. R﹀
We pray for the sick, the sorrowful, captives and exiles:—show them
your power and compassion. R﹀

We pray for those who have lost you in the maze of life:—let them know once more the joy of coming home. R̦

Crucified and risen Saviour, you will come again in judgment:—be merciful to us sinners. R̦

We pray for all the living,—and for those who have left this world in the hope of the resurrection. R̦

Our Father

Concluding Prayer

Lord God,
grant your people constant joy
in the renewed vigour of their souls.
They rejoice because you have restored them
to the glory of your adopted children:
let them look forward gladly
in the certain hope of resurrection.
(We make our prayer) through our Lord.

Invitatory

Ant. The Lord has truly risen, alleluia.

MORNING PRAYER

Hymn for Eastertide.
Psalms and canticle with proper antiphons as in the psalter.

Scripture Reading   *Acts 10:40-43*
God raised Jesus from death on the third day and caused him to appear. He was not seen by all the people, but only by us who are the witnesses that God had already chosen. We ate and drank with him after God raised him from death. And he commanded us to preach the gospel to the people, and to testify that he is the one whom God has appointed Judge of the living and the dead. All the prophets spoke about him, saying that everyone who believes in him will have his sins forgiven through the power of his name.

Short Responsory

R̷ Have mercy on us, Christ, Son of the living God, alleluia, alleluia.
Repeat R̷
V̷ You have risen from the dead. R̷ Glory be. R̷

Benedictus Antiphon

It was necessary that Christ should suffer and on the third day rise
from the dead, alleluia.

Intercessions

Let us pray to Christ, the author of life. God raised him from the
dead, and he himself will raise us to life by his own power. R̷ Christ
our life, save us.

Christ, you are the light that drives out darkness and draws men to
holiness;—let us make this day a living hymn of praise. R̷

Lord, you followed the way of suffering, even to the cross;—grant
that we may die with you and come to life with you. R̷

Our master and our brother, you have made us a kingdom of priests
to serve God our Father;—let us offer to you with joy the sacrifice of
praise. R̷

King of glory, we look forward to the day of your coming;—grant
that we may see your face and share in your splendour. R̷

Our Father

Concluding Prayer

Lord God,
grant your people constant joy
in the renewed vigour of their souls.
They rejoice because you have restored them
to the glory of your adopted children:
let them look forward gladly
in the certain hope of resurrection.
(We make our prayer) through our Lord.

EVENING PRAYER II

Hymn for Eastertide.
Psalms and canticle with proper antiphons as in the psalter.

Scripture Reading   *Heb 10:12-14*
Christ has offered one single sacrifice for sins, and then taken his place for ever at the right hand of God, where he is now waiting until his enemies are made into a footstool for him. By virtue of that one single offering he has achieved the eternal perfection of all whom he is sanctifying.

Short Responsory
R̶/ The Lord has truly risen, alleluia, alleluia. *Repeat* R̶/
V̶/ He has appeared to Simon. R̶/ Glory be. R̶/

Magnificat Antiphon
Jesus said to his disciples, 'Bring some of the fish you have just caught.' Simon Peter went aboard and dragged the net to the shore, full of fish, alleluia.

Intercessions
Let us pray with joy to Christ the Lord. He rose from the dead and is living now to intercede for us. R̶/ Victorious king, hear us.
Christ, you are the light of the world and the salvation of nations;
—set us on fire with your Spirit as we proclaim the wonder of your resurrection. R̶/
Let Israel recognize in you the Messiah they have longed for:—fill all men with the knowledge of your glory. R̶/
Keep us united in the communion of saints;—may we find rest with them, when life's work is done. R̶/
You have overcome death, the last enemy of man;—destroy everything in us that is at enmity with God. R̶/
Christ, our Saviour, you became obedient to death, but God raised you to the heights;—receive our brothers into the kingdom of your glory. R̶/
Our Father

The concluding prayer as at Morning Prayer.

MONDAYS
OF THE EASTER SEASON

Weeks 2 and 6: Psalter, Week 2
Weeks 3 and 7: Psalter, Week 3
Week 4: Psalter, Week 4
Week 5: Psalter, Week 1

Invitatory ant. The Lord has truly risen, alleluia.

MORNING PRAYER

Hymn for Eastertide.
Psalms and canticle with the antiphons for Eastertide as in the psalter.

Scripture Reading   *Rom 10:8b-10*
It is on your lips, it is in your heart, meaning by that the message of
faith which we preach. You can find salvation, if you will use your
lips to confess that Jesus is the Lord, and your heart to believe that
God has raised him up from the dead. The heart has only to believe,
if we are to be justified; the lips have only to make confession, if we
are to be saved.

Short Responsory
R⁷ The Lord has risen from the dead, alleluia, alleluia. *Repeat* R⁷
V For our sake he died on the cross. R⁷ Glory be. R⁷

Benedictus Antiphon
I tell you solemnly, unless a man is born again he cannot see the
kingdom of God, alleluia.

Intercessions
Let us pray to the Father, whose glory was displayed in the death
and resurrection of his Son. R⁷ Lord, enlighten our minds and hearts.
God, Father of light, you have illumined the world with the glory of
Christ;—may the light of faith shine in our lives today. R⁷

Through the resurrection of your Son you have opened man's way to everlasting life;—may all our work today be filled with the hope of your kingdom. R̸

Through your risen Son you sent the Holy Spirit into the world;—set our hearts on fire with his divine love. R̸

By hanging on the cross, your Son won our lasting freedom;—may he stay with us today as our Saviour and Redeemer. R̸

Our Father

Concluding Prayer

Almighty, ever-living God,
we confidently call you Father as well as Lord.
Renew your Spirit in our hearts,
make us ever more perfectly your children,
so that we may enter upon the inheritance you have promised us.
(We make our prayer) through our Lord.

EVENING PRAYER

Hymn for Eastertide.
Psalms and canticle with antiphons for Eastertide as in the psalter.

Scripture Reading   *Heb 8:1b-3a*

This high priest of ours is one who has taken his seat in heaven, on the right hand of that throne where God sits in majesty, ministering now in the sanctuary, in that true tabernacle which the Lord, not man, has set up. After all, it is the very function of a priest to offer gift and sacrifice.

Short Responsory

R̸ The disciples rejoiced, alleluia, alleluia. *Repeat* R̸
℣ They saw the Lord. R̸ Glory be. R̸

Magnificat Antiphon

What is born of the flesh is flesh; what is born of the Spirit is spirit, alleluia.

Intercessions

Rejoicing, let us pray to Christ the Lord, who sheds glory on the universe through his resurrection. ℟ Christ, our life, hear us.

Lord Jesus, you joined your disciples on the way to Emmaus;—accompany your Church on her journey through life. ℟

May we, your faithful, not be slow to believe;—give us the courage to proclaim your victory over death. ℟

Look upon those who have not recognized your presence in their lives;—let their hearts rejoice in the knowledge of their Saviour. ℟

You are the judge of the living and the dead;—grant to the faithful departed forgiveness of their sins. ℟

Our Father

The concluding prayer as at Morning Prayer.

TUESDAYS
OF THE EASTER SEASON

Invitatory ant. The Lord has truly risen, alleluia.

MORNING PRAYER

Hymn for Eastertide.

Scripture Reading   *Acts 13:30-33*

God raised Jesus from the dead and for many days he was seen by those who had travelled with him from Galilee to Jerusalem. They are now witnesses for him to the people of Israel. And we are here to bring the Good News to you: what God promised our ancestors he would do, he has now done for us, who are their descendants, by raising Jesus to life. As it is written: You are my son, Today I have become your Father.

Short Responsory

℟ The Lord has risen from the dead, alleluia, alleluia. *Repeat* ℟
℣ For our sake he died on the cross. ℟ Glory be. ℟

Benedictus Antiphon

I am the Alpha and the Omega, the beginning and the end; I am of the house and family of David, the bright star of the morning, alleluia.

Intercessions

Let us pray to God the Father, whose Son became the Lamb without blemish to take away the sins of the world. R℣ God of life, save us.

Father, be mindful of your Son, who died on the cross and was raised again to life;—hear him interceding for us now. R℣

Let us cast out the leaven of corruption and malice;—let us celebrate Christ's passover in purity and truth. R℣

May we overcome today all envy and dissension;—help us to take care of our brothers in their every need. R℣

Place deep in our hearts the spirit of the gospel;—may it inspire us to keep your commandments today and always. R℣

Our Father

Concluding Prayer

Almighty God,
give your Church the grace
to proclaim the power of Jesus, our Risen Lord.
We have received the first fruits of his grace:
prepare us for the full revelation of his gifts.
(We make our prayer) through our Lord.

EVENING PRAYER

Hymn for Eastertide.

Scripture Reading   *1 Pet 2:4-5*

He is the living stone, rejected by men, but chosen by God and precious to him; set yourselves close to him so that you too, the holy priesthood that offers the spiritual sacrifices which Jesus Christ has made acceptable to God, may be living stones making a spiritual house.

Short Responsory

R℣ The disciples rejoiced, alleluia, alleluia. *Repeat* R℣
℣ They saw the Lord. R℣ Glory be. R℣

Magnificat Antiphon

Did not our hearts burn within us as Jesus talked to us on the road,
alleluia.

Intercessions

Let us pray to Christ, who by his resurrection strengthens his people
in hope. R℣ Ever-living Christ, hear us.

Lord Jesus, from your opened side there poured out blood and
water;—cleanse the Church, your bride, from every stain of sin. R℣

Good shepherd, risen from the dead, you gave to the apostle Peter
the care of your flock;—may Pope N. be ever strengthened in charity
and zeal. R℣

Beside the lake of Galilee, you directed your disciples to a great catch
of fish;—direct the work of your disciples today, and give them your
abundant blessing. R℣

On the shore of the lake you prepared food for your disciples;—help
us to find your joy in caring for others. R℣

Jesus, the last Adam, life-giving Spirit, conform the dead to your
likeness;—make their joy complete. R℣

Our Father

The concluding prayer as at Morning Prayer.

WEDNESDAYS
OF THE EASTER SEASON

Invitatory ant. The Lord has truly risen, alleluia.

MORNING PRAYER

Hymn for Eastertide.

Scripture Reading   *Rom 6:8-11*

If we have died with Christ, we have faith to believe that we shall share his life. We know that Christ, now he has risen from the dead, cannot die any more; death has no more power over him; the death he died was a death, once for all, to sin; the life he now lives is a life that looks towards God. And you, too, must think of yourselves as dead to sin, and alive with a life that looks towards God, through Christ Jesus our Lord.

Short Responsory

R⁷ The Lord has risen from the dead, alleluia, alleluia. *Repeat* R⁷
℣ For our sake he died on the cross. R⁷ Glory be. R⁷

Benedictus Antiphon

God loved the world so much that he gave his only Son, so that everyone who believes in him may not be lost but may have eternal life, alleluia.

Intercessions

Let us pray to God, who manifested to the apostles the glory of the risen Christ. R⁷ Glorify us. Lord, with the glory of Christ.

Father, we praise you today with grateful hearts, because you have called us into your own marvellous light;—help us always to see your loving-kindness. R⁷

Through your Holy Spirit strengthen and purify men;—give them new heart in their struggle to improve the quality of life. R⁷

May we pour out our lives in the service of men:—bless our efforts, that the whole of humanity may become a sacrifice acceptable to you. R⁷

At the start of the day fill our hearts with your love;—let the praise of your glory be the joy of our lives. R⁷

Our Father

Concluding Prayer

Year by year, Lord,
we recall the mystery of Easter,
the mystery which restored mankind to its lost dignity

and brought the hope of resurrection.
Grant that we may possess eternally in love
what we now worship in faith.
(We make our prayer) through our Lord.

EVENING PRAYER

Hymn for Eastertide.

Scripture Reading   *Heb 7:24-27*
Jesus, because he remains for ever, can never lose his priesthood. It
follows, then, that his power to save is utterly certain, since he is
living for ever to intercede for all who come to God through him.
To suit us, the ideal high priest would have to be holy, innocent
and uncontaminated, beyond the influence of sinners, and raised
up above the heavens; one who would not need to offer sacrifices
every day, as the other high priests do for their own sins and then
for those of the people, because he has done this once and for all by
offering himself.

Short Responsory
R/ The disciples rejoiced, alleluia, alleluia. *Repeat* R/
V/ They saw the Lord. R/ Glory be. R/

Magnificat Antiphon
The man who lives by the truth comes into the light, so that it may
be plainly seen that what he does is done in God, alleluia.

Intercessions
In Christ, who was raised from the dead, the Father has opened for
us the way to eternal life. Let us pray to him: R/ Save your people
through the victory of Christ.
God of our fathers, in the resurrection you glorified your Son;—
grant us true repentance that we may walk in newness of life. R/
You have brought us to Christ, the shepherd and guardian of our
souls;—keep us faithful to him, under the guidance of our pastors.
R/

From the Jewish people you chose Christ's first disciples;—show the children of Israel that your promises are fulfilled. ℟

Remember the orphans, the widows and the homeless of our world; —your Son has reconciled men with God, do not abandon them now. ℟

You called Stephen to yourself as he bore witness to Jesus;—welcome the faithful departed who have loved and desired you. ℟

Our Father

The concluding prayer as at Morning Prayer.

THURSDAYS
OF THE EASTER SEASON

Invitatory ant. The Lord has truly risen, alleluia.

MORNING PRAYER

Hymn for Eastertide.

Scripture Reading   *Rom 8:10-11*

If Christ lives in you, then although the body be a dead thing in virtue of our guilt, the spirit is a living thing, by virtue of our justification. And if the Spirit of him who raised up Jesus from the dead dwells in you, he who raised up Jesus Christ from the dead will give life to your perishable bodies too, for the sake of his Spirit who dwells in you.

Short Responsory

℟ The Lord has risen from the dead, alleluia, alleluia. *Repeat* ℟
℣ For our sake he died on the cross. ℟ Glory be. ℟

Benedictus Antiphon

The Father loves the Son, and has entrusted everything to him, alleluia.

Intercessions

Let us pray with confidence to God our Father. In Christ he has
given all his children the pledge of resurrection. R℣ May the Lord
Jesus be our life.

Father, by a pillar of fire you led your people through the desert:
—may the risen Christ be the light of our lives. R℣

Through the voice of Moses you spoke on the mountain;—may the
risen Christ be our word of life. R℣

With the gift of manna you fed your wandering people;—may the
risen Christ be our bread from heaven. R℣

You drew water from the rock to save your children;—may the
risen Christ fill us with his Spirit. R℣

Our Father

Concluding Prayer

God of mercy,
let the mystery we celebrate at Eastertide
bear fruit for us in every season.
(We make our prayer) through our Lord.

EVENING PRAYER

Hymn for Eastertide.

Scripture Reading *1 Pet 3:18,22*

Christ himself, innocent though he was, died once for sins, died for
the guilty, to lead us to God. In the body, he was put to death, in
the spirit he was raised to life. He has entered heaven and is at God's
right hand, now that he has made the angels and Dominations and
Powers his subjects.

Short Responsory

R℣ The disciples rejoiced, alleluia, alleluia. *Repeat* R℣
℣ They saw the Lord. R℣ Glory be. R℣

Magnificat Antiphon

Anyone who believes in the Son has eternal life, alleluia.

Intercessions

Let us pray to Christ, who is our living hope of rising from the dead.

R/ King of glory, hear us.

Lord Jesus, by shedding your blood and rising from death you entered into your glory;—let us go with you into the presence of your Father. R/

You sent your disciples into the world, their faith made strong by the resurrection;—grant that bishops and priests may be faithful ministers of your gospel. R/

Through your resurrection you united the faithful in one hope and love;—may we share in your ministry of peace and reconciliation. R/

Through your resurrection you healed the cripple who begged at the entrance to the temple;—look with pity on the sick and display in them your glory. R/

You are the first to rise from the dead, the first of many brothers;—share your glory with those who have hoped in you. R/

Our Father

The concluding prayer as at Morning Prayer.

FRIDAYS
OF THE EASTER SEASON

Invitatory ant. The Lord has truly risen, alleluia.

MORNING PRAYER

Hymn for Eastertide.

Scripture Reading   *Acts 5:30-32*

The God of our fathers raised Jesus from death, after you had killed him by nailing him to a cross. And God raised him to his right side as Leader and Saviour, to give to the people of Israel the opportunity to repent and have their sins forgiven. We are witnesses to these things—we and the Holy Spirit, who is God's gift to those who obey him.

Short Responsory

R̸ The Lord has risen from the dead, alleluia, alleluia. *Repeat* R̸
V̸ For our sake he died on the cross. R̸ Glory be. R̸

Benedictus Antiphon

Jesus took the loaves, gave thanks and distributed them to th
people as they sat there, alleluia.

Intercessions

Through his Spirit God raised Jesus from the dead and he will giv
life to our own mortal bodies. Let us pray to him, saying: R̸ Lord
give us life through your Holy Spirit.

Father, you accepted the sacrifice of your Son, raising him from th
dead;—receive our morning offering and lead us to eternal life. R̸
Reveal your presence in our work this day;—may we do everything
for your glory and for the sanctification of our world. R̸
Do not allow our work to come to nothing;—let it serve our fellow
men and bring us to your kingdom. R̸
Open our eyes to see our brother's need;—warm our hearts that we
may offer him our love. R̸

Our Father

Concluding Prayer

By your will, Lord God,
your Son underwent the agony of the cross
to break the power of Satan over man.
Give your people grace to rise again with Christ,
who lives and reigns with you and the Holy Spirit,
God, for ever and ever.

EVENING PRAYER

Hymn for Eastertide.

Scripture Reading   *Heb 5:8-10*

Although he was Son, Christ learnt to obey through suffering; but
having been made perfect, he became for all who obey him the

source of eternal salvation and was acclaimed by God with the title
of high priest of the order of Melchizedek.

Short Responsory

R⁷ The disciples rejoiced, alleluia, alleluia. *Repeat* R⁷
V They saw the Lord. R⁷ Glory be. R⁷

Magnificat Antiphon

By submitting to death on the cross he destroyed the power of hell;
he has covered himself in glory by rising on the third day, alleluia.

Intercessions

Let us pray to Christ, the fount of life and the source of virtue.
R⁷ Lord, restore your kingdom in the world.
Jesus, our Saviour, in the body you were put to death, in the Spirit
you were raised to life;—grant that we may die to sin, and live in the
power of your resurrection. R⁷
You sent your disciples to proclaim throughout the world the gospel
of salvation;—may all who preach your word be alive with the Holy
Spirit. R⁷
You received all power in heaven and on earth to bear witness to the
truth;—guide in the spirit of truth the plans of governments and
rulers. R⁷
Keep our eyes fixed on the new heaven and the new earth;—make
us care more deeply for our world and its future. R⁷
You descended into hell to bring the dead good news;—let the
faithful departed come to you, their joy, their hope, their glory. R⁷
Our Father

The concluding prayer as at Morning Prayer.

SATURDAYS
OF THE EASTER SEASON

Invitatory ant. The Lord has truly risen, alleluia.

MORNING PRAYER

Hymn for Eastertide.

Scripture Reading   *Rom 14:7-9*
None of us lives for himself only, none of us dies for himself only
if we live, it is for the Lord that we live, and if we die, it is for the
Lord that we die. Whether we live or die, then, we belong to the
Lord. For Christ died and rose to life in order to be the Lord of the
living and of the dead.

Short Responsory
℞ The Lord has risen from the dead, alleluia, alleluia. *Repeat* ℞
℣ For our sake he died on the cross. ℞ Glory be. ℞

Benedictus Antiphon
Peace be with you, it is I, alleluia; do not be afraid, alleluia.

Intercessions
Let us pray to Christ, who has revealed to us the knowledge of
everlasting life. ℞ Lord, may your resurrection enrich us with your
grace.
Eternal Shepherd, strengthen us for the coming day with the bread
of your word;—nourish us with the bread of the eucharist. ℞
May your voice find a response in our hearts;—do not let your
word be silenced by rejection or indifference. ℞
You are at work in those who spread the gospel, confirming the
truth of their message;—help us to manifest your resurrection by
our way of living. ℞
You yourself are the joy that can never be taken away;—may we
leave behind the sadness of sin and experience eternal life. ℞
Our Father

Concluding Prayer
Since it is from you, God our Father,
that redemption comes to us, your adopted children:

424

ook with favour on the family you love,
ive true freedom to us and to all who believe in Christ,
nd bring us all alike to our eternal heritage.
We make our prayer) through our Lord.

THE ASCENSION OF THE LORD

Solemnity

EVENING PRAYER I

Magnificat ant. Father, I have made your name known to the men
ou gave me; now I pray for them, not for the world, since I am
oming to you, alleluia.

The concluding prayer as at Morning Prayer.

MORNING PRAYER

Benedictus ant. I am ascending to my Father and your Father, to my
God and your God, alleluia.

Concluding Prayer
Almighty God,
ll us with a holy joy,
each us how to thank you with reverence and love
n account of the ascension of Christ your Son.
You have raised us up with him;
vhere he, the head, has preceded us in glory,
here we, the body, are called in hope.
We make our prayer) through our Lord.

EVENING PRAYER II

Magnificat ant. King of Glory, Lord Almighty, today you have
ascended victoriously above the heavens; do not leave us as orphans
vithout a guide, but send the one whom you promised, the gift of
he Father, the Spirit of Truth, alleluia.

The concluding prayer as at Morning Prayer.

PENTECOST SUNDAY

Solemnit

EVENING PRAYER I

Hymn for Pentecost.

PSALMODY

Ant. 1: On the day of Pentecost they were all together in one place alleluia.

PSALM 112(113

Práise, O sérvants of the Lórd,*
práise the náme of the Lórd!
May the náme of the Lórd be bléssed*
both nów and for évermóre!
From the rísing of the sún to its sétting*
práised be the náme of the Lórd!

Hígh above all nátions is the Lórd,*
abóve the héavens his glóry.
Whó is like the Lórd, our Gód,*
who has rísen on hígh to his thróne
yet stóops from the héights to look dówn,*
to look dówn upon héaven and éarth?

From the dúst he lífts up the lówly,*
from his mísery he ráises the póor
to sét him in the cómpany of prínces,*
yés, with the prínces of his péople.
To the chíldless wífe he gives a hóme*
and gláddens her héart with chíldren.

Ant. On the day of Pentecost they were all together in one place alleluia.

Ant. 2: There appeared to the apostles what seemed like tongues o
fire, and the Holy Spirit came upon each of them, alleluia.

Praise the Lórd for hé is góod;†
sing to our Gód for hé is lóving:*
to hím our práise is dúe.

The Lórd buílds up Jerúsalem*
and bríngs back Ísrael's éxiles,
he héals the bróken-héarted,*
he bínds up áll their wóunds.
He fíxes the númber of the stárs;*
he cálls each óne by its náme.

Our Lórd is gréat and almíghty;*
his wísdom can néver be méasured.
The Lórd ráises the lówly;*
he húmbles the wícked to the dúst.
O síng to the Lórd, giving thánks;*
sing psálms to our Gód with the hárp.

He cóvers the héavens with clóuds;*
he prepáres the ráin for the éarth,
making móuntains spróut with gráss*
and with plánts to sérve man's néeds.
He provídes the béasts with their fóod*
and young rávens that cáll upón him.

His delíght is nót in hórses*
nor his pléasure in wárriors' stréngth.
The Lórd delights in thóse who revére him,*
in thóse who wáit for his lóve.

Ant. There appeared to the apostles what seemed like tongues of
fire, and the Holy Spirit came upon each of them, alleluia.
Ant. 3: The Holy Spirit, who comes from the Father, will glorify me,
alleluia.

Great and wonderful are your deeds,*
O Lord God the Almighty!
Just and true are your ways,*
O King of the ages!

Who shall not fear and glorify your name, O Lord?*
For you alone are holy.
All nations shall come and worship you,*
for your judgments have been revealed.

Ant. The Holy Spirit, who comes from the Father, will glorify me,
alleluia.

Scripture Reading   *Rom 8:11*
If the Spirit of God who raised up Jesus from the dead dwells in you,
he who raised up Jesus Christ from the dead will give life to your
perishable bodies too, for the sake of his Spirit who dwells in you.

Short Responsory
R⁊ The Holy Spirit is the Advocate, alleluia, alleluia. *Repeat* R⁊
Y He will teach you everything. R⁊ Glory be. R⁊

Magnificat ant. Come, Holy Spirit, fill the hearts of your faithful,
and enkindle in them the fire of your love; though the peoples spoke
different tongues you united them in proclaiming the same faith,
alleluia.

Intercessions
The apostles waited and prayed for the coming of the Spirit.
Gathered together in their company, we pray for his coming tonight,
and joyfully proclaim the greatness of God. R⁊ Father, send us your
Spirit.
In Christ you restored the universe which you made;—through your
Spirit renew the faith of the earth. R⁊
You breathed into Adam the breath of life:—breathe your Spirit
into the Church, that the world may find life in her. R⁊
May your Spirit bring light to our darkness;—turn hatred into love,

orrow into joy, and doubt into hope. R̷

Cleanse and refresh us in the waters of the Spirit;—where there is anguish and sin, bring healing and rebirth. R̷

Through the Holy Spirit you bring men to life and glory:—may the dead enter their home in heaven to enjoy your love forever. R̷

Our Father

Concluding Prayer

Almighty, ever-living God,
you ordained that the paschal mystery
be completed by the mystery of Pentecost.
Gather together, by your gift of grace,
the scattered nations and divided tongues
to one faith in your Name.
(We make our prayer) through our Lord.

Invitatory

Ant. Alleluia, the Spirit of the Lord has filled the whole world.
Come, let us adore him, alleluia.

MORNING PRAYER

Hymn

A mighty wind invades the world,
So strong and free on beating wing:
It is the Spirit of the Lord
From whom all truth and freedom spring.

The Spirit is a fountain clear
For ever leaping to the sky,
Whose waters give unending life,
Whose timeless source is never dry.

The Spirit comes in tongues of flame,
With love and wisdom burning bright,
The wind, the fountain and the fire
Combine in this great feast of light.

O tranquil Spirit, bring us peace,
With God the Father and the Son.

We praise you, blessed Trinity,
Unchanging, and for ever One.

Ant. 1: How good and how kind, Lord, is your Spirit in us, alleluia

Psalms and canticle from Sunday: Week 1.

Ant. 2: Let every spring of water bless the Lord; let everything that
lives in water sing a hymn to God, alleluia.

Ant. 3: The apostles spoke in different tongues and proclaimed the
wonderful deeds of God, alleluia.

Scripture Reading   *Acts 5:30-32*
The God of our fathers raised Jesus from death, after you had killed
him by nailing him to a cross. And God raised him to his right side
as Leader and Saviour, to give to the people of Israel the opportunity
to repent and have their sins forgiven. We are witnesses to these
things—we and the Holy Spirit, who is God's gift to those who obey
him.

Short Responsory
R꜠ They were all filled with the Holy Spirit, alleluia, alleluia.
Repeat R꜠
V꜠ They began to speak. R꜠ Glory be. R꜠

Benedictus ant. Receive the Holy Spirit. Those whose sins you
forgive will be forgiven them, alleluia.

Intercessions
On this day of Pentecost, the Church is filled with joy. Strengthened
with measureless hope, we pray to Christ, who is calling his Church
together in the Holy Spirit. R꜠ Lord, renew the face of the earth.
Lord Jesus, raised on the cross, you poured out the water of rebirth
for the life of the world.—Quicken the life of all men with the gift
of the Spirit. R꜠
Raised up to God's right hand, you bestowed on the apostles the
Father's Gift;—your Church now waits for the same Gift, the same
hope. R꜠

You breathed your Spirit upon the apostles, and gave them the power
of forgiveness:—set all men free today from the prison of sin. R⁄
You promised to send us the Spirit of truth, that we might become
your heralds throughout the world.—Through his presence in the
Church may we bear faithful witness to you. R⁄

Our Father

Concluding Prayer

Lord God,
you sanctify your Church in every race and nation
by the mystery we celebrate on this day.
Pour out the gifts of the Holy Spirit on all mankind,
and fulfil now in the hearts of your faithful
what you accomplished
when the Gospel was first preached on earth.
(We make our prayer) through our Lord.

EVENING PRAYER II

Hymn for Pentecost.

PSALMODY

Ant. 1: The Spirit of the Lord has filled the whole world, alleluia.

Psalms and canticle from Sunday: Week 1.

Ant. 2: Send forth your power, Lord, from your holy temple in
Jerusalem, and bring to perfection your work among us, alleluia.

Ant. 3: They were all filled with the Holy Spirit and began to speak,
alleluia.

Scripture Reading   *Eph 4:3-6*

Do your best to preserve the unity which the Spirit gives, by the
peace that binds you together. There is one Body and one Spirit,
just as there is one hope to which God has called you. There is one
Lord, one faith, one baptism; there is one God and Father of all
men, who is Lord of all, works through all, and is in all.

431

Short Responsory

R⍣ The Spirit of the Lord has filled the whole world, alleluia, alleluia.
Repeat R⍣
℣ It is he who holds all things in being and understands every word
that is spoken. R⍣ Glory be. R⍣

Magnificat ant. This is the day of Pentecost, alleluia; today the Holy
Spirit appeared to the disciples in the form of fire and gave to them
his special gifts; he sent them into the world to proclaim that whoever believes and is baptized will be saved alleluia.

Intercessions

We know that the Father is with us because of the Spirit he has given
us. With this confidence we turn to you in prayer: R⍣ Father, send
your Spirit into the Church!
Father, you want to unite all men by baptism in the Spirit;—draw all
believers together in mind and heart. R⍣
You sent the Spirit to fill the earth with your love;—let men build
the human city in justice and peace. R⍣
Lord God, Father of all men, bring to your scattered children unity
of faith:—make the world alive with the power of your Spirit. R⍣
By the work of the Spirit you create all minds afresh:—heal the sick,
comfort the afflicted, and bring all men to salvation. R⍣
Through the Holy Spirit you raised your Son from the dead.—Raise
us by the power of your Spirit when we come to your kingdom. R⍣
Our Father

Concluding Prayer

Lord God,
you sanctify your Church in every race and nation
by the mystery we celebrate on this day.
Pour out the gifts of the Holy Spirit on all mankind,
and fulfil now in the hearts of your faithful
what you accomplished
when the Gospel was first preached on earth.
(We make our prayer) through our Lord.

The invitation to leave is:
Go in the peace of Christ, alleluia, alleluia.
R⍣ Thanks be to God, alleluia, alleluia.

FEASTS OF THE LORD
IN ORDINARY TIME

Sunday after Pentecost
THE MOST HOLY TRINITY

Solemnity

EVENING PRAYER I

Magnificat ant. We give you thanks, O God; we give thanks to you the one and true Trinity, the one and highest God, the one and all-holy Unity.

The concluding prayer as at Morning Prayer.

MORNING PRAYER

Benedictus ant. Blessed be the creator and ruler of all things, the holy and undivided Trinity, both now and for ever and for ages unending.

Concluding Prayer
God our Father,
you revealed the great mystery of your godhead to men
when you sent into the world
the Word who is Truth
and the Spirit who makes us holy.
Help us to believe in you and worship you,
as the true faith teaches:
three Persons, eternal in glory,
one God, infinite in majesty.
(We make our prayer) through our Lord.

EVENING PRAYER II

Magnificat ant. With our heart and lips we praise you, we worship you and we bless you, God the Father unbegotten, only-begotten Son, and Holy Spirit Paraclete: all glory is yours for ever.

The concluding prayer as at Morning Prayer.

Thursday after Holy Trinity
(In Australia, Sunday after Trinity Sunday)
THE BODY AND BLOOD
OF CHRIST

EVENING PRAYER I

Magnificat ant. Lord, how good you are and how gentle is your spirit. When you wished to show your goodness to your sons you gave them bread from heaven, filling the hungry with good things and sending the rich away empty.

The concluding prayer as at Morning Prayer.

MORNING PRAYER

Benedictus ant. I am the living bread which came down from heaven; whoever eats this bread will live for ever, alleluia.

Concluding Prayer
Lord Jesus Christ,
you gave your Church an admirable sacrament
as the abiding memorial of your passion.
Teach us so to worship
the sacred mystery of your Body and Blood,
that its redeeming power
may sanctify us always.
Who live and reign with the Father and the Holy Spirit,
God, for ever and ever.

EVENING PRAYER II

Magnificat ant. O sacred feast in which we partake of Christ: his sufferings are remembered, our minds are filled with his grace and we receive a pledge of the glory that is to be ours, alleluia.

The concluding prayer as at Morning Prayer

Friday after the Second Sunday after Pentecost
THE MOST SACRED HEART
OF JESUS

Solemnity

EVENING PRAYER I

Magnificat ant. I have come to spread fire on earth, and how I wish it were blazing already.

The concluding prayer as at Morning Prayer.

MORNING PRAYER

Benedictus ant. In his tender mercy God has visited us; he has redeemed his people, alleluia.

Concluding Prayer
Almighty God and Father,
we glory in the Sacred Heart of Jesus, your beloved Son,
as we call to mind the great things his love has done for us.
Fill us with the grace that flows in abundance
from the Heart of Jesus, the source of heaven's gifts.
(We make our prayer) through our Lord.

EVENING PRAYER II

Magnificat ant. The Lord has received us into his own self, into his heart, remembering his mercy, alleluia.

The concluding prayer as at Morning Prayer.

THE ORDINARY SUNDAYS
OF THE YEAR

THE ORDINARY SUNDAYS
OF THE YEAR

WEEK 1

Psalter: Week 1

The Feast of the Baptism of the Lord takes the place of the Sunday.

SUNDAY 2

Psalter: Week 2

EVENING PRAYER I

Magnificat ant. Behold the Lamb of God who takes away the sins of the world, alleluia.

The concluding prayer as at Morning Prayer.

MORNING PRAYER

Benedictus ant. The disciples went and saw where Jesus was staying, and they spent the rest of the day with him.

Concluding Prayer
Almighty God,
ruler of all things in heaven and on earth,
listen favourably to the prayer of your people,
and grant us your peace in our day.
(We make our prayer) through our Lord.

EVENING PRAYER II

Magnificat ant. There was a wedding at Cana in Galilee, and Jesus was there with Mary his mother.

The concluding prayer as at Morning Prayer.

SUNDAY 3

Psalter: Week 3

EVENING PRAYER I

Magnificat ant. Jesus preached the gospel of the kingdom of God, and cured those who were in need of healing.

The concluding prayer as at Morning Prayer.

MORNING PRAYER

Benedictus ant. Come, follow me, the Lord; I will make you fishers of men.

Concluding Prayer
All-powerful, ever-living God,
direct our steps in the way of your love,
so that our whole life may be fragrant
with all we do in the name of Jesus, your beloved Son,
who lives and reigns with you and the Holy Spirit,
God, for ever and ever.

EVENING PRAYER II

Magnificat ant. The spirit of the Lord rests upon me; he has sent me to preach his gospel to the poor.

The concluding prayer as at Morning Prayer.

SUNDAY 4

Psalter: Week 4

EVENING PRAYER I

Magnificat ant. When Jesus saw the crowds he went up the mountain; his disciples came and gathered round him and he began to teach them.

The concluding prayer as at Morning Prayer.

MORNING PRAYER

Benedictus ant. The people were astounded at his teaching because he taught them with authority.

Concluding Prayer

Lord our God,
make us love you above all things,
and all our fellow-men
with a love that is worthy of you.
(We make our prayer) through our Lord.

EVENING PRAYER II

Magnificat ant. Everyone was astonished at the words that came from the mouth of God.

The concluding prayer as at Morning Prayer.

SUNDAY 5

Psalter: Week 1

EVENING PRAYER I

Magnificat ant. You are the light of the world. Let your light shine before men; let them see your good works and give honour to your Father in heaven.

The concluding prayer as at Morning Prayer.

MORNING PRAYER

Benedictus ant. Jesus got up early in the morning and left the house. He went to a deserted place and prayed there.

Concluding Prayer

Guard your family, Lord, with constant loving care,
for in your divine grace we place our only hope.
(We make our prayer) through our Lord.

EVENING PRAYER II

Magnificat ant. Master, we have worked hard all night and have caught nothing; but if you say so, I will let down the nets.

The concluding prayer as at Morning Prayer

SUNDAY 6

Psalter: Week 2

EVENING PRAYER I

Magnificat ant. If you are offering your gift at the altar and there remember that your brother has something against you, leave your offering there before the altar, go and be reconciled with your brother first, and then come and present your offering, alleluia.

The concluding prayer as at Morning Prayer.

MORNING PRAYER

Benedictus ant. Lord, if it is your will, you can make me clean. Jesus answered: It is my will, may you be clean.

Concluding Prayer
To those who love you, Lord,
you promise to come with your Son
and make your home within them.
Come then with your purifying grace
and make our hearts a place where you can dwell.
(We make our prayer) through our Lord.

EVENING PRAYER II

Magnificat ant. Blessed are you who are in need; the kingdom of God is yours. Blessed are you who hunger now; you shall be satisfied.

The concluding prayer as at Morning Prayer.

SUNDAY 7

Psalter: Week 3

EVENING PRAYER I

Magnificat ant. Pray for those who persecute you and for those who treat you badly; in this way you will be sons of your Father in heaven, says the Lord.

The concluding prayer as at Morning Prayer

MORNING PRAYER

Benedictus ant. The paralytic took up the bed on which he was lying and gave praise to God. When the people saw this they also praised God.

Concluding Prayer
Grant, almighty God,
that with our thoughts always on the things of the Spirit
we may please you in all that we say and do.
(We make our prayer) through our Lord.

EVENING PRAYER II

Magnificat ant. Do not judge, and you will not be judged, says the Lord; as you judge others, so you also will be judged.

The concluding prayer as at Morning Prayer.

SUNDAY 8

Psalter: Week 4

EVENING PRAYER I

Magnificat ant. Set your hearts first on the kingdom of God, and on keeping his commandments, and then all these other things will be given you as well, alleluia.

The concluding prayer as at Morning Prayer.

MORNING PRAYER

Benedictus ant. No man puts new wine into old wineskins; new wine must be kept in new skins.

Concluding Prayer
In your mercy, Lord, direct the affairs of men so peaceably
that your Church may serve you in tranquillity and joy.
(We make our prayer) through our Lord.

EVENING PRAYER II

Magnificat ant. A good tree cannot bear bad fruit; a bad tree cannot bring forth good fruit.

The concluding prayer as at Morning Prayer.

SUNDAY 9

Psalter: Week 1

EVENING PRAYER I

Magnificat ant. It is not the man who says to me, 'Lord, Lord', who will enter the kingdom of heaven: but the man who does the will of my Father will enter the kingdom of heaven.

The concluding prayer as at Morning Prayer.

MORNING PRAYER

Benedictus ant. The sabbath day was made for man, not man for the sabbath.

Concluding Prayer
Lord God, by whom our lives are governed with unfailing
   wisdom and love,
take away from us all that is harmful

and give us all that will be for our good.
(We make our prayer) through our Lord.

EVENING PRAYER II

Magnificat ant. Lord, I am not worthy to have you under my roof;
only say the word and my servant will be healed.

The concluding prayer as at Morning Prayer.

SUNDAY 10

Psalter: Week 2

EVENING PRAYER I

Magnificat ant. Mercy is what I want, not sacrifice. For I did not
come to call the virtuous, but sinners.

The concluding prayer as at Morning Prayer.

MORNING PRAYER

Benedictus ant. Whoever does the will of God is my brother, and my
sister, and my mother.

Concluding Prayer
Lord God, source of all good,
hear our prayer:
inspire us with good intentions,
and help us to fulfil them.
(We make our prayer) through our Lord.

EVENING PRAYER II

Magnificat ant. A great prophet has risen up among us and God has
come to visit his people.

The concluding prayer as at Morning Prayer.

SUNDAY 11

Psalter: Week 3

EVENING PRAYER I

Magnificat ant. Go, preach the gospel of the kingdom; you received without cost, you must give without charge, alleluia.

The concluding prayer as at Morning Prayer.

MORNING PRAYER

Benedictus ant. The kingdom of heaven is like a mustard seed which is the smallest of all seeds; yet it grows into the biggest shrub of all.

Concluding Prayer
Lord God, strength of those who hope in you,
support us in our prayer:
because we are weak and can do nothing without you,
give us always the help of your grace
so that, in fulfilling your commandments,
we may please you in all we desire and do.
(We make our prayer) through our Lord.

EVENING PRAYER II

Magnificat ant. Jesus said to the woman, 'Your faith has saved you. Go in peace.'

The concluding prayer as at Morning Prayer.

SUNDAY 12

Psalter: Week 4

EVENING PRAYER I

Magnificat ant. If any man bears witness to me before men, I also will bear witness to him in the presence of my Father.

The concluding prayer as at Morning Prayer.

MORNING PRAYER

Benedictus ant. Save us, Lord, we are in danger; O God, give the command, and there will be peace.

Concluding Prayer
Lord God,
teach us at all times to fear and love your holy name,
for you never withdraw your guiding hand
from those you establish in your love.
(We make our prayer) through our Lord.

EVENING PRAYER II

Magnificat ant. If any man wishes to come after me, he must deny himself and take up his cross, and in that way he must follow me.

The concluding prayer as at Morning Prayer.

SUNDAY 13

Psalter: Week 1

EVENING PRAYER I

Magnificat ant. Whoever receives you, receives me; and whoever receives me, receives the one who sent me, says the Lord.

The concluding prayer as at Morning Prayer.

MORNING PRAYER

Benedictus ant. Jesus turned round and saw the woman. He said, 'Take courage, daughter: your faith has saved you, alleluia.'

Concluding Prayer
Lord God,
since by the adoption of grace,
you have made us children of light:

do not let false doctrine darken our minds,
but grant that your light may shine within us
and we may always live in the brightness of truth.
(We make our prayer) through our Lord.

EVENING PRAYER II

Magnificat ant. The Son of Man came not to destroy souls but to
save them.

The concluding prayer as at Morning Prayer.

SUNDAY 14

Psalter: Week 2

EVENING PRAYER

Magnificat ant. My yoke is easy and my burden is light, says the
Lord.

The concluding prayer as at Morning Prayer.

MORNING PRAYER

Benedictus ant. Many were astonished when they heard the teaching
of Jesus. They said, 'How is it that all this has come to him? Surely
this is the carpenter, the son of Mary?'

Concluding Prayer
Lord God,
when our world lay in ruins
you raised it up again
on the foundation of your Son's passion and death;
give us grace to rejoice in the freedom from sin
which he gained for us,
and bring us to everlasting joy.
(We make our prayer) through our Lord.

EVENING PRAYER II

Magnificat ant. The harvest is great, but the labourers are few. Pray to the Lord of the harvest that he may send labourers into his harvest.

The concluding prayer as at Morning Prayer.

SUNDAY 15

Psalter: Week 3

EVENING PRAYER I

Magnificat ant. The seed is the word of God and Christ is the sower; whoever listens to this word will live for ever.

The concluding prayer as at Morning Prayer.

MORNING PRAYER

Benedictus ant. The disciples set out to preach repentance; and they anointed many sick people with oil and cured them.

Concluding Prayer
God and Father,
to those who go astray you reveal the light of your truth
and enable them to return to the right path:
grant that all who have received the grace of baptism
may strive to be worthy of their Christian calling,
and reject everything opposed to it.
(We make our prayer) through our Lord.

EVENING PRAYER II

Magnificat ant. 'Master, what is the greatest commandment in the Law?' Jesus said to him, 'You must love the Lord your God with all your heart, alleluia.'

The concluding prayer as at Morning Prayer.

SUNDAY 16

Psalter: Week 4

EVENING PRAYER I

Magnificat ant. The kingdom is like the yeast a woman took and mixed in with three measures of flour till it was leavened all through.

The concluding prayer as at Morning Prayer.

MORNING PRAYER

Benedictus ant. Jesus saw the great multitude and he was moved to compassion for them because they were like a flock of sheep with no shepherd.

Concluding Prayer
Be gracious, Lord, to us who serve you,
and in your kindness increase your gifts of grace within us:
so that fervent in faith, hope and love
we may be ever on the watch
and persevere in doing what you command.
(We make our prayer) through our Lord.

EVENING PRAYER II

Magnificat ant. Mary has chosen the better part and it will never be taken from her.

The concluding prayer as at Morning Prayer.

SUNDAY 17

Psalter: Week 1

EVENING PRAYER I

Magnificat ant. The kingdom of heaven is like a merchant seeking good pearls; when he has found one of great value he sells everything else and buys it.

The concluding prayer as at Morning Prayer.

MORNING PRAYER

Benedictus ant. When those men saw the sign that Jesus had given, they said, 'This really is the Prophet who is to come into the world.'

Concluding Prayer
Lord God, protector of those who hope in you,
without whom nothing is strong, nothing holy,
support us always with your love.
Guide us so to use the good things of this world,
that even now we may hold fast to what endures for ever.
(We make our prayer) through our Lord.

EVENING PRAYER II

Magnificat ant. Ask, and you will receive; seek and you will find; knock, and the door will be opened to you, alleluia.

The concluding prayer as at Morning Prayer.

SUNDAY 18

Psalter: Week 2

EVENING PRAYER I

Magnificat ant. A great crowd had gathered about Jesus, and they had nothing to eat. He called his disciples and said to them, 'I feel compassion for all these people.'

The concluding prayer as at Morning Prayer.

MORNING PRAYER

Benedictus ant. Do not work for food that cannot last, but work for food that endures to eternal life.

Concluding Prayer
We recognize with joy
that you, Lord, created us,
and that you guide us by your providence.
In your unfailing kindness
support us in our prayer:
renew your life within us,
guard it and make it bear fruit for eternity.
(We make our prayer) through our Lord.

EVENING PRAYER II

Magnificat ant. If you wish to be truly rich, my brothers, then seek true riches.

The concluding prayer as at Morning Prayer.

SUNDAY 19

Psalter: Week 3

EVENING PRAYER I

Magnificat ant. 'Lord, bid me to come to you on the waters.' Jesus reached out his hand and took hold of Peter. He said, 'Man of little faith, why did you doubt?'

The concluding prayer as at Morning Prayer.

MORNING PRAYER

Benedictus ant. Truly I say to you, 'Whoever has faith in me has eternal life, alleluia.'

Concluding Prayer
Almighty, ever-living God,
we confidently call you Father as well as Lord.
Renew your Spirit in our hearts,

make us ever more perfectly your children,
so that we may enter upon the inheritance you have promised us.
(We make our prayer) through our Lord.

EVENING PRAYER II

Magnificat ant. Wherever your treasure is, there also will your heart
be, says the Lord.

The concluding prayer as at Morning Prayer.

SUNDAY 20

Psalter: Week 4

EVENING PRAYER I

Magnificat ant. Woman, your faith is great; let it be done for you
as you have asked.

The concluding prayer as at Morning Prayer.

MORNING PRAYER

Benedictus ant. I am the living bread which has come down from
heaven. If any man eats of this bread he will live for ever, alleluia.

Concluding Prayer
Lord God,
you have prepared for those who love you
what no eye has seen, no ear has heard.
Fill our hearts with your love,
so that loving you above all and in all,
we may attain your promises
which the heart of man has not conceived.
(We make our prayer) through our Lord.

EVENING PRAYER II

Magnificat ant. I have come to spread a fire on earth, and how I wish it were blazing already.

The concluding prayer as at Morning Prayer.

SUNDAY 21

Psalter: Week 1

EVENING PRAYER I

Magnificat ant. 'You are the Christ, the Son of the living God.' 'Blessed are you, Simon, Bar Jona.'

The concluding prayer as at Morning Prayer.

MORNING PRAYER

Benedictus ant. To whom shall we go, Lord? You have the words of eternal life. We believe and we know that you are the Christ, the Son of God, alleluia.

Concluding Prayer
Lord, by your grace we are made one in mind and heart.
Give us a love for what you command
and a longing for what you promise,
so that, amid this world's changes,
our hearts may be set on the world of lasting joy.
(We make our prayer) through our Lord.

EVENING PRAYER II

Magnificat ant. Many will come from the east and from the west to take their places with Abraham and Isaac and Jacob in the kingdom of heaven.

The concluding prayer as at Morning Prayer.

SUNDAY 22

Psalter: Week 2

EVENING PRAYER I

Magnificat ant. What does it profit a man if he gains the whole world, but suffers the loss of his own soul?

The concluding prayer as at Morning Prayer.

MORNING PRAYER

Benedictus ant. Listen, and understand these traditions which the Lord has given to you.

Concluding Prayer
Father of might and power,
every good and perfect gift
comes down to us from you.
Implant in our hearts the love of your name,
increase our zeal for your service,
nourish what is good in us
and tend it with watchful care.
(We make our prayer) through our Lord.

EVENING PRAYER II

Magnificat ant. When you are invited to a marriage feast sit in the lowest place, so that the one who invited you can say to you, 'Friend, take a higher place.' Then everyone with you at table will see you honoured, alleluia.

The concluding prayer as at Morning Prayer.

SUNDAY 23

Psalter: Week 3

EVENING PRAYER I

Magnificat ant. Where two or three are gathered together in my name, I am there in their midst, says the Lord.

The concluding prayer as at Morning Prayer.

MORNING PRAYER

Benedictus ant. He has done all things well: he made the deaf hear and the dumb speak, alleluia.

Concluding Prayer
Since it is from you, God our Father,
that redemption comes to us, your adopted children:
look with favour on the family you love,
give true freedom to us and to all who believe in Christ,
and bring us all alike to our eternal heritage.
(We make our prayer) through our Lord.

EVENING PRAYER II

Magnificat ant. Whoever does not take up his cross and follow me, cannot be my disciple, says the Lord.

The concluding prayer as at Morning Prayer.

SUNDAY 24

Psalter: Week 4

EVENING PRAYER I

Magnificant ant. Jesus said to Peter, 'I do not say to you that you should forgive seven times, but rather seventy-seven times.'

The concluding prayer as at Morning Prayer.

MORNING PRAYER

Benedictus ant. Whoever loses his life for my sake and for the sake of the gospel, will save it, says the Lord.

Concluding Prayer
Look upon us, Lord, creator and ruler of the whole world:
give us grace to serve you with all our heart
that we may come to know the power of your forgiveness and love.
(We make our prayer) through our Lord.

EVENING PRAYER II

Magnificat ant. I say to you that there is great joy among the angels when one sinner repents.

The concluding prayer as at Morning Prayer.

SUNDAY 25

Psalter: Week 1

EVENING PRAYER I

Magnificat ant. You also must go into my vineyard; and I will pay you what is just.

The concluding prayer as at Morning Prayer.

MORNING PRAYER

Benedictus ant. The greatest among you must be your servant, says the Lord. Anyone who humbles himself will be exalted, alleluia.

Concluding Prayer
Father,
you summed up the whole law
as love of you and of our neighbour.
Grant that by keeping this commandment of love,

456

we may come to eternal life.
(We make our prayer) through our Lord.

EVENING PRAYER II

Magnificat ant. No man can serve two masters. You cannot serve both God and money.

The concluding prayer as at Morning Prayer.

SUNDAY 26

Psalter: Week 2

EVENING PRAYER I

Magnificat ant. It is not the man who says to me, 'Lord, Lord,' who will enter the kingdom of heaven, but the man who does the will of my Father, alleluia.

The concluding prayer as at Morning Prayer.

MORNING PRAYER

Benedictus ant. Whoever gives you a drink of water in my name, because you follow Christ, will not lose his reward, says the Lord.

Concluding Prayer
Lord,
you reveal your mighty power
most of all by your forgiveness and compassion:
fill us constantly with your grace
as we hasten to share the joys you have promised us in heaven.
(We make our prayer) through our Lord.

EVENING PRAYER II

Magnificat ant. My son, remember that you received good things during your life, just as Lazarus received bad things.

The concluding prayer as at Morning Prayer.

SUNDAY 27

Psalter: Week 3

EVENING PRAYER I

Magnificat ant. He will bring those wretched men to a wretched end and lease the vineyard to other tenants who will deliver the fruits to him at the proper season.

The concluding prayer as at Morning Prayer.

MORNING PRAYER

Benedictus ant. Let the little children come to me; for the kingdom of heaven belongs to such as these.

Concluding Prayer
Almighty, ever-living God,
whose love surpasses all that we ask or deserve,
open up for us the treasures of your mercy.
Forgive us all that weighs on our conscience,
and grant us more even than we dare to ask.
(We make our prayer) through our Lord.

EVENING PRAYER II

Magnificat ant. Say to yourselves, 'We are useless servants, we only did what we had to do.'

The concluding prayer as at Morning Prayer.

SUNDAY 28

Psalter: Week 4

EVENING PRAYER I

Magnificat ant. A certain man prepared a great feast and invited many guests. When everything was ready and the time for the feast had come he sent his servant to call those who had been invited, alleluia.

The concluding prayer as at Morning Prayer

MORNING PRAYER

Benedictus ant. You, who have left everything and have come after me, will receive a hundredfold in return and will possess eternal life.

Concluding Prayer
Lord God,
open our hearts to your grace.
Let it go before us and be with us,
that we may always be intent upon doing your will.
(We make our prayer) through our Lord.

EVENING PRAYER II

Magnificat ant. When one of them saw that he had been made clean, he went back and gave praise to God with a loud voice, alleluia.

The concluding prayer as at Morning Prayer.

SUNDAY 29

Psalter: Week 1

EVENING PRAYER I

Magnificat ant. Give to Caesar the things that belong to Caesar, and to God the things that belong to God, alleluia.

The concluding prayer as at Morning Prayer.

MORNING PRAYER

Benedictus ant. The Son of Man did not come to be served but to serve, and to give up his life to redeem many.

Concluding Prayer
Almighty, ever-living God,
make us ever obey you willingly and promptly.
Teach us how to serve you
with sincere and upright hearts
in every sphere of life.
(We make our prayer) through our Lord.

EVENING PRAYER II

Magnificat ant. When the Son of Man comes, do you think he will find faith on earth?

The concluding prayer as at Morning Prayer.

SUNDAY 30

Psalter: Week 2

EVENING PRAYER I

Magnificat ant. 'Master, what is the greatest commandment in the Law?' Jesus said to him, 'You must love the Lord your God with all your heart, alleluia.'

The concluding prayer as at Morning Prayer.

MORNING PRAYER

Benedictus ant. 'Have mercy on me, Son of David,' 'What do you wish me to do for you?' 'Lord, that I may see.'

Concluding Prayer
Lord God, deepen our faith,
strengthen our hope,
enkindle our love:
and so that we may obtain what you promise

make us love what you command.
(We make our prayer) through our Lord.

EVENING PRAYER II

Magnificat ant. The publican went home justified, for everyone who exalts himself will be humbled, but the man who humbles himself will be exalted.

The concluding prayer as at Morning Prayer.

SUNDAY 31

Psalter: Week 3

EVENING PRAYER I

Magnificat ant. You have only one master and he is in heaven: Christ, the Lord.

The concluding prayer as at Morning Prayer.

MORNING PRAYER

Benedictus ant. You must love the Lord your God with all your heart. You must love your fellow man as yourself. There is no other commandment that is more important than these.

Concluding Prayer
God of power and mercy,
by whose grace your people give you praise and worthy service:
save us from faltering on our way
to the joys you have promised.
(We make our prayer) through our Lord.

EVENING PRAYER II

Magnificat ant. The Son of Man came to seek out and to save that which was lost.

The concluding prayer as at Morning Prayer.

SUNDAY 32

Psalter: Week 4

EVENING PRAYER I

Magnificat ant. At midnight a cry was raised: 'Behold, the bridegroom is coming, go out and meet him.'

The concluding prayer as at Morning Prayer.

MORNING PRAYER

Benedictus ant. That poor widow gave more than all the others, for in her poverty she gave all she had.

Concluding Prayer
Defend us, Lord, against every distress
so that unencumbered in body and soul,
we may devote ourselves to your service in freedom and joy.
(We make our prayer) through our Lord.

EVENING PRAYER II

Magnificat ant. He is God, not of the dead, but of the living: because for him all things are alive, alleluia.

The concluding prayer as at Morning Prayer.

SUNDAY 33

Psalter: Week 1

(If this is the last Sunday of the Year the solemnity of Christ the King, pp 357 ff, is celebrated.)

EVENING PRAYER I

Magnificat ant. Well done, my good servant, you have proved yourself faithful in small things. Enter into the joy of your Lord.

The concluding prayer as at Morning Prayer.

MORNING PRAYER

Benedictus ant. They will see the Son of Man coming on the clouds of heaven with great power and glory.

Concluding Prayer
Lord our God,
give us grace to serve you always with joy,
because our full and lasting happiness
is to make of our lives
a constant service to the Author of all that is good.
(We make our prayer) through our Lord.

EVENING PRAYER II

Magnificat ant. Your endurance will win you your lives, says the Lord.

The concluding prayer as at Morning Prayer.

Last Sunday of the Year
CHRIST THE KING

EVENING PRAYER I

Magnificat ant. The Lord God will give him the throne of David, his ancestor; he will reign in the house of Jacob for ever and his kingdom will know no end, alleluia.

The concluding prayer as at Morning Prayer.

MORNING PRAYER

Benedictus ant. He made us a kingdom for his God and Father; he is the firstborn from the dead, the leader of the kings of the earth, alleluia.

Concluding Prayer
Almighty, ever-living God,
it is your will
to unite the entire universe
under your beloved Son,
Jesus Christ, the King of heaven and earth.
Grant freedom to the whole of creation,
and let it praise and serve your majesty for ever.
(We make our prayer) through our Lord.

EVENING PRAYER II

Magnificat ant. All authority in heaven and on earth has been given to me, says the Lord.

The concluding prayer as at Morning Prayer.

SAINTS OF THE GENERAL CALENDAR

SOLEMNITIES AND FEASTS

2 February

THE PRESENTATION OF THE LORD

Feast

If this day is a Sunday:

EVENING PRAYER I

Magnificat ant. The old man held the child, but the child was his king; the virgin bore the child, yet remained a virgin after the birth; she adored as her God the child she bore.

The concluding prayer as at Morning Prayer.

MORNING PRAYER

Benedictus ant. When his parents brought in the child Jesus, Simeon took him in his arms and gave thanks to God.

Concluding Prayer
Almighty, ever-living God,
on this day your Only-begotten Son
was presented in the temple,
in flesh and blood like ours:
purify us in mind and heart
that we may meet you in your glory.
(We make our prayer) through our Lord.

EVENING PRAYER II

Magnificat ant. Today the Blessed Virgin Mary presented the child Jesus in the temple; there Simeon took him in his arms and gave thanks to God.

The concluding prayer as at Morning Prayer.

19 March
SAINT JOSEPH
Husband of the Blessed Virgin Mary
Solemnity

EVENING PRAYER I

Magnificat ant. Behold the faithful and wise servant, whom the Master placed over his household (alleluia).

The concluding prayer as at Morning Prayer.

MORNING PRAYER

Benedictus ant. Joseph settled in a town called Nazareth. This was to fulfil the words spoken about Christ by the prophets: He will be called a Nazarene (alleluia).

Concluding Prayer
Almighty God,
at the beginnings of our salvation,
when Mary conceived your Son and brought him forth into the
    world,
you placed them under Joseph's watchful care.
May his prayer still help your Church
to be an equally faithful guardian of your mysteries,
and a sign of Christ to mankind.
(We make our prayer) through our Lord.

EVENING PRAYER II

Magnificat ant. When Jesus started to teach, he was about thirty years old, being the son, as it was thought, of Joseph (alleluia).

The concluding prayer as at Morning Prayer,

25 March

THE ANNUNCIATION OF THE LORD

Solemnity

EVENING PRAYER I

Magnificat ant. The Holy Spirit will come upon you, Mary, and the power of the Most High will overshadow you (alleluia).

The concluding prayer as at Morning Prayer.

MORNING PRAYER

Benedictus ant. God loved us so much that he sent his own Son in a mortal nature like ours (alleluia).

Concluding Prayer
Shape us in the likeness of the divine nature of our Redeemer,
whom we believe to be true God and true man,
since it was your will, Lord God,
that he, your Word,
should take to himself our human nature
in the womb of the Blessed Virgin Mary.
(We make our prayer) through our Lord.

EVENING PRAYER II

Magnificat ant. The angel Gabriel said to Mary: Hail, full of grace: the Lord is with you. You are the most blessed of all women (alleluia).

The concluding prayer as at Morning Prayer.

24 June
THE BIRTHDAY OF
SAINT JOHN THE BAPTIST
Solemnity

EVENING PRAYER I

Magnificat ant. When Zachary had entered the temple of the Lord, the angel Gabriel appeared to him, standing on the right of the altar of incense.

The concluding prayer as at Morning Prayer.

MORNING PRAYER

Benedictus ant. Zachary opened his mouth and spoke this prophecy: Blessed be the Lord, the God of Israel.

Concluding Prayer
Almighty God and Father,
you sent Saint John the Baptist to the people of Israel
to make them ready for Christ the Lord.
Give us the grace of joy in the Spirit,
and guide the hearts of all the faithful
in the way of salvation and peace.
(We make our prayer) through our Lord.

EVENING PRAYER II

Magnificat ant. The child that is born to us today is greater than any prophet: this is he of whom the Saviour said, 'Among those born of women there was no man greater than John the Baptist.'

The concluding prayer as at Morning Prayer.

29 June
SAINTS PETER AND PAUL
Apostles

Solemnity

EVENING PRAYER I

Magnificat ant. Glorious are the apostles of Christ; they loved each other in this life; they are not separated in death.

The concluding prayer as at Morning Prayer.

MORNING PRAYER

Benedictus ant. Simon Peter said, 'Lord, to whom shall we go? You have the words of eternal life; we believe and we know that you are the Christ, the Son of God,' alleluia.

Concluding Prayer
Almighty, ever-living God,
you give us the great joy of devoting this day
to the honour of the apostles Peter and Paul.
Grant that your Church
may follow their teaching to the full,
because these are the men
who first taught us to worship you in Christ, your Son,
who lives and reigns with you and the Holy Spirit,
God, for ever and ever.
(Who lives and reigns for ever and ever.)

EVENING PRAYER II

Magnificat ant. Peter the apostle and Paul the teacher of the nations taught us your law, Lord.

The concluding prayer as at Morning Prayer.

6 August
THE TRANSFIGURATION
OF THE LORD

Feast

EVENING PRAYER I
(Said when this feast occurs on a Sunday)

Magnificat ant. Jesus Christ is the radiant light of the Father's glory and flawless expression of his nature, sustaining the universe by his powerful word; now he has destroyed the defilement of sin and appeared in glory today on the high mountain.

The concluding prayer as at Morning Prayer.

MORNING PRAYER

Benedictus ant. A voice came from the cloud, saying, 'This is my beloved Son, with whom I am well pleased; listen to him', alleluia.

Concluding Prayer
Father,
at the Transfiguration in glory of your Only-begotten Son,
you confirmed the mysteries of faith
by the witness to Jesus
of the prophets Moses and Elijah.
You foreshadowed there what we shall be
when you bring our sonship to its perfection.
Grant that by listening to the voice of Jesus
we may become heirs with him,
who lives and reigns with you and the Holy Spirit,
God, for ever and ever.

EVENING PRAYER II

Magnificat ant. When the disciples heard they fell on their faces, overcome with fear. But Jesus came up and touched them, saying, 'Stand up and do not be afraid,' alleluia.

The concluding prayer as at Morning Prayer.

15 August
THE ASSUMPTION OF THE BLESSED VIRGIN MARY
Solemnity

EVENING PRAYER I

Magnificat ant. Behold, all generations will call me blessed, for he who is mighty has done great things for me, alleluia.

The concluding prayer as at Morning Prayer.

MORNING PRAYER

Benedictus ant. See the beauty of the daughter of Jerusalem, who ascended to heaven like the rising sun at dawn.

Concluding Prayer
Almighty, ever-living God,
you have taken the mother of your Son,
the immaculate Virgin Mary,
body and soul into the glory where you dwell.
Keep our hearts set on heaven
so that, with her, we may share in your glory.
(We make our prayer) through our Lord.

EVENING PRAYER II

Magnificat ant. Today the Virgin Mary was assumed into heaven; rejoice and be glad, for she will reign for ever with Christ.

The concluding prayer as at Morning Prayer.

14 September
THE EXALTATION OF
THE HOLY CROSS

Feast

EVENING PRAYER I
(When the feast occurs on a Sunday)

Magnificat ant. It was fitting that Christ should suffer and rise from the dead, and so enter into his glory.

The concluding prayer as at Morning Prayer.

MORNING PRAYER

Benedictus ant. We venerate your cross, Lord: we praise and glorify your holy resurrection: because of the wood of the cross, joy has come into the world.

Concluding Prayer
God our Father,
in obedience to your will
your Only-begotten Son endured the cross for our salvation.
Grant that as we have come to know the mystery of the cross here
　　on earth,
we may receive its rewards in heaven.
(We make our prayer) through our Lord.

EVENING PRAYER II

Magnificat ant. Hail holy cross, standard of victory. Lead us to the triumph of Christ Jesus in the kingdom of heaven.

The concluding prayer as at Morning Prayer.

1 November
ALL SAINTS

EVENING PRAYER I

Magnificat ant. The glorious band of apostles, the noble company of prophets, the white-robed army who shed their blood for Christ and all the saints in heaven together proclaim: We praise you, Holy Trinity, one God.

The concluding prayer as at Morning Prayer.

MORNING PRAYER

Benedictus ant. The just will shine out, clear as the sun, in their Father's kingdom, alleluia.

Concluding Prayer
Almighty, ever-living God
we are celebrating with joy
the triumph of your grace in all the saints.
With so vast a multitude praying for us,
may we receive from you
the fulness of mercy we have always desired.
(We make our prayer) through our Lord.

EVENING PRAYER II

Magnificat ant. How full of splendour is the kingdom where all the saints exult with Christ! The white-robed throng follows the Lamb of God in all his ways.

The concluding prayer as at Morning Prayer.

2 November
ALL SOULS DAY

When 2 November is a Sunday, even though Mass may be of the Commemoration of All Souls, the Office celebrated is that of the Sunday, and the Office for the Dead is omitted. However, Morning Prayer and Evening Prayer for the Dead, in which the people participate, may be celebrated.

From the Office for the Dead, 477 ff.

9 November
DEDICATION OF
THE LATERAN BASILICA

Feast

EVENING PRAYER I

Magnificat ant. Rejoice with Jerusalem and exult in her for ever all you who love her (alleluia).

The concluding prayer as at Morning Prayer.

MORNING PRAYER

Benedictus ant. 'Zacchaeus, make haste and come down; for I must stay with you today.' He came down with great haste and received the Lord joyfully in his house. Today salvation has come from God to this house, alleluia.

Concluding Prayer
In the dedicated church only
Almighty God,
as we recall with joy
the dedication of this house of yours
on each recurring anniversary:
listen to your people's prayer,
and grant that our worship here
may be a sincere and holy service,
honouring your name
and bringing us the fulness of redemption.
(We make our prayer) through our Lord.

Outside the dedicated church itself
Lord God,
you choose men as living stones to become an eternal dwelling,
built to the glory of your name.
Increase your gifts of grace to the Church,
and let your faithful people throng in ever greater numbers
to form the heavenly Jerusalem.
(We make our prayer) through our Lord.

Alternative
Lord God,
you have called your people to become your Church,
grant that all who are gathered in your name
may fear you and love you,
may follow you and, under your guidance,
attain to your promises in heaven.
(We make our prayer) through our Lord.

EVENING PRAYER II

Magnificat ant. The Lord has made holy the place where he dwells;
this is the house of God in which his name will be invoked; as it is
written: My name shall be there, says the Lord (alleluia).

The concluding prayer as at Morning Prayer.

8 December
THE IMMACULATE CONCEPTION OF THE BLESSED VIRGIN MARY

Solemnity

EVENING PRAYER I

Magnificat ant. All generations will call me blessed, for the Almighty has done great things for me, alleluia.

The concluding prayer as at Morning Prayer.

MORNING PRAYER

Benedictus ant. The Lord God said to the serpent: I will put enmity between you and the woman, between your seed and her seed. She will crush your head, alleluia.

Concluding Prayer
Father,
we rejoice in the privilege of our Lady's Immaculate Conception,
which preserved her from the stain of sin
by the power of Christ's redeeming death,
and prepared her to be the Mother of God.
Grant that through her prayers
we ourselves may come to you,
cleansed from all sin.
(We make our prayer) through our Lord.

EVENING PRAYER II

Magnificat ant. Hail, Mary, full of grace: the Lord is with you. You are the most blessed of all women, and blessed is the fruit of your womb, alleluia.

The concluding prayer as at Morning Prayer.

THE OFFICE FOR THE DEAD

The concluding prayers are to be changed in gender and number according to circumstances.
In Eastertide, Alleluia may be added, if judged fitting, to the end of antiphons, versicles and responsories.

INVITATORY

Ant. Come, let us adore the King for whom all men are alive.

MORNING PRAYER

Hymn

Remember those, O Lord,
Who in your peace have died,
Yet may not gain love's high reward
Till love is purified.

With you they faced death's night,
Sealed with your victory sign,
Soon may the splendour of your light
On them for ever shine.

Sweet is their pain, yet deep,
Till perfect love is born;
Their lone night-watch they gladly keep
Before your radiant morn.

Your love is their great joy;
Your will their one desire;
As finest gold without alloy
Refine them in love's fire.

For them we humbly pray:
Perfect them in your love.
O may we share eternal day
With them in heaven above.

PSALMODY

Ant. 1: The bones you have crushed will rejoice in you, Lord.

PSALM 50(51)

Have mércy on me, Gód, in your kíndness.*
In your compássion blot óut my offénce.
O wásh me more and móre from my guílt*
and cléanse me fróm my sín.

My offénces trúly I knów them;*
my sín is álways befóre me.
Against yóu, you alóne, have I sínned;*
what is évil in your síght I have dóne.

That you may be jústified whén you give séntence*
and be withóut repróach when you júdge
O sée, in guílt I was bórn,*
a sínner was Í concéived.

Indéed you love trúth in the héart;*
then in the sécret of my héart teach me wísdom.
O púrify me, thén I shall be cléan;*
O wásh me, I shall be whíter than snów.

Make me héar rejóicing and gládness,*
that the bónes you have crúshed may revíve.
From my síns turn awáy your fáce*
and blót out áll my guílt.

A púre heart creáte for me, O Gód,*
put a stéadfast spírit withín me.
Do not cást me awáy from your présence,*
nor depríve me of your hóly spírit.

Give me agáin the jóy of your hélp;*
with a spírit of férvour sustáin me,
that I may téach transgréssors your wáys*
and sínners may retúrn to yóu.

O réscue me, Gód, my hélper,*
and my tóngue shall ríng out your góodness.

O Lórd, ópen my líps*
and my móuth shall decláre your práise.

For in sácrifice you táke no delíght,*
burnt óffering from mé you would refúse,
my sácrifice, a cóntrite spírit.*
A húmbled, contrite héart you will not spúrn.

In your góodness, show fávour to Síon:*
rebuíld the wálls of Jerúsalem.
Thén you will be pléased with lawful sácrifice,*
hólocausts óffered on your áltar.

Ant. The bones you have crushed will rejoice in you, Lord.
Ant. 2: Rescue my soul, Lord, from the gate of death.

CANTICLE: IS 38:10-14,17-20

I said, In the noontide of my days I must depart;†
I am consigned to the gates of Sheol*
for the rest of my years.

I said, I shall not see the Lord*
in the land of the living;
I shall look upon man no more*
among the inhabitants of the world.

My dwelling is plucked up and removed from me*
like a shepherd's tent;
like a weaver I have rolled up my life;*
he cuts me off from the loom;

From day to night you bring me to an end;*
I cry for help until morning;
like a lion he breaks all my bones;*
from day to night you bring me to an end.

Like a swallow or a crane I clamour,*
I moan like a dove.
My eyes are weary with looking upward.*
O Lord, I am oppressed; be my security.

Lo, it was for my welfare*
that I had great bitterness;
but you have held back my life*
from the pit of destruction,
for you have cast all my sins*
behind your back.

For Sheol cannot thank you,*
death cannot praise you;
those who go down to the pit*
cannot hope for your faithfulness.

The living, the living, he thanks you†
as I do this day;*
the father makes known to the children your faithfulness.

The Lord will save me,*
and we will sing to stringed instruments
all the days of our life,*
at the house of the Lord.

Ant. Rescue my soul, Lord, from the gate of death.
Ant. 3: I will praise God all my days.

PSALM 145(146)

My sóul, give práise to the Lórd;†
I will práise the Lórd all my dáys,*
make músic to my Gód while I líve.

Pút no trúst in prínces,*
in mortal mén in whóm there is no hélp.
Take their bréath, they retúrn to cláy*
and their pláns that dáy come to nóthing.

He is háppy who is hélped by Jacob's Gód,*
whose hópe is in the Lórd his Gód,
who alóne made héaven and éarth,*
the séas and áll they contáin.

It is hé who keeps fáith for éver,*
who is júst to thóse who are oppréssed.

480

It is hé who gives bréad to the húngry,*
the Lórd, who sets prísoners frée,

the Lórd who gives síght to the blínd,*
who ráises up thóse who are bowed dówn,
the Lórd, who protécts the stránger*
and uphólds the wídow and órphan.

It is the Lórd who lóves the júst
but thwárts the páth of the wícked.
The Lórd will réign for éver,
Sion's Gód, from áge to áge.

Ant. I will praise God all my days.

Alternative psalm
Ant. 3: Let everything that lives praise the Lord.

PSALM 150

Práise Gód in his hóly pláce,*
práise him in his míghty héavens.
Práise him for his pówerful déeds,*
práise his surpássing gréatness.

O práise him with sóund of trúmpet,*
práise him with lúte and hárp.
Práise him with tímbrel and dánce,*
práise him with stríngs and pípes.

O práise him with resóunding cýmbals,*
práise him with cláshing of cýmbals.
Let éverything that líves and that bréathes*
give práise to the Lórd.

Ant. Let everything that lives praise the Lord.

Scripture Reading   *I Thess 4:14*
We believe that Jesus died and rose again; so we believe that God
will bring with Jesus those who have died believing in him.

481

Short Responsory

R̸ I will praise you, Lord. You have rescued me. *Repeat* R̸

V̸ You have changed my mourning into gladness. R̸ Glory be. R̸

Benedictus ant. I am the resurrection and the life; he who believes in me, though he die, yet shall he live, and whoever lives and believes in me shall never die.

Alternative for Eastertide

Christ has risen; he is the light of his people, whom he has redeemed with his blood, alleluia.

Intercessions

God, the Father almighty, raised Jesus from the dead and he will give life to our own mortal bodies. We pray to him in faith: R̸ Lord, bring us to life in Christ.

Holy Father, we have been buried with your Son in baptism to rise with him in glory;—may we always live in Christ and not see death for ever. R̸

Father, you have given us the living bread from heaven to be eaten with faith and love;—grant that we may have eternal life and be raised up on the last day. R̸

Lord, when your Son was in agony you sent an angel to console him; —at the hour of our death take away all fear and fill our hearts with hope. R̸

You delivered the three young men from the blazing furnace;—free the souls of the dead from the punishments their sins have deserved. R̸

God of the living and the dead, you brought Jesus back to life;— raise up the faithful departed, and let us come with them into your heavenly glory. R̸

Our Father

Concluding Prayer

Grant, Lord, we pray,

that as our faith is built on the Risen Christ,

so too may our hope be steadfast,

as we await the resurrection of your servant N. from the dead.

(We make our prayer) through our Lord.

Alternative: For a Man
God, our Father,
by whose Son's death and resurrection we have been redeemed,
you are the glory of your faithful, the life of your saints:
have mercy on your servant N.,
and as he professed his faith in the mystery of our resurrection,
so may he gain possession of eternal joy.
(We make our prayer) through our Lord.

For a Woman
God, our Father,
by whose Son's death and resurrection we have been redeemed,
you are the glory of your faithful, the life of your saints:
have mercy on your servant N.,
and as she professed her faith in the mystery of our resurrection,
so may she gain possession of eternal joy.
(We make our prayer) through our Lord.

Alternative: Through the Year
For a Man
Let our prayer come into your presence, Lord,
as we humbly ask for mercy:
and as in your love
you counted your servant N. among your people in this world,
so bring him now to the abode of peace and light,
and number him among your saints.
(We make our prayer) through our Lord.

For a Woman
Let our prayer come into your presence, Lord,
as we humbly ask for mercy:
and as in your love
you counted your handmaid N. among your people in this world,
so bring her now to the abode of peace and light,
and number her among your saints.
(We make our prayer) through our Lord.

Eastertide
God of mercy and power,
whose Son of his own free will
underwent a human death on our behalf:
let your servant N.
share in the admirable victory of Christ's resurrection.
(We make our prayer) through our Lord.

For several deceased
Lord God,
who gave your only-begotten Son
his place on high as conqueror of death:
grant to your servants N. and N. who have died,
that they in their turn may triumph over death,
and may live forever before you, their creator and redeemer.
(We make our prayer) through our Lord.

For Brethren, Relatives and Benefactors
Lord God,
as you are the fount of mercy and wish all men to be saved:
have mercy then on our deceased brethren, relatives and
    benefactors.
Through the intercession of Blessed Mary ever-virgin,
and of all your saints,
bring them to the fellowship of eternal joy.
(We make our prayer) through our Lord.

EVENING PRAYER

Hymn

Merciful Saviour, hear our humble prayer,
For all your servants passed beyond life's care;
Though sin has touched them, yet their weakness spare.

Refrain:
O grant them pardon, Jesus Saviour blest,
And give their spirits light and endless rest.

O gentle Saviour, Lamb for sinners slain,
Look on your brothers, cleanse their hearts of stain:
Your cross has won them everlasting gain. (*Refrain:*)

Lord, at your passion love did conquer fear;
Now share that triumph with these souls so dear:
Banish their sorrows, let your light appear. (*Refrain:*)

PSALMODY

Ant. 1: The Lord will guard you from every evil, he will guard your soul.

PSALM 120(121)

I líft up my éyes to the móuntains:*
from whére shall come my hélp?
My hélp shall cóme from the Lórd*
who made héaven and éarth.

May he néver állow you to stúmble!*
Let him sléep not, your guárd.
Nó, he sléeps not nor slúmbers,*
Ísrael's guárd.

The Lórd is your guárd and your sháde;*
at your ríght side he stánds.
By dáy the sún shall not smíte you*
nor the móon in the níght.

The Lórd will guárd you from évil,*
he will guárd your sóul.
The Lórd will guárd your góing and cóming*
both nów and for éver.

Ant. The Lord will guard you from every evil, he will guard your soul.

Ant. 2: If you, O Lord, should mark our guilt, Lord, who would survive?

PSALM 129(130)

Out of the dépths I crý to you, O Lórd,*

485

Lórd, hear my vóice!
O lét your éars be attentive*
to the vóice of my pléading.

If you, O Lórd, should márk our guílt,*
Lórd, who would survíve?
But with yóu is fóund forgíveness:*
for thís we revére you.

My sóul is wáiting for the Lórd,*
I cóunt on his wórd.

My sóul is lónging for the Lórd*
more than wátchman for dáybreak.
Let the wátchman cóunt on dáybreak*
and Ísrael on the Lórd.

Becáuse with the Lord there is mércy*
and fúlness of redémption,
Ísrael indéed he will redéem*
from áll its iníquity.

Ant. If you, O Lord, should mark our guilt, Lord, who would survive?

Ant. 3: As the Father raises the dead and gives them life, so the Son gives life to anyone he chooses.

CANTICLE: PHIL 2:6-11

Though he was in the form of God,*
Jesus did not count equality with God a thing to be grasped.

He emptied himself,†
taking the form of a servant,*
being born in the likeness of men.

And being found in human form,*
he humbled himself and became obedient unto death,*
even death on a cross.

Therefore God has highly exalted him*
and bestowed on him the name which is above every name,

That at the name of Jesus every knee should bow,*
in heaven and on earth and under the earth,

And every tongue confess that Jesus Christ is Lord,*
to the glory of God the Father.

Ant. As the Father raises the dead and gives them life, so the Son gives life to anyone he chooses.

Scripture Reading   *I Cor 15:55-57*
Death, where is your victory? Death, where is your sting? Now the sting of death is sin, and sin gets its power from the Law. So let us thank God for giving us the victory through our Lord Jesus Christ.

Short Responsory
R/ In you, O Lord, I take refuge. Let me not be lost for ever.
Repeat R/
V/ I will rejoice and be glad because of your merciful love. R/ Glory be. R/

Alternative
R/ Show them your merciful love, Lord, give them eternal rest.
Repeat R/
V/ You are coming to rule over both the living and the dead. R/ Glory be. R/

Magnificat ant. All that the Father gives me will come to me; and I will never turn away the one who comes to me.

Alternative in Eastertide
Christ was crucified and rose from the dead; he has redeemed us, alleluia.

Intercessions
Let us pray to Christ who gives us the hope that our mortal bodies will become like his in glory. R/ Lord, you are our life and our resurrection.
Christ, Son of the living God, you raised your friend Lazarus from the dead;—grant life and glory to the faithful departed, redeemed by

your precious blood. R̸ Lord, you are our life and our resurrection.
Compassionate Saviour, you wiped away all tears when you gave
back to the widow of Naim her only son;—comfort those who
mourn because the one they love has died. R̸
Christ, our Redeemer, destroy the reign of sin in our mortal bodies;
—let us not receive the wages of death but the reward of eternal
life. R̸
Christ, our Saviour, look on those who live without hope and do not
know you;—let them believe in the resurrection and the life of the
world to come. R̸
You restored sight to the man born blind and opened the eyes of his
faith;—reveal your face to the dead who have not seen your glory.
R̸
Lord, be merciful to us when we leave this earthly dwelling;—make
for us a home in heaven that will last for ever. R̸
Our Father

The concluding prayer as at Morning Prayer.

NIGHT PRAYER

All as on a Sunday, After Evening Prayer II, pp 322 ff.

MEMORIAL OF THE BLESSED
VIRGIN MARY ON SATURDAY

On ordinary Saturdays Through the Year on which optional Memorias are allowed, an optional Memoria of the Blessed Virgin Mary may be celebrated.

INVITATORY

Ant. Christ is the Son of Mary; come, let us adore him.

Alternative
Come, ring out our joy to the Lord, as we venerate the Blessed Virgin Mary.

MORNING PRAYER

Hymn for the Blessed Virgin Mary.

Antiphons, psalms and canticle from the current Saturday.

The Scripture Reading with its short responsory may be chosen from among the following:

Scripture Reading   *Gal 4:4-5*
When the appointed time came, God sent his Son, born of a woman, born a subject of the Law, to redeem the subjects of the Law and to enable us to be adopted as sons.

Short Responsory
℟ After the birth of your child you remained a virgin. *Repeat* ℟
℣ Mother of God, intercede for us. ℟ Glory be. ℟

Alternative
Scripture Reading   *Cf Is 61:10*
I will greatly rejoice in the Lord, my soul shall exult in my God; for he has clothed me with the garments of salvation, he has covered me with the robe of righteousness. as a bride adorns herself with her jewels.

Short Responsory

R℣ The Lord chose her. He chose her before she was born. *Repeat R*
℣ He made her live in his own dwelling place. R℣ Glory be. R℣

Alternative
Scripture Reading   *Rev 12:1*

A great sign appeared in heaven: a woman, adorned with the sun
standing on the moon, and with the twelve stars on her head for a
crown.

Short Responsory

R℣ Hail Mary, full of grace: the Lord is with you. *Repeat R℣*
℣ You are the most blessed of all women and blessed is the fruit of
your womb. R℣ Glory be. R℣

Benedictus Antiphon

One of the following may be chosen:

1 Let us celebrate the commemoration of the Blessed Virgin Mary,
that she may intercede for us with the Lord Jesus Christ.

2 Blessed are you, O Virgin Mary, above all women on earth. The
Lord God himself has chosen you.

3 Through you, immaculate Virgin, the life we had lost was returned
to us. You received a child from heaven, and brought forth to the
world a Saviour.

4 Hail Mary, full of grace; the Lord is with you. You are the most
blessed of all women, alleluia.

5 How shall I fittingly praise you, holy and immaculate virginity of
Mary? Through you we received our Redeemer, our Lord Jesus
Christ.

6 You are the glory of Jerusalem! You are the joy of Israel! You are
the highest honour of our race.

Intercessions

Let us proclaim the greatness of our Saviour who chose to be born
of the Virgin Mary. Confident that he will hear us, we ask: R℣ Lord,
may your mother pray for us.

Sun of justice, you showed your day was dawning in the immaculate

Virgin Mary;—help us to walk in the daylight of your presence. R̷
Eternal Word, in the living flesh of Mary you found a dwelling
place on earth;—remain with us for ever in hearts free from sin. R̷
Christ, our Saviour, you willed that your mother should be there
when you died;—through her intercession may we rejoice to share
your suffering. R̷

Loving Saviour, while hanging on the cross, you gave your mother
Mary to be the mother of John;—let us be known as her children
by our way of living. R̷

Our Father

Alternative

Let us proclaim the greatness of our Saviour who chose to be born
of the Virgin Mary. Confident that he will hear us, we ask: R̷ Lord,
may your mother pray for us.

Saviour of the world, by your redemptive power you preserved your
mother Mary from every stain of sin;—deliver us from the evil that
lies hidden in our hearts. R̷

Christ, our Redeemer, you made the Virgin Mary the sanctuary of
your presence and the temple of the Spirit;—make us bearers of your
Spirit, in mind, heart and body. R̷

Eternal Word, you taught your mother Mary to choose the part that
was best;—let us follow her example and hunger for the food of
everlasting life. R̷

King of kings, you assumed Mary into heaven to be with you
completely in body and soul;—may we seek the things that are above
and keep our lives fixed on you. R̷

King of heaven and earth, you placed Mary at your side to reign as
queen for ever;—grant us the joy of sharing in your glory. R̷

Our Father

Concluding Prayer

One of the following may be chosen:

Grant us, Lord, we pray
the joy of continued health of mind and body:
and through the intercession of Blessed Mary ever-virgin,
free us of this present sadness,
fill us with eternal joy.
(We make our prayer) through our Lord.

Alternative
Forgive the sins of your people, Lord,
and as nothing we can do is worthy in your sight,
save us through the intercession of the Mother of our Lord
    Jesus Christ
who lives and reigns with you and the Holy Spirit,
God, for ever and ever.

Alternative
Come to help us in our weakness, God of mercy,
and as we celebrate the memory of the Mother of God,
may we rise from our sins by the help of her prayer.
(We make our prayer) through our Lord.

Alternative
Let the gracious intercession of Blessed Mary ever-virgin help us,
    Lord:
may she protect us in all dangers
and make us rejoice in your peace.
(We make our prayer) through our Lord.

Alternative
Lord God,
as we venerate the memory of the Virgin Mary, now in glory,
grant that by her intercession
we ourselves may share in the fulness of your grace.
(We make our prayer) through our Lord.

Alternative
Almighty God,
grant that your faithful who rejoice in the protection of the
    Blessed Virgin Mary,
may be delivered from every evil here on earth through her prayer,
and come to the enduring joys of heaven.
(We make our prayer) through our Lord.

The Benedictus

Blessed be the Lord, the God of Israel!*
He has visited his people and redeemed them.

He has raised up for us a mighty saviour*
in the house of David his servant,
as he promised by the lips of holy men,*
those who were his prophets from of old.

A saviour who would free us from our foes,*
from the hands of all who hate us.
So his love for our fathers is fulfilled*
and his holy covenant remembered.

He swore to Abraham our father to grant us,*
that free from fear,
   and saved from the hands of our foes,
we might serve him in holiness and justice*
all the days of our life in his presence.

As for you, little child,*
you shall be called a prophet of God,
   the Most High.
You shall go ahead of the Lord*
to prepare his ways before him,

To make known to his people their salvation*
through forgiveness of all their sins,
the loving-kindness of the heart of our God*
who visits us like the dawn from on high.

He will give light to those in darkness,†
those who dwell in the shadow of death,*
and guide us into the way of peace.

The Magnificat

My soul glorifies the Lord,*
my spirit rejoices in God, my Saviour.
He looks on his servant in her lowliness;*
henceforth all ages will call me blessed.

The Almighty works marvels for me.*
Holy his name!
His mercy is from age to age,*
on those who fear him.

He puts forth his arm in strength*
and scatters the proud-hearted.
He casts the mighty from their thrones*
and raises the lowly.

He fills the starving with good things,*
sends the rich away empty.

He protects Israel, his servant.*
remembering his mercy,
the mercy promised to our fathers,*
to Abraham and his sons for ever.